CATHOLICS AND ANTI-CATHOLICISM
IN CHOSŎN KOREA

HAWAI'I STUDIES ON KOREA

Catholics and Anti-Catholicism in Chosŏn Korea

DON BAKER
with FRANKLIN RAUSCH

University of Hawai'i Press, Honolulu
and
Center for Korean Studies, University of Hawai'i

Paperback edition 2018

Printed in the United States of America

23 22 21 20 19 18   1 2 3 4 5 6

Library of Congress Cataloging-in-Publication Data

Names: Baker, Don, author. | Rausch, Franklin, contributor.
Title: Catholics and anti- Catholicism in Chosŏn Korea / Don Baker with
   Franklin Rausch.
Other titles: Hawai'i studies on Korea.
Description: Honolulu : University of Hawai'i Press : Center for Korean Studies,
   University of Hawai'i, [2017] | Series: Hawai'i studies on Korea | Includes a
   complete translation of an anti-Catholic essay and an annotated translation of
   the Silk letter of Hwang Sayŏng. | Includes bibliographical references and index.
Identifiers: LCCN 2016054294 | ISBN 9780824866266 (cloth ; alk. paper)
Subjects: LCSH: Anti-Catholicism—Korea—History—19th century. | Catholic
   Church—Korea—History—19th century. | Hwang, Sayŏng, 1775–1801.
Classification: LCC BX1775.K6 B35 2017 | DDC 282/.51909034—dc23 LC record
   available at https://lccn.loc.gov2016054294/

ISBN 978-0-8248-7926-6 (pbk.)

The Center for Korean Studies was established in 1972 to coordinate and develop
resources for the study of Korea at the University of Hawai'i. Reflecting the diversity
of the academic disciplines represented by affiliated members of the university
faculty, the Center seeks especially to promote interdisciplinary and intercultural
studies. Hawai'i Studies on Korea, published jointly by the Center and the University
of Hawai'i Press, offers a forum for research in the social sciences and humanities
pertaining to Korea and its people.

University of Hawai'i Press books are printed on acid-free paper and meet the
guidelines for permanence and durability of the Council on Library Resources.

CONTENTS

ACKNOWLEDGMENTS

This translation of *A Conversation on Catholicism* by Ahn Chŏngbok and *The Silk Letter of Hwang Sayŏng* (hereafter referred to as the *Silk Letter*) has its roots in the doctoral dissertation Don Baker wrote at the beginning of his career in the early 1980s. That dissertation examined the Korean Confucian reaction to Catholicism up to 1791. However, he was not able to continue that story up to the major anti-Catholic persecution of 1801 until the Academy of Korean Studies approached him in 2006 and asked him to prepare an annotated English translation of the *Silk Letter*, a first-person account of the 1801 persecution by one of its last victims.

The ensuing project to translate and annotate the *Silk Letter* was supported by the Academy of Korean Studies (AKS) Promotion Service Grant funded by the Ministry of Education of the government of the Republic of Korea, grant number AKS-2007-AC-3002. That funding made it possible to also translate and annotate another important document, *A Conversation on Catholicism*, which provided much of the ideological justification for the anti-Catholic movement. Thanks to the support from the AKS, Baker was also able to write an introduction to those two documents that places them in their historical context.

The funding from the AKS allowed Baker to enlist the support of his graduate students at the University of British Columbia in this project. Franklin Rausch was his primary assistant. Together they worked on the translation of the *Silk Letter*, and Dr. Rausch (he received his Ph.D. for a doctorate on Hwang Sayŏng and Ahn Chunggŭn in 2011) also translated important material from the court records of the Chosŏn dynasty and uncovered important biographical information about many of the names that appear in the *Silk Letter*. The AKS also funded the research of another graduate student, Jee-yeon Song, who contributed to this project by uncovering information about the leading Korean anti-Catholic officials at the time the *Silk Letter* was written.

This work could not have been completed with the help of the staff of the Asian Library of the University of British Columbia. Research for this book was also conducted at the Library of Congress and was facilitated by the staff of the Asian Reading Room. In addition, funding from the AKS allowed both Don Baker and Franklin Rausch (who received additional funding from the Korea Foundation and Fulbright Korea) to visit libraries and consult with scholars in Korea in order to locate important material and learn about the latest Korean scholarship on the *Silk Letter* and the anti-Catholic persecution in Korea in the eighteenth and early nineteenth centuries. The Center for Research in Korean Church History, associated with the Seoul archdiocese, was particularly helpful, as were the scholars Cho Kwang and Yŏ Chinch'ŏn. Thanks are also due to the anonymous readers for the University of Hawai'i Center for Korean Studies who made many useful suggestions for improving this manuscript. Don Baker, the senior author and translator, accepts full responsibility for any errors and infelicitous phrases that remain.

PREFACE

On the fifth day of the eleventh month of the first full year of the reign of King Sunjo (r. 1800–1834), according to the lunar calendar, a young Korean man named Hwang Sayŏng (1775–1801), who had once appeared to have ahead of him a sterling career as a civil servant, was decapitated by his government's official executioner for his activities on behalf of Korea's young and persecuted Roman Catholic community. Today, over two centuries later, the Korean attitude toward the Catholic Church is very different. In August 2014, Pope Francis traveled from the Vatican to South Korea to honor many of those whom Hwang had worked with and whose martyrdom in the anti-Catholic persecution of 1800–1801 Hwang had chronicled. Pope Francis was welcomed by hundreds of thousands of cheering Koreans, many of them the descendants of those who had persecuted those the Pope came to Korea to honor.[1]

Catholicism is clearly no longer a prohibited religion in Korea (at least in the southern half of the peninsula). In fact, public opinion polls in the first decade of the twenty-first century have found that the Catholic Church is the most respected religious community in South Korea, and also the fastest growing.[2] Yet there were no practicing Catholics in Korea until the late eighteenth century. Even half a century ago, there were fewer than one million Catholics on the entire Korean peninsula. However, according to an official South Korean government census in 1995 and another in 2005, membership in the Korean Catholic Church grew from slightly less than three million in 1995 to more than five million in 2005, an increase of almost 75 percent over just one decade. Though growth has somewhat slowed since then, the Korean Catholic Church remains a dynamic element of Korea's diverse religious culture, claiming over 10 percent of the fifty million people who live in South

Korea, making Catholicism Korea's third largest religion, behind Buddhism and Protestantism.

The current success of Catholicism in Korea is remarkable in light of the difficulties Catholics faced over the course of their first century in Korea. When Catholicism first appeared in Korea in 1784, it encountered a hostile Neo-Confucian government that considered that religion, and its believers, a threat to the political as well as ethical foundations of its power. Over the course of the next century, thousands of Koreans were executed for refusing to yield to government pressure to renounce their faith.

The first pope to visit Korea was John Paul II, who flew to Seoul in May 1984 to announce official recognition of the price the first generations of Korean Catholics had paid for their fidelity. He elevated to sainthood 103 members of the Korean Catholic Church (including ten French missionaries who were killed in the nineteenth century for ministering to the struggling Korean Catholic Church).

The martyrs formally recognized as saints in 1984 gave their lives during the great persecutions of 1839, 1846, and 1866. But 1839 was not the first major persecution. The Confucian government of Korea began executing Catholics in 1791 and carried out a major persecution in 1801. Nevertheless, it was not until 2014 that Rome formally recognized the sacrifice those earlier Korean martyrs had made. When he visited Seoul in August of 2014, Pope Francis raised to Blessed status (one step below full recognition as saints in Heaven) 124 additional martyred members of the Korean Catholic community, beginning with Paul Yun Chich'ung (1759–1791), who was martyred in 1791. Among those on that list are eighty-six men and women who died professing their faith in the face of government hostility before 1839, including fifty-two who were killed during the 1801 persecution that also claimed the life of Hwang Sayŏng.

The elevation to Blessed status of Korea's first martyrs is important as a formal recognition of the distinctive origins of the Korean Catholic community. Korea's Catholics are proud that the first Catholic community on Korean soil emerged in 1784, when there were no foreign missionaries in Korea. Catholicism was brought to Korea by a Korean layman who had been baptized in Beijing, not by a foreign priest. Moreover, except for the period between 1795 and 1801, when a lone Chinese priest ministered to Korea's beleaguered Catholics before he was executed in an anti-Catholic persecution, Korean Catholics were a community of only lay believers for most of their first half century, until the 1830s. This makes the history of Catholicism in Korea unique in the global history of the Roman Catholic Church. Honoring those early lay Catholics as Blessed is a sign that Rome recognizes the essential role the laity plays in church life.

Information confirming that those early martyrs maintained fidelity to their faith up through their executions can be found in two types of sources. We have government accounts, both interrogation records and official reports to the king, detailing how the Catholics who were arrested and tortured responded to that treatment at the hands of officials. We also have a remarkable document called *The Silk Letter of Hwang Sayŏng,* a first-hand account by the young man whose execution opened this chapter.

Even though information contained in Hwang's *Silk Letter* (so called because it was written on a single piece of silk a little more than two feet wide and a foot long to make it easier to smuggle out of Korea and into the hands of the bishop of Beijing) was important in documenting the steadfastness of the early martyrs, and Hwang himself was executed near the end of that persecution, still professing his faith in God, Hwang himself does not appear on that list of martyrs from 1801 declared Blessed. Political considerations may be the reason Hwang Sayŏng is not on that list.

Hwang's letter never made it to Beijing. Instead, he was arrested and his letter was read by Korean government officials. They were alarmed by what they read, and generations of Koreans after them have also been troubled when they learned what Hwang wrote. At the end of his *Silk Letter,* after detailing how his fellow Catholics dealt with government hostility from 1791 through 1801, Hwang asked the Portuguese bishop of Beijing to arrange for Western naval forces to sail to Korea and threaten to shell Korean soil if the persecution was not halted. That appeal for foreign military threats against the Korean government makes Hwang a controversial figure in Korean history. To some Catholics, he was a brave fighter for religious freedom. To most non-Catholics, he was a traitor who placed his personal religious beliefs ahead of national sovereignty.[3] To include him among those declared Blessed would have introduced a political dispute into what was intended to be a purely religious celebration in Seoul in the summer of 2014.

However his role in Korean history is evaluated, it is widely recognized that the *Silk Letter* he authored is an important eyewitness account of a seminal moment in modern Korean history. It therefore deserves to be introduced to the wider world; hence this English translation. Before presenting that translation and delving into the intricacies of the political dispute surrounding Hwang and his *Silk Letter,* an explanation of why Hwang wrote that letter is in order.

This volume places Hwang's actions in their historical context by examining the religious, political, and social institutions that shaped the society in which he lived and died. This book also traces the short history of Catholicism in late eighteenth-century Korea in order to make it easier to understand why Hwang and a few other Koreans abandoned Confucianism for Catholicism despite the danger that entailed, and why their non-Catholic compatriots found Catholic beliefs and practices so philosophically, politically, and morally obnoxious that they responded by torturing and killing Catholics in large numbers.

So that the reader can appreciate the philosophical obstacles Catholics had to overcome living in a staunchly Confucian Chosŏn dynasty society, we also provide here a translation of a sharp criticism of Catholic beliefs and practices written shortly before anti-Catholicism turned violent. *A Conversation on Catholicism* was written by Ahn Chŏngbok (1712–1791), a respected Confucian scholar who was personally acquainted with many of the first Catholics and was concerned about their deviation from the Confucian path.

Both the *Silk Letter* and *A Conversation on Catholicism* provide a glimpse into the minds of Koreans, in particular their beliefs and values, before Korea encountered the modern world. These texts, therefore, are enlightening reading for anyone who wants to understand recent Korean history, especially what Korea was like before it embarked on the journey that has led to the modern Korea we see today.

NOTES ON THE TRANSLATED TEXTS
AND ROMANIZATION

A Conversation on Catholicism [Ch'ŏnhak mundap 天 學 問 答] is taken from Volume 17 (8a–26a) of *Sunam sŏnsaeng munjip* [The collected works of Sunam Ahn Chŏngbok 順庵先生文集], also known as simply *Sunamjip*. Compiled by Ahn's disciple Hwang Tŏkkil, it was published by Ahn's fifth-generation descendant Ahn Chongyŏp in 1900. It is available in the online database of Korean classics (http://db.itkc.or.kr/) maintained by the Institute for the Translation of Korean Classics (한국 고전번역원). We also used a printed version of the *Sunamjip* (Seoul: Sŏnggyun'gwan taehakkyo, Taedong munhwa yŏn'guwŏn, 1970).

For the *Silk Letter* (*Hwang Sayŏng Paeksŏ* [黃嗣永帛書]), we have relied on the version in Yŏ Chinch'ŏn, *Nuga chŏhŭirŭl wirohae chugessŭmnikka?* [Who will comfort us?] (Seoul: Kibbŭn sosik, 2002). The original letter written by Hwang was confiscated by the Korean government in 1801 and placed in the archives of the State Tribunal [Ŭigŭmbu]. In 1894, when an inventory of those archives brought it to their attention, the Korean government decided to give it to Gustave Mutel, the head of the Catholic Church in Korea. In 1925, Bishop Mutel sent the original letter to the Vatican, after making a copy in 1924 that was the exact same size. That copy is kept in the Museum of the Martyrs at Ch'ŏltu-san in Seoul. The original has been held in the Folk Museum in the Vatican.

Other versions of the *Silk Letter* appeared over the course of the nineteenth century, including the version found in the records of the interrogation of Hwang Sayŏng as well as a much shorter version, cleansed of elements that might cause trouble for the Koreans, that was sent by the Seoul government to Beijing to counter any rumors that might have spread in China about what was happening in Korea, particularly the execution of the Chinese subject Zhou Wenmo.[1] The best-known version is the one that first appeared in the middle of the nineteenth century in an anti-Catholic work, the *Pyŏgwip'yŏn* [In defense of the right against the wrong]. There are many omissions and incorrect Sino-Korean characters in that version but it is the version that, ironically, was used by the authors of the first histories of the Catholic Church in Korea. Yŏ Chinch'ŏn compared the various versions and based his annotated translation into Korean on what he has determined is the original wording of Hwang's letter.[2]

There are currently two competing systems for writing Korean in English letters. The older system, and the one most scholars in Europe and North America still use, is the McCune-Reischauer system that uses the breve to distinguish between o and ŏ as well as between u and ŭ and also distinguishes between voiced and unvoiced consonants by writing, for example, p and b for the same Korean phonetic symbol, depending on whether it is voiced or not.

At the turn of the twenty-first century, the government of the Republic of Korea (ROK) proposed a different system, which does not use the breve but instead uses eo for ŏ and eu for ŭ, and does not distinguish clearly between voiced and unvoiced consonants at the beginning of a word. (Thus Korea's second-largest city is spelled Pusan in the McCune-Reischauer system but Busan in the ROK system.)

We have decided to use the McCune-Reischauer system, since most foreign scholars prefer that older system. However, we have deviated from the system for two surnames. The surname that should be written "Sin" according to McCune-Reischauer is written here as "Shin," as in the name "Shin Hudam." That surname sounds more like the English word "shin" and, besides, we thought it might be confusing in a text on Christianity to fail to distinguish morphologically between "sin" and "shin." We also decided to write the surname that should be written "An" according to the McCune-Reischauer system as "Ahn," in order to distinguish it from the common English indefinite article "an."

For the Christian names of the baptized, we provide the English equivalent rather than the romanization of the Korean version of that name. We also follow the Korean Catholic custom of putting the baptismal name first, followed by the surname and then the Korean personal name (which is usually two syllables).

For the few Chinese terms that appear in this work, we use pinyin romanization.

PART I

THE ROAD TO PERSECUTION

CHAPTER 1

Korea at the End of the Eighteenth Century

W hen Hwang was executed at the age of twenty-six, he was only slightly older than the Korean Catholic Church for which he had died. This church was founded only in 1784, more than a century after the emergence of Catholic communities in China, Japan, Vietnam, and the Philippines. Before 1784, a few Koreans had heard about Catholicism, primarily through Catholic missionary publications published in Chinese in China that had been brought to Korea by Koreans who had gone to the Chinese capital of Beijing on diplomatic missions. However, though some of the information in those Catholic publications on Western mathematics, geography, medicine, and astronomy aroused the curiosity of Korean readers, most agreed with the respected Neo-Confucian scholar Yi Ik (1681–1763) that when those Catholic authors departed from discussions of the natural world to talk about God and other Catholic religious doctrines, they added "grains of sand and pieces of grit" to what would otherwise be acceptable scholarship.[1] Korean members of the *yangban* political and social ruling class tended to remain satisfied with the Neo-Confucian philosophy their ancestors had imported from China in the fourteenth and fifteenth centuries. Outside of that scholarly male elite, Buddhism and the folk religion, which includes shamanism, satisfied the religious needs of the majority of the Korean population at that time.

Christianity, when it finally arrived in Korea in the last quarter of the eighteenth century, represented a radical challenge to the religious attitudes prevalent on the peninsula at that time. Christianity is monotheistic, demanding worship of one God and one God only. It draws clear boundaries between itself and all other religious communities, forbidding

Christians from participating in non-Christian religious rituals or join-ing non-Christian religious organizations. It demands belief in specific clearly defined articles of faith, differentiating itself from other religious communities along doctrinal as well as behavioral lines. And it stresses the importance of the individual soul, and that soul's personal relation-ship to the One God above.

RELIGION IN KOREA BEFORE CHRISTIANITY ARRIVED

These defining characteristics of Christianity are the opposite of what we see in traditional Korean religion. For instance, monotheism was absent in pre-Christian Korea. Koreans before the nineteenth century tended to believe either in many gods and spirits, or no gods at all. There are a multitude of gods and spirits in the folk religion, ranging from vil-lage guardian deities to disease-causing spirits. Though some of those supernatural beings were believed to be more powerful than others, no one god reigned supreme. Popular Buddhism, the Buddhism of the peas-antry, was equally polytheistic. The many statues found in typical Bud-dhist temples in Korea even today testify to the traditional practice of visiting temples to pray for assistance from the different Buddhas and Bodhisattvas represented by those statues. Neo-Confucianism, on the other hand, insisted that whether God or gods existed was not particu-larly important, since human beings should focus on cultivating their own innate ability to live moral lives. Similarly, philosophical Buddhism tended to treat the statues of various Buddhas as tools for focusing the mind for the more important task of meditation that would produce insight into the true nature of reality. Neither the popular Buddhist and shamanistic polytheists nor the Neo-Confucian and philosophical Buddhist nontheists demanded the worship of one God and only one God that Catholicism demands.[2]

Monotheistic religions, such as Christianity, Judaism, and Islam, tend to worship a jealous God, a God who does not tolerate the worship of, or even interaction with, other gods on the part of His devotees. In polytheistic religions, on the other hand, there is no one god powerful enough to enforce such a limitation on who and what can be worshipped. With no such restrictions on how many supernatural beings an individual may interact with, the boundaries between what outside observers might see as separate and distinct religious traditions are blurred. The average villager during the Chosŏn dynasty (1392–1910) saw no contradiction between praying at a Buddhist temple in the morning and asking for the help of a local spirit during a shaman ritual in the afternoon. Moreover, most Koreans before the twentieth century didn't normally see themselves as members of any particular religious community to the exclusion of any other. Traditionally, only those who were ritual specialists, such as Buddhist monks, shamans, or Confucian scholars, identified with a specific religious community. Catholics were the first group in Korea to place a religious label on ordinary laypeople.

Another aspect of traditional Korean religiosity that distinguishes it from Christianity is the pre-Christian lack of concern for dogma. Shamans don't question those who have come to watch a shamanic ritual what they believe about the gods that appear during that ritual. Nor do Buddhist monks demand that those who pray in their temples affirm belief in certain core Buddhist teachings. There were no catechisms for Buddhists or for those who patronized shamans. Even Confucian scholars, despite their focus on certain classical texts, were more concerned with what Confucians did, whether or not they acted in accordance with Confucian moral principles and performed Confucian rituals properly, than they were with mere differences of opinion over how to interpret those classical texts. Catholicism was the first religion in Korea to insist that those who participate in its rituals must first affirm their belief in certain doctrinal statements about the meaning of those rituals.[3]

Finally, Catholicism startled Koreans in the eighteenth century with its insistence on the primacy of the individual soul. Buddhist philosophy taught that belief in a separate and distinct identity was a mistake that was responsible for the suffering that human beings endure. Though the less philosophical popular Buddhism and folk religion were not that explicit in denying ultimate reality to individual existence, those religious traditions assumed that human beings were primarily social beings, defined in terms of whom they were related to, what village they lived in, and what role they were assigned in society. They did not share the Catholic stress on the individual. Neo-Confucianism went even farther and made the assumption that human beings are social beings the core of its moral philosophy. According to Neo-Confucianism, a human being was nothing more than the sum total of his or her relationships with other human beings and therefore there could be no individual soul separate and distinct from those relationships. In fact, Neo-Confucians argued, the primary cause of evil in the world was a tendency of human beings to forget that they were social beings and act instead as if they were the separate and distinct individuals Catholics insisted they were.

This is the religious ground on which the Catholic seed fell in Korea in the last quarter of the eighteenth century. It was not at first very fertile ground, since Catholics appeared not just different, but also antisocial. Catholics refused to participate in traditional family and village rituals, putting the salvation of their individual souls above the expectations of their family and neighbors. In their most shocking departure from traditional Korean religiosity, Catholics refused to honor their ancestors in the manner Koreans had honored their ancestors for centuries.

Chosŏn dynasty Koreans, in accordance with Confucian tradition, created "spirit tablets" (wood plaques on which the names of the deceased were written) for their deceased parents and grandparents and, on certain days designated for ritual displays of respect and filial piety, offered food and drink to those spirit tablets and bowed before them.[4] However, Catholics were told by the Pope in Rome, whom they believed was the representative of Jesus Christ on earth, that offering food to those tablets and bowing before them was idolatry, the worship of false gods and, as such, was a violation of the first of the Christian Ten Commandments.[5] Catholics, therefore, were not permitted to participate in such a ritual. Such nonparticipation was an offense not only against Korean customs but also against Korean law.

The decision whether or not to honor deceased parents, grandparents, and other ancestors with a traditional Confucian memorial service was a matter of public law rather than personal preference because, in premodern Korea, the state exercised both ethical and ritual hegemony. The state, rather than religious communities, defined both the ethical and the ritual obligations of its subjects. Since the government of Chosŏn dynasty Korea defined itself as a Confucian government, that meant that Confucian morality and Confucian rituals were both mandatory.

Under the ethical hegemony of the state, ethical demands generated by specific religious traditions were not allowed to override the behavioral demands of the state. Rather than serving as a primary, or even an alternative, source of moral guidance, as it had in the West, religion in traditional Korea, just as in traditional China and traditional Japan, had to accept the subordinate role of reinforcing the moral code promoted by the government. Religions could make additional moral demands, such as Buddhism did when it encouraged Buddhists to refrain from eating meat. However, by definition, any religion that contradicted such Confucian values as loyalty to the king or filial respect and support for parents was immoral and therefore both unacceptable and illegal. This became clear in the late eighteenth century, when a few Koreans who had converted to Catholicism began claiming that their obligation to obey what they perceived as God's laws to refrain from bowing before ancestral tablets superseded the Confucian injunction to show proper ritual respect for deceased ancestors. Those early Catholics were executed as criminals for violating the government's demand that religious beliefs support rather than determine moral obligations.[6]

Under the ritual hegemony of the state, the state determined how loyalty to the king and filial respect to parents was displayed. The state reserved for itself the right to determine which spirits could be worshipped, by whom they could be worshipped, and how, when, and where they could be worshipped. For example, though Chosŏn Korea's Confucian government condemned both Buddhism and shamanism, it permitted some Buddhist and shamanic rituals when they were performed with the permission of the state. Those same rituals, however, were illegal when they were performed without official sanction.

For example, a few decades after it was founded, in the middle of the fifteenth century, the Chosŏn dynasty government declared that heads of households hosting shamanic rituals would suffer legal consequences.[7] Yet the same government that declared private shamanic ritual illegal occasionally mobilized shamans to participate in a number of state-sanctioned rituals, such as rituals for rain in times of drought, for the recovery of the health of an ill member of the royal family, or in honor of local guardian deities.[8] Clearly, the staunchly Confucian

Chosŏn government did not outlaw religious activity or persecute religious practitioners per se. However, it also clearly did not allow religious freedom. Instead, it looked upon religious activity as no different from any other activity taking place within the territory under its control, granting religious organizations no more autonomy than it granted merchants, scholars, or slaves, and availing itself of their services whenever and wherever it saw fit.

Moreover, the ritual hegemony exercised by the premodern Korean state was not restricted to determining which rituals could legally be performed. The state also required that certain rituals had to be performed, and stipulated who had to perform them and when. Among the required rituals was the Confucian ancestor memorial service, with its spirit tablets. Those early Korean Catholics who refused to place such ancestor tablets on memorial altars in their homes and then bow before those tablets on the days designed for such ritual homage were not only deemed immoral for refusing to display proper ritual devotion to their ancestors, they were also condemned for their refusal to obey the laws of their country, which were seen as direct orders from the king himself. Catholics, therefore, were doubly criminal. They were considered to be both unfilial and disloyal. A common phrase used to criticize Catholics was *"mubu, mugun"* [無父無君, literally, "they have no parents and no ruler], meaning that they show no respect for their parents or their ruler.[9]

MORAL FRAILTY AND THE APPEAL OF CATHOLICISM

Yet, despite all these religious and legal barriers that Catholicism faced in Korea, a few Koreans, among them some of the brightest young men of their day, were drawn to that alien religion. What was it about Catholicism that attracted them? We can identify two major reasons for conversions to Catholicism. First, among the *yangban* (Confucian scholars eligible to vie for high-level government posts and their closest family members) elite, a growing sense of frustration with their inability to realize the Confucian promise that they could achieve moral perfection through their own efforts made a few of them receptive to the Catholic promise of divine assistance in overcoming human moral frailty. Some of the other Catholics were attracted more by the promise that death was not final, that eternal life in paradise awaited those who had been faithful servants of God.

"Moral frailty" is not a term that appears as such in the writings of premodern Korean thinkers. According to both Buddhism and Neo-Confucianism, as they were taught and practiced in Korea, human beings are born with the natural ability to overcome the temptations of the world on their own and to achieve moral perfection. Therefore an explicit acknowledgment that we might find it difficult, if not impossible, to overcome our innate ignorance and selfish tendencies would signal a sharp break with mainstream thought. However, a close study of what some Korean Buddhists and Neo-Confucians wrote about what was the most effective way to ensure that we consistently think and act in the most appropriate and ethical manner reveals that they recognized that the task was more difficult than their tradition would at first make it appear.

Within Korean Buddhism, we can find, starting with the influential Koryŏ monk Chinul (1158–1210), a recognition that a practitioner needed to diligently cultivate a moral character even after enlightenment had been achieved. As Chinul warned a disciple, "Although he has awakened to the fact that his original nature is no different from that of the Buddhas, . . . [habits of thought and behavior] are extremely difficult to remove suddenly and so he must continue to cultivate while relying on this awakening."[10] In other words, even after enlightened Korean Buddhists realized that they are actually Buddhas, and therefore should be perfect examples of proper behavior, they still needed to work hard to eradicate the bad habits they had acquired before they achieved that realization. This belief that sudden enlightenment had to be followed by gradual cultivation was not unique to Korea. However, the emphasis on the need for gradual cultivation even after enlightenment appears to have been stronger in Korea than elsewhere, reflecting a greater Korean awareness of how difficult it was to consistently think and act the way we know we should think and act.

We find that awareness in Korea's Neo-Confucian tradition as well. T'oegye Yi Hwang (1501–1570) and Yulgok Yi I (1536–1584), two giants of the Korean Neo-Confucian tradition, agreed that human beings are essentially good, but they also recognized that we do not always act in accordance with our innate goodness. Their counterpart to the Buddhist question of why we do not always think and act like Buddhas, even after we have become enlightened to our Buddha nature, was to ask why we seldom think and act like sages, even though we have studied the words of the Sages and pledged to live lives modeled on theirs. Though they agreed that human beings are generally not perfect, they disagreed over the cause of such moral failures, especially over how much to blame the body, and the emotions it produces, for our moral shortcomings.

Yulgok, reflecting the holistic tendency of mainstream Neo-Confucianism, refused to split human beings between a moral heart-and-mind that produces virtuous instincts that encourage us to act properly and a dangerous body that generates emotions that can only lead us astray. Instead, he argued that all human instincts and emotions are generated by interactions between our bodies and the material world in which they are immersed. Whether those instincts and emotions lead us to do good or evil is determined by whether or not we ensure they are guided by *li* (理), the Neo-Confucian term for the patterns of appropriate interaction that direct us to behave appropriately in every situation. T'oegye, on the other hand, believed that, since our bodies are what distinguish us from other human beings and other objects and therefore are what make us separate and distinct individuals, they are by their very nature morally dangerous. According to the standard Confucian view, morality consisted of always acting for the common good, never letting considerations of personal benefit sway us into acting one way or another. In T'oegye's view, since our bodies, as individual objects, always encourage us to think of ourselves as separate and distinct individuals, they inevitably pull us in an individualist, selfish direction. Our hearts-and-minds, on the other hand, are nothing other than *li* and as such let us know how we should act to promote the good of our community and live a moral life.

Over the next several centuries, Korean Neo-Confucianism was split into those whose preferred Yulgok's approach and those who preferred T'oegye's. Yulgok's followers tended to place less stress on human moral frailty than did the followers of T'oegye. Yulgok's holistic approach encouraged his followers to accept the fact that they could not avoid living in a material world and to recognize furthermore that it had some positive aspects, since it provided the arena within which moral action could take place. T'oegye's followers, on the other hand, moved in an opposite direction.

Within the T'oegye school, particularly the political and scholarly faction known as the Southerners (Namin), there was a growing tendency to emphasize the moral danger that existence as an individual in the material world entailed. Their increasing distrust of the human body, for example, encouraged them to move in an ascetic direction. One leading eighteenth-century disciple of T'oegye, Sŏngho Yi Ik, advocated severe restraint on the exercise of even those normal human desires for food and sex that are necessary to the survival of the human race. For example, he encouraged husbands and wives, after they had brought a son into the world, to move into separate sleeping quarters in order to make it easier for men to resist the pull of the flesh. He also suggested that men eat less than one full bowl of rice at every meal so that they will become accustomed to leaving physical desires less than completely satisfied.[11]

Moreover, some of the Southerners began to feel that their bodies were not the only threat. They were worried that the universe in general is full of material stuff that coagulates into separate and distinct entities, generating differentiation within the universal network of intertwined patterns formed by *li*. Differentiation, because it separates things from one another, is the fertilizer of selfishness. This was a matter of grave concern since, in the Neo-Confucian worldview, selfishness is responsible for the inappropriate thoughts and actions that constitute evil. However, they also recognized that it was impossible to be completely sheltered from the temptations emanating from the body and the material world. Therefore, though for the most part they continued to assert agreement with the Neo-Confucian assumption that human beings have an innate ability to live moral lives despite all the temptations to selfish thoughts and actions that surround them, they grew increasingly concerned about how difficult it is to actually live up to that Neo-Confucian promise.

The first Catholics in Korea emerged from among Southerner disciples of T'oegye and Sŏngho. Their heightened sense of moral frailty, of how difficult it is to live a moral life, stimulated them to search outside mainstream Confucian tradition for help in living up to the high moral standards set by that tradition. One of those Southerners, an early Catholic, though he later apostatized when the anti-Catholic persecution grew deadly, is widely recognized today as one of the greatest philosophers in all Korean history. Chŏng Yagyong (1762–1836), often called by his literary name, Tasan ("tea mountain"), never explicitly defends his Catholic youth in his extant writings. He and one of his brothers, Chŏng Yakchŏn (1758–1816), were both tortured and then exiled in 1801 for their involvement in the early Catholic community, though they had both left that Catholic community many years earlier. Another brother of his, Chŏng Yakchong (1760–1801), remained an active Catholic and was executed. So Tasan was circumspect in what he wrote about his beliefs and spiritual practices.

Nevertheless, we can still see from the commentaries on the Confucian classics he wrote while he was in exile that he had moved far beyond his Southerner predecessors to openly challenge the assumption that it is natural, and therefore should be easy, for human beings to be virtuous. Moreover, his recognition of human moral frailty led him to what was in Confucian circles a novel solution: belief in God Above (whom he called *Sangje*, 上帝, a term taken from the ancient Confucian classics).

In his commentaries on the seminal Confucian classics the *Mencius* and the *Doctrine of the Mean*, Tasan argued that when we say that human nature is innately good, we mean only that human beings have an innate desire for what is good. That includes moral good, of course, but Tasan points out that it also includes what feels good. He insists that when Confucians in the ancient past used the term "human nature," they meant "human desires," both moral desires and the desire for physical pleasure.[12] Moreover, often those two desires are in conflict. For example, he pointed out that if someone offers us a gift that could be interpreted as a bribe and therefore we know it would be wrong to accept it, we are torn between a desire for the pleasure that gift would give us and the desire to act appropriately and decline it. Similarly, if we find ourselves in a difficult situation, but we know we should deal with that situation, we nevertheless are tempted to simply flee and abdicate our responsibilities.[13] As a result, we often find that consistently following the right way and sticking to the moral path is as difficult as climbing up a steep hill, while following our preference for physical pleasure is as easy as rolling down that same hill.[14]

How can we then ensure that we always choose the moral course? Tasan provided an untraditional answer, grounded in his untraditional reading of the Confucian classics. He wrote that we need to be shamed into being moral all the time. And the only way we can be sure that we will be ashamed every time we do something wrong is if we keep in mind that, always and everywhere, we are being watched to see if we think and act properly. Who can possibly watch us always and everywhere? There is only one possible answer: God Above.

> There is no human being born on this earth without base desires. What keeps us from following those desires and doing whatever we feel like doing? It is the fear that our misbehavior will be noticed. Noticed by whom? Whose gaze keeps us in a state of constant caution and apprehension? We are cautious and apprehensive because we know there are enforcement officers responsible for making sure rules are followed. We are cautious and apprehensive because we know our ruler can punish us if we behave improperly. If we did not think there was someone watching us, would we not simply abandon all sense of moral responsibility and just do whatever we felt like doing?
>
> But what makes us behave properly even in the privacy of our own room and make sure that even our thoughts are proper thoughts? The only reason why a superior person is watchful over his thoughts and behavior even in the privacy of his own room is that he knows that there is a God Above [*Sangje*] watching him.[15]

No one else in his day was as explicit as Tasan in arguing that we need to believe that God Above is watching us in order to be motivated enough to consistently think and act the way we should. However, we know that the first Catholics were Confucians just as Tasan was. Moreover, Tasan and other founding members of the Korean Catholic Church had studied Confucian texts together before they formed Korea's first Catholic community.[16] It is not unreasonable to assume that some of his fellow Southerner disciples of T'oegye came to believe in God for the same reason Tasan did. They, too, may have found belief in God helpful for overcoming moral frailty.

However, not all of the early Korean Catholics were as motivated by frustration over personal moral frailty as Tasan was. Some of them were less concerned about that than they were attracted to the possibility of leaving behind the material world and gaining eternal life. Among those was Tasan's own older brother Yakchong. We read in Hwang Sayŏng's *Silk Letter* that, when Chŏng Yakchong

> was young, he wanted to learn about the immortals and their techniques of prolonging life. At that time, he believed in the false theory of the Great Transformation, the end of this universe and birth of another. But, realizing there was a problem with that theory, he sighed and said "When the cosmos undergoes this great transformation, even the immortals will not be able to escape destruction. In the end there is no way to live in this body forever. It's not worth studying those techniques." Then he heard of Catholicism and gained new hope for eternal life. He became a sincere Catholic.[17]

Yakchong was not alone. In fact, many of Korea's early Catholics made clear when they were being interrogated that they had joined the church because they wanted to go to Heaven when they died and were willing to hasten that transition by refusing to renounce their Catholic beliefs, even though that meant they would be executed. The Confucian prosecutors noticed that this unusual attitude was characteristic of Catholics. The official statement summing up the persecution of 1801 noted that "Those Catholics are deluded into believing in heaven and hell. . . . . Though it is normal for human beings to love life and fear death, when they are brought to the execution ground they look on it as a comfortable place to lie down and take a rest!"[18] Some recent observers have even described early Korean Catholics as "in pursuit of martyrdom."[19]

If that was their wish, they got what they wanted. The few dozen deaths described in the *Silk Letter* were followed by thousands more over the course of the nineteenth century. What was the nature of the government that could kill so many people because of their religious beliefs and practices?

THE GOVERNMENT OF KOREA IN
THE TIME OF THE *SILK LETTER*

Korea before the modern era was not a democracy. The government of the Chosŏn dynasty, which ended in 1910, was a monarchy. That is not surprising, since the vast majority of governments on earth at that time were monarchies. However, the monarchy of premodern Korea had its own distinctive features. Outwardly, in the formal structure of its government institutions as well as the titles of its government officials, it looked very similar to China. The ruler in Korea was called a king rather than an emperor, but below the ruler there were striking similarities in both structure and nomenclature. Confucianism was the official philosophy in both China and Korea. Both China and Korea had six primary ministries, one each for personnel administration, revenue, public works, law enforcement, military affairs, and rites (which was also in charge of education and foreign relations). In both China and Korea the officials who staffed those central government agencies were bureaucrats chosen mostly on the basis of their performance on civil service examinations that tested their command of Confucian traditions. Moreover, the titles for their respective posts were, for the most part, the same in Korea as in China. And, just as in China, the central government dispatched officials from the capital to serve as the heads of various local government agencies, ranging from provincial governors to county magistrates. Those local officials bore the same titles in both Korea and China.

However, the Korean government worked in distinctively Korean ways. Hereditary social status played a much larger role in the government of premodern Korea than it did in China, and, as a result, the king exercised less power over his bureaucrats than the emperor of China did over his.

Though, theoretically, the civil service examinations were open to almost all educated males, in Korea, unlike in China, in the second half of the Chosŏn era the higher-level civil service examinations were for all practical purposes limited to members of the *yangban* elite. The *yangban* were defined as those whose fathers and mothers, and grandfathers and grandmothers, were *yangban*. Since "*yangban*" refers to those who were related to present or past officeholders, that meant that usually the only people who were allowed to take the civil service examination were those whose parents and paternal and maternal grandparents had either held a central government bureaucratic post themselves or were directly descended from someone who had held such a post. In a further difference from China, the status of a potential government official's mother was as important as the status of his father. The son of a *yangban* father and a non-*yangban* mother was barred from all high-level positions in the government bureaucracy. So was the son of a mother who was a remarried widow, no matter what her original social status may have been.

Such a restriction on whom the king could appoint to work for him greatly limited his ability to select officials whom he trusted to carry out his policies in the ways he wanted them carried out. Moreover, there were even more restrictions on whom he could bring into the government to help him govern. By the second half of the dynasty, the *yangban* elite of Korea had divided into two groups: those who usually lived in the capital region and had ancestors within just a few generations who had held high government office, and those in the countryside, whose last ancestor to hold a high government office was several generations back. Men from the latter group could take the examination but, even if they passed it, they had little hope of actually being appointed to a post in the central government. Instead, those posts tended to be monopolized by families who lived either in or near the capital and had a family history of holding high government posts. And even within that elite group, factional affiliation often determined a successful examination passer's actual chances of winning an important government post. If a bright young man were a member of a faction that was out of power when he was in his prime office-holding years, he had little chance of actually becoming an important government official. Moreover, since factional affiliation was, to a large degree, hereditary, he could not easily change his factional affiliation in order to better his chances for appointment.

As a result of all of these restrictions on whom the king could choose to work with him at court or as the head of a local government agency, the king often found himself unable to rule as he saw fit. Instead, if his officials firmly resisted his proposed policies, he often had to give in to their demands, since he would find it difficult to hire replacements if he dismissed them or they resigned. One example of a king unable to impose his wishes on his own government was King Chŏngjo (r. 1776–1800). He was on the throne when a Catholic community emerged in Korea. He was concerned that the dispute that arose during his reign over who was tainted by association with Catholicism and who was not would further restrict his ability to appoint to office those whom he believed were best suited for those posts. However, despite his many calls for his officials, as well as out-of-office *yangban*, to stop flooding the court with requests for a wide-ranging search for, and punishment of, anyone who was in any way involved with the birth of Catholicism in Korea, those requests continued to pour in.[20] The king found himself at times forced to dismiss from office, or demote from a central government post to one in the distant countryside, someone whose talents he valued but who had come under attack for alleged pro-Catholic sympathies.[21]

The king also had to deal with his Censorate. Censorate is a general term used in a Korean context to refer to three different governments agencies that assumed responsibility for ensuring that government policies, as well as the personal lives of government officials, were in accord with Confucian moral principles. The Office of the Censor-General was one such agency, but it shared censoring duties with the Office of the Inspector-General and the Office of Special Counselors. The concept of a Censorate, which acquired its name from its power to deem certain documents and actions unacceptable, emerged first in China, where it was intended to aid the emperor of China in fighting corruption among his officials. It was supposed to identify those whom the emperor should not trust. However, in Korea, the Censorate often aimed its criticisms at the king himself. The king might be accused of lacking filial piety if he proposed significant changes to the policies of his predecessors, he might be accused of not showing Confucian scholars proper respect if he tried to raise taxes on the *yangban*, and he might be accused of insufficient dedication to preserving and promoting Confucianism if he failed to be as aggressive against Catholics as the censors thought he should be.

The history of the Chosŏn dynasty cannot be comprehended apart from the struggle between the kings and their censors.[22] Often, the censors won. A monarch ignored the demands of the censors at his own peril. One Chosŏn dynasty king, Yŏnsan'gun (r. 1494–1506), was over-thrown because of a number of actions he took that turned his officials against him, but the last straw may have been his prohibition of any criticism directed at him. Almost three centuries later, censors were among the first, and the most vociferous, of the voices demanding that Catholics be punished as harshly as possible for their challenge to Con-fucian beliefs and values. King Chŏngjo tried his best to tone down anti-Catholic rhetoric, but he could not totally ignore what his censors were telling him. If he had turned a deaf ear to remonstrance from the Censorate, he would have been accused of lacking respect for Confu-cian moral principles, and that would have called into question his suit-ability for serving as the ruler of a Confucian state.

Despite the relative weakness of the Korean monarch in his dealings with his top officials, including the censors, the Chosŏn dynasty govern-ment overall was quite strong in its dealings with those it governed, par-ticularly in the area of criminal law. Premodern Korea had a multilayered system for identifying criminals, arresting them, and punishing them. In Seoul, the State Tribunal was responsible for investigating crimes by *yangban*, particularly when they were charged with treason or any other activity that threatened the government, while the Police Bureau was in charge of investigating criminal activity by other members of society. Outside of Seoul, the local district magistrate was the chief law enforce-ment officer in his district. He served as the chief investigator, judge, and jailer. However, he was not allowed to execute any criminals in his care without specific authorization from the king.

Much of our information on the persecution of Catholics comes from the transcripts of the interrogations of *yangban* Catholics by the State Tribunal as well as reports from local district magistrates on their interrogation of *yangban* Catholics under their jurisdiction. We know much less about what happened to non-*yangban* Catholics once they were arrested, since neither the Police Bureau nor local government offi-cials felt any need to keep detailed records on them. In fact, we do not even know the names of many of the commoner and lower-class Catho-lics who were executed.

THE LAW ENFORCEMENT SYSTEM

We do know, however, how Catholics of all ranks were treated once they were in custody. Interrogation in premodern Korea almost always involved what we would today call torture: the deliberate inflicting of severe pain, including beating with clubs. The purpose of such harsh interrogation was twofold: the interrogators wanted to make sure those they were interrogating gave them the names of anyone else involved in their criminal activity or even knew about it but had failed to inform the authorities. They also wanted the accused to confess that they were guilty as charged. Often the last information in the official records about a suspect before their execution is a first-person account of their crimes.

Among the tortures the accused often had to endure was the "leg screw," which was often quite effective since it caused extreme pain but usually did not kill or even cause unconsciousness. In this particular form of torture, the accused sat on a chair with his or her legs tied together tightly at the ankles and the knees. Then two sturdy sticks were placed between the legs below the knees and twisted so that they forced the legs apart. This would force the shinbones to slowly and painfully bend outward. However, if it were done the way it was intended, those bones would not break, so this procedure could be repeated over and over again until the accused told the interrogators whatever they wanted to hear.[23]

Flogging was also used, both in interrogations and also as a form of punishment. It was somewhat riskier, since it would often leave the subject of an interrogation unconscious and therefore unable to answer any questions. That made it necessary for the interrogators to wait until the accused regained consciousness so they could again interrogate, and beat, them. Sometimes the flogging went too far, and the accused, or the convicted, died. Nevertheless, it was considered an essential tool of law enforcement, if used correctly.

Chŏng Yagyong experienced flogging both as a subject of an official interrogation, when he was accused of being pro-Catholic in 1801, and as an official who supervised its use on others. In a guide for district magistrates he wrote after 1801, while he was in exile, he complained that flogging often was done incorrectly. He noted, "the magistrates are inexperienced in administration and the clerks are so ignorant that they do not hesitate to thrash the suspect with lashes and paddles when they take the deposition from the offender. Sometimes they smash the ribs of the suspect by using a truncheon that is too thick, causing pain too extreme to bear."[24] However, he was not opposed to flogging done properly. He noted approvingly, "in the beginning of our dynasty there was no fixed rule for the number of strokes in flogging during interrogation. In the third year of King Sejong's reign, the Chief Magistrate of the State Tribunal Pak Ŭn requested that the number of times the accused is clubbed at the first interrogation be limited to thirty."[25] That seemed a reasonable number to Chŏng.

If someone were accused, interrogated, and beaten, and then found innocent, they could not sue the government for improper treatment. There were no legal limits on the power of the state vis-à-vis its subjects, and therefore subjects did not have inalienable legal rights they could accuse the government of violating. That meant they also did not enjoy any right to be free from government interference in matters that today are often seen as private and outside of any government's legitimate exercise of authority. Among the areas considered to be within the jurisdiction of the government of Chosŏn Korea were religion and ritual. As we have already seen, this led to the persecution of Catholics who refused to honor their ancestors in the manner prescribed by their government. The Catholic attempt to erect a wall between church and state in order to carve out space for religious and ritual freedom clashed with a long-standing Confucian assumption that control of ritual was essential to the preservation of governmental authority. Around two thousand years before the Chosŏn dynasty began persecuting Catholics for violating ritual regulations, an early Chinese history had already noted that "the great matters of concern for the state are ritual and the use of force."[26] When Catholics claimed that they should be free to follow their own conscience in religious and ritual matters, they were undermining one of the two pillars that held up Confucian states. That made them subject to the full force of the staunchly Confucian Chosŏn dynasty's law enforcement system.

Despite its strong commitment to Confucian beliefs and values, and its willingness to use force to protect those beliefs and values, Chosŏn dynasty Korea departed sharply from the official Confucianism of China, the country that had created and defined it, on two issues: the role of heredity in determining social status and its toleration of factions.

THE SOCIAL STRUCTURE

Confucianism was not egalitarian. It assumed that men were inherently superior to women, at least in the public sphere. It also required the young to defer to those older than them. And, it granted scholars higher social status than it awarded to technicians, artisans, peasants, and merchants. However, although Confucianism in China opened the civil service examinations to almost all adult males, Korea, as we have already seen, did not. Instead, Korea restricted its civil service examinations to the sons of *yangban* parents. This created a hereditary governing class. Moreover, the *yangban* were more than just the governing class. They were also the major landowners in Korea. Since agriculture was the mainstay of the economy of premodern Korea, that made the *yangban* the wealthiest class as well.

The *yangban* were not a monolithic group. Within their ranks there were subgroups that were also largely defined along hereditary lines. We have already noted the distinction between those *yangban* who lived in the capital region and those who lived in the countryside. Sons and daughters of *yangban* from the capital region tended to marry the sons and daughters of other *yangban* from the capital region. The son or daughter of a rural *yangban* usually ended up marrying someone from another rural *yangban* family. Moreover, even within the capital elite, there was a distinction between those who held high civil posts, or were related to those who had held such posts, and those who held high military posts or were related to those who had held such posts. That distinction determined marriage partners as well, with few sons of military officers marrying daughters of high civil officials. Daughters were more likely to be able to marry outside of their particular subgroup, but generally marriages linked families within the same small social circle, creating communities defined along occupational and hereditary lines.

This emphasis on heredity, and the association of heredity with occupation, determined the lower rungs of the social ladder as well. We have already noted that the sons of *yangban* fathers and non-*yangban* mothers were not allowed to take the higher-level civil service examination. They ended up forming a separate social class of their own. The sons of *yangban* fathers were discouraged from becoming merchants, since the open pursuit of profit was considered beneath the dignity of even someone who was half *yangban*. As a result, many of them used the education they had received in their *yangban* family to work as clerks in central government offices or as lower-level officials, filling posts in the central government bureaucracy that such men were allowed to hold.

Over the generations, some of the descendants of these "secondary sons" ended up dropping one more rung down the social ladder into the class of technical specialists working for the government. Mathematicians, geographers, translators, physicians, artists, and others with technical skills needed by the government formed a class called *chungin,* the "middle people," since originally many of them had lived in the middle of Seoul. They also tended to marry among themselves, so they came to form another group defined by both the work they did and whom their ancestors were. Since male *chungin* were educated in the same literary Chinese used by the *yangban,* they could, and often did, socialize with *yangban* and secondary sons. However, they did not forge marriage ties with *yangban* families. They also did not tend to intermarry with another group that was sometimes also called *chungin.* Those other *chungin* were the subordinates of *yangban* officials in government offices in the countryside. They, too, were a hereditary group, but in their case they inherited low-level positions requiring them to aid rural *yangban* government officials by collecting taxes and administering the punishments they decreed. Their status in society was lower than that of the *chungin* who were technical specialists working directly for the central government. One reason the capital-based *chungin* enjoyed a higher status is that they, unlike the local clerks, earned their position by taking a special civil service examination for technical specialists. It was not the same examination as the one on the Confucian classics that *yangban* officials were required to pass, but it was an examination nonetheless, and therefore it provided social status for those who passed it. Just as was the case with the Confucian examination, those who passed that technical examination tended to come from a very narrow segment of society. In fact, mathematicians tended to come from the families of mathematicians, physicians tended to come from the families of physicians, geographers tended to come from the families of geographers, and so on. Even at the level of technical expertise, family background determined both what job you could hold and what sort of person you could marry.[27]

Beneath the *chungin* were the commoners, called "the good people" in most Korean Confucian writings. Commoners included peasants, fisherfolk, artisans, and merchants, though theoretically peasants and fisherfolk enjoyed higher social status than did artisans and merchants. The restrictions against marriage across status boundaries tended to blur within the commoner class. However, commoners avoided marriage with those of lowest status, the group consisting of people involved in despised occupations. Butchers, grave diggers, shamans, entertainers, and slaves were all ranked below commoners, artisans, and merchants, with butchers and grave diggers placed at the very bottom.

The position of women in society was not quite as rigidly defined as it was for men. The social status of a woman was largely defined by that of her father, and to a lesser extent by that of her husband. It was not uncommon for a woman to marry into a family of higher status than her natal family. However, a woman who moved into the household of a man of higher status, such as when a non-*yangban* female became the secondary spouse of a *yangban* male, would not move up to the same rank as her husband. Only the primary wife, who had to come from a *yangban* family, would enjoy full *yangban* status. In fact, as we have noted already, even the children of the secondary wife would be lower down on the social ladder than their *yangban* father, since they were not eligible for high-level government posts, though they might have higher social standing than their mother. Nevertheless, such a wife would be treated with more respect than if she had stayed a peasant, for example.

FACTIONALISM

In addition to this un-Confucian stress on hereditary status, Korea also tolerated factions in court politics to a much greater extent than Confucian China did.[28] "Faction" is a derogatory term often used to dismiss a political group as more concerned with personal benefit than for what is best for society as a whole. Confucians, both in China and in Korea, often called for the elimination of factions. However, the existence of factions is inevitable in any political climate in which there are more qualified applicants for government posts than are available, causing people to look for a group of like-minded potential officials they can join in the hope that, by helping each other, they all can advance into the official positions they desire. Factions also arise because there will always be differences of opinion over which policies a government should adopt, and those who share a similar policy stance will tend to work together to promote that policy. Nevertheless, Confucian political philosophers condemned the forming of such groups, arguing that there was always only one correct political course a government should follow in any particular situation and everyone in government or who hoped to be in government should support that policy. Those who did not, or who formed minority groups within the bureaucracy, were condemned as placing personal self-interest ahead of the common good and therefore were deemed immoral.

Factionalism became a serious problem in Korea because, due to the Korean stress on heredity, Korea's factions stayed together over generations. *Yangban* in the second half of the Chosŏn dynasty generally were members of the same faction their ancestors had been in. There might have been a split within a faction, but it was rare to see someone actually move to a faction completely different from that of their father and grandfather. Moreover, people tended to marry within their faction, and considered their own faction morally superior to all others. In fact, even though they might use a faction title for themselves and their friends and relatives, they would often deny that their group was actually a faction. That label was reserved for all the other factions. Because of the stress on filial piety in Confucian Korea, members of a faction could not accept a charge that their paternal and material ancestors had been part of a faction, by definition an immoral group. They would adamantly reject the charge that the group to which they and their ancestors belonged was an "evil faction."

Historians usually trace the roots of the factionalism that prevailed in eighteenth- and nineteenth-century Korea to 1575, when the opposing sides in a battle for control of the positions in the Ministry of Personnel responsible for nominating candidates for official posts coalesced into hereditary cliques. Since the leaders of those factions lived in different parts of Seoul, their followers became known as Easterners and Westerners, depending on which direction their allegiance lay. A decade and a half after the Easterners separated from the Westerners, the Easterners underwent fission once again, this time into the similarly named Namin (Southerners) and Pugin (Northerners). Almost a century later, when the Westerners could not agree on how long the Queen Dowager should mourn the recently deceased king (King Hyojong, r. 1649–1659), they ruptured as well, separating into hostile Noron (Patriarchs) and Soron (Disciples) camps.

As a result of these various disputes, the Chosŏn dynasty entered the eighteenth century with four irreconcilable groups, called the "Four Colors," differentiated not only by what their political positions were but also by what the political positions of their ancestors had been. These hereditary factions sought to place as many of their own members in high government posts as possible while excluding as many members of opposing factions as they possibly could. Kings naturally opposed this, since they would prefer to be surrounded by ministers more inclined to follow the king's policy preferences than by ministers more interested in promoting the narrow agenda of a particular faction.

The history of the eighteenth century is therefore a history of a constant struggle between the throne and the bureaucracy, with kings trying to claim supreme authority over their government but facing resistance from officials trying to bend the bureaucracy to serve factional interests.

Royal attempts to strengthen the authority of the reigning monarch were made more difficult in the eighteenth century because three kings in a row had family backgrounds that made them appear, in the eyes of many, unsuitable to sit on the throne. King Kyŏngjong (r. 1720–1724) was the son of Lady Chang, who was believed to have used black magic to cause the death of Queen Inhyŏn, her rival for the affection of his father, King Sukchong (r. 1674–1720).[29] That made Kyŏngjong the son of a criminal.

Kyŏngjong died in 1724, after coming down with a severe bout of diarrhea shortly after eating some crabs pickled in soy sauce his half-brother had sent him. That half-brother then ascended the throne as King Yŏngjo (r. 1724–1776), immediately raising suspicions that Kyŏngjong's death was not accidental. No one could prove that those pickled crabs were poisonous. However, there were some among Kyŏngjong's supporters who remembered that the person who had first reported Lady Chang's use of black magic, and thus was indirectly responsible for the death of Kyŏngjong's mother, was the mother of Yŏngjo, who as crown prince gave King Kyŏngjong those crabs.

Yŏngjo thus became king with his legitimacy compromised by rumors of fraternal regicide. Moreover, his mother was not only an informer, she had been a lowly servant girl in the palace before she caught King Sukchong's eye. To the scholar-officials who stressed proper pedigree, her low social status made her an unacceptable mother for a king, and thus raised doubts about her son's right to claim to throne.

In 1749 King Yŏngjo handed over many of his royal duties to his son Prince Sado, naming him regent in the hope that ambitious officials would cluster around the regent and allow the king to escape their constant attention. Unfortunately, the crown prince suffered from a mental disease, which made him unsuitable for such a responsibility. In fact, he was so unsuitable that, since he was Yŏngjo's only surviving son and therefore his one and only heir, his survival threatened the survival of the dynasty itself. He began to engage in behavior even a king could not engage in, including random acts of murder. Such behavior by a leading member of the royal family undermined the aura of virtue that the Yi family needed in order to rule over the Confucian government of Korea. In order to save the Yi family claim to the Chosŏn throne, in 1762 King Yŏngjo ordered his son sealed into a rice chest to die of dehydration.[30] Unfortunately, with that command, he not only caused the death of his only son, he also caused two new factions to appear when his grandson took the throne in 1776. Those new factions, which crossed previous factional lines, came to be known as the "Flexible Faction" (時派 Sip'a), which supported the right of the son of that prince in the rice chest to succeed Yŏngjo, and the "Intransigent Faction" (僻派 Pyŏkp'a), which did not.

That new king, King Chŏngjo, like his grandfather Yŏngjo and his granduncle Kyŏngjong before him, ascended the throne under a cloud of doubts about the legitimacy of his claim. Unlike his two predecessors, he was the son of a respectable mother from a family that had produced many top officials. Like his granduncle, however, he was the child of someone who had been condemned as a criminal. However, in his case, his parentage was more problematic than Kyŏngjong's, since patriarchal Korea was more interested in someone's father than their mother. His father's death in that rice chest, and the conviction of many officials and scholars that Prince Sado's execution was the inevitable and appropriate consequence of his unacceptable behavior, cast a shadow over Chŏngjo's claim to monarchial virtue. Chŏngjo tried to overcome that handicap of doubtful legitimacy by rising above factionalism and implementing a policy of "Grand Harmony." By the middle of his reign, Chŏngjo had successfully forced the three most powerful factions, the Patriarchs, the Disciples, and the Southerners, to share the top ministerial posts, though the Patriarchs remained the most powerful faction in the central government bureaucracy overall.

However, Chŏngjo clearly remained concerned that doubts about his legitimacy or his attempts to break the grip of particular factions on government posts might lead to attempts to overthrow him. In 1785 he downgraded the royal guard unit that was under the control of his officials and replaced it with a new unit, the *Chang'yong'yŏng* ("Stout young braves garrison"), which was under his direct control.[31] A few years later, he began making plans to move his capital from Seoul to a new fortress he ordered built south of Seoul in what is now the city of Suwŏn.[32] He apparently hoped that such a move would put him beyond the reach of the old elite who would stay behind in Seoul. In addition, he created a Royal Library (Kyujanggak), modeled after the Imperial Library of Song China, and used the young scholars assigned to work there to provide him with advice directly, bypassing the normal bureaucratic channels. All of those moves angered the Patriarchs Faction, which had been the dominant faction since 1740.

The Intransigent Faction, led by Sim Hwanji (1730–1802) from the Patriarchs Faction, was probably bothered more by Chŏngjo's attempt to gain supremacy over the entrenched power of high officials and elite families in Seoul than they were by his tainted ancestry. The Flexible Faction, on the other hand, supported the king's strengthening of royal authority because a stronger king would mean more opportunities for scholars from weaker factions to advance through government ranks. The stage was thus set for factional battles. King Chŏngjo further exacerbated matters by insisting, in the last year of his reign, that, despite centuries of Korean tradition, officials were supposed to obey their king, not argue with him. When Chŏngjo declared, as he did on the last day of May 1800, that he was the personification of Heavenly Principle on Earth, the August Monarch around which government revolved, anger among the Intransigent Faction reached unprecedented levels.[33] When he went further and hinted that he might declare that their faction was responsible for the death of his father, they also began to fear that they would soon lose what little political power they still wielded.

It is no wonder that when King Chŏngjo died in June 1800, less than a month after demanding unquestioning obedience from his officials, many suspected that his death was no accident. (The fact that the physician who treated the king on his deathbed was related to Sim Hwanji appeared to some to be more than a coincidence.) Whether King Chŏngjo died a natural death or had been murdered made not much difference to the members of the Flexible Faction. The king who had brought them into his government was gone, and as a result they faced a dramatically different political environment. The new king, Sunjo (r. 1800–1834), was only eleven years old when he replaced his father on the throne. That put the court in the hands of the oldest living queen, who happened to be Queen Chŏngsun (1745–1805), one of the queens of King Yŏngjo and the daughter of a Patriarchs Faction family, which was allied with the Intransigent Faction.

The Flexible Faction was rendered particularly vulnerable by the fact that among their ranks were the leaders of Korea's Catholic Church. Catholicism had appeared in Korea only fifteen years earlier, when a young member of the Southerner Faction accompanied a diplomatic mission to Beijing and met some French missionaries there. Converted by those priests, he returned to Korea and began converting his friends and relatives. Within a decade there was an underground Catholic community on the peninsula several thousand strong. Those Catholics violated Korean law, refusing to mourn their dead in the prescribed Confucian manner because the Pope in Rome had told them Confucian mourning rituals were idolatrous. On top of that, they had smuggled a foreigner, a Chinese Catholic priest, into Korea in 1794 and tried to arrange for even more foreigners, including French troops, to come to Korea to force the Korean government to grant them religious freedom.

Such violations of both Confucian ethics and Korean sovereignty practically invited a bloody persecution.

However, King Chŏngjo tried to mitigate the persecution of Catholics, fearing that charges of Catholic connections would be wielded as a weapon by the Intransigent Faction against the Flexible Faction. Once he was dead, his fears were realized. The Intransigent Faction seized control of the government and used its prosecutorial authority to decimate the Flexible Faction, killing those it could prove were active Catholics and exiling many others. The Flexible Faction's connection with Catholicism became a perfect weapon to use against them. The conventions of Korean politics stipulated that the new monarch could not directly attack the policies of the previous king. However, since King Chŏngjo had condemned Catholicism as a violation of Confucian norms and had even permitted the execution of two Catholics in 1791 for failing to hold a funeral in the prescribed Confucian manner, the Intransigent Faction was able to attack the Catholics as being disloyal to King Chŏngjo, citing the late king's anti-Catholic statements.

Ironically, the Intransigent Faction was also able to draw on anti-Catholic writings by members of the same Southerners Faction to which most Catholic *yangban,* and many members of the Flexible Faction, belonged to justify a bloody persecution of Catholics. Chapter 2 examines those writings to see why even many of those who were in the same political camp as most of the *yangban* Catholics nevertheless felt that Catholicism was a threat to the foundations of Chosŏn Korea's state and society and therefore felt morally compelled to condemn Catholicism and those who believed in it.

CHAPTER 2

Confucian Criticisms of Catholicism

Confucius (551–479 BCE) warned 2,500 years ago that "The study of strange teachings is harmful indeed!"[1] The word Confucius used in denouncing "strange teachings" is *idan* (異端). Shin Hudam (1702–1761), writing over two millennia later, used the same term when, denouncing Catholicism and other departures from mainstream Confucianism, he declared, "There are thousands of deviant teachings [*idan*], all different, yet all flowing from the common spring of selfishness."[2]

Confucius spoke in vague generalities when he condemned harmful teachings in the sixth century BCE. In eighteenth-century Korea, his followers were more specific in their denunciations. An influential early disciple of Confucius, Mencius (371–289 BCE), in the fourth century BCE had rejected as *idan* the ideas of Yang Zhu (440?–360?) and Mozi (479?–381?). Mencius criticized Yang Zhu for not placing enough priority on the common good, and Mozi for erring in the other direction by insisting that every human deserved the same love and respect from us, even though, Mencius insisted, we had a special relationship with members of our own family. In twelfth-century CE China, Zhu Xi (1130–1200), whose grand synthesis of the ideas of earlier Confucians gave birth to Neo-Confucian, had condemned Buddhism and Daoism as *idan* for ignoring the importance of our obligations to our fellow human beings. T'oegye Yi Hwang, whom some considered the Korean Zhu Xi, warned against the positions taken by Wang Yangming (1472–1529), writing that Wang fell into *idan* when he argued that Zhu Xi was wrong to insist on looking for the patterns of appropriate interaction in the world around us rather than within our own hearts-and-minds. Shin and some of his contemporaries wanted to add "Western Learning" to the list of deviant teachings. They charged that the Catholicism preached by European missionaries in China, under the names

"Celestial Learning" (Ch'ŏnhak) and "Western Learning" (Sŏhak) and propagated in Korea through missionary-authored Chinese-language texts, was also *idan*.

Idan was a term Koreans applied to all ideas and practices that did not follow the way laid down by the Sages of ancient China.[3] Arthur Waley translated the statement by Confucius that opens this chapter as "He who sets to work upon a different strand destroys the whole fabric."[4] Waley's rendition preserves the metaphor that Confucius used to warn his listeners that his teachings were sewn from a common thread that must be preserved intact lest the moral order thus woven unravel. During the staunchly Neo-Confucian Chosŏn dynasty, Koreans heeded this warning from Confucius and carefully evaluated all novel ideas to determine if they were a help or a hindrance to the promotion of the Confucian moral order.

Korean Neo-Confucians had two primary criteria for testing ideas to determine whether they were *idan* or acceptable, whether they followed or threatened the thread of Confucian tradition. First of all, orthodoxy, correct ideas, had to be accompanied by orthopraxis, correct behavior, to merit recognition as true orthodoxy. Only those ideas, assertions, and claims, whether psychological, philological, philosophical, ontological, or ethical, that encouraged proper behavior, or at least did not discourage such behavior, could be accepted as truly orthodox. The traditional Confucian values of loyalty, filial piety, and unselfish dedication to the common good were the touchstones, forming the court before which all ideas had to come to plead their case for acceptability. This pragmatic approach is inherited from T'oegye's vision of truth as primarily a guide to proper behavior.[5] As Sŏngho Yi Ik explained, what difference did it make whether people were "orthodox" or not if they did not do what they were supposed to do?[6] Sŏngho's disciple Sunam Ahn Chŏngbok (1712–1791) made a similar point, writing to a friend in 1783 that he should not rely on verbal arguments alone in deciding what to believe but should instead test the practical applicability of ideas in order to determine their acceptability.[7]

Equally critical was fidelity to a plausible reading of the Confucian canon. There was some dispute over how much weight was to be assigned to Song dynasty (960–1279) commentaries from China relative to the original Confucian classics they were commenting on. By the seventeenth century, there were already some in Korea as well as in China who questioned whether those classics had to be approached only through later commentaries or whether they could be approached directly.[8] Nevertheless, there was broad agreement that Confucian tradition, grounded in the classics, provided a standard against which ideas, assertions, and claims could be evaluated. As Ahn Chŏngbok stated, "Anything that is not Confucian is heterodox [idan]."[9] Just as Catholics and Protestants have argued over whether the Bible should be interpreted by the individual reader or through the medium of centuries of Christian tradition but have agreed on the primacy of the Bible's words, so too Korean Neo-Confucians accepted the recorded words of Confucius and Mencius as definitive. Supporting this canonical criterion for orthodoxy, another Sŏngho disciple, Hwang Tŏkkil (1750–1827), wrote that true Confucians would not say anything or do anything the great men of old would not have said or done. Moreover, he, like other mainstream Confucians, insisted this was the only way to preserve the moral order. "We illuminate the great Confucian Way in order to block the self-centered tendencies existence as an individual stimulates, and we promote orthodoxy [chŏnghak] in order to expose non-canonical theories."[10]

These first two criteria were interrelated. The behavior that orthodoxy promoted was deemed proper because it was ordained by the classics. And the moral message of the classics was respected and protected because they taught men the proper way to behave. Consequently, any statements or claims that undermined fidelity to the Confucian moral code enshrined in the classics were idan, "heterodoxy."

In addition to textual and behavioral evidence for orthodoxy, Koreans also expected ideas claiming orthodox status to appear in Chinese dress. Orthodoxy had to have some connection with China. If it did not originate in China, it at least had to have undergone some measure of Sinification. Imported ideas appealing for acceptance by Korean Neo-Confucians could not come to Korea directly, but could only approach the peninsula through China. A Chinese pedigree alone was not sufficient grounds for acceptance, of course. The Korean rejection of Wang Yangming is evidence of that. However, proof of either Chinese ancestry, or at least Sinification, was a necessary, though not a sufficient, condition for acceptance by Sŏngho and like-minded Confucians in eighteenth-century Korea. As Sunam argued in a letter to a disciple who was flirting with Catholicism, "I have heard of China transforming barbarians but I have never heard of barbarians transforming China."[11] Shin Hudam echoes that rejection of Catholicism as Western, and therefore inferior to Confucianism: "The various states of Europe are nothing but barbarian tribes on the fringes of civilization. Europeans have no basis for claiming for themselves or their civilization the same respect which China and Chinese receive."[12]

This third criterion is related to the fourth. To win a positive hearing, ideas should not only be Sinified but also well aged. Novel ideas were automatically suspect. The only way new ideas could win a hearing was to disguise them in old clothing. All else being equal, the older the better. That is why some Koreans were intrigued by the arguments of Matteo Ricci (1552–1610) and other Jesuit missionaries in China that Catholic teachings were more faithful to the earliest Confucian texts than the later commentaries of the Song were.[13] However, that patina of age, like a Chinese pedigree, was a necessary but not a sufficient condition for acceptance as orthodoxy. After all, the heterodox teachings of Buddhism, Mozi, and Yang Zhu could also claim a long history. Sunam wrote his "An Examination of Celestial Learning" to show that, though many of the ideas and practices Catholics espoused in their Celestial Learning resembled ideas and practices mentioned in Chinese records from centuries past, those ideas and practices had been rejected back then, so they should be rejected again by his contemporaries.[14]

Those last two criteria of historical and cultural coloring would usually only come into play after the first two of ethical and canonical compatibility had been applied. In Chosŏn Korea, the two questions Neo-Confucians asked most often in testing ideas to determine whether they were orthodox or heterodox, whether they followed or threatened the thread of Confucian tradition, were: Did those ideas encourage or discourage proper behavior? Did they contradict or support the moral message of the Confucian classics? If they discouraged proper behavior or contradicted the moral message of the Confucian classics, they were *idan*.

As is often the case with key Confucian terms, there is no precise English equivalent for *idan*. Dictionaries today may define *idan* as "heresy" but neither heresy nor "heterodoxy" carries the full meaning *idan* had for Koreans in the seventeenth and eighteenth centuries. Both *idan* and heterodoxy indicate unacceptable opinions and beliefs. However,

idan designated dangerous teachings that not only departed from orthodox Confucian beliefs and values but challenged them in actual behavior
as well. When missionaries from the Roman Catholic Society of Jesus, the
Jesuits, sailed to China in the seventeenth and eighteenth centuries,
they hoped to convince the people of China that Catholicism represented
the true religion. Though they were able to convince a few Chinese to
accept their claim, most Chinese, and most Koreans as well, concluded
instead that the Jesuits and their followers held unacceptable beliefs and
values that led to unacceptable behavior.

The Neo-Confucian conception of *idan* differed significantly from
the notion of heresy prevalent in the West that the Jesuit missionaries in
China had traveled from. There was no equivalent to Rome in Korean
Neo-Confucianism. There were no ecclesiastical authorities defining
specific doctrines Neo-Confucians had to believe and other ideas they
were not allowed to entertain. In the Neo-Confucian world, outside of
the state itself, there was no organization entrusted with the power to
use force to establish, safeguard, foster, and defend orthodoxy. Moreover, a Confucian state normally did not demand rigid adherence to
specific formulations of Confucian teachings. Free debate by scholars
could be and often was permitted. Only when the political authority of
the state, or the rituals and morals that were the core of Confucian practice, was challenged did the government feel compelled to intervene in
intellectual disputes.[15] The state was more concerned about orthopraxy
than it was about orthodoxy.

The Jesuit missionaries who traveled to China from Europe to pros-
elytize for Roman Catholic monotheism in the seventeenth and eighteenth centuries entered a world that generally tolerated private deviation from mainstream thinking but condemned such nonconformity if
it went beyond the realm of ideas into public action. What a person
believed in the privacy of his own heart was of no concern to the Confucian state. What a person did with others was. Buddhism, for example, was *idan*, yet Buddhists were not punished merely for believing in
Buddhism. However, when they met secretly with other Buddhists at
night and proclaimed that the coming of the Maitreya [the Buddha who
would rule in the future] was at hand, they violated the laws of the state
and risked official censure and punishment.[16] The Chinese state had
learned from experience that secretive Buddhist sects could turn rebel-

lious, so they had to be controlled. Likewise, Confucian governments chastised those who violated the regulations governing ritual or disobeyed the moral rules governing human relationships, since ritual and social morality were the glue that held Confucian society together. Confucian officials acted vigorously to protect the social order. They showed less concern for how closely the thinking of the masses mirrored the orthodox interpretations of Confucian philosophy. Challenges to the accepted ethical norms were prohibited, though disagreement on minor philosophical or doctrinal issues was permitted as long as that disagreement remained within the boundaries delineated by the dominant moral code. Religious pluralism was tolerated, as long as moral and ritual orthopraxy was maintained.[17]

This is quite different from the Christian approach to differences of opinion. Since Christians believe that correct belief, particularly belief in God and His revelations, is important for salvation, Church authorities felt obligated to ensure that everyone believed in God as the church defined Him, and believed in only those doctrines that the church identified as authentic divine teachings. After all, salvation depended on obedience to God's commands, and it was more difficult for someone to obey God if he or she did not even know who He was. Those who refused church guidance in such matters were condemned as heretics and punished for their recalcitrance as a lesson to others. Purity of dogma was not the only concern, of course. Until the Reformation forced the Papacy and the governments of Europe reluctantly to tolerate religious pluralism, theological dissent was more than just a religious problem. It was also seen as a threat to the political and social order of Christendom. Nonetheless, judgments of heresy were always couched in terms of doctrine, for that was how Christianity and heresy were differentiated.[18]

A modern student of Christianity and Confucianism has noted perceptively, "Christianity is constituted by the belief in the God of Jesus, whereas ethical values—rather than belief in God—determine who is Confucian."[19] Jesuit missionaries came from Europe to teach the Chinese what to believe, to show the Chinese that their Neo-Confucianism was untrue. Most Neo-Confucians were more interested in how the Jesuits and their fellow Catholics behaved than in what Christians believed. Neo-Confucians tended to judge Catholicism according to the morality its teachings implied and the ethics its adherents followed.

Idan, therefore, was primarily ethical rather than doctrinal deviation. Probity was the standard more than truth. Philosophical differences with mainstream Confucianism were less important than ideas or practices that were seen as preventing, discouraging, or distracting men from the performance of their moral responsibilities to society, in determining what was, or was not, *idan.* Catholics had to prove that they were not promoting *idan,* that their religion and behavior were consistent with and supportive of Confucian classical ethical principles, before they could win a hearing in educated circles in China and Korea.

PRECEDENTS FOR JUDGMENT

In evaluating Celestial Learning, Korean Neo-Confucians relied on precedents from Chinese tradition as well as their own. Those who declared Catholicism *idan* invariably directly or indirectly compared it to one or more of the teachings condemned as immoral in the past. For example, the charge that European religion lacked proper respect for rulers and parents echoed Mencius's complaint against Yang Zhu and Mozi.[20] Yang Zhu taught that each man should think of himself first, that self-interest should be paramount. Mencius argued that such selfishness was a denial of the just claim of a ruler, as the leader of our community, to our loyalty and obedience. Mozi went to the opposite extreme, in Mencius's view. By advocating that men should love everyone equally, Mozi denied the special claim parents have on the heart. Mencius concluded that to refuse to acknowledge special obligations to rulers and to parents was to show oneself more beast than human.[21] Catholics in the Confucian world had to show both in their writings and in their actions that they, unlike Yang Zhu and Mozi, recognized the importance of loyalty and filial piety.

Another accusation revived from the past to be used against Catholics was that they, like the Buddhists and the Daoists before them, destroyed the moral bonds that made a human community possible.[22] The Confucian revival in Song China in the eleventh and twelfth centuries gave birth to a Neo-Confucianism that, though it borrowed some terminology and philosophical concepts from Buddhism and Daoism, condemned Buddhism and Daoism for denying the validity and significance of those virtues that governed all human relationships. Buddhism, by teaching that this world was essentially an illusion and not ultimate reality, and Daoism, by encouraging men to leave their villages and pursue personal immortality in distant mountains and forests, were denounced for going even further than Yang Zhu and Mozi in undermining the very foundations of morality by denying every human being's duties to society.[23]

Cheng Hao (1032–1085), Cheng Yi (1033–1107), and Zhu Xi, the fathers of the philosophical Confucianism now called Neo-Confucianism, recognized some similarities between their teachings and Buddhist doctrines. In particular, they respected some Buddhist techniques for mental discipline. However, they believed Buddhists erred in failing to apply the self-control gained from meditation to the affairs of the real world. "In the learning of the Buddhists there is a seriousness to straighten the internal life but no righteousness to square the external life."[24] Such neglect of the ethical rules governing a human being's interactions with fellow human beings was alone enough to merit condemnation, without further need to ponder the truth or falsity of Buddhist doctrine. If Catholics could not show that they, unlike Buddhists and Daoists, took seriously the world of human relationships as the main arena for moral action, they too would be dismissed as preaching immoral doctrines unworthy of the attention of a true Confucian gentleman.

Koreans also had their own tradition of criticism of Buddhism. Chosŏn dynasty Confucians blamed Buddhism for the social disorder that brought about the fall of the Koryŏ dynasty in 1392. They argued that Buddhism had led to an erosion of social ethics and a misdirecting of individual moral efforts. One prominent theme in Korean Neo-Confucian attacks on Buddhism was that Buddhists frightened people with talk of Heaven and Hell. They warned that the false hope of a future reward or fear of imaginary future punishment turned human beings' attention away from the real world. Another frequent accusation was that the Buddhist mode of self-cultivation, because of its stress on individual enlightenment, encouraged selfish withdrawal from society.[25] Both themes reappeared in the eighteenth century when Korean Neo-Confucians saw Celestial Learning as bearing a dangerous resemblance to the Buddhism their forerunners had condemned.[26]

Though Koreans relied heavily on Chinese precedents in distinguishing orthodox teachings from the heterodox, they did not limit themselves to pious repetitions of Chinese judgments. They felt enough confidence in their own command of Confucian teachings to decide for themselves if doctrines even the Chinese tolerated fit Korean Neo-Confucian criteria for orthodoxy. They not only rejected all of the schools of thought the Chinese Confucian tradition condemned, but also branded as *idan* some ideas Chinese had found acceptable. For example, Sŏngho and Shin Hudam mistakenly believed that Catholicism was flourishing in China, since there were European priests serving as official astronomers in Beijing and many of the Jesuit books that had made their way into Korea included laudatory prefaces by Chinese Confucian officials. They rejected the religious implications of Celestial Learning anyway. Moreover, some Koreans felt that they should proudly proclaim their rejection of Catholicism so that the whole world would know that in Korea, at least, there were still scholars who held fast to the legacy of Confucius, Mencius, and Zhu Xi and had not been deluded by evil doctrines.[27]

The eighteenth-century rejection of Catholicism was not the first time Korean thinkers had differed from their fellow Neo-Confucians in China. Three centuries earlier, T'oegye Yi Hwang had condemned the teachings of Wang Yangming, which were popular in China at that time. Wang insisted on the unity of the mind-and-heart with the patterns of appropriate interaction, and of knowledge with conduct, as well as innate knowledge of the good. He taught further that there was no need to engage in the exhaustive examination of *li* [理, the dynamic patterns of appropriate interaction that shaped the universe] in external things and events that Zhu Xi had demanded, since *li* resided within our own minds. T'oegye insisted that Wang Yangming was wrong to challenge so many of Zhu Xi's interpretations of the classics, particularly those dealing with the *Great Learning*. T'oegye charged that Wang's suggested emendations to Zhu Xi's commentary on that revered Confucian classic as well as his alterations of Zhu's commentaries on other classics were not only a distortion of the original meanings of the words under dispute but also would lead to a denial of fundamental Confucian behavioral guidelines.

To T'oegye, Wang's stress on *li* within, on innate knowledge of the good, was dangerously one-sided and self-centered. He wrote that unless subjective insights into *li* were confirmed with the objective *li* in the external world, the original impartial mind-and-heart that alone makes human beings truly human would be led astray. T'oegye cautioned that Wang Yangming would have men turn inward, as the Zen Buddhists do, rather than reaching outward with their moral strength, as good Confucians should do.[28] Wang Yangming's philosophical errors disturbed T'oegye less than the behavioral implications of those errors. As T'oegye saw it, Wang was not only incorrect, his teachings were morally tainted and had to be condemned alongside those of Mozi, Yang Zhu, Buddha, and Laozi (the legendary first Daoist philosopher).

T'oegye's writings shaped mainstream Korean Neo-Confucian thought for the rest of the Chosŏn dynasty. Never was Wang Yangming to have in Korea the respectability he won in China. T'oegye's influence was particularly strong among that small group in the eighteenth century that debated the merits and demerits of Heavenly Learning. Ahn Chŏngbok's advice to his disciple Hwang Tŏkkil is indicative of the respect many Koreans accorded T'oegye: "Treat the words of Confucius and Mencius as you would the laws of the land, the words of Zhu Xi and the Cheng brothers as the moral direction of a stern teacher, the words of T'oegye as the admonitions of a kind father."[29]

Those Korean scholars who attacked Celestial Learning as a dangerous *idan* believed they were following T'oegye's example in defending orthodoxy. Hwang Tŏkkil, for example, praised Ahn for furthering that tradition of refutation of evil doctrines with his anti-Catholic writings: "When Wang Yangming was gaining attention in Korea, T'oegye was the first to point out the damage his teachings would do. When Western books first began to come into Korea, Sŏngho was the first to criticize their absurdities. Now you have continued the task they began and further clarified that the standard they used was the same."[30]

What was that standard, the yardstick used to measure the worth of moral and philosophical teachings in the Neo-Confucian world, particularly among those who traced their philosophical lineage through Sŏngho to T'oegye as the Southerners did? Underlying the four criteria for distinguishing between *idan* and non-*idan* discussed above was the implicit assumption that the degree to which an idea represented *kong* (公, public mindedness) or *sa* (私, selfishness) determined whether that idea was acceptable or *idan*. Any idea that focused on or encouraged the pursuit of personal benefit without regard for the needs of society as a whole was immoral and therefore unacceptable. Only ideas that placed the needs of the community above those of the individual were moral and therefore were not *idan.*

Kong means much more than its usual English translation as "self-lessness" indicates. In English, selflessness implies a willingness to sacrifice one's own interests for the good of others. It also suggests a lack of excessive longing for the rewards of power, prestige, and money. In Neo-Confucianism, *kong* meant all that "selflessness" implies and more. *Kong* implied not just deference to the needs of others, but identification with others. A person infused with a *kong* spirit knows that he or she exists only as part of a much larger whole and therefore thinks and acts morally and correctly only when he or she thinks and acts as a member of society rather than as an isolated individual. Not only will such a person be unselfish, a person motivated by *kong* will also be impartial. By identifying with the world around them, those who are unselfish will be able to react to, and judge, people and events appropriately rather than viewing the people and the world around them through the distortion of the lens of personal self-interest.

Sa also means more than its English counterpart, "selfishness," indicates. People dominated by *sa* not only put their own interests first, greedily pursuing personal profit at the expense of others, they also turn inward, away from the external world, and thus deny a very important part of themselves. Those absorbed in self-centered thoughts and actions isolate themselves from the social and material environment that surrounds and shapes them. People with minds distorted by *sa* reveal themselves by their biases, by their incomplete understanding of how everything, including themselves, relates to everything else. Unable to fully comprehend that which is going on around them and unwilling to recognize their responsibilities, they fail to properly develop the social vision that would enable them to become truly human and truly moral.[31] Understood in this way, *sa* is both an ethical and a cognitive flaw.[32] Ideas rooted in selfishness are irrational as well as immoral. Such was the Neo-Confucian conception of *idan.*

The first paragraph in this chapter included a statement by Shin Hudam that all deviant doctrines flow from the common spring of selfishness. Shin went on to explain the selfish elements in the various *idan* schools. In Yang Zhu, the selfishness was obvious, since Yang argued openly that one should not give up even one hair from his or her body to benefit others.[33] In Mozi, Shin found selfishness not in his advocacy of universal love but in his call for frugality in ritual. Shin believed that anyone who scrimped and saved on funeral rites showed that he thought more of his own purse than of his parents. Among the Daoist followers of Zhuangzi and Liezi, selfishness sprouted in their incessant search for eternal physical life. The Buddhists, too, selfishly hungered for eternal life, though they were more sophisticated and attributed immortality to an immaterial soul rather than to the body. Shin argued:

> As for these teachings of Europeans, they are nothing more than the dregs of Buddhist doctrine. Those Europeans have made a few cosmetic changes to give themselves the appearance of greater rationality, but they cannot hide their unseemly greed for life and distaste for death. If scholars only realize that Celestial Learning is rooted in selfishness, and if they do not let themselves be moved by dreams of life after death, it will have no attraction for them at all.[34]

Other critics of Celestial Learning also pointed to the Christian doctrines of Heaven, Hell, and the immortality of the soul to prove that this Western religion was *idan*. For Ahn Chŏngbok, as it was for Shin, it was not so much that it was foolish to believe in personal survival after death as that it was immoral to adhere to ethical guidelines out of a selfish desire for eternal happiness.

> The doctrines that are introduced in Western books appear profound at first glance, but further analysis shows them to be *idan*. The only reason we Confucians do good and avoid evil is that that is what we are supposed to do. We never for even one moment do so in order to earn some reward in life after death. The only reason Catholics do good is that they expect to be judged later by God for what they do in this life. This "Celestial Learning" is totally unlike our Confucianism.[35]

YI IK

Shin Hudam and Ahn Chŏngbok shared more than just an aversion to Catholicism. They were both disciples of Yi Ik. It was as disciples of Yi Ik that they came to know of Catholicism, and also to condemn it.

Yi Ik, usually referred to by his literary name, Sŏngho, was an influential Neo-Confucian scholar in eighteenth-century Korea and the intellectual mentor of the Southerner Faction.[36] Though his great grandfather, his grandfather, and his father all held responsible government posts, Yi himself was kept from a career of public service by bitter factional disputes that ravaged political circles in his day. His father, who had risen as high as Inspector General, died in exile in the far northwestern corner of Korea a year after Yi Ik was born. While Yi was still in his twenties, an older brother died as a result of a beating ordered by government officials angered by a memorial he had submitted to the king. Understandably wary, Sŏngho declined the two minor government posts that were offered him over his long lifetime. Yi apparently preferred the secure and stable life of a rural scholar. He stayed on his few acres of rice land in the countryside, out of the limelight, and quietly wrote essays, letters, and short notes on topics ranging from metaphysics and ethics to natural science and socioeconomic reform.[37]

Sŏngho was remarkable in his time for his willingness to accept help from any quarter in pursuing Confucian aims. He read at least twenty Jesuit-authored works, including moral and religious tracts, scientific treatises, and introductions to world geography and Western technology.[38] Idle curiosity may have motivated some of his reading. The *Zhifang waiji* [World geography] of Guilio Aleni (1582–1649) and the *Tianzhu shiyi* [The true meaning of the Lord of Heaven] of Matteo Ricci (1552–1610) offered little information or advice that Sŏngho would have found relevant to the cultivation of moral self-perfection or socioeconomic stability.[39] Such was not the case, however, with some of the other Catholic books Sŏngho read and wrote about. The suppression of selfish desires preached by Diego de Pantoja (1571–1618) in *Qike* (Seven victories), for example, won praise from Sŏngho for its similarity to the Confucian morality of self-denial. Pantoja's *Qike*, first printed in 1614, stressed morality over theology, extolling the seven cardinal virtues of humility, charity, patience, compassion, temperance, diligence, and self-restraint with which the vices common to all men could be controlled.[40] Pantoja's portrayal of the moral man leading a simple and frugal life in which reason has firm control over passion appealed to the Chinese literati, who had been taught to respect the Confucian ideal of the philosopher-scholar whose mind rules his body. Sŏngho was impressed as well.

Sŏngho wrote that *Qike* surpassed all Confucian writings in its use of similes to elucidate the relationship between vice and virtue. "This book will be a great help to our effort to restore proper behavior. It is surprising, though, to find talk of god and spirits mixed up in this otherwise fine work. If we excise all such non-essential bits of grit and copy down only the parts in it that are worthwhile, then we can treat it as orthodox Confucianism."[41]

Western writings impressed Sŏngho when they advocated the frugality and self-discipline he believed essential to a healthy and moral society. However, when they included references to Catholic theological doctrines, he found them much less impressive. As far as he was concerned, those "bits of grit," as Sŏngho labeled Catholic teachings on God, the soul, and the afterlife, should be excised. A true Confucian should extract techniques for moral self-cultivation from the Catholic religious teachings that accompanied them. Catholic techniques were useful. Catholic theological assertions were not.

Sŏngho was much more tolerant of non-canonical practices than most of his contemporaries were. For example, Sŏngho wrote that the Confucians of his day could learn much from Daoists and Buddhist monks. He agreed that a good Neo-Confucian should not believe what a Daoist or a Buddhist teaches. He could, however, imitate certain Daoist and Buddhist ascetic practices. In fact, Sŏngho wrote, some Buddhist monks he had seen far surpassed most Confucians in their compassion, their respect for their teachers, and their self-control.[42]

Sŏngho stands apart from most of his fellow Korean Neo-Confucians in his willingness to apply non-Confucian means in his moral practice in order to achieve Confucian ends. Sŏngho put aside the non-Confucian character of Buddhist and Daoist beliefs to praise some of their practices. This ability to see some good in what is not Confucian, to find something useful even in non-canonical beliefs and practices, marks Sŏngho's response to Celestial Learning as well. Despite his conviction that Catholic religious teachings were a threat to Confucian values, he nevertheless insisted that there was much in Western writings that could be beneficial to Korea.

SHIN HUDAM

Shin Hudam had a much less benign view of Jesuit works. An admiring disciple of Sŏngho, Shin argued with his mentor over the value of Western books the first time they met. When Shin met Sŏngho in 1724, Sŏngho praised some Jesuit writings. His curiosity aroused, Shin then read Ricci's *Tianzhu shiyi*, Aleni's *Zhifang waiji*, and *Lingyan lishao* (On the soul), a Thomistic explanation of the nature of the human soul and its faculties by Francis Sambiasi (1582–1649). Neither Ricci's theology, Aleni's world geography, nor Sambiasi's psychology particularly impressed Shin. He decided that the West had little to offer Korea besides strange and dangerous ideas.[43]

Shin was two decades younger than Sŏngho. He was born in 1702 in Seoul into a family of minor officeholders. His father had once held the rank of section chief in the Board of War, and his grandfather on his mother's side had held a sinecure as an official at a royal tomb.[44] Shin spent his youth reading widely in both Confucian and heterodox sources. Late in his teens, following a series of reprimands from his father, he abandoned his reading of Daoism and Buddhism and became totally absorbed in Neo-Confucianism. Though he passed the preliminary examinations for government service and was awarded the *chinsa* (literary licentiate) degree at the age of twenty-two, Shin abandoned further examination preparation and retired to his home, where he engaged in moral cultivation through intensive reading of the Confucian classics and the practice of strict Confucian self-discipline.[45]

Shin spent the rest of his life in determined pursuit of moral perfection. After Shin's death at the age of sixty, Sŏngho said of him, "Whether at home or outside managing his affairs, Shin always maintained a cautious and conscientious attitude."[46] At twenty-four, Shin posted a list of his moral faults on the wall of his room as a constant reminder of his need for further self-improvement. He chided himself for not being cheerful enough when serving his parents, not getting along well enough with his brothers, being too casual and insincere in his dealings with friends and too loose in his conversations, and for not being consistent in following through on resolutions previously made.[47] Even Sŏngho, who was well known for holding himself to very demanding moral standards, seems to have thought that Shin went too far at times. In 1725 Sŏngho advised his young disciple to practice quiet sitting and not keep himself in a continual state of anxiety, frustration, and distress. Shin at that time apparently had worked himself into a state of physical and mental exhaustion in his frustrating efforts to become a paragon of Confucian virtue.[48]

Neo-Confucian thought balanced on the two poles of moral perfection within and sagehood without. A complete Neo-Confucian ideally would be both a scholar and a statesman, concerned both with recovering his innate goodness by overcoming selfish tendencies and with promoting a peaceful, harmonious, and prosperous society. Sŏngho paid equal attention to both goals, writing about self-cultivation as well as political and socioeconomic issues. His student Shin was more one-sided. Sihn's preoccupation with nurturing his personal virtue blinded him to the possible benefits to society of non-canonical scholarship.

In their 1724 discussion of Western learning (they both preferred that term to the Celestial Learning preferred by European missionaries in China), Shin argued that Catholicism, because of its fundamental absorption with Heaven, Hell, and the fate of the individual immortal soul, was no better than Buddhism. Sŏngho responded with a defense of Catholicism, saying that such coincidental similarities between Catholicism and Buddhism should not cause them to overlook the great difference between the nihilism of Buddhism and the practicality of Western learning. Shin refused to admit that there was anything to be gained from the study of Western books unless Sŏngho could show him that the West provided techniques for governing the state as grand as the Way of the legendary rulers of ancient China. Sŏngho then pointed out that the Jesuits had made advances in calendrical science, for example, that surpassed anything any man, Chinese or barbarian, had ever accomplished before. When he spoke of the practical benefits that Western books offered, Sŏngho explained, he was referring primarily to books on astronomy and mathematics, both important in governance.[49]

Shin viewed the West through eyes focused more on the moral than the political strands in the Neo-Confucian tradition. He was dismayed that a respectable Confucian scholar such as Sŏngho would brush aside the serious moral threat Western writings posed simply because those books contained, amid their absurdities, some bits of useful information that might be of interest to the technicians and artisans of the state. After Shin read *Tianzhu shiyi, Zhifang waiji,* and *Lingyan lishao,* he wrote out a long Neo-Confucian critique of Catholic thought, condemning it as dangerous, erroneous, and immoral.[50] Shin's proud descendants later wrote that Shin's *Sŏhakpyŏn* [On Western Learning] deserved to be ranked alongside Zhu Xi's denunciation of Buddhism and Mencius's condemnation of Yang Zhu and Mozi, though they noted that others more favorably inclined to Christianity saw Shin simply as stubborn and inflexible.[51]

The forty-two-year-old Sŏngho was not swayed by the twenty-two-year-old Shin's essay. When they met again in 1725, Sŏngho told his young disciple that he was disappointed to learn that Shin still did not realize that Catholicism was different from those non-canonical teachings that do nothing more than delude the people. Sŏngho insisted moreover that there were a lot more similarities between the Catholic God and the Lord Above (*Sangje*) of the Confucian classics than Shin was admitting. He concluded, "I am afraid you been rather superficial in your examination of Western Learning."[52] Yi was so unimpressed by Shin's anti-Catholic essay that when he wrote Shin's obituary forty years later, he did not include the *Sŏhakpyŏn* among the many titles of Shin's works he judged worthy of mention, although Yi did give the titles of five separate works by Shin dealing with the *Book of Changes* alone.[53]

Having failed to convince Sŏngho of the foolishness of his weakness for Western books, Shin made no further excursions into Jesuit literature, except for a brief glance shortly before his death at an introduction to astronomy by Emmanual Diaz (1574–1659), the *Tianwen lüe* [A survey of the heavens], and a world atlas by Ferdinand Verbiest (1623–1688), the *Kunyu tushuo* [An illustrated discussion of the geography of the entire world]. His appraisal of the West had not changed over the decades. In his comments on those books, Shin repeated his charge that Catholicism was essentially no different from Buddhism. He warned that the Jesuits might be quite detailed in their discussions of the natural world, but not everything they said could be believed.[54]

AHN CHŎNGBOK

Shin was not the only disciple with whom Yi Ik discussed Western learning. Sunam Ahn Chŏngbok also sought Sŏngho's opinion on the value of Western ideas and techniques. Unlike Shin, Sunam (the literary name of Ahn Chŏngbok) did not object to Sŏngho's interest in Jesuit writings. He agreed with Sŏngho that there were useful elements in Western scholarship that could be extracted from the theological nonsense in which they were embedded.[55]

Sunam did not meet Sŏngho until 1746, but they quickly established a close master-disciple relationship.[56] It was Sunam who edited Sŏngho's vast encyclopedic collection of essays into the more manageable form that cemented Sŏngho's reputation, the *Sŏngho sasŏl yusŏn* [A selection of the classified writings of Sŏngho Yi Ik]. And it was Sunam who defended Sŏngho's reputation as an orthodox Neo-Confucian scholar when, after Sŏngho's death, the popularity of Catholic books among some young Namin raised suspicion in some quarters that Yi himself had been too tolerant of heterodoxy.

Sunam, like Sŏngho and Shin Hudam, was a rural scholar. He spent most of his life at his farm in Kwangju near Seoul and held no important government posts until late in his life, when he was appointed tutor to the Crown Prince in the last years of King Yŏngjo's reign and then was sent to Mokch'ŏn in Ch'ungch'ŏng province as magistrate soon after King Chŏngjo (r.1776–1800) ascended the throne.[57] Sunam read widely in a variety of areas, from frivolous fiction to serious philosophy, but he remained committed to the Neo-Confucianism of Zhu Xi.[58] Unlike Sŏngho, who read and wrote much about politics, economics, and natural science, or Shin Hudam, who dedicated most of his scholarly energy to explicating the *Book of Changes*, Sunam devoted much of his attention to history. His *Tongsa kangmok* (An outline of Korean history), which covered the beginnings of Korean history to the end of the Koryŏ dynasty in 1392, is respected today for pioneering the critical analysis of primary sources in Korean historiography.[59]

Sunam exchanged a couple of letters with Sŏngho on Western Learning in the 1750s, but it was not until the 1780s that Sunam began to seriously examine and criticize Catholic writings.[60] It was then that Catholicism became more than an exotic novelty to spice up conversation among Southerners and began to be practiced seriously as a religion by some. Among Korea's first Catholics, converted soon after Yi Sŭnghun (1756–1801) returned from Beijing in 1784, brandishing the newly bestowed Christian name of Peter, were Sunam's son-in-law Kwŏn Ilsin (1742–1791), as well as Kwŏn's older brother Ch'ŏlsin (1736–1801), one of Sunam's disciples. Also attracted to the new religion from the West were two more of Sunam's disciples, Yi Kiyang (1745–1802) and Yi Kahwan (1742–1801), the latter a grandnephew of Sŏngho.

In 1785 Sunam wrote two treatises on Catholicism in which he pointed out the flaws in that European religion from a Sinocentric Neo-Confucian perspective. In *Ch'ŏnhakko* (An examination of Celestial Learning), Sunam turned his vast store of historical knowledge into a powerful weapon aimed at the Jesuit claim that Catholicism, "Celestial Learning," had parallels in orthodox Confucian tradition. Citing Chinese records from the Han dynasty through the Qing, he argued that Catholicism resembled such barbarian religions as Islam, Nestorianism, and the idol worship of central Asia more than it did Confucianism. He supported this rejection of the Christian pretense to orthodoxy by quoting explicit criticism of Catholicism by the Chinese scholar Gu Yanwu (1613–1682) and by Sunam's own predecessors in Korea, Yi Sugwang (1563–1628) and Sŏngho.[61]

Sunam explained at the beginning of the *Ch'ŏnhakko* why he had prepared his historical survey of East Asian reactions to Western religions.

> Western books have been coming into Korea since the end of the reign of King Sŏnjo (r. 1567–1608). There is no respected official or learned scholar who has not looked upon them as belonging to the same category as Daoist and Buddhist works, books best left on a library shelf for amusement. All they have to offer are some techniques in mathematics and the study of the heavens. Recently a young scholar picked up some of those books while in Beijing on a diplomatic mission and brought them back into Korea. Subsequently, in the last couple of years [1784–1785], a group of bright young men have begun preaching that the Lord Above descended to the earth as a divine messenger and other such Catholic doctrines.

What a tragedy! They spend their entire lives studying the works of the Sages of China and then, in just one morning, throw it all away for such strange teachings. That is as bad as someone who goes off to study for three years and then, when he returns home, impudently addresses his mother by her given name. It is really a pity. I have selected some records from history and compiled this *Ch'ŏnhakko* to show them that this "celestial learning" has been around China for quite some time. It even reached Korea a long time ago. It is nothing new.[62]

In his *Ch'ŏnhakko* Sunam tried to convince Kwŏn Ch'ŏlsin and others sympathetic to Catholicism that they had been fooled by Jesuit writings into believing that Catholicism was accepted in China and acceptable in Korea, when actually Chinese and Koreans had been condemning it and similar immoral religions for centuries. In his other anti-Catholic polemic, *Ch'ŏnhak mundap* (A conversation on Catholicism), Sunam attacked the specifics of Catholic doctrine that offended his Confucian values.

The *Ch'ŏnhak mundap*, which is translated in Chapter 6 of this volume, takes the form of a dialogue in which Sunam responded to over thirty questions about Catholic thought and practices. His anonymous questioner asked his opinion of the Catholic claim to be the true Celestial Learning, teaching the proper way to show the respect for Heaven that Confucianism demands. Sunam replied that, quite the contrary, Catholicism was immoral, irrational, illogical, antisocial, unrealistic, selfish, and superstitious; in a word, *idan*.[63]

Sunam Ahn Chŏngbok died in 1791, just before the first major anti-Catholic persecution took the lives of three *yangban*, including his son-in-law Kwŏn Ilsin. There had been an arrest of some Catholics in 1785, for which Sunam disclaimed responsibility, though there were those among his former associates who nevertheless blamed Sunam for the authorities' discovery of a Catholic service in progress at the home of the *chungin* Kim Pŏmu (1751–1787).[64] It was not Sunam's intention to expose to official punishment those among his disciples who had defected to Catholicism. Rather, he hoped to win them back to the mainstream Confucian fold before word of their unacceptable views spread too far. Sunam shared Sŏngho's belief that the Catholic teachings about Heaven and Hell were dangerous because they led men to place the salvation of their individual soul above the needs of society as a whole. For Sŏngho, that concern was purely theoretical since there were no Catholics in Korea while Sŏngho was alive. Sunam felt a greater urgency. The spread of Catholic ideas among his own disciples and in-laws compelled him to write a condemnation of Catholicism more strident and detailed than Sŏngho had ever written.

When the seventy-three-year-old Sunam took up his pen in 1785 and wrote the *Ch'ŏnhakko* and the *Ch'ŏnhak mundap,* he intended his essays to awaken the Catholics to the error they had fallen into. Sunam had been shocked and saddened by the dangerous turn his friends, relatives, and students had taken. Though his essays were more polemical than Shin Hudam's earlier philosophical critique, Sunam nevertheless wrote to persuade more than to condemn. At first Kwŏn Ilsin and the others were willing to sit and discuss the merits and demerits of Catholic teachings with Sunam, but by 1785, Sunam complained to Yi Kiyang, they had grown tired of arguing with him and would not even answer his letters anymore. "Their Jesus is called the Messiah. That means that he wants to save the world by guiding the ignorant to enlightenment. So how can they refuse to answer my questions, keeping their beliefs secret and denying enlightenment to me in my ignorance? Is that how their Lord of Heaven intends to save the world?"[65]

Sunam also had a practical, political motive for writing his anti-Catholic essays. He believed that Confucians who converted to Catholicism not only debased themselves, they also endangered their friends and associates. In the heated factional politics of the latter half of the Chosŏn dynasty, it was not wise for any group, especially one as weak as Sunam's to become associated with ideas and practices that departed from mainstream Confucianism. Kwŏn Ch'ŏlsin and most of the early Catholic *yangban* were members of Sunam's Southerner Faction. Yet prudence demanded that the Southerners maintain a safe distance from even the hint of such deviation. In an admonitory letter, Sunam warned Kwŏn Ch'ŏlsin that, considering the factional rivalries of their day, Catholicism could easily be seized by their enemies as a weapon for slandering and destroying all the Southerners. He reminded Kwŏn that Christians had been killed by the tens of thousands in Japan and even in the West. He then asked the rhetorical question, "Could the Lord of Heaven save them if the same fate threatened them in Korea?"[66]

In 1783 Sunam wrote Ch'ae Chegong (1720–1799), the highest-ranking Namin in the government, to join with him in his anti-Catholic campaign. Sunam informed Ch'ae that many talented Southerners were dabbling in that new religion, proclaiming it the true Way. If he and Ch'ae did not work together to put a stop to the spread of such alien teachings in their ranks, Sunam wrote, the entire Southerner Faction could be in danger.[67] Sunam showed an astute understanding of traditional Korean politics with that expression of concern, for what he feared came to pass in the great persecution of 1801. Those Southerners tainted by the slightest contact with Catholicism were purged from power. Many, including some who had renounced or never accepted Catholicism, were executed. Ch'ae himself, though he had risen as high as Second State Councilor before his death in 1799, was posthumously stripped of all his titles and honors in 1801 because he had not acted firmly enough in suppressing Catholicism.[68] Sunam, on the other hand, received a posthumous promotion to the post of Sixth State Councilor for his contribution to the fight against the Catholic *idan*.[69]

A third reason Ahn was so active in refuting and condemning Catholic teachings was his concern for his teacher's reputation. Since so many of those espousing Catholicism had been Sŏngho's followers, Sunam was afraid that Sŏngho would be branded as the man responsible for their folly. At the end of his *Ch'ŏnhak mundap*, Sunam appended a defense of Sŏngho, saying that those who read Sŏngho's admiration for Western science and technology as praise for Western religion were wrong. Sunam argued that there was nothing wrong in recognizing Western expertise in astronomy or noting that Western craftsmen surpassed the Chinese in some areas, since China traditionally had relied on barbarian monks for such skills. Since Sŏngho had clearly condemned such Catholic doctrines as the afterlife as *idan*, there was no justification for accusing him of believing in or tolerating Catholicism.[70]

Sŏngho Yi Ik, Shin Hudam, and Sunam Ahn Chŏngbok provided the ideological framework for an anti-Catholic movement in Korea in the last quarter of the eighteenth century. As Sunam noted, many read the Catholic books from China. Few, however, believed what those books taught about God, the human soul, virtue, or human nature. The position laid out by Sŏngho, Shin, and Sunam became the majority view. When Celestial Learning veered away from science, mathematics, and technology and began talking about God, Heaven, and Hell, becoming the Western "Religion of the Lord of Heaven" (Catholicism), it was seen as contaminated by selfish interest in personal salvation and therefore had no rightful place in their Neo-Confucian world.

MORE THAN A LANGUAGE BARRIER

Though Sŏngho, because of his broader range of interests and greater tolerance for diversity, was willing to entertain what the West had to say on matters concerning statecraft, nature, and self-discipline, he was no more willing than Shin or Sunam were to ingest Western theological fare. He differed from Sunam and Shin primarily in being less wary of the power of Catholicism to spread its "poison" through other than theological offerings and more confident of the power of Confucianism to successfully resist the selfishness he believed Catholicism promoted.

Why did Catholicism fail to escape condemnation even by someone as open-minded as Sŏngho Yi Ik? The Jesuit policy of accommodation to Confucian culture through the presentation of Catholic theology in Confucian language failed to disguise the *idan* character and foreign origin of Catholic concepts. Many of the Jesuit missionaries in China wrote their arguments for their faith in eloquent prose garnished with liberal quotations from the revered Confucian classics. Yet Sŏngho, Shin Hudam, and Sunam represented a majority Korean view that beneath that beautiful prose lay an ugly immorality. Matteo Ricci's strategy in his *Tianzhu shiyi* failed to take into account the semantic gap between what the Jesuits intended by the Chinese characters they wrote and what connotations their Confucian audience usually read into those words.

A common language requires more than just a shared lexical, phonemic, and grammatical base. A linguistic bridge can join two cultures only when it is supported by pillars of mutually compatible, fundamental assumptions. Only those who invest their words with the same meanings can truly understand one another. The European missionaries in China in the seventeenth and eighteenth centuries, though they wrote in the Chinese language of their Neo-Confucian audience, appeared unable or unwilling to use that language in the same sense in which most Neo-Confucian scholars of that time used it and understood it.

Most Confucians who read Jesuit books could not totally understand them. Many of those who did understand what the Jesuits were trying to say were more disturbed than convinced by the Christian message. Catholicism in Confucian terminology remained Roman Catholicism, an alien religion in a Sinocentric world.

The differences between Catholicism and Confucianism were more than differences of language. The primary Korean Confucian objection to Catholicism was that it was rooted in selfishness. Shin Hudam denounced Catholic writings as nefarious glorification of self-interest. He charged that when Catholics outwardly conformed to moral principles, they did so only because they expected to be rewarded for their good behavior in this life or after death. Shin insisted that Catholics showed Confucian respect for the Lord Above only because they believed that God determines how long they live, whether they are favored with good fortune or stricken with bad luck while they live, and whether they will gain eternal happiness or endless misery after death. "What they call reverence is not the reverence that comes from a sincere heart. . . . All they care about is winning happiness and avoiding suffering." In Shin's judgment, Catholic teachings were the product of minds bent on the pursuit of personal interest. He declared that such selfishness clearly could not be compared to the sincerity with which the Sages of old addressed Heaven.[71]

Sunam made a similar point in a letter to his pro-Catholic disciple Kwŏn Ch'ŏlsin. Sunam, too, objected to Catholic belief in Heaven and Hell, "two realms whose reality no man can verify." Sunam argued that when Catholics talked of salvation, they really were talking only about the individual rewards such salvation promised and were therefore teaching the same selfishness that perverted Daoist and Buddhist teachings. "Their so-called 'salvation' is as different from what the Sages have done to clarify virtue and renew the people as *kong* [public-mindedness] is from *sa* [egocentricity]." Sunam warned that such doctrines try to replace the real with the imaginary and the genuine with the fraudulent and could delude men as badly and as dangerously as Buddhist millenarianism had done.[72]

The Confucian employment of the moral criteria of public-mindedness versus egocentricity to judge and condemn Catholicism contrasts sharply with the Jesuit denunciation of Neo-Confucianism on doctrinal grounds. The first Jesuit missionaries were careful not to condemn outright the Confucian moral code, which they read as incomplete but largely in accord with natural law. Nicolas Trigault (1577–1628) noted that Matteo Ricci, the founder of the Jesuit mission to China, "Did not find fault with the literary sect; on the contrary, he praised them and particularly their great philosopher, Confucius, who preferred to observe silence relative to the future life, rather than put forth erroneous ideas about it, and to explain the law by offering precepts for regulating the life of the individual, for the direction of the family, and for the proper government of the kingdom."[73] Ricci instituted a missionary policy in China of presenting Christianity not as a replacement for Confucianism but as a supplement to it and perfection of it.[74] He preached that Catholic doctrine would complete, not contradict, the ethical foundations of Confucianism.

To those who argued that belief in Heaven and Hell was unnecessary or even detrimental for a moral life, Ricci responded that only those who accepted this Catholic doctrine of reward and retribution after death were true gentlemen. To his Confucian questioner in *Tianzhu shiyi* who at first assumed that simply acting as a gentleman was enough to merit that appellation, Ricci offered a quotation from the *Odes*. Since the *Odes* described the Sage King Wen as reverently serving the Lord on High, Ricci argued that all men who aspired to be gentlemen had to imitate King Wen's faith in God. Moreover, God, as God, exemplified benevolence and impartiality (*in* [仁] and *kong*) and such a God necessarily showed his benevolence by rewarding the good with eternal happiness and his impartiality by punishing the evil with eternal misery. Therefore those who shared King Wen's belief in God had to also believe in Heaven and Hell. Otherwise, they rejected both the message of the classics and the force of logic.[75] Proper Confucian behavior had to be coupled with correct Catholic belief for a man to earn the title of gentleman: that was the core of the Riccian case for Catholic theology.

Of course, there were areas of Confucian practice that Ricci and other missionaries condemned as immoral. Concubinage, even if necessary to fulfill the Confucian obligation of producing an heir to continue one's family line, was not acceptable. Nor would the missionaries accept the Confucian toleration of Daoist divination or Buddhist idols.[76] The papal condemnation of Confucian mourning ritual in the eighteenth century, because it involved bowing before, and offering food and drink to, ancestral spirit tablets, is perhaps the best-known example of conflict between Catholic and Confucian moral standards.[77]

Yet the thrust of the Catholic disagreement with Confucianism was doctrinal. The Jesuits were apparently unaware that most Neo-Confucians viewed disputes with Europeans over dogma as a reflection of a basic moral antagonism. The missionaries wrote, preached, and proselytized as though their differences were more over what to believe than over what to do. They more often condemned Neo-Confucianism as wrong than as immoral. A century and a half after Ricci arrived in Beijing, the Jesuit priest Alexander de la Charme (1695–1767) listed over twenty-five reasons why Neo-Confucianism should be condemned, all of them doctrinal. The idolatrous implications of ancestor memorial services appeared to him less relevant than the failure of Neo-Confucian metaphysics to admit the existence of the Creator. "These books on nature and principle [性理, sǒngni, i.e., Neo-Confucianism] talk only of i [理] and ki [氣] and do not push beyond them to their origin in the Creator. The harm they do is far worse than that done by the pagan religions which worship false gods."[78] This Catholic missionary believed that it was better to worship false gods than to deny the existence of any god at all, for atheism was the ultimate impiety. For de la Charme, as for Ricci, errors in Chinese thought were more in need of rectification than errors in Chinese behavior.

From Matteo Ricci to Alexander de la Charme, the Jesuit missionaries in China consistently argued that Catholicism was the true religion, more faithful both to the dictates of reason and to the unadulterated sense of the original Chinese classics than was the Neo-Confucianism then dominant in China and Korea. Just as Neo-Confucians did in China, Korean Neo-Confucians resisted this attempt to force the debate between Confucianism and Christianity into a battle of competing truth claims. Shin Hudam and Sunam instead shifted the focus of the dispute to morality, charging that the fundamental difference between Confucianism and Catholicism was best seen in terms of concern for society versus selfish egotism. The Korean refusal to accept the Jesuit terms for the debate reveals that Catholicism and Neo-Confucianism were divided by contrasting assumptions regarding the nature of truth itself.

Catholicism was rejected by most Korean Confucians because it appeared to conflict with the requirement of Confucian social morality that men always act without regard for their own personal benefit. By Confucian standards, the Catholic doctrines of Heaven, Hell, and individual salvation were immoral and therefore could not and should not be believed. The missionaries argued, however, that truth should determine moral judgments, rather than moral presuppositions determining what is accepted as true.

The core argument by the Jesuits in their Chinese language writings was that God exists and lived on earth as Jesuit Christ, the savior of all mankind, and that His words are found in the Bible, which promises eternal life to all those who love and obey God. To the Jesuits, the divine revelation found in the Bible determines what is good, since morality is nothing other than the will of God codified for man. In the Thomistic Catholicism that Korea encountered in the eighteenth century, there can be no moral good independent of the will of God.[79] The Jesuit position was that God has told man both in the Bible and indirectly in the Confucian classics that He intends to reward the good in Heaven and punish the wicked in Hell after their death, so men are morally justified in reflecting God's will by seeking that eternal reward and have no moral or logical justification for denying the existence of Heaven and Hell or repudiating their role in moral decisions.[80]

Shin and Sunam could not understand this argument. For them, morality was the given, the unquestioned assumption on which all other judgments were based. Any assertions that appeared to contradict the tenets of Confucian morality could not be true, as Confucians conceived truth. In their world, truth was determined by the good. That which conformed to basic ethical principles was true. That which challenged those principles was false. Ethical consequences were more important than logical considerations in evaluating the worth of an idea.

In the anti-Catholic essays of Shin Hudam and Sunam, there are countless examples of greater concern for questions of good and evil than of truth and falsity. Heaven and Hell were not the only Catholic doctrines attacked as immoral. Sunam wrote that the Catholic belief in the devil should be dismissed on the same grounds. He believed that if men believed in a devil, they would be tempted to attribute their own moral weakness to external pressure and would neglect their own obligation to cultivate their innate goodness through rigorous self-control.[81] Whether or not a devil really existed was less important to Sunam than what the consequences would be of the belief that he existed.

Shin Hudam used a moral standard to criticize certain biblical accounts of God's intervention in human affairs. An essential element of Confucian morality was impartiality. The Christian claim that God selected the Jews to be His chosen people and that God appeared to human beings only in Palestine and left the rest of the world to receive His guidance secondhand made the God of Christianity appear guilty of favoritism.[82]

Nor did God's treatment of the inhabitants of the town of Sodom reflect well on His claim to perfect goodness and justice. According to Aleni's *Zhifang waiji*, the people of Sodom had angered God with their licentious ways and their open display of contempt for morality by their shameless practice of homosexuality, so God destroyed their city and all who lived there, sparing only the family of a particularly just man named Lot.[83] Shin agreed that homosexuals should be punished, but he condemned the indiscriminate destruction of an entire town for the sins of some of its citizens. "Sodom must have had within its walls some children only seven or eight years old as well as some old men in their seventies and eighties. How could these children and old men have been guilty of homosexuality? Yet they were destroyed along with the others."[84]

A God who could be so partial to the Jews and unfair to the Sodomites was a dangerous God indeed, for if God were allowed to act with such disregard for the fundamental principles of fairness, so were human beings. Shin preferred to believe that an immoral God was no god at all and that the biblical tales were in error, since they depicted an immoral deity. Accordingly, the Bible could not be the infallible revelation of God the Jesuits claimed it to be.

Because the Jesuits could not convince mainstream Neo-Confucians like Shin Hudam and Sunam to accept their premise that theology preceded ethics, that God provided the standards by which all else was judged, the Christian message encountered more resistance than acceptance in Neo-Confucian Korea. Until Neo-Confucians abandoned their belief that religion was the handmaid of morality rather than its master, few Koreans could read Catholic arguments for Christianity with sympathetic eyes. The Catholic hope of selling monotheism and religious dogma to men who recoiled at the implied price to Confucian moral values was doomed to disappointment. Instead of wide acceptance, in Korea Catholicism met bloody persecution.

CHAPTER 3

The Birth of the Korean Catholic Church

Although most of their fellow Confucians were convinced that Confucianism and Catholicism were incompatible, Korea's first Catholics were drawn to Catholicism because of, not in spite of, their Confucian values. They, just as the anti-Catholics did, read Jesuit writings with eyes trained in Neo-Confucian schools. In their initial reactions to those writings, they neither forsook their heritage nor forgot their education. However, their peculiar visions of those Confucian values engendered unconventional responses to Catholicism.

The first Catholics in Korea were *yangban*. In other words, they had been educated as Confucian scholars. Their Confucian orientation led them to embrace Catholicism out of a belief at first that it supported Confucianism. These Confucians reached out to the Christian God hoping to ground Confucian ethics in an external, immutable, personal source that could offer them strength and security as they strove to meet stringent Confucian moral demands. For them, belief in the Christian God originally was a means to a Confucian goal. However, some of them later moved from a Confucianism that sought support from Catholicism to a Catholicism that superseded Confucianism. Such Catholics, for whom Catholicism came to provide both their fundamental beliefs and their primary moral principles, became convinced that God was the personification of selflessness, the supreme ethical value, and therefore His commands superseded all human rules and regulations. They came to consider themselves Catholics rather than Confucians. On the other hand, those Confucians who accepted Catholic ideas and practices only in so far as they appeared helpful in living up to the high moral demands of Confucianism returned to operating within the parameters of mainstream Confucianism and renounced their earlier interest in Catholicism when the ethical demands of Catholicism and Confucianism came into conflict. Nevertheless, both those who abandoned Confucianism for Catholicism and those who put aside their youthful attraction to Catholicism in order to stay loyal to Confucianism suffered for contributing to the establishment of a Catholic community in Korea. As you will read in Hwang Sayŏng's *Silk Letter,* the anti-Catholic persecution of 1801 embraced faithful Catholics and "apostates" alike.

Not all schools of Confucianism in Korea were equally receptive to Catholicism. The particular brand of Korean Neo-Confucianism most open to Catholic ideas was found in the school stemming from the thinking, writing, and teachings of Sŏngho Yi Ik. Sŏngho has been mentioned frequently in this book as the dominant intellectual influence on Southerner circles in the eighteenth century. As noted previously, Sŏngho displayed a remarkable receptivity to the moral self-cultivation techniques associated with non-mainstream schools. His persuasive presentation of the merits of adopting valuable ideas, wherever they were found and whatever their pedigree, encouraged the interest many Southerners demonstrated in Jesuit publications. As pointed out in the preceding chapter, Sŏngho was no Catholic. However, an ascetic strand in Sŏngho's thought, discussed earlier, seems to have had particular relevance for those drawn to Catholicism. Sŏngho preached a Neo-Confucian puritanism that went beyond the usual Confucian uneasiness over the desires and pleasures of the body. This asceticism made those of his followers who attempted to implement Sŏngho's rigid moral principles, including his call for strict control over the body's desire for sex and food, receptive to the Catholic teachings of the moral frailty of man and to the missionaries' insistence that human beings need to rely on help from God if they are to overcome evil. Sŏngho raised ethical demands so high that failure was inescapable. Out of frustration, Southerners who could not reach Sŏngho's standards of moral perfection through their own efforts in Confucian self-cultivation began to seek assistance elsewhere.

THE MEETING AT CHUŎSA

A few Southerner disciples of Sŏngho gathered in a Buddhist hermitage in the winter of 1779 to discuss more effective techniques for moral cultivation. Chǒng Yakchǒn, Yi Pyǒk (1754–1786), and, according to some, Yi Sǔnghun, along with six other followers of Sǒngho, met in the abandoned Ch'ǒnjin hermitage of Chuǒsa [Chuǒ temple] not far from Kwangju in Kyǒnggi province in order to discuss a number of issues relevant to self-cultivation, the elimination of selfishness, and the relationship of human beings to the cosmos. Father Charles Dallet, in his mid-nineteenth-century history of Korean Catholicism, writes that this group of eager young Confucian students spent over ten days at that temple debating among themselves questions concerning Heaven, this world, and the nature of human beings.[1] Despite drawing on the works of many scholars before them, on the writings of the ancient Chinese Sages, and despite benefiting from the guidance of a senior member of the Sǒngho branch of Korean Neo-Confucianism, Kwǒn Ch'ǒlsin, they found they still could not find satisfactory answers to the serious questions that troubled them. According to Father Dallet, they therefore turned to the books written by Catholic missionaries dealing with philosophy, mathematics, and religion.

Lacking a Catholic priest or even a layman properly instructed in the faith, and possessing only a few Western publications, many of the group at Chuǒsa felt they did not have enough information about Catholicism to adequately understand it. They did attempt for a while to implement the little they thought they knew. They observed a Sabbath of rest, abstention from meat, and meditation on the seventh, fourteenth, twenty-first, and twenty-eighth of every month. They followed that regimen for only a short time, however, before tiring of it and abandoning that practice. Nevertheless, the few days of reading and discussion in the winter of 1779 had whetted their appetites for more knowledge of the West and its religious and ethical teachings.[2]

That, anyway, is the Catholic account of that meeting, several decades after it took place. Tasan's description of this meeting is somewhat different. Tasan was not present at Chuǒsa, but he later heard first-person accounts from some who were. Tasan wrote that the young Confucian students at that retreat concentrated on tracing the ideas of Zhu Xi back to their roots in original Confucianism. He claimed that Yi Yunha (1738–1793), who was Sǒngho's grandson by adoption; Yi Sǔnghun, who was a distant maternal relative of Yi Ik; and Chǒng Yakchǒn, who was Yi Sǔnghun's brother-in-law and Tasan's older brother, organized that meeting.[3] They asked Yi Yunha's brother-in-law Kwŏn Ch'ŏlsin to lead their retreat.

Kwŏn agreed and set up a strict schedule for them to follow during their seminar. According to Tasan, Kwŏn had them arise before sunrise, wash their faces and hands in ice water, and then recite the "Admonition on Rising Early and Retiring Late" by the Song Neo-Confucian Chen Bo. When the sun came up, they chanted Zhu Xi's "Admonition to Mindfulness." At noon they intoned the "Four Things Not Done." And at sunset they chanted the "Western Inscription" of Zhang Zai (1020–1077). Yi Pyŏk, who later played a pivotal role in the birth of a Catholic church in Korea, heard of their meeting and hurried to join them, traveling over one hundred *li*[4] and hiking over snow-covered mountain trails to join his friends in the reciting of Neo-Confucian admonitions and discussions of the Confucian classics from early morning until late at night.[5]

Tasan's account of the Chuŏsa meeting reveals much about the intellectual climate in which the Korean Catholic Church was born. An examination of those admonitions so faithfully recited at that retreat provides a glimpse of the basic values of this particular group of eighteenth-century Koreans. "The Western Inscription," for example, presented the metaphysical basis of Neo-Confucian ethics. Written in China in the eleventh century, it introduced the doctrine that human beings form one substance with Heaven and earth and that the practice or violation of virtue has cosmic repercussions. It opens with the statement that "Heaven is my father and Earth my mother," goes on to say that "All people are my brothers and sisters, and all things my companions," and from this draws the exhortation, "Do nothing shameful in the recesses of your own home and thus bring no dishonor to them." The "Western Inscription" is a call to be virtuous toward everything and everyone, everywhere and at all times.[6]

The three admonitions offer more specific ethical guidance. "The Four Things Not Done" of Cheng Yi (1020–1077) is an elaboration of the command in the *Analects* that, if something is contrary to propriety, do not look at it, listen to it, say it, or do it.[7] Cheng Yi stressed the constant self-control necessary to avoid those four temptations to impropriety. He warned that any contact with the world outside the mind, any external sensation, was a potential threat to the calm and purity that was the foundation of intrinsic virtue. He taught that only through rigorous self-discipline could human beings protect their innate goodness from disturbances originating in the external world.[8]

Chen Bo's "Admonition on Rising Early and Retiring Late" furnished precise rules governing every period of the day. Chen wrote that on awakening, people should lie in bed for a while to compose their minds for the coming tests the day will pose to their ability to remain serious, solemn, and composed in the midst of activity. Before rising, he advised reflecting on faults and weaknesses revealed on previous days. In the evening, he suggested, when the time has come to go to bed, people ought to lie with their hands at their sides and their feet together and let neither their bodies nor their minds relax or wander.[9]

Further encouragement to constant watchfulness over thought and behavior is found in Zhu Xi's "Admonition to Mindfulness." Zhu directed his followers to always keep a calm and focused mind, as though in the presence of the Lord Above. He warned them to be constantly cautious and careful never to relax their guard, for the consequences of even the slightest slip were awesome: "Falter for a single moment and selfish desire will burst forth in full force . . . Make the slightest mistake and Heaven and earth will be turned upside down, destroying the basic moral principles governing society and bringing about the collapse of civilization."[10] Attention to these admonitions was not new. T'oegye had included all but the "Four Things Not Done" in his *Sŏnghak sipto* (Ten diagrams on the learning of the Sages), an influential systematic survey of Neo-Confucian ethical thought. What was new was the seriousness and literalness with which the group at Chuŏsa took those texts. Whereas previously Neo-Confucian demands for constant vigilance against the slightest slip into selfishness had been treated as the ultimate goals toward which all men should strive, this small band of Sŏngho's disciples read those admonitions as demands that had to be met perfectly every day. Just as few Christians, outside of pacifist sects such as the Quakers, have tried to immediately implement Christ's command to love one's enemies, so, too, few Neo-Confucians had truly expected to immediately gain total mastery over the distractions of the mind and the selfish desires of the body. Chŏng Yakchŏn, Yi Sŭnghun, Yi Pyŏk, and Yi

Yunha were the impatient exceptions. With the impetuosity of youth, they expected to be able to achieve instant moral perfection.

Such stringent moral expectations created feelings of guilt in those unable to remain constantly calm and unperturbed and filled with nothing but selfless thoughts twenty-four hours a day. Tasan once recalled a conversation with his brother Yakchŏn in which Yakchŏn told him, "I have a lot to repent. Every day I remind myself of all that I have done wrong." Tasan commented that his brother's remark caused him to reflect on the frailty of man. He noted that human beings are unable to reach perfection, no matter how wise or diligent they are, since they are not just a disembodied mind but also possess a body filled with passion and carnal urges. Even the Sages of ancient China were not perfect. If they had been perfect, they would not have been human. But, Tasan went on, human beings can turn this evil into good. Regret can serve to fertilize minds. If human beings constantly remind themselves of serious mistakes they have made in the past, even mistakes they no longer commit, then that feeling of remorse can stimulate them to reform. Guilt and repentance can build virtue from the sins we commit.[11]

Tasan's recognition of the weakness inherent in the human condition, along with his resulting assumption that guilt was an inescapable yet useful feature of the human condition, contradicts one of the fundamental assumptions of Confucian ethics: that human beings are inherently perfectible. Frustration arising from repeated failures to conform to the Neo-Confucian vision of rectitude led to guilt. That guilt led to disillusionment with one of the cornerstones of Neo-Confucian thought. Conventional Neo-Confucian moralists presumed that all human beings have within themselves the strength to eventually become a sage, to form a moral creative force equal to that of, and cooperating with, Heaven and earth.[12] Tasan and his friends asked if all human beings can be Sages, why then are not all people Sages? Especially, they asked themselves, why were they, who tried their best to eliminate self-centered biases and act in accordance with moral principles, unable to go through even a single day without going astray at least once in thought or action? The guilt these men felt at their inability to live up to the high demands of the Sŏngho school of Neo-Confucianism stimulated them to question if their Neo-Confucianism actually did provide the only truly effective path to righteousness.

The Korean Catholic Church was not born at that meeting at Chuǒsa, despite the claims to that effect that have been made in recent years.[13] Though some of those at that retreat, such as Yi Pyŏk, Chŏng Yakchŏn, and Kwŏn Ch'ŏlsin, later went on to participate in the founding of the Korean Catholic Church five years later, others at that meeting joined in the attacks on Catholics. For example, Kim Wŏnsŏng, one of the six people Tasan says were there, later became one of the earliest critics of Catholicism.[14] Moreover, an examination of those admonitions Tasan tells us were so faithfully recited at the retreat reveals that it was all about Confucian self-cultivation rather than the worship of the Catholic God or even the reading of Catholic publications. One scholar has argued that, if in fact that gathering did veer away from the Neo-Confucian mainstream, it was toward the philosophy of the Ming thinker Wang Yangming rather than toward Catholicism.[15]

If we define a Catholic as someone who was baptized a Catholic and intends to participate regularly in Catholic rituals, then the Korean Catholic Church came into existence in early 1784, when Yi Sŭnghun returned from a trip to Beijing as Peter Yi. He had accompanied his father to Beijing as part of a diplomatic mission. Before he left, his friend Yi Pyŏk, who had been reading some Catholic publications from China, urged him to drop by one of the Catholic churches in that city to see what they might give him. Yi Sŭnghun did that and was given some Catholic publications by the European priests he met there. He found those books interesting enough that he returned several times to discuss what those books said. (Neither Yi nor the priests he talked with tell us exactly what those books said that he found most persuasive. We are told, however, that he originally approached the European missionaries in the hope of obtaining some books on mathematics, not religion or philosophy.) After just a few such visits, he decided to become a Catholic and, after promising to forego the common practice among the *yangban* of having a concubine or two in addition to a primary wife, was baptized as Peter by Father Jean-Joseph de Grammont (1736–1812).[16]

When he returned to Korea, he shared his faith with Yi Pyŏk, who also decided to try to put into practice what the Catholic books Yi Sŭnghun had brought back from Beijing taught, even though there was no priest available to say Mass for them in Korea or even explain in detail what those books taught. Nevertheless, Yi Pyŏk and Yi Sŭnghun soon convinced Chŏng Yakchŏn and Chŏng Yagyong that Catholicism offered some interesting ideas and techniques for achieving the ethical goals of Confucianism. Yi Pyŏk then turned to the man who should have been his mentor, Kwŏn Ch'ŏlsin, and converted both Ch'ŏlsin and his younger brother Kwŏn Ilsin.

Notice the connections linking those first Catholics. There were many followers of Sŏngho's philosophy in late eighteenth-century Korea. However, most of them were not converted to Catholicism, despite a common heritage of political frustration and philosophical asceticism. The conversions spread among those of Sŏngho's followers who were related to one another, either by blood or by marriage. For example, Yi Pyŏk's sister had married Chŏng Yakhyŏn (1751–1821), the older brother of Chŏng Yakchŏn and Chŏng Yagyong. The daughter of Yakhyŏn and Yi's sister became the wife of Hwang Sayŏng. (Yi Pyŏk himself is said to have married a daughter of Kwŏn Ŏm [1729–1801], an official who later became one of the chief persecutors of Korea's Catholics.)[17] Yi Sŭnghun was related through marriage to Yi Pyŏk's brother-in-law Chŏng Yakhyŏn, since Yi Sŭnghun had married a sister of the Chŏng brothers. And the mother of the Chŏng brothers was the aunt of Yun Chich'ung (1759–1791), who was martyred in 1791 for following the dictates of his Catholic faith rather than the laws of his country.

Perhaps because participation in non-Confucian rituals was so dangerous for *yangban* that only relatives and close friends could be trusted, or perhaps simply because personal networks in traditional Korea tended to be formed through ties of blood or marital kinship, such ties provided the channels through which the Catholic Church spread out throughout the peninsula. The pattern seen with Yi Pyŏk and Yi Sŭnghun repeated itself over and over again—the seeds of Catholicism fell on barren ground until one member of a family was converted, and then very quickly several relatives of that new Catholic were also converted. However, not every member of every family with a convert became a Catholic, for example, one of Sunam's sons-in-law was Kwŏn Ilsin, an early Catholic. Nor was every convert necessarily related to some previous convert. Nevertheless, the history of the spread of Catholicism in eighteenth- and nineteenth-century Korea is in general a history of relatives converting relatives and therefore cannot be understood outside of a genealogical framework.

THE KOREAN CATHOLIC CHURCH IS BORN

When Yi Sŭnghun returned from Beijing in early spring of 1784 and showed his Catholic books to Yi Pyŏk, it was Yi Pyŏk, not Yi Sŭnghun, who became the most active proselytizer. Apparently bolder and more fervent than Yi Sŭnghun in his conviction that Catholicism offered a superior path to becoming a moral person, Yi Pyŏk began proselytizing his discovery among his friends and relatives right away.[18]

Among those friends and relatives was his brother-in-law Tasan. Tasan and his brother Yakchŏn joined Yi Pyŏk at a memorial service for Yi's sister in April (by the lunar calendar) of 1784. (The wife of Chong Yakhyŏn, she had died in 1780.)[19] During a boat ride on their way back to Seoul from that traditional Confucian ritual in the countryside, Yi shared with Tasan and Yakchŏn what he had learned from the Catholic books Yi Sŭnghun had brought back from Beijing. After they reached Seoul, Yi showed them some of his collection of Catholic works, including Ricci's *Tianzhu shiyi* and Pantoja's *Qike* [Seven victories]. Tasan later confessed that he and his brother found the conversation on the boat fascinating and those books a pleasure to read. He records that they were intrigued by the information Yi said those books contained about the creation of the universe, about the difference between material and spiritual beings, and about life and death.[20] He was only twenty-two years old at that time.

Within a year, Tasan had joined with Yi Pyŏk, his brother Yakchŏn, his brother-in-law Yi Sŭnghun, and a few others to meet regularly to perform what they thought were Catholic rituals. (Since there was no Catholic priest in Korea at that time, they tried to create what they hoped was an appropriate form of Sunday worship.) However, they soon faced consequences for doing so. In the spring of 1785, a Seoul city policeman was passing by a house in Seoul, near what is now the Myŏngdong cathedral, when he heard what he thought were the sounds of drinking and gambling coming from that house. He rushed into the home of the *chungin* translator Kim Pŏmu to find out what was going on and discovered a group of young men sitting on the floor with powder on their faces and dark pieces of cloth over their heads. They were all listening intently to another young man wearing a dark cloth over his head from his forehead back to his shoulders. These young men all held books in their hands and gave the speaker their undivided attention, "with a demeanor more solemn than that of Confucian students at the feet of their teacher."[21] However, though they were mostly the sons of respectable *yangban* families, they were not listening to a traditional exegesis of some Confucian classic. The portrait of Jesus in the room made that obvious. So did the Catholic books and various other religious articles in that house. These young men were listening to Yi Pyŏk explain Catholic doctrines and practices. Kim Pŏmu, as the host of this gathering, was beaten severely and then sent into exile, where he died the next year.[22]

The *yangban* at that gathering were scolded by the minister of the Board of Punishments, who ordered them to return to the true path of Confucianism and then sent them on their way. Their fathers grew worried about possible further repercussions of such involvement with non-Confucian practices. They warned their sons about involvement with this dangerous behavior and asked them to stop.[23] It was at this point that Yi Pyŏk, though he was one of the founders of the Catholic community and one of its most active members, withdrew from further involvement with Catholicism. Yi Pyŏk's father threatened to hang himself unless his son abandoned his practice of Catholicism. Torn between love for father and respect for the teachings of his faith, Yi Pyŏk broke off all contact with the friends he had introduced to Catholic teachings. A year later, in 1786, Yi Pyŏk died of typhus at the age of thirty-three, estranged from the church he had done so much to establish in Korea.[24]

However, many of his friends continued to meet to read and discuss Catholic books, under the pretense of studying for the upper-level civil service exams (many of them were students at the Sŏnggyun'gwan, the Royal Confucian Academy, where young Confucian scholars prepared for the qualifying examinations for government service). They even established a pseudo-ecclesiastical hierarchy for a couple of years (1786–1788), appointing some of their group to act as priests before they learned that such clerical self-appointments were illegitimate.[25]

In 1787 word of those meetings spread to their fellow students at the Sŏnggyun'gwan. A friend and fellow Southerner student, Yi Kigyŏng (1756–1819), grew concerned and tried to talk his colleagues out of their infatuation with Catholicism. When they failed to heed his advice, he turned to another Namin student at the Sŏnggyun'gwan, Hong Nagan (1752–1811), and told him about his anxiety over the spread of Western ideas among their fellow students. Hong's reaction was that they should immediately draft a memorial asking the government to condemn those deviants. Yi talked him out of that dangerous action at that time.[26] (Hong would later file a written complaint with the government that would lead to the execution of Tasan's cousin Yun Chich'ung in 1791 for violating the regulations governing Confucian mourning ritual.) However, word spread about these meetings nonetheless, and eventually the court had to take notice of them.

As rumors spread of alien practices among some Sŏnggyun'gwan's students, Chŏng Yagyong wrote an angry letter to Yi Kigyŏng, blaming Yi for being behind rumors linking Chŏng and his associates to immoral activity. Chŏng wrote that though he had made a serious mistake in placing too much trust in Yi (he had lent Yi some of his Catholic books), Yi had made the graver error of judging others too quickly. "Without even a full day's reflection, you decided that we were miles apart in matters of morality and proper behavior."[27]

Yi defended himself by reiterating to Chŏng his warning of the dangers of Catholicism. Yi pointed out that the Ten Commandments of Christianity did not say anything specifically about serving one's ruler, and they listed the command to honor one's father and mother in fourth place, instead of at the top of the list where it belonged. Such blindness to the proper moral priorities was not something that a true gentleman could accept. Moreover, he noted some of those who were studying Catholic books were hiding that fact from their fathers and older brothers and that was not the way a true gentleman should behave. He summed up his objections to Chŏng's dabbling with Catholicism by declaring, "it perverts the moral rules governing human relationships and does not make any sense at all."[28]

Yi Kigyŏng's letter to Chŏng Yagyong is representative of the Korean Neo-Confucian reaction to Catholicism. Yi did not display much concern for arguing the truth or falsity of Catholic statements about the existence of God, the divinity of Jesus Christ, or the immortality of man's soul. He was more concerned with the moral consequences of those beliefs. Catholicism, he argued, led men to slight their responsibilities to their parents and superiors. That reason alone made it unacceptable to a Confucian moralist.

However, the first person to formally ask the government to take action against Catholics was not Yi Kigyŏng or Hong Nagan but Yi Kyŏngmyŏng, an official in the Office of the Censor-General. In 1788, he reported to the court that "Western Learning" was spreading rapidly all over the kingdom.[29] Fortunately for the small band of Catholics, the king responded that there was no need to take drastic action against those who appeared to be drawn to those teachings. Instead, he said a two-pronged approach of outlawing Catholic books in private hands, on the one hand, and promoting true Confucianism, on the other, would cause this threat to subside.[30]

With no immediate serious threat to their small community, the Catholics continued to meet for a while, and even added to their numbers. Chŏng Yakchong followed his brothers Yakchŏn and Tasan into the church in 1786 and became an active proselytizer.[31] Their cousin Yun Chich'ung was baptized by Yi Sŭnghun the next year, in 1787, and also began attracting others to the Catholic community.[32]

Then, in 1790, a letter arrived from Bishop Alexandre de Gouvea in Beijing that shook the Korean Church to its foundation. That letter informed the Catholics in Korea that the Pope had forbidden the use of spirit tablets, an essential element of Confucian ancestor memorial rituals.[33] That Catholic rejection of Confucian ritual regulations set the stage for an open confrontation with the government, and the first deliberate execution of Korean Catholics. It also caused many of those who were Confucians first and Catholics second, those who had joined the Catholic community to become better Confucians, to leave the church. Yi Sŭnghun withdrew from active leadership of the church upon hearing this news, turning his responsibilities over to Kwŏn Il-sin.[34] Chŏng Yagyong and his brother Yakchŏn also withdrew from further participation in Catholic activities after the announcement of the ban on Confucian ancestor rites, although their brother Yakchong remained an active leader of the church until his execution in the 1801 persecution.[35]

THE ANCESTOR MEMORIAL SERVICE

Korea's first Catholics had been converted primarily by books written by Jesuit missionaries in the seventeenth century who stressed compatibility rather than incompatibility between Confucianism and Catholicism. However, the Pope in Rome had ruled in 1704 against that Jesuit policy of accommodation, demanding instead that Asian Catholics make a complete break with their non-Christian culture. Rejecting the Jesuit argument for toleration of cultural diversity, the Pope insisted that all members in good standing of the Catholic Church in East Asian desist from participation in the Confucian ritual of bowing and offering bowls of food and wine to tablets on which were inscribed the names of ancestors.[36]

What was the nature of this rite that caused so much difficulty for the Catholic Church, both in Korea and in China? It is often referred to as "ancestor worship," but that translation of the Korean word *chesa* [祭祀] is misleading. No worship of ancestors was involved. Family members and descendants of the deceased simply gathered together in remembrance of their ancestors as an expression of filial piety and family unity. The ancestor memorial service was the glue that held Confucian society together. It was this ritual that reinforced the recognition that men were not individuals living isolated and alone on this planet but were members of a family and a community, with all the duties, responsibilities, benefits, and rewards that entailed.

Confucians looked upon society as an extension of the family. Filial sons in the families of the nation meant subjects loyal to the throne. To refuse to honor ancestors according to the prescribed ritual, as Korean Catholics were ordered to do, was to challenge the core of the Confucian political, moral, and social order. To be moral and loyal in eighteenth-century Korea meant, above all, to show filial piety by serving, honoring, and obeying parents faithfully, before and after their death. The refusal to perform these rites meant a refusal to show proper respect for parents, a refusal to carry out the duties of a loyal subject of the sovereign, and a refusal to act in a manner befitting a respectable member of society.

The element in the ancestor memorial service that most offended the Pope in Rome was the wooden ancestral tablet representing the spirit of the ancestor being honored. During the mourning period and on the anniversary of the death of the person being honored, direct descendants and relatives of the deceased to the fourth generation, led by the eldest surviving direct male descendant, were supposed to perform the ancestor memorial service before the appropriate tablet. That service essentially consisted of placing on a low table a tablet on which the name of the deceased had been written, arranging bowls of food and drink on that table as an offering in front of that tablet, and bowing several times to show respect for the person the tablet represented while offering the food and drink to the spirit of the ancestor being remembered.[37] The Catholic Church in the eighteenth century chose to interpret this service as a religious ritual that entailed worship of an ancestral spirit who was actually present in the wooden tablet. This literal interpretation made this ritual a form of idolatry, and therefore forbidden to all Catholics. The early Jesuit missionaries in China had recognized the importance of this rite in family-oriented Confucian society and had argued that, as educated scholars viewed it, the ritual did not offend against any points of Catholic doctrine, since their Confucian informants told them no worship was involved. According to those informants, participants in such rituals acted as though their ancestors were present before them, but they did not believe their dead relatives actually resided in those tablets.

In retrospect, the Jesuit understanding of the actual significance of the ancestor memorial service appears to have been a more accurate representation of what most educated scholars in China believed about that ritual. Kangxi, the Manchu emperor of China from 1661 to 1722, declared in 1700 that veneration of ancestors was an expression of love and filial remembrance, not intended to bring protection to the worshiper. Furthermore, there was no idea, when an ancestral tablet was erected, that the soul of the ancestor dwelled in that tablet.[38] Emperor Kangxi was not placing a new rationalistic interpretation on an old superstitious Chinese practice with his statement. Almost two thousand years earlier, the *Li Ji* (Book of rites) had declared, "The idea of sacrifice is not something that comes from without. It issues from within, being born in the heart. When the heart is deeply moved, expression is given to it in ceremonies."[39] The ancestor memorial ritual was described even in early Confucian classics as more an expression of the filial piety of the living than an assertion of the presence of the soul of the dead in a wooden tablet. As the sociologist C. K. Yang noted of the early rationalist tradition in Confucian philosophy, "All the ritual behavior and offerings made to the spirits were to be interpreted as an expression of longing for the continued existence of the dead without belief in the actual existence of the soul."[40]

Korean Confucians also understood the psychological nature of the ancestor memorial ritual. They recognized that the motive and state of mind of the person performing the ritual were more important than any belief or skepticism about the survival of the soul. In a short essay entitled "the principles behind ancestral rites," Sŏngho pointed out that the ancestor memorial ceremony was more for the living than for the dead. He argued that the Sages established that ritual to allow the living to express proper respect for their ancestors. Through proper performance of the ancestor memorial rite a filial son was able to express the depth of the gratitude he felt toward the parents who gave him life. It was this sincere expression of filial sentiments that provided the foundation of morality and social order in the Confucian world. Whether or not a soul existed to accept the ritual offerings of food and drink was of secondary importance.[41]

Sŏngho's disciple Sunam showed a similar concern for the sincerity with which the ancestor rites were performed in his criticism of Catholic doctrine and practices. Writing before the Catholics in Korea had been informed that they were forbidden to play any role whatsoever in ancestral rites, Sunam reported that Catholics already had been criticizing as absurd the placing of food before ancestral tablets. Furthermore, the Catholics were advising their friends to take part in such "superstitious" Confucian ceremonies only under silent protest, inwardly turning toward Heaven and asking God's forgiveness for not being able to resist the social pressure to participate in this Confucian ritual. Calling such advice "a perversion of our rituals and a slander against Confucianism," Sunam declared that the Catholics did not understand the moral principles by which the Sages in ancient China established ancestor memorial rites to show respect for forefathers.[42] Sunam argued that the ritual was meaningful only if the participants sincerely desired to show through their performance of the traditional ceremonies their filial gratitude to the ancestors who gave them life. The reluctant participation the Catholics advised implied to Confucian observers an immoral lack of respect for ancestors and contempt for time-honored tradition. That alone would have been enough to convince staunch Neo-Confucians that the government should act to stop the spread of such a challenge to the moral foundations of Korea's Confucian state and society.

The Catholic interpretation of the ancestor memorial service as based on the assumption of the actual presence of the spirit of those ancestors at that ritual was not completely unjustified. Confucians assumed that the spirits of the dead still existed as an attenuated form of energy (ki, 氣) for a while after the death of their physical body. In fact, they assumed that it was the fact that we and our ancestors had the same ki that made it possible for us to feel that our ancestors responded to our displays of gratitude and respect in an ancestor memorial service. However, educated scholars would not call those displays of reverence for ancestors "worship," since the ancestors were not viewed as divine beings who could respond to the pleas of the living by directly intervening in the affairs of this world and granting requests for assistance. In other words, educated Confucian scholars did not pray to their ancestors, and therefore it would be a mistake to label the ancestor memorial service as understood and performed by most Confucian scholars to be a form of idolatry.

That may not have been the case with the less-educated members of the population in both China and Korea. Those missionaries in China who convinced Rome that the ancestor memorial services constituted a form of idolatry because participants in those services assumed that the spirits were present and could respond to their words and actions may have been relying on what the less educated told them about their reasons for engaging in such rituals. The first Catholics in Korea may have made a similar observation. They may have noticed that commoners often treated those wooden ancestral tablets as though spirits were actually present in them, and as though those spirits could interact with the living. That would have made the use of such tablets appear unacceptable in the eyes of those who believed that only God (or his designated intermediaries, such as his mother Mary or the saints) could be the object of prayers.

However the ancestor memorial service is understood, whether it is seen as worship of spirits or simply as a display of respect for the dead, the fact remains that many early Catholics in Korea were uncomfortable with that ritual even before they learned that the use of spirit tablets had been forbidden by the Pope. Moreover, whether or not the ancestor rites issue had arisen, Catholicism would still have found Korea an unfriendly environment, though their objection to the use of spirit tablets heightened the animosity toward them. Before 1790, when Korea's Catholics first learned of the papal prohibition, Shin Hudam, Sunam, Yi Kigyŏng, and Hong Nagan had already condemned Catholicism as an immoral deviation from the path of righteousness. Matteo Ricci had been naive when he argued that Confucian values and Catholic doctrines were compatible. The conflict over the proper procedure for honoring deceased parents was a symptom, not a cause, of the moral friction between the doctrinal, supernatural orientation of Catholicism and the moralistic, humanistic focus of Neo-Confucianism. The fact that Catholics placed their duty to obey God above their duty to obey their parents and their secular ruler was enough to ensure that Catholics would be accused of not paying proper respect to parents and rulers (*mubu, mugun*). The papal decision against the Jesuit policy of accommodation in matters of rituals merely guaranteed that the Catholic challenge was more flagrant than it otherwise might have been.

THE ARREST AND MARTYRDOM OF PAUL YUN AND JAMES KWŎN

After 1790, Koreans sympathetic to Catholicism could no longer ignore the choice that faced them. They could either be loyal to their new religion or at peace with their government and their society. They could no longer view Catholic teachings as merely an aid to more consistent adherence to Confucian moral demands. The letter from Bishop de Gouvea made clear that faithful adherence to the directives of the church would inevitably lead to conflict with their society, with their family, friends, and neighbors. Two who made the decision to risk that confrontation were Yun Chich'ung, baptized Paul, and Kwŏn Sang'yŏn, baptized James (1751–1791). In May of 1791, Paul Yun's mother, who was also James Kwŏn's aunt, died. Paul and his cousin James decided that they would follow all the customary Confucian mourning rituals except the rites involving the ancestral tablets. Going beyond the instructions from Bishop Gouvea in Beijing, they not only did not make a tablet for Yun's mother, they burnt all the ancestral tablets in their possession and buried the ashes. Given the central role of the tablets in the mourning ceremonies, their absence could not go unnoticed by relatives who came to the village of Chinsan in Chŏlla province to join Yun in mourning the loss of his mother.[43]

Soon rumors spread of Yun and Kwŏn's violation of the requirements of Confucian mourning ritual. These rumors reached the ears of Hong Nagan, Yi Kigyŏng's friend, who in 1787 had wanted to punish Yi Sŭnghun and Tasan for their participation in the Catholic study group at the Sŏnggyun'gwan National Confucian Academy. In 1791, Hong was a minor official in the royal secretariat. He apparently felt that his post gave him the authority and the responsibility to demand strict adherence to Confucian norms from the members of Korea's literati elite. He sent a long letter voicing his opinion to Ch'ae Chegong, who was then the leading Namin official in King Chŏngjo's court. In that private letter, Hong demanded that Ch'ae, as the highest ranking member of their Southerner Faction, take drastic action against Yun and Kwŏn before the Catholic disease spread further and threatened both the Namin and the entire society and government of Korea.

In his letter, Hong charged that Catholics treated their fathers and their rulers as no different from strangers they might happen to pass on the street. "They have thrown away their moral principles as if they were worth no more than a pair of old shoes." Asserting that moral principles were eternal and unalterable and that Korea had taken ritual and righteousness as the foundation of the nation for thousands of years, he wrote, "Even the most perverse and immoral have not dared to violate the rules of propriety that require them to serve their parents while they are alive and to bury them properly when they die." Yun and Kwŏn had lowered themselves to the level of beasts and barbarians. They had let their belief in their "strange and monstrous god" deceive them into refusing to follow the proper burial and mourning procedures. Not only had they refused to make an ancestral tablet for Yun's mother, they had gone even further and burnt the ancestral tablets they already had.[44]

What a tragedy! Nothing this bizarre has happened since time began. The laws of our land declare that the crime of destroying an ancestral tablet is as serious an offense as murder. The laws also say that anyone who deliberately destroys his father's ancestral tablet with his own hands should be treated exactly the same as someone who rebels against the throne. Even if Yun and Kwŏn were shown to be insane, we could not let them escape the full penalty the law demands. They openly condemn the way of our ancestors and embrace perversion without hesitation or restraint. Look closely at the evil nature of their crime. It is one hundred times worse than rebellion. If we do not exterminate them now, then the moral bonds among men will be destroyed everywhere and this land where ritual and righteousness have prevailed for four thousand years will fall into ruin and become fit only for savages and wild animals.[45]

Hong's charges were too serious to be ignored. An official search was made of Yun's and Kwŏn's homes and no ancestral tablets were found. Warrants for their arrest were issued immediately. Near the end of November, Yun and Kwŏn were taken into custody by the magistrate of Chinsan county. That magistrate, Shin Sawŏn, had reluctantly arrested Yun and Kwŏn, doing so only after receiving explicit instructions from Seoul. He obviously did not want the embarrassment of official recognition that *idan* had sprouted in the county under his jurisdiction.

In the notes Yun Chich'ung took of his interrogation by Magistrate Shin, the magistrate appears to have tried to save his prisoners' reputations and his own by having them renounce their more extreme actions and provide an explanation of their Catholic beliefs that would make this Western religion completely compatible with Confucian orthodoxy. But Yun and Kwŏn held fast to their convictions. Shin reminded them of the Confucian injunction to filial sons to protect the body their parents had given them. To allow themselves to suffer torture and death, argued the magistrate, would bring ruin and disgrace on their families and show a lack of proper filial respect for the lives that they had received from their parents. Unmoved, Yun countered with his belief that filial piety meant always acting in accordance with what was right, even at the cost of torture and death. Magistrate Shin, seeing that he could not convince Yun or Kwŏn to abandon their religion, placed cangues around his prisoners' necks and sent them to Chŏnju, where they were turned over to the provincial governor Chŏng Minsi.[46]

In Chŏnju, Yun continued to deny that he had done anything wrong. He attempted to justify the destruction of ancestral tablets by using logic and reason to show the absurdity of the ancestor memorial service. Yun's defense, adopted from the Western insistence on the "irrational and superstitious" character of Confucian ritual, clashed with the Confucian concern for the psychological and ethical significance of the rite. The account of the interrogation shows the interrogator and the interrogated talking past each other rather than to each other. Yun kept insisting that he had done what he had done in order to ensure that his actions were in accordance with what he believed was true. The governor kept insisting that Yun admit that what he had done and what his Catholic books taught were immoral. Yun could not understand how actions that offended against logic and reason could be moral. The governor could not understand how considerations of truth or falsity could affect a person's performance of his social obligations.[47]

Yun first argued that it was an affront to the dignity owed his father and mother to treat pieces of wood as though they held their spirits. He noted that the Fourth Commandment ordered Catholics to honor their fathers and mothers. If their parents were actually present in those wooden ancestral tablets, then Catholics would be obligated to show respect for the tablets. But those tablets were made of wood. "They have no flesh and blood relationship with me. They did not give me life nor educate me. . . . How can I dare to treat these man-made pieces of wood as though they were actually my mother and father?"[48]

Yun argued further that it was foolish to place food and drink before a block of wood, even if a spirit of a deceased parent were present in it. Yun pointed out that a spirit is not a material object and could get no nourishment from material goods. No matter how delicious the wine and nutritious the meat, that spirit could get no benefit from the offering. Furthermore, even the most filial son did not try to serve his parents food and drink when they were asleep. "If people cannot eat while they sleep, how much more foolish is it to offer food to our parents when they are dead? How can anyone who is sincere in his filial piety try to honor his parents with such an absurd practice?"[49]

This Catholic Korean even dared to challenge the fundamental assumption of Confucian morality that made filial piety and loyalty to the ruler the absolutes from which all other value and virtue were derived. He denied that those two virtues were complete and axiomatic in themselves but instead argued that "the basis of loyalty to the ruler is the laws of God, and the basis of filial piety towards one's parents is also the laws of God."[50] This was a radical contradiction of the core of Confucian thought. Rather than accepting the virtues of filial piety and loyalty as the standards by which all else was to be judged, Yun claimed that filial piety and loyalty were themselves only conditional obligations, binding on man only because God, the source of all value, has so willed.

Paul Yun did not completely escape the behavioral orientation of the Confucian world that placed concern for what should be done ahead of concern for what should be believed. When told to provide a short summary of Catholic teachings, he replied not with an account of the divinity of Jesus Christ and his power to redeem human beings from their sins, but with the statement "What we practice can be reduced to the ten commandments and the seven virtues."[51] For the purpose of arguing with his Confucian interrogator, Yun thus reduced Catholicism to its moral commands and presented it as essentially a collection of guidelines for ethical behavior.

The ethical behavior Catholicism demanded differed from that which Confucianism required. Catholicism, unlike Confucianism, was more oriented toward the next world than toward this one. Yun's view of Catholic morality placed him in fatal conflict with his Confucian society, since he placed his obligations to God above his obligations to his fellow human beings. Yun was asked by his interrogator to state the Ten Commandments by which Catholics regulated their conduct. The governor immediately noticed that there was no specific mention of the relationship between subjects and their rulers. He demanded that Yu explain this deficiency. Yun's reply, that the king was like the father of his realm and therefore his subjects owed him the same respect and loyalty they owed their parents as enjoined by the Fourth Commandment, did not satisfy his interrogator. Yun was ordered to write down in greater detail the Catholic principles of morality, keeping in mind the need to "emphasize the principles of loyalty to the king and filial piety so that you might be able to save your life."[52]

Yun responded with a written statement in which he declared that the Lord of Heaven was the Creator and Father of all men. Since he recognized God as his Father, he could not disobey any of God's orders. God had forbidden his children to have ancestral tablets in their homes or to offer meat and wine to the spirits of the dead represented by such tablets. He had to obey that divine command. There was no moral alternative to doing so. Yun also explained the difference between Confucian and Catholic expressions of filial piety. He said that Catholics emphasized diligent application to the practice of virtue instead of participation in rituals of doubtful merit. This Catholic interest in the sincere practice of virtue, Yun argued, should be seen as the expression of loyalty and filial piety that it was, not as rebellious and immoral. After all, Yun noted, commoners and impoverished *yangban* were not harshly punished if they did not carry out the mourning ritual strictly according to regulations. Why should those who were only obeying the commands of their God in the privacy of their own homes be threatened with capital punishment and charged with defying the laws of the land?[53]

Though the arguments of Paul Yun might seem reasonable to people in the twenty-first century, they appeared irrelevant to Confucian officials in 1791. Few well-educated scholars then needed to be convinced that the souls of the dead were not actually present in the wooden ancestral tablets. They had long been following the injunction of Confucius to show respect for spirits as if they were present without worrying about whether those spirits were really available for interactions or not.[54] Yun's contentions did not in the least mitigate the impression in their Confucian eyes that both Yun and Kwŏn were guilty of a grave offense against both the laws of their state and the mores of their society. Yun's claim that he had not violated Confucian moral principles, properly understood, was dismissed out of hand.[55] From Magistrate Shin on up, Yun's jailers and judges recognized that Catholicism was not just Confucian morality cloaked in Western theological rhetoric. As they saw it, Catholicism led to actions that challenged the basic assumptions of Confucian morality. Yun's actions, even more than his beliefs, sealed his fate. As Governor Chŏng pointed out to him, King

Chŏngjo had ordered the destruction of all Catholic books in 1788.[56] By reading books that the king himself had condemned, Yun had displayed disloyalty. But that was a minor mistake compared to the more grievous error of acting on the precepts taught in those forbidden writings. When Yun refused to perform a proper mourning ritual, destroying his family's ancestral tablet instead, he lowered himself to the level of beasts and brought on himself the most severe of punishments.[57]

The language of the many memorials demanding the death penalty for Yun and Kwŏn further supports the conclusion that it was what Yun and Kwŏn did and did not do, more than what they did and did not believe, that provoked the animosity of so many of Korea's Neo-Confucian scholars both in and out of the government. The most common charge levied against them was not merely that they held unacceptable ideas but that they acted contrary to fundamental moral principles, "wounding morality and perverting righteousness [*sangnyun p'aeŭi* 傷倫悖義]."[58] And, when King Chŏngjo agreed to order their execution, the reason he gave was that they had behaved immorally, not that they held noncanonical beliefs. It was their destruction of ancestral tablets in accordance with their Catholic faith, more than their Catholic faith itself, which provided the grounds for their beheading.[59]

If Yun had merely entertained Catholic ideas while continuing to follow Confucian rules of morality and ritual, he might have escaped with no more than a severe warning for dabbling in strange theories.[60] However, he was not content to merely believe in Catholicism. He was determined to practice it as well. Yun's redefinition of acceptable ideas and practices, grounding them in belief in God's existence and obedience to God's will rather than in the cosmic network of appropriate interrelationships and interaction (*li*) that underlay Confucian behavior and ritual, allowed Catholic theological doctrine to dictate his behavior. His Catholic conception of orthodoxy thus became the framework for a challenge to the very foundations of Neo-Confucian morality that could not be overlooked. By rejecting the traditional subordination of religion to morality, Yun brought on his own death sentence.

The governor of Chŏnju reported to Seoul that Paul Yun Chich'ung and James Kwŏn Sang'yŏn had indeed destroyed their ancestral tablets and had abandoned the Confucian ways of their fathers. On December 3, 1791, King Chŏngjo commanded that Paul Yun and James Kwŏn be beheaded without delay.[61] Five days later, the thirty-two-year-old Yun and the forty-one-year-old Kwŏn were decapitated, and then their heads were exposed for five days to make the general population aware of the enormity of their crime. Their belief that religious truths determined morality and their denial that Confucian moral presuppositions determined what could and could not be believed cost them their lives.[62]

The persecution of Catholics did not stop there. Kwŏn Ilsin was brought in for questioning. Under the torture he endured as part of his interrogation, he condemned the destruction of ancestral tablets.[63] Though he had been a leader of the Catholic community, he was a Confucian first and a Catholic second. He had embraced Catholicism primarily for the support it seemed to offer to fundamental Confucian moral values. After several days of torture and interrogation, followed by a threat of exile to Chejudo that would have separated him from his dying mother, Kwŏn Ilsin made a faint and ambiguous renunciation of Catholicism. His sentence was then changed to exile at a site closer to his mother's home. Soon thereafter he died of his wounds while on his way to exile in Ch'ungch'ŏng province.[64]

Ch'oe P'ilgong (1744–1801), a *chungin* Catholic leader, was brought in for questioning about the same time as Kwŏn Ilsin. Unlike Kwŏn, Ch'oe initially proudly proclaimed his commitment to Catholicism. He defended his religion for asking nothing more of its adherents than that they show respect for Heaven and live virtuous lives. He also called the Lord of Heaven the Father of the universe and said that there could be no greater display of filial piety than to die for such a God. Ch'oe suffered imprisonment and torture for a full month before he finally relented and made a formal statement renouncing Catholicism, although he later returned to his faith and was martyred in 1801.[65]

Several other Catholics were also tortured into at least temporarily abandoning Catholicism in the immediate aftermath of the Yun-Kwŏn incident.[66] Others abandoned their faith completely and never returned to Catholicism. The Korean Catholic community was a very different community after 1791 than it had been before Yun and Kwŏn were executed.

CHAPTER 4

A Decade of Hopes and Fears

The 1791 persecution led many of those who had played a major role in establishing a Catholic Church on Korean soil, such as Yi Sŭnghun and Chŏng Yagyong, to withdraw from active involvement with the Catholic community once they realized that they had to choose between Catholicism and Confucianism. However, new leaders stepped up to take their place alongside those of the old leaders who chose Catholicism over Confucianism. Among those new leaders was Chŏng Yakchong, who joined the church after his two brothers Yakchong and Yakchŏn did but was much more fervent than either of them and played a leading role in keeping the Catholic community alive in the decade between 1791 and 1801. Another was Hwang Sayŏng. Hwang, as noted earlier, was married to a daughter of yet another Chŏng brother, Chŏng Yakhyŏn, who was never a member of Korea's Catholic community. Hwang was only in his teens when Paul Yun and James Kwŏn were executed. He had been a Catholic for only a few months when those two men were killed because of their Catholic beliefs. However, undeterred by that foreshadowing of what would happen to him someday, he not only stayed faithful to his choice of Catholicism over Confucianism but went on to play an increasingly important role in the Catholic community over the decade leading up to his own execution in 1801.

Chŏng Yakchong and Hwang were both of *yangban* stock. There were a few other *yangban* from among those who had helped organize the Korean Catholic Church before 1791 who decided that they would rather be Catholic than Confucian when that choice had to be made in 1791. They included Hong Nangmin (1751–1801) and the brothers Yu Hanggŏm (1756–1801) and Yu Kwan'gŏm (1768–1801) and their cousin Yun Chihŏn (1764–1801). Yun Yuil (1760–1795) was also of rural *yang-ban* background. Other leaders were *chungin*, including Ch'oe Ch'anghyŏn

(1754–1801), who had been one of the self-appointed "priests" in the late 1780s. Other important *chungin* Catholics who were active after 1791 include Yi Chonch'ang (1759–1801), Ch'oe In'gil (1764–1795), and Ch'oe P'ilgong. In addition, a woman, Kang Wansuk (1761–1801), became an important figure in the Korean Catholic Church in the 1790s. Kang was neither *yangban* nor *chungin* but somewhere in the middle. She was from a family line descended from *yangban* paternal ancestry but non-*yangban* maternal ancestry.[1]

Several prominent *yangban* who had been associated with the Catholic community in the beginning found that, even though they had left the church by 1791, they could not escape the taint of having once been Catholic. Though both Yi Sŭnghun and Chŏng Yagyong managed to win appointments to governments posts in the 1790s, they both were often forced out of government service temporarily when their Catholic past was brought up. Even Yi Kahwan (1742–1801), who had never formally joined the Catholic Church and who kept an even greater distance between himself and the Catholic community after 1791 than he had before 1791, found that he, too, faced barriers in his political career because of accusations that he was secretly a leader of the Korean Catholic community. All three men publicly denounced Catholicism and even persecuted Catholics when they were given administrative responsibility for local districts in which Catholics lived. Yet in 1801 Yi Sŭnghun was executed, Chŏng was exiled, and Yi Kahwan, who was Yi Sŭnghun's uncle, died from the rough treatment he endured while he was being interrogated.[2]

Those who remained active in the Catholic community after 1791 realized they had to do two things if the Korean Catholic Church was going to survive and even grow. They had to convince the government to change its anti-Catholic attitude and at least tolerate the existence of a Catholic community on its territory. They also needed to bring a priest to Korea. The Catholic Church teaches that certain sacraments (sacred rituals), such as Confession and the Eucharist, are very important for salvation, yet they can be performed only by an ordained priest. Without a priest, Korea's Catholics feared it would be difficult for them to escape eternal damnation.

It was clear to the small group of beleaguered Catholics in Korea that their government would not grant them religious toleration or allow the presence of a priest unless it was forced to do so. The Korean Catholic community was too small to exert enough pressure on their government to force it to change its policies. There were only around four thousand Catholics in Korea in the mid-1790s, out of a population of several million, and, despite active underground proselytizing, that community had only grown to ten thousand by the beginning of the nineteenth century.[3] They realized that they had to rely on external pressure, on requests or even demands (backed up by armed force) from Western countries (which they assumed were all Roman Catholic countries), if they were to get their government to stop persecuting them and allow them to practice their faith openly. The history of the Korean Catholic Church in the 1790s, therefore, is a history of the attempts by Korea's Catholics to bring a priest to Korea (which they succeeded in doing in 1795) and to get the government to stop jailing, torturing, and killing them (which they were not able to do).

Korea's Catholics did not realize that the Catholic West was not as strong as they thought it was. Not only was eighteenth-century Europe not 100 percent Catholic, since several countries in Europe were ruled by Protestant Christians, but even Catholic countries did not necessarily have governments willing to use military force to help Catholic communities overseas. Among those Catholic countries, France was the country on which they placed their greatest hopes. Korea's Catholics did not realize that since the French Revolution in 1789, France was in no position to, nor eager to, offer official assistance to them. Moreover, the situation for Catholics in China was not as healthy as they thought it was.[4] The Society of Jesus (the Jesuits), whose missionaries wrote most of the books Korean Catholics had been reading, had been suppressed by the Pope in 1773. The Catholic Church in China was now under the supervision of Franciscans and Dominicans, two religious orders not as favorably inclined to support accommodation with Confucian cultures as the Society of Jesus had been. The bishop in Beijing with whom Korean Catholics communicated, Bishop Alexandre de Gouvea (1751–1808), was Portuguese, as many of the Jesuits in China had been, but he was a Franciscan.[5] Moreover, the church in China was having its own difficulties in the eighteenth century. The presence of priests in Beijing was tolerated because they provided technical assistance in astronomical and calendrical matters to the Imperial Court, not because the Chinese government had a policy of religious toleration. In fact, Catholics, both foreign priests and Chinese priests and laypeople, sometimes faced persecution of their own outside the Chinese capital.[6]

BRINGING A PRIEST TO KOREA

Even if the Catholics in Korea had realized that the situation for Catholicism was much more complicated than they thought it was, and that the Catholic Church outside Korea was much less prepared to render the assistance to Korea they desperately needed, they still would have embarked on their project to bring a priest to Korea. The presence of a priest was absolutely essential. A Catholic community without a priest is not a complete Catholic community.

Yun Yuil, a neighbor and disciple of Kwŏn Ch'ŏlsin, was the first to carry to Beijing the request for the dispatch of a priest. He made his first trip to Beijing in 1789 to deliver letters from Yi Sŭnghun, Yu Hanggŏm, and Kwŏn Ilsin. While there, he was baptized and confirmed (another Catholic sacrament). He made another trip in January 1790, at which time he met Father Nicolas-Joseph Raux (1754–1801), a Lazarist missionary working in the North Church in Beijing. On that same trip, he handed over a letter asking that a Western warship bring a priest to Korea.[7] He went back to Beijing later that year and finally was able to obtain a promise from Bishop de Gouvea that a priest would be sent to Korea.[8] Bishop de Gouvea tried to fulfill that promise the next year. He assigned to Korea a Chinese priest from Macao, Father Wu, also known by his Portuguese name, Jean dos Remedios. Father Wu left Beijing for Korea in February 1791, and reached the Sino-Korean border twenty days later. However, he was unable to meet with the Korean Catholics who were supposed guide him across the border into the peninsula. Father Wu passed away in 1793, before he could schedule another rendezvous with Korean Catholics, leaving Korea in the same priestless state it had been since the founding of the Korean Catholic Church almost a decade earlier.[9]

Bishop de Gouvea then turned to another Chinese priest, Father Zhou Wenmo (1752–1801). Unlike Father Wu, Zhou Wenmo was from China, not Macao. He was born in 1752 in the Suzhou district in Jiangsu. His mother died in 1757, and his father died soon afterward, in 1758. He then went to live with his Catholic aunt. At the age of twenty, in 1771, he married, but his wife died two years later. Sometime after 1785 he entered a new seminary in Beijing and trained to become a priest. He was the first person to graduate from that seminary and was ordained a priest sometime between 1791 and 1794.[10]

In 1793 Chi Hwang (1766–1795) traveled to Beijing and learned that Father Wu had passed away, but that another priest, Father Zhou, would soon be sent to Korea. One year later, Zhou walked from Beijing to the Willow Palisades, a twenty-day trek. The Willow Palisades marks the northern limits of the Chinese portion of the Manchu Empire. He was still a nine days' walk from the border with Korea, but Koreans were allowed to travel to the Willow Palisades, if they traveled as members of diplomatic embassies or merchants.[11] While he waited for Korean Catholics to meet him and also waited for the Yalu River marking the Korean border to freeze over so he could walk across it, he ministered to Chinese Catholics in various churches in the Liaodong area. Finally, on January 3 (by the solar calendar), he met Chi Hwang in Ŭiju, a town across the river from Korea. Dressed like a Korean, he walked across the Yalu River into Korea and, guided by Chi, arrived at Seoul on January 14.[12]

FATHER ZHOU WENMO IN KOREA

Once in Seoul, Zhou settled in the home of the *chungin* Catholic leader Ch'oe In'gil. He met a number of Korean Catholics at this time, including Hwang Sayŏng. On Easter Sunday, 1795, he baptized those who had been waiting for a priest to baptize them, and also rebaptized those who had been baptized under the old "pseudo-ecclesiastical hierarchy" established before 1791. He also "heard" confessions (he had to receive written notes, since he could not understand much spoken Korean at that point), giving Catholics the comfort of having their sins absolved, something they believed could only be done through the sacrament of confession administered by a priest.[13] That same year, Zhou also created lay organizations to help him manage the affairs of the growing Korean Catholic community. He named Kang Wansuk the head of a Catholic women's association, and also named Ch'oe Ch'anghyŏn (1759–1801) the general secretary and chief catechist of the Korean Catholic Church.

The next month, however, Zhou had to leave Seoul and go into hiding in the countryside. The government had learned that a Chinese priest had been smuggled into Korea and issued an order to apprehend him. He spent an entire year, from May 1795 to May 1796, with Catholics in the provinces outside of Seoul. Among the homes he stayed in were those of Yu Yunil, Yi Chonch'ang, and Yu Hanggŏm.[14] When he returned to Seoul, he spent most of his time hiding in Kang Wansuk's house, assuming that the government would not expect to find him in the home of a respectable Korean woman.

In the meantime, the three men who had been the most helpful in smuggling him into Korea were arrested, tortured, and killed. Yun Yuil, Chi Hwang, and Ch'oe In'gil were all arrested and taken to the Seoul P'odoch'ŏng on May 12, 1795. (The P'odoch'ŏng, literally "the office for apprehending thieves," served as both police station and jail for dealing with common criminals. Normally, *yangban* accused of criminal activity as well as others accused of such serious crimes as treason and rebellion were dealt with by the State Tribunal instead.) There they were beaten repeatedly in an effort to convince them to divulge where Father Zhou had gone. Their silence brought their death. On June 18, all three died from the mistreatment they had endured. Chi was twenty-nine years old, Yun was thirty-six, and Ch'oe was thirty-one. After they died, their bodies were tossed in the Han River south of Seoul. They were not even given the courtesy of a decent burial.[15]

When it was discovered that a foreign priest had been smuggled into Korea, the calls for action against Catholics, cries that had fallen quiet after 1791, began to be heard at court again. The central government felt compelled to remove three men from its ranks who were widely (but erroneously) believed to be the secret leaders of Korea's Catholic community in the 1790s. Yi Kahwan, Yi Sŭnghun, and Chŏng Yagyong had all been appointed to important positions in the civil service. They were not banned from government service entirely, since there was no evidence to substantiate the charges against them, but they were temporarily demoted. Yi Sŭnghun was exiled to Yesan. He claimed later that he wrote condemnations of Catholicism in both classical Chinese and Han'gŭl, which he distributed around Yesan. He bragged that his attacks on Catholicism, particularly his criticism of the doctrines of the incarnation and of Heaven and Hell, stopped the spread of Catholicism there.[16] Chŏng Yagyong was sent down to be superintendent of the post station in Kŭmjŏng, where he too adopted a public stance of opposing Catholicism.[17] Yi Kahwan, since he had held a higher position in the central government bureaucracy than either Yi Sŭnghun or Chŏng Yagyong had, was demoted only to the post of district magistrate of Ch'ungju, where he, too, adopted a public anti-Catholic stance, even using the leg screw torture on one recalcitrant Catholic.[18]

Back in Seoul, Father Zhou continued to minister to the needs of the frightened Catholic community as best he could. In 1797, at the request of Kang Wansuk, he baptized two residents of the Yangje Palace. (The Yangje Palace had been the palace of Prince Ŭnŏn, King Chŏngjo's stepbrother, but it was no longer considered an official palace, since the son of that prince had been accused of plotting to overthrow the king. That son was executed and his father was sent into exile on Kanghwa Island.) Maria Song (?–1801) was the wife of the ill-fated prince, and Maria Shin (?–1801) was her daughter-in-law. They had been introduced to Catholicism by Kang Wansuk and had the highest social status of the entire Korean Catholic community. As members (through marriage) of the royal family, they were allowed to take poison rather than being decapitated when the full-scale persecution of Catholics broke out in 1801.[19]

That same year, Father Zhou gave permission to Yu Chungch'ŏl (1779–1801) and Yi Suni (1782–1802) (they were both children of early converts) to live in a celibate marriage. This was done because they both preferred to live lives of celibacy dedicated to the church but realized that, if they remained unmarried, their non-Catholic neighbors would be suspicious of them.[20] While he was hiding from government law enforcement and ministering to the spiritual needs of Korea's small group of Catholics, Zhou also helped Chŏng Yakchong write the first comprehensive catechism in the Korean alphabet, Han'gŭl. The *Chugyo yoji* [Essential Elements of the Lord's teachings] provided a broad overview of Catholic doctrine in terms that even less-well-educated Koreans could understand, and it remained in wide use in the Korean Church well into the twentieth century.[21]

Chŏng Yakchong begins, not with the usual Confucian exhortations to the cultivation of virtue, but with logical arguments for God's existence.[22] Even the Trinitarian doctrine of three persons in one God is introduced early in this text, long before the ethical implications of the assertion of God's existence are addressed.[23] The first moral principles Chŏng Yakchong specifically mentions are the need to worship the one true God and the related sin of worshipping false gods.[24] Worship of the true God is thus given clear priority over loyalty to political rulers or filial piety to parents, a sharp break with Korean tradition.

The rest of the Ten Commandments are not ignored, but they clearly take a back place to the demands of monotheism. The only commandments to which Chŏng devotes much attention are the ones that impose ethical obligations not found in Neo-Confucianism. The relationship of human beings to God, the obligation to worship the one true God and to refrain from worshipping false gods, is given much more emphasis than those commandments that echo Confucian concerns about relations among human beings. The other commandments are given only a glancing mention, showing how much the *oryun* [五倫, the five moral principles that govern the five basic human relationships] have retreated into the background in this theological conception of orthodoxy.

Chŏng fills most of his pages with theological issues such as God's omniscience and with the details of God's life on earth as Jesus. He even discusses at length the crucifixion of Jesus, a topic Jesuit publications downplayed in their efforts to present Catholicism as compatible with Confucianism. Chŏng also devotes more attention to attacking Buddhist beliefs that contradict Catholic doctrine than he does to pointing out any overlap of Confucianism and Catholic moral principles. As a result of this subordination of morality to theology, of orthopraxy to orthodoxy, when Chŏng was later arrested in 1801, he was condemned not for doctrinal heresy but for moral perversion, accused of promoting evil teachings that undermined the ethical foundations of society.[25]

INVITING WESTERN WARSHIPS

Though there had been some discussion earlier of inviting Western warships to Korea, that had usually been in the context of bringing a missionary or two to Korea. After Father Zhou arrived, talk of Western warships shifted to using them to pressure the Korean government to stop persecuting Catholics. According to at least one Korean Catholic, Yu Hanggŏm (himself accused of being the one who broached that idea), that idea came from Zhou himself.[26] One year after Zhou arrived, Hwang Sim (1756–1801) left on the first of his many trips to Beijing to carry messages between Korea and Beijing. Among the messages he carried in 1796 was a request to Bishop de Gouvea to arrange for European warships to sail to Korea. However, the bishop told him that would not be possible in the near future.[27]

Hwang Sim was a commoner from Onyang in Ch'ungch'ŏng who had been converted to Catholicism by Yi Chonch'ang. He was an official horse handler for the government, an occupation that allowed him to accompany diplomatic delegations to Beijing. However, he usually had to bribe someone in order to be appointed as a horse handler for a tribute mission to Beijing. He was able to visit Beijing in October 1797, October 1798, and October 1799. Each time, he brought messages from Korea to Beijing and then brought messages from Beijing back to Korea.[28] He was not the only messenger ferrying letters between Father Zhou and Bishop de Gouvea. A man named Kim Yusan (1761–1801) made two trips as well, in 1798 and 1799. And Ok Ch'ŏnhŭi (1767–1801) made three trips, in 1799, 1800, and 1801 (just before full-scale persecution broke out).[29] Ok Ch'ŏnhŭi was a low-level worker in a government post station and was able to travel to Beijing as a groom for the horses.[30] Not all of the messages carried back and forth dealt with the request for European warships to sail into Korean waters and force the Korean government to stop harassing and killing Catholics. However, that was a recurrent theme.

The hope that a Western military could be used to force religious toleration on the part of the Korean government intensified after September 6, 1797. That was the day the British warship, the *Providence*, approached Tongnae, Yongdangp'o, on the southeastern coast of Korea. A Catholic named Hyŏn Kyehŭm (1763–1801), who also came from a family of official interpreters, sailed out to look over that ship for the government and reported back that it was as strong as any one hundred ships Korea had. A couple of months later, in November, Yu Kwan'gŏm mentioned to Yi Ujip (1762–1801) that Western warships had a lot of firepower, so if the Korean government did not do what they asked, they would face "a decisive moment." He also claimed that the West was so rich it could build a church in Korea with materials it brought from the

West and would not have to use any Korean resources.[31] Yu Kwan'gŏm apparently believed that, with the help of the West, Korean Catholics could build a church on Korean soil with Western tools such as a Western-style pulley (a pulley had already been used by Chŏng Yagyong in the construction of the fortress that stands in Suwŏn today). And he believed such a church would have what he called "music without drums," a possible reference to an organ.[32]

Some of the Catholics had even more grandiose plans. Under interrogation in 1801, Yi Ujip slipped up and told interrogators about the hope that the appearance of Western warships off Korean shores would bring about a "decisive change." Yi also told his interrogators that some Catholics had talked about one thousand Western ships sailing to Korea to establish a Catholic church in Korea, including erecting a church on the grave site of Yun Chich'ung, and instituting an exam for selecting officials (probably a reference to clergy).[33]

The government was unaware, before Yi Ujip revealed Catholic hopes in 1801, that Korea's Catholics planned to use Western naval forces to transform the traditional relationship between the state and religious communities in Korea. However, even though they were not yet aware of how much of a threat to Korea's sovereignty Catholics posed, they continued to persecute individual Catholics when they found them, especially if they suspected those Catholics of sheltering Father Zhou.

One example of such persecution is Yi Chonch'ang. Originally of *chungin* status, he came to the government's attention in 1791 and was tortured until he renounced his Catholicism. Despite that renunciation, he was demoted to commoner status. That appears to have been a verbal renunciation only, however, since government officials in his local district of Kongju suspected that he was still practicing and proselytizing Catholicism and brought him in for interrogation and torture in 1795. Between 1795 and 1799 he was locked up in the local jail. He was released for a while in 1799, but then jailed again when he again began acting like a Catholic. Finally, in February 1801, after the outbreak of the major anti-Catholic persecution, he was executed. He was only forty-three years old at the time.[34]

There were other local persecutions as well. One scholar estimates that twenty-one people had already died for their Catholic faith before the major persecution of 1801.[35] A list of Korean martyrs on a website devoted to hagiography provides names for only fourteen of those who died before 1801. Of those fourteen, eight died in persecutions in Ch'ungch'ŏng province in 1788 and 1800, persecutions Hwang Sayŏng refers to in the sixth line of his *Silk Letter*.[36]

FULL-SCALE PERSECUTION

The increasingly bloody anti-Catholic activities in the countryside were an indication that the situation for Catholics throughout Korea was growing more tense. First of all, most of the *yangban* Catholics belonged to the Flexible Faction, and the split between the Flexible Faction and the Intransigent Faction began growing wider after ten thousand scholars in the southeastern part of Korea sent a memorial to King Chŏngjo in 1792 asking that the reasons for the death of King Chŏngjo's father in 1762 be clarified, an indirect call to blame the Patriarchs Faction, many of whom were members of the Intransigent Faction, for the king's father's death.[37] Also King Chŏngjo began threatening the traditional balance of power between the king and his *yangban* officials by starting construction of a new capital south of Seoul, creating a new military unit directly under royal command, and creating a new advisory body of young scholars to bypass the entrenched senior leadership of the bureaucracy. Moreover, King Chŏngjo began challenging the virtual monopoly over high government posts the Patriarchs Faction had enjoyed for decades by employing such Southerners as Ch'ae Chegong (1720–1799), Yi Kahwan, and Chŏng Yagyong.

Ch'ae Chegong rose as high as prime minister, which made the Catholics relax a bit. He was not pro-Catholic. In fact, he had called for the execution of Yun Chich'ung and Kwŏn Sangyŏn in 1791. However, he was a member of the Southerner Faction and wanted to protect his fellow faction members as much as he could. It was therefore a matter of concern for the Catholic community when he retired from his government post in 1797 and then died in early 1799. Even more worrisome was the fact that, a few months before Ch'ae left the government, a relatively moderate head of the Intransigent Faction, Yun Sidong (1729–1797), died and was replaced as head of that faction by the more hardline

Sim Hwanji (1730–1802). Then King Chŏngjo died in June 1800. His eleven-year-old successor, King Sunjo, was too young to actually wield power. Instead, the oldest living queen assumed a regency over the throne. That was bad news for the many Catholic Southerners, since she was the sister of a man who had died in exile during King Chŏngjo's reign, and she blamed the Southerners for his death.[38]

The formal funeral for King Chŏngjo wasn't held until November. Soon after that, the anti-Catholic atmosphere heated up.[39] We can date the beginning of the persecution in Seoul to December 17, 1800, when Ch'oe P'ilgong was re-arrested and taken to the Seoul Police Station on the charge of being a secret Catholic. However, there was a warning sign several months earlier. The previous spring Yi Chungbae (1752?–1801), who lived away from Seoul in the town of Yŏju, had celebrated Easter with a little too much exuberance, loudly singing Christian songs on a hillside with fellow Catholics. He was arrested as well. Nevertheless, both Ch'oe P'ilgong and Yi Chungbae were alive at the beginning of 1801. They were only executed when anti-Catholicism reached a fever pitch in 1801.[40] The formal launching of the full-scale persecution of Catholics came on January 10, 1801, a day after the chief catechist Ch'oe Ch'anghyŏn was arrested in Seoul. January 10 was the day the Queen Dowager, acting as regent for King Sunjo, issued a call to identify Catholics throughout Korea and force them to recant. If they still insisted on clinging to their "deviant ways," she declared, they should be viewed as rebels against the state and dealt with accordingly.[41]

The Queen Dowager declared:

> The previous king always said that, if proper scholarship were illuminated, then deviant schools would disappear on their own. But we have learned that the particular type of deviancy he was referring to has not gone away. It has spread from the capital into the provinces of Kyŏnggi [the capital region] and Honam [the southwestern region] and is growing stronger every day. Morality is what makes a human being a human being. Promoting morality is what makes a country a country. This thing we label "deviant" shows no respect for fathers and rulers, undermines morality, blocks efforts to promote moral behavior, and causes people to act like barbarians and wild animals rather than like human beings. Ignorant people have been infected with these errors and led astray. How can we stand by and do nothing

about this? If a child fell into a well, how could we not take pity on it and be heartbroken? It's the same situation here.

Governors and magistrates, carefully admonish your people. Have those who are followers of those deviant teachings change their ways and get back on the right track. Have those who have not yet been infected be cautious and apprehensive lest they, too, become infected. In this way, the many accomplishments by the late king in educating the people will not be for naught. If, even though that deviant way of thinking and behaving has been strictly forbidden, there are still some who do not mend their ways, then we will deal with them in accordance with the law against rebels. Each magistrate should group the families in the area under his jurisdiction into groups of five families each. If there is anyone in one of those families who continues to be involved with deviancy, the head of that five-family group should report them to the government, which will then punish such deviants to the full extent of the law. Report this to the spirits of the ancestors at the ancestral temple and inform the people outside the capital as well.

Directly following the edict is an explanation of why it was promulgated:

Before it came to Korea, the so-called "Learning of Jesus, the Lord of Heaven" bewitched the people in the West with talk of Heaven and hell, taught them to disrespect their parents, led them to act out of harmony with the cosmic pattern, and wrecked havoc with the normative cosmic patterns and moral principles. This is really a strange school of thought. It has no moral principles. Books teaching this nonsense were brought from China into our country. Some people were infected by those books and ended up believing the rubbish those books contained. This deviancy was strictly forbidden during the reign of King Chŏngjo. However, there is still a group of people who believe in it. They continue to call people together to teach them this deviant scholarship, infecting others with their errors. This was revealed when many of them were captured by the officials of the Seoul police station. Therefore, we issued this edict.[42]

The Queen Dowager placed the Seoul Police Station in charge of the arrest and interrogation of Catholics. She did that because it traditionally was in charge of violations of the moral code as well as bandit gangs. Moreover, the police station was not under the Ministry of Punishments but under the Ministry of War, implying that the Catholic community was a threat to national security.[43]

The persecution broke out in full force a few days later when Chŏng Yakchong became worried that his home might be raided. He had his servant Im Taein put all incriminating documents in a bamboo box and take them to the home of Hong Kyoman (1737–1801). However, Hong grew worried as well and gave them to Im to return to Chŏng Yakchong's home. Im was intercepted, and those letters were discovered. Im had covered the box with dried pine needles and disguised himself as a seller of firewood. However, the box could be seen through that thin cover of pine needles, and a policeman stopped Im, thinking that he was smuggling meat into Seoul. Im was arrested on January 19. When the box was opened, the letters were discovered, including letters from Father Zhou.[44] That led to the arrest of Yakchong on February 11 and his execution shortly thereafter, on February 26. Yi Sŭnghun, Ch'oe Ch'anghyŏn, and Hong Kyoman were executed along with him.[45]

Even though Yi Sŭnghun had left the Catholic community a decade earlier and had even publicly denounced Catholic beliefs, he was executed along with Yakchong because he was seen as the man who had introduced Catholicism to Korea. Among those who called for his execution were a member of the Disciples (Soron) Faction, Yi Pyŏngmo, who sat on the State Council, as well as Southerners such as Yi Igun, the governor of Kyŏnggi province and a close associate of the late Ch'ae Chegong. Even more remarkably, Kwŏn Ŏm, Yi Pyŏk's father-in-law, who was then the Third Minister without Portfolio, rounded up sixty-three names on a petition calling for severe punishment for Yi Sŭnghun for bringing Catholic books to Korea and spreading all sorts of unhealthy ideas and practices. Mok Manjung, another senior Southerner official, joined in the chorus of calls for Yi to be harshly punished.[46] However, most of the high officials in the new government that emerged under the regency of Queen Chŏngsun after the death of King Chŏngjo were Patriarchs, who were bitter enemies of the Southerners and were happy to be able to use the charge of Catholicism against their factional enemies.

When Yi was brought in for interrogation in February 1801, he aggressively declared his innocence, pointing out that his father had made him burn all his Catholic books in the 1780s and that, since 1791, he had viewed Catholicism as an enemy of his family, "so how could he have remained involved with the Catholic community? Why would he continue to have anything to do with something that disregarded the proper relations between parents and children and between rulers and subjects, undermined moral principles, and obscured the moral constants? . . . How could he possibly believe that absurd story that Heaven descended to earth and took human form?" However, realizing that, no matter what he said, he would still have to pay the ultimate price for importing so many Catholic books into Korea and sharing them with friends and family, he gave up the struggle to stay alive and said, "if you decide that I am responsible for distributing those books in Korea, and therefore I am the reason these evil ideas have taken root here, then I will accept my execution as just."[47]

Yi Kahwan and Kwŏn Ch'ŏlsin were arrested at the same time Yi Sŭnghun was. Both died shortly thereafter from wounds suffered during their interrogations. Chŏng Yakchŏn and Chŏng Yagyong were also arrested at that time. However, they were more fortunate than either Yi Sŭnghun, Yi Kahwan, or Kwŏn Ch'ŏlsin.

In February, Yakchŏn was subjected to harsh interrogation and then exiled to an island not far from the Korean coast. However, after the government found out that Hwang Sayŏng, the husband of his niece, had planned to send a letter to the Catholic bishop in Beijing asking for a French fleet to be sent to Korea to threaten the king, Yakchŏn was exiled even farther away, to Hŭksan-do, which is about as far west as you can be and still be in Korean waters. He spent the remaining fifteen years of his life there, never to see his brothers nor his wife or son again.[48]

Yakchŏn's younger brother Yagyong suffered a similar fate. He was originally exiled to Kyŏngsang province. He had only been there for a few months when the capture of Hwang Sayŏng led to even harsher measures against Korea's Catholics and those associated with them. Though no evidence linking him to Hwang's letter was found, he was exiled even farther away, this time to remote Kangjin in Chŏlla province. He stayed there for eighteen years, kept away from his family and from the career in Seoul he had coveted for so long.

In March 1801, Father Zhou turned himself over to the authorities. Originally, when the persecution intensified after the discovery of

Yakchong's letterbox, Zhou fled toward Hwanghae province. He hoped that, since there were few Catholics in that northwestern corner of Korea, no one would look for him there. He got as far as Hwangju in Hwanghae-do. But then he turned back when he realized the government would keep grabbing, torturing, and killing Catholics in a search for him. So, on March 12, he surrendered in the hope that would put an end to the persecution. He may have also thought that, once the government realized he was Chinese, rather than killing him, they would extradite him to China. He was wrong. He was decapitated on April 19.[49]

His death did not bring an end to the anti-Catholic persecution. Kang Wansuk had been arrested along with her entire household on February 24. She was executed almost three months later, on May 22.[50] Moreover, the search continued for Hwang Sayŏng. He was arrested on September 29, after being on the run for almost half a year. He was found in Paeron, a potter's village, hiding inside a large earthenware pot. On him was the letter he planned to give to Hwang Sim for delivery to Ok Ch'ŏnhŭi, who was supposed to take that letter to Bishop de Gouvea in Beijing. However, Hwang Sim was already under arrest at this time. In fact, it was Hwang Sim who told the authorities how to find Hwang Sayŏng. Hwang Sim had assumed that Hwang Sayŏng had already left Paeron when he told his interrogators to check there. He probably was not pleased that his information turned out to be accurate, since the name on that letter that so upset the government was Hwang Sim's name, not Hwang Sayŏng's. Hwang Sayŏng had put Hwang Sim's name on that letter because, he told his interrogators, the priests in Beijing knew Hwang Sim but did not know him.[51]

The letter found on Hwang Sayŏng was written in black ink on a single piece of silk a little more than twenty-five inches wide and not quite fifteen inches long, so that it could be hidden under clothing and smuggled out of Korea. Despite its small size, it contains a lot of information. Using over 13,300 Sino-Korean characters distributed over 122 vertical lines, the *Silk Letter* provides a detailed account of the history of the Korean Catholic Church up to 1801, including information on the many people Hwang knew who had died for their faith. Hwang's purpose in devoting most of that letter to stories of persecution and martyrdom was twofold. First of all, he hoped that Europeans who learned of the suffering Korean Catholics were enduring would be so impressed by the courage they were showing in the face of a bloody perse-cution that they would immediately rush to their aid. Moreover, he also wanted to leave a record of who had died still professing their faith in the hope that later they might be officially recognized by the church as saints. That is the reason he often notes in the *Silk Letter* when he can and when he cannot confirm that someone died without renouncing their Catho-lic beliefs.

However, the part of the letter that most alarmed the government comes at the end, when Hwang gives the European bishop of Beijing seven different suggestions for supporting the Catholic community in Korea and forcing the government of Korea to stop persecuting Catho-lics. Korean Catholics today tend to focus on the main body of the letter, on the accounts of brave and faithful martyrs. Many non-Catholics, on the other hand, focus on the last few lines and accuse Hwang Sayŏng of betraying his country. Hwang's seven suggestions that alarmed the gov-ernment of Chosŏn Korea in 1801 continue to make Hwang a contro-versial figure today.

First of all, he asked the bishop to arrange for foreign (i.e., European) financial support for the beleaguered Korean Catholic community (line 96). Then he went a little further and suggested that a Chinese Catholic be sent to the northern reaches of the Chinese empire to meet secretly with Korean Catholic travelers (line 99). His third suggestion was to teach a Chinese priest to speak Korean and then have him enter Korea illegally (line 98). Then he made some even bolder proposals. His fourth suggestion was that the Pope ask the emperor of China to order the king of Korea to stop persecuting Catholics (lines 100–101). Fifth, he pro-posed advising the Manchu rulers of China that it was in their best in-terest to absorb Korea, so that they would treat Korea the same way they treated China. Hwang believed that making Korea directly subject to Chinese rulers would allow Catholics the freedom to practice their reli-gion that he believed they enjoyed in China under Manchu rule (lines 105–106). If the Manchu could not be convinced that it was in their best interest to absorb Korea, then, Hwang suggested, they should be in-formed that Korea was violating the conditions of its subordinate status in the Sinocentric world. Then the Manchu would surely want to punish Korea by abolishing its power to control its own internal affairs (lines 107–108). Finally, if none of those proposals were adopted or if they were ineffective, then Hwang suggested that the Pope organize an armada of European ships and warriors to sail to the Korean peninsula and force the Chosŏn government to stop persecuting Catholics (line 110–111).

The reaction of the government officials who read these proposals was not unexpected. Earlier Catholics had been strangled or decapitated (if they had not died first from the beatings they suffered while they were being interrogated). Hwang, and all those directly involved in this project to invite foreign military forces to threaten Korea, were condemned to the worst punishment possible, the "slow and lingering death." That is the literal translation of the term for execution that leaves the body in pieces. Normally, however, the person to be sliced up is beheaded first. Only after he is dead is his body cut up. This is considered the worst possible capital punishment because Confucians are told that they should strive to keep their bodies intact as a show of respect for the parents who gave them their bodies. To be strangled is preferable because at least the body remains intact. Beheading is worse than strangulation since the body is divided into two pieces. Death by slicing is the worst because it suggests that the person executed had no respect for his or her parents.[52]

Confucians are also told that, even if they die, they need to keep their family intact. Hwang Sayŏng was unable to do that. After he was executed on November 5 (by the lunar calendar), his mother was exiled to Kŏje Island, his wife to Cheju Island (where she became a slave), and his son to Ch'ujado, a small island between Cheju Island and the Korean Mainland.[53]

CHAPTER 5

Nationalism and Evaluations of Hwang Sayŏng and His *Silk Letter*

This book opened with a brief reference to the decapitation of Hwang Sayŏng. The chapter immediately preceding this one ended with what happened to Hwang's family after his execution. As we have seen, Hwang was not the first member of Korea's *yangban* elite to be put to death by his own government, nor was he the last. His name could have been buried in the long list of those executed over the more than five centuries the Chosŏn dynasty ruled over the Korean peninsula. However, Hwang attracts more attention today than most of the names on that list because, before he was arrested, he wrote the *Silk Letter*, an eyewitness account of the persecution that was decimating the small Korean Catholic community at the beginning of the nineteenth century. His account provides information on this important event that we cannot find in any other source. In fact, it is one of the few detailed descriptions we have of a bloody conflict between the Chosŏn government and its subjects told from the standpoint of a victim. Normally, we can only hear the voices of resisters as filtered through the interrogation records produced by the government. Hwang's *Silk Letter* allows us to hear the voice of a resister unfiltered by state interpretation.

The *Silk Letter*, therefore, though it is an account of an anti-Catholic persecution written by a devout Catholic, has significance far beyond its value as a primary document providing information essential for the study of the early history of the Korean Catholic Church. Its detailed account of the first decades of Korea's Catholic community provides a personal, close-up look at the impact of government policies on not just members of the male *yangban* elite but also on *yangban* women and on the members of other social classes. In particular, it opens a window on religious life in general in late eighteenth-century Korea, shedding light on the relationship between the state and religion in a Confucian society.

Hwang relates in great detail how the staunchly Confucian Korean government at that time dealt with the few Catholics on its soil, and how those Catholics reacted to the demands their government made of them. His letter constitutes a thick description of life in Korea at the end of the eighteenth century. As such, it can help us come to a more comprehensive understanding of the relationship between the Chosŏn dynasty government and the ritual life of those it governed, which in turn yields insight into the broader relationship between individuals and the state on the peninsula at that time in history. Hwang's letter reveals how the Chosŏn dynasty concept of government, the prevailing assumptions about the responsibilities of government and its limitations, differs from present-day understandings of the role of government in society. This letter also reveals how different the nationalism of the present generation of Koreans is from the attitudes of Koreans two centuries ago, particularly in terms of where the ultimate focus of the loyalty of subjects was expected to lie. Hwang openly called for Western military intervention in the internal affairs of his country, raising questions about how much Koreans two centuries ago such as Hwang identified with their government.

Though Hwang's commitment to Catholicism would not make him a criminal in the eyes of Korea's current government, more than two centuries after he was executed, he still remains a controversial figure. He remains so because Koreans do not agree how to evaluate the passages in his *Silk Letter* in which Hwang calls for foreign intervention to force the Chosŏn government to stop persecuting Catholics. To many of the more than five million Korean Catholics today, he was a brave young man who was unjustly persecuted because he tried to build a Catholic community on Korean soil and accepted death rather than renounce his faith in God. Most non-Catholic Koreans, on the other hand, tend to agree with the Chosŏn government that Hwang was a traitor to the Korean nation, since he was willing to compromise the sovereignty of Korea if that was the only way he would be able to practice his Catholic faith openly.

The non-Catholic description of Hwang's *Silk Letter* is accurate. It did ask for foreign intervention in Korea's internal affairs. However, the Catholic view of Hwang is also accurate. He was killed primarily because he was a Catholic, and he never renounced that faith, even when he knew he would be killed because of it. Both the positive and negative evaluations of Hwang and his actions are based on what he actually did. Since he can arguably be labeled both a martyr and a traitor, someone who was more dedicated to his religious beliefs than he was to the independence of his country, it is likely that Koreans will continue for quite some time to disagree over whether he should be condemned or be revered.

A wide range of opinions exists in Korea today over how Hwang should be remembered. A website[1] points visitors to Hwang's tomb on the northern outskirts of Seoul. Along the way small road signs in both English and Korean announce you are approaching the tomb of "the martyr Alexsio Hwang Sayeong, a sacred site." However, the spot where the bones of Hwang are interred does not appear to be very sacred. All that is there is a grass-covered dirt mound (the standard shape of a Korean tomb) in a small field approached via a dirt path that winds its way between two "motels," the Korean name for hotels that charge by the hour. A sign by that mound announces that this was the tomb of Alexander Hwang Sayŏng. ("Alexander" is the way his baptismal name used to be spelled in English. Recently it has been changed to "Alexius.") That sign also explains that the tomb was built in 1988 by the Korean Committee to Exalt the Martyrs of Korea (*Han'guk sun'gyoja hyŏnyang wiwŏnhoe*) after Hwang's remains had been identified below the remains of some of his more illustrious ancestors who had been buried there. Hwang remains controversial enough that the Catholic Church in Korea has not yet felt it appropriate to expend the funds necessary to purchase the land around the site in order to provide a more attractive and uplifting environment of the sort that would draw more attention to it, and to the man who was buried there.[2] His "sacred site" stands in sharp contrast to the architectural homage paid to the tombs of some other martyrs who worked with him in the last decade of the eighteenth century to establish a Catholic church on the Korean peninsula.[3]

A search for Hwang's birthplace provides an even stronger confirmation that Koreans do not agree over how to view Hwang, whether to honor him or to try to forget about him. A website listing sacred sites that Korean Catholics should visit sends readers to Kanghwa Island, to the west of Seoul in the estuary of the Han River. That website claims that Hwang was born in a place that still hosts the Hwang family clan shrine.[4] The site also promises that there is a sign at the entrance to that shrine noting that this was the birthplace of the martyr Hwang Sayŏng. However, the sign announces only that this was the birthplace of one of Hwang's most illustrious ancestors. Hwang Hyŏng (1459–1520), identified on the sign by his posthumous title, Hwang Changmu (Stately Military Force), was a leading military official in Korea in the early sixteenth century. However, he was twelve generations removed from Hwang Sayŏng. Moreover, there is no mention of Hwang Sayŏng in the shrine itself. The local Catholic Church confirmed that there had been a sign identifying that spot as Hwang Sayŏng's birthplace, but the branch of the Hwang family that still lived there insisted that it be taken down, since they are not Catholic and do not want to be associated with someone they do not consider a particularly admirable figure. Apparently Hwang was actually born in Seoul, though the exact sites of his birth and childhood have not yet been determined, and there does not appear to be any concerted effort to find these sites.[5]

NATIONALISM AND ANACHRONISM

The disagreement over how to remember Hwang Sayŏng today, with even contemporary members of the Hwang clan wanting to disown him and Catholics not as eager to honor him as they are other Catholics who died for their faith, is exacerbated by the fact that Hwang is often judged today according to modern values that were not relevant two centuries ago. One value in particular that many twenty-first-century Koreans tend to apply in their evaluations of Hwang is nationalism, which they think of as a value that Koreans have always held, rather than as a recent product of the specific historical circumstances of the modern age.

Even though nationalism is relatively new both in the West and in Korea, it is popularly assumed that the Korean people have always been nationalistic, and therefore Korean attitudes toward their government in centuries past, as well as their attitudes toward non-Korean interference in Korean affairs, are interpreted through a nationalistic lens, and judged accordingly. Moreover, even if they are sophisticated enough to recognize that modern nationalism is a relatively recent phenomenon in historical terms, many Koreans frequently nonetheless assume that Korea's progress toward modern nationalism unfolded in the same way it unfolded in the West. They often view their history through the implicit assumption that the process that led Koreans to replace the notion of the state as the personal property of the royal family with a conception of the state as an impersonal political entity happened in the same way it happened in the West. Similarly, they frequently write histories shaped by the assumption that their ancestors moved from distinguishing themselves from their neighbors living in other kingdoms primarily in cultural terms toward distinguishing themselves from those neighbors primarily in political terms for the same reasons Westerners made that same transition. Such an understanding of the history of nationalism in Korea distorts Korean history and creates a misunderstanding of the actions of Hwang Sayŏng and his role in Korean history.[6]

DEFINING MODERN NATIONALISM AND THE NATION-STATE

We use the term nation-state to refer to the recent phenomenon of the linking of a government and the people it governs. The nation-state combines people and power in a way that was not common before the last few centuries. Different from a traditional monarchy, a nation-state derives its legitimacy from its claim that it represents the people it governs. Similarly, the people it governs, because they see that state as representing them, adopt the state as part of their personal identity to such an extent that they are willing to give their lives for their nation, and their national identity becomes just as much a part of them as their family identity.

There are other characteristics of the modern nation-state that also distinguish it from countries and governments of the past. First of all, the modern nation-state sees itself, and is seen as, existing within a relationship of legal equality with other nation-states. As such, it has clearly defined borders that separate it from other nation-states, and those borders are inviolable. As a result, citizens of nation-states feel justified, and even compelled, to use military force to defend their borders and protect themselves from external interference.

This kind of state is also defined more by its territorial and political identity than by its cultural values. The nation-state may share religious and other cultural values with neighboring states, but that does not lead to porous borders. Canada and the United States share a lot in common, but they maintain a clearly marked border between them. Moreover, even though religion may have played an important role in constructing the early nation-state, modern states generally have embraced as full-fledged members of their national community all those within their borders, including those with different religious beliefs. At the same time, in order to escape from the restraints religious leaders may try to impose on them, the leaders of most modern states have separated religious from secular power and granted secular power the dominant role. There are some modern states in Europe that still grant a special status to a particular branch of Christianity by requiring the monarch in those constitutional monarchies to profess faith in their favored form of Christianity. That is the case with both Anglicanism in England and Lutheranism in Norway, for example. However, neither the UK nor Norway, nor other modern states in Europe allow religious leaders or religious organizations to interfere with the secular business of the government, or to monopolize spiritual or ritual activity within their borders (the Vatican is the one obvious exception!). By the same token, secular rulers of modern nation-states do not issue theological directives or require everyone within their borders to affirm affiliation with the same religion. One more characteristic of a modern nation-state, therefore, is that it is defined more by its territorial and political identity than by its religious orientation.[7]

Modern nationalism arose with the emergence of the modern nation-state. Before modern nationalism appeared, most governments in the world were what can be labeled "predatory governments." They were run for the benefit of the ruling class, not for the benefit of the ruled. For example, they saw no need to provide the sort of medical and educational services for the general population we expect the nation-state to provide today. Governments run according to Confucian philosophy may have been somewhat less predatory, at least in appearance and rhetoric, since Confucian governments were supposed to provide basic economic security for those they governed. But they, too, were run mainly for the benefit of the rulers. (Any measures taken to protect the health or security of the general population should usually be interpreted as intended to maintain a stable population of taxpayers rather than being motivated by any concern for actually improving the lives of those they ruled over, and even less by any concern for being chosen by those taxpayers to rule over them.) As a result, the common person, unlike the members of the ruling elite, normally did not identify with their government. It was not seen as "their government" in the sense that it was expected to represent them. Instead, it was simply something they had to accept and had to pay taxes to without expecting to get much in return.

More striking, the premodern state was often seen as the personal property of the ruling family. That is why countries changed their names when the ruling family changed (from Koryŏ to Chosŏn, for example) and why, in Europe, countries changed their boundaries when kings married into the ruling family of a neighboring territory. And that is why the boundaries between the royal family treasury and the government treasury were often not very clear. When the state is viewed as the personal property of a royal family, it is difficult for the average person to see that state as his or her state as well, especially when the average person is denied even a symbolic role in influencing the decisions made by the state.

Moreover, before the modern nation-state, the governments of the world did not have the same sense of legal equality and inviolable borders we see today. In East Asia, China was seen as the Central Kingdom. Korea and Vietnam were autonomous, but they also saw themselves as "small countries" in contrast to the big country they were obligated to ritually recognize as superior. In Europe, until the weakening of the papacy, which made the Protestant Reformation possible, kings often had to accept interference in their kingdom's affairs by a foreign pontiff, the Pope. There could be no United Nations, with one vote per nation, under such an international system.

Modern nationalism, with the modern nation-state, arose first in Europe, partially because the weakening of papal authority and then the Protestant Reformation made possible sharper dividing lines on the map of Europe. In order to stop the religious wars that were causing so much damage in Europe in the aftermath of the Protestant Reformation, in the middle of the 17th century leaders of predominantly Roman Catholic and Protestant countries negotiated a series of treaties creating what is known as the Peace of Westphalia. The Peace of Westphalia created the modern notion of sovereign nation-states, which respected each other's sovereignty despite religious differences. At first this acceptance of religious diversity was based on the understanding that the ruler of a kingdom determined which religion the majority of the people of his kingdom had to follow. This created sharper divisions between kingdoms, with political distinctions, such as who was empowered to collect taxes, reinforced by religious differences.[8]

At the same time, the Protestant Reformation created alternative forms of Christianity within what had been a united Christendom in Europe, which stimulated a rise in a more individualist concept of religious faith. When people saw that their religious orientation was different from that of others living on the same continent, they began to see their faith as part of their distinctive personal identity. When that faith coincided with the religion supported by their government, religious and political identities began to merge, and people began to identify with their government since it shared, and defended, their faith. Later, as governments became less predatory and more accountable to those they governed and started to try to actively promote the welfare of those living within the territory they controlled, religion become just one of many factors relevant to people's identification with their government. By the 18th century, people across Europe were beginning to believe that their general welfare was linked to the fortunes of their government, and therefore they identified with their nation-state much more than their ancestors had generations earlier.[9] Thus was born modern nationalism, which spread to the non-Western world in the 19th and 20th centuries.

We can therefore define modern nationalism, first of all, as the identification of a people (the masses, not just the elite) with their government to the extent that they link their own personal self-interest to the interests of their national government. (This is why we see national volunteer armies in modern times.) Modern nationalism is also distinguished from premodern feelings of loyalty to the state in two more ways: first of all, in the case of modern nationalism, the people view their nation as primarily an impersonal political entity that is separate and distinct from whatever person or family happens to be ruling it at the time. They do not expect their country to change its name when its leaders change. Second, modern nationalism recognizes the legal equality of all nation-states, leading the people of a particular country to resist real or imagined foreign interference or even perceived insults to their country's equal standing in the global community of nations.

By this definition, Korea was not nationalistic before the twentieth century. We might say it was "protonationalist," in the sense of having many but not all of the prerequisites of modern nationalism.[10] In fact, despite the difficulties Korea encountered in trying to adapt to modern nationalism in the last decades of the Chosŏn dynasty, it may have been better prepared than most countries were in premodern times. Koreans have identified as a separate and distinct people with an autonomous government for many centuries. Korea was fortunate in that it had fairly stable borders (partially thanks to being a peninsula) for almost a thousand years and, as a result, the people living in Korea had many centuries of a shared political history. Moreover, Korea had within its borders a linguistic and cultural community that was quite different from what lay beyond those borders, and it was also relatively ethnically and linguistically homogenous internally. Koreans did not need to re-imagine themselves as one people when they built a modern nation-state. They already had the basic building blocks of a national community that could provide the foundation for such a state.[11]

Nevertheless, before the twentieth century Korea had not yet developed the nationalism we see today. In a truly national community, you would expect to see national organizations independent of the government. The only nongovernmental organizations in Korea that were national in scope prior to the twentieth century were kinship organizations, and they promoted lineage rather than national identity. Factional groupings were centered on Seoul rather than being active throughout the country, and they emphasized rivalry with other factions rather than promoting a vision of a united Korea. Religion, unlike in other countries, did not promote national consciousness. We do not see in Chosŏn Korea national Confucian or Buddhist hierarchies independent of the government that could provide another way of imagining the nation. Nor do we see, before the twentieth century, Korean Confucians or Buddhists defining their traditions as distinctively Korean. Therefore, until a little more than a century ago, Korea's "protonationalism" had not yet evolved into modern nationalism.

Proto-nationalism is not nationalism, in that we do not see in it the conflating among the masses of individual self-interest with the fortunes of their government. Nor does the protonationalism of Chosŏn Korea envision Korea as a member of a community of nations, in which each nation is treated as the equal of every other member nation. We can distinguish in the *Silk Letter of Hwang Sayŏng* and the reactions to it two forms of protonationalism, both of which agreed that Korea existed within a hierarchical international order, though they did not agree on what that order was. There was the protonationalism of the court, which defined Korea as a small country serving the great country of China while at the same fighting to maintain autonomy in its internal affairs. There was also the protonationalism of Hwang Sayŏng, who sought to move Korea beyond the Sinocentric world and link it to the larger Catholic global community, which, Hwang believed, would be much better for the average Korean.

Though neither of these protonationalisms is "nationalistic" in the current sense, since both assumed a subordinate status for the Korean state on the global stage, both can be seen as stages on the distinctive road Korea followed to modern nationalism in that they were based on an understanding of Korea as a separate and distinct political entity, albeit one that needed to be part of a larger political community. However, such limited steps toward the modern notion of the nation-state do not justify imposing nationalistic terminology on a protonationalist past.

THE SHOCK OF THE *SILK LETTER*

At first glance, especially with modern eyes, the *Silk Letter of Hwang Sayŏng* does appear to justify subjecting it to a negative nationalist evaluation. After all, when the Chosŏn government launched a full-scale persecution of Catholics after the death of King Chŏngjo in 1800, Hwang escaped the first wave of arrests and fled to the countryside, where he penned his *Silk Letter* pleading with the Portuguese bishop of Beijing for help in bringing an end to that bloody persecution, and detailing how much suffering Catholics were enduring for the sake of their Catholic faith. As noted in the previous chapter, Hwang's purpose in devoting most of that letter to stories of persecution and martyrdom was religious: he wanted Catholics in other countries to, first of all, be aware of how strong the faith of Korea's Catholics was and, secondly, he wanted the Catholics in other countries to put pressure on the Korean government to force it to stop persecuting the devout Catholics.

However, it was the political ramifications of the ways Hwang proposed Catholics outside Korea could help Catholics in Korea that most alarmed the government. When Hwang gives the European bishop of Beijing his suggestions for relying on either the Manchu rulers of China or European military might to force the government of Korea to stop persecuting Catholics, he appears to many modern eyes to be disloyal to his country. Korean Catholics today tend to focus on the main body of the letter, on the accounts of brave and faithful martyrs. Many non-Catholics, on the other hand, focus on the last few lines, in which Hwang suggests both that the Manchu put Korea under their direct control and that Western naval forces be used to force Korea to stop persecuting Catholics.

THE ABSENCE OF NATIONALISM IN BOTH HWANG AND HIS PROSECUTORS

When viewed through twenty-first-century eyes, Hwang looks like a traitor. He appears to suggest subjecting Korea to foreign intervention in its internal affairs. However, to read Hwang's *Silk Letter* as a deliberate betrayal of the Korean nation is to assume that Hwang saw Korea as a modern nation-state, one that was the legal equal of all other states and therefore was completely independent and autonomous. Such an assumption is anachronistic. A close reading of Hwang's letter reveals that he did not look at his country and his government the way people today look at their country and government. He did not apply the modern concept of the nation-state to the Korea of his day.

First of all, it is obvious that Hwang did not share the modern notion of the separation of secular and sacred power. Just as the emperor of the Chinese empire was seen by Confucians as both a political and a ritual and cultural leader, Hwang saw the Pope as both a religious and a political leader, similar to the emperor of China but superior to him. For example, he believed that if the Pope asked the emperor of China to order Korea to accept missionaries from the West, the emperor would do what the Pope asked him to. And he also believed that the Pope could order several hundred warships loaded with fifty or sixty thousand elite troops and weapons to sail to Korea to force them to stop persecuting Catholics.

Second, Hwang did not separate the royal family from the country it ruled, though he did distinguish between the royal family and those he believed were corrupt officials. That is why he could suggest in the *Silk Letter* that "If Korea were absorbed into China, then the disdainful looks of the wicked officials towards the king would cease of their own accord and the royal house of Yi would find itself in a much better position." He saw his proposals as actually helping rather than hurting the royal family, and, since he didn't clearly distinguish between the royal family and his country, as helping Korea in the long run.

Of course, the officials he considered corrupt, as well as the royal family that utilized those officials to exercise autonomous power within Korea's borders, did not agree. That is why Hwang and his fellow Catholics were frequently accused of being people who did not respect either their parents or their rulers (*mubu, mugun*). Notice, however, that the Catholics were not accused of showing a lack of respect for their country (*muguk*, 無國). The anti-Catholics as well as the Catholics shared the premodern identification of the royal family, the ruler, with the state.

A third feature of Hwang's view of Korea that makes his view different from the modern view is that he clearly did not believe in the legal equality of states. Rather, he believed that states were placed in different slots within an international hierarchy, and Korea was on a middle rung, not at the top. That is clear in his attempt to use Korea's position within the Sinocentric tributary order to force Korea to stop persecuting Catholics. It is also clear in the way he writes about the role of the Pope in the West.

It would be anachronistic to accuse Hwang of being a traitor to the Korean nation. The way he envisioned his country did not require him to support its complete autonomy and independence. In fact, he shared with the Korean government officials who interrogated and then executed him the concept of Korea as immersed in a world order in which Korea was under the political and religious overlordship of another country. He also shared with them an understanding of Korea as more the personal possession of the royal family rather than an impersonal political entity whose survival was not inextricably linked to the survival of the royal family. He differed from his fellow Koreans in the government primarily over who that overlord should be (the emperor of China or the Pope in Rome) and which religion should have hegemony (Confucianism or Catholicism). He was not a traitor, since he was not trying to destroy Korea. He was simply trying to shift its position horizontally in the global political and religious order.

KOREAN AND EUROPEAN PATHS TO THE MODERN NATION-STATE

The way Koreans, both Hwang and his enemies, conceived of Korea and its place in the world at the beginning of the nineteenth century was not very different from the way Europeans had conceived of their countries a couple of centuries earlier. Before the seventeenth century, secular authority and sacred authority were not clearly demarcated in Europe. The Pope often exercised secular power, and the Holy Roman Empire claimed dominion over much of Europe for centuries, though its power tended to be more contested than that of the Chinese empire. Moreover, the fact that we talk about dynasties in early modern Europe, just as we do in Korea and China, reveals that no clear lines had yet been drawn in Europe between the state and the family that controlled it. A prime example are the Habsburgs, who controlled portions of Europe for centuries but eventually were weakened by their own desire to keep their territories within the family by intermarrying, which led to genetic problems in that family (though one Habsburg monarchy survived into the twentieth century).

Moreover, until the seventeenth century, the borders of the kingdoms of Europe were even more porous than the boundaries of East Asia. Prior to the Peace of Westphalia agreements of 1648, sovereignty was not mutually exclusive in Europe. The spiritual power of the Pope was not hindered by the political boundaries defining the reach of a secular monarch's power. Korea was quite different. The only outside force that could legitimately breach Korean boundaries was that of the emperor in the capital in China. However, for most of the Chosŏn dynasty, that was more theoretical than actual interference. So the Korean government actually enjoyed much more unbridled sovereignty, in the modern sense, before the seventeenth century than European kingdoms did at the same time.

Nevertheless, no one who reads official messages sent by the king of Korea to the emperor of China would conclude that Korea was totally independent of Chinese political influence. Nor would Korea have made that claim at that time. Korea was very proud of its tradition of "serving the great" and regularly reminded China that it was a faithful junior member of the Sinocentric community.

Europe may have begun moving away from the premodern concept of the state with porous boundaries earlier than Korea did but they eventually both moved in the same direction. However, they moved for different reasons. Religion, as we noted earlier, was a spur to the creation of separate and distinct nations in Europe, with the Reformation stimulating some kingdoms to define themselves as Protestant and others Catholic. In Korea, on the other hand, Hwang tried to use religion to link Korea more closely to other nations. Though most of his fellow Koreans did not agree with Hwang's religious preference, they, too, saw religion, if we can call Confucianism a religion, as transcending national borders (at least in the case of the border between China and Korea) rather than erecting them. So neither Hwang nor his enemies can be seen as promoting the modern notion of the nation-state.

Unlike Europe, Korea was propelled toward nationalism and the nation-state by secularization. As long as Korea defined itself as a Confucian country, it had a difficult time seeing itself as a nation-state on a par with its neighbor China. It was only in the late 19th century, when Koreans began moving away from the definition of Korea as a Confucian state and society, that Korea began moving toward defining itself as a modern nation-state. Though many of Korea's first modern nationalists were Christians, and they may have hoped that the majority of the Korean population would become Christian, they did not seek to create a Christian government for Korea. Their religious commitment was separate from their determination to gain for Korea membership as an equal partner in the secular community of nations. Though the first president of the Republic of Korea was a Christian, he did not use Christianity to delineate his republic's borders (except when he wanted to contrast the ROK with the godless DPRK [North Korea]). The Republic of Korea arose in opposition to both the Confucian nature of the Chosŏn dynasty and the Shinto support of the Japanese colonial government and therefore has been adamantly secular.

Saying that the modern Korean nation-state, unlike Europe nation-states, did not emerge from a search for protection for one religion against another does not mean that the deadly dispute between Hwang and the Chosŏn government made no contribution to the transformation of Korea. Hwang deserves some credit for pushing Korea slightly along the road to the modern nation-state. As a Catholic, he demanded that the state stop interfering in the ritual practices of the Catholic community and stop trying to force Catholics to perform Confucian rituals. This has been described as a call for religious freedom, and Hwang an advocate of religious freedom. That is anachronistic, since neither Hwang nor the global Catholic Church of his day supported complete religious liberty. All Hwang was asking was that *Catholics* be left alone. He said nothing about religious freedom for shamans or Buddhists. If he had been asked his preference, Hwang would not have said that rulers had no authority over religious matters. He would probably have argued instead that his king should abdicate that authority to a superior ruler, the Pope!

In this, Hwang was not much behind the West. After all, "religious freedom" emerged in Europe first as the religious freedom of the ruler—he could choose his version of Christianity (no other choices were permitted), but his subjects had to follow his choice. That meant that the subjects of a Catholic ruler were supposed to be Catholics, and the subjects of Anglican or Lutheran rulers were supposed to be Anglicans or Lutherans. It was not until the seventeenth century that the notion that individuals should be free to choose their own religion emerged, and even then it took a while for most of Europe to follow the path that Holland pioneered once it had broken free of the grip of Catholic Spain.

Even though he cannot be praised as an early advocate of religious freedom, Hwang's challenge to the traditional control of its subjects' ritual activities by the Korean state can be seen as a step toward modernity. As noted in chapter 1, Hwang lived at a time when the Korean government used deadly force to control the ritual lives of its subjects. Korea, and most of the rest of the world, is different now. In both East Asia and in the West, the nation-state is now seen as standing above questions of religious belief and religious practices. The secular nation-state leaves such issues to the conscience of the individual, as long as social order is not disturbed. An essential first step toward the religious neutrality of the modern nation-state was having the state relinquish ritual hegemony.

Another contribution to Korea's modernization, albeit a small one, was Hwang's attempt to free Korea from the Sinocentric world of which it was an integral part. However, instead of taking a step toward the modern concept of the nation-state, he wanted Korea to become part of what he thought was a world order under the leadership of the Pope. Hwang was not interested in reinforcing national boundaries. Instead, he wanted Korea to become part of the transnational Catholic community. He wanted the Korean king to be subject to Rome rather than being fully autonomous.

EVALUATING HWANG SAYŎNG

In 1801, for his challenge to the specifics of Korea's place in the world order at that time, Hwang was charged with rebellion and executed as a traitor. However, it is not clear if he was seen as a traitor to Korea per se or as a traitor to the royal family and the officials who served it. He was accused of threatening to harm the people who lived in Korea, the "hundred names," but that harm is usually expressed as damaging them morally rather than physically. The closest we see to a charge that he threatened Korea's political sovereignty (rather than the royal family itself) is the accusation that he invited foreign warships to penetrate Korea's borders. However, that accusation is overshadowed by the many accusations of immoral conduct, of refusing to show the respect due to his parents and his ruler. Today, most Koreans say Hwang betrayed Korea, but Korea then was not the impersonal and autonomous political entity we see today. He "betrayed" Korea only by trying to shift Korea from subordination to China to subordination to Rome, in the process making Korea's traditional subordinate status more explicit, and by proposing a closer link between the royal families of China and Korea than had existed in Korea after the Mongol era.

Arguing that contemporary standards of nationalistic behavior should not be applied to Hwang does not mean that we should excuse his behavior, either. Conversely, we should neither condemn nor excuse the actions of those who killed Hwang and his fellow Catholics. It is not unusual to read about modern Koreans, particularly those who admire Hwang for having the courage of his convictions, accusing the anti-Catholics of the late eighteenth century of being so stubborn and close minded that they irrationally blocked the door to new ideas that could have solved many of the social, economic, and political problems Korea faced in the last centuries of the Chosŏn dynasty.[12] Just as it is anachronistic to accuse Hwang of not being a nationalistic, so, too, it is anachronistic to accuse his enemies of failing to foresee the problems that lay ahead for the Chosŏn dynasty in the last quarter of the nineteenth century. Instead, we should avoid both forms of anachronism and approach the past with all due humility, trying to understand it on its own terms and refraining from imposing our moral standards and political beliefs on those who lived in a time with different moral standards and different political beliefs. We should attempt to understand history, not judge it.

That is the reason we have decided to include a translation of an anti-Catholic document, Ahn Chongbok's *A Conversation on Catholicism*, alongside the *Silk Letter*. Ahn was not among those who tortured and killed Catholics. He died before the persecution began. However, he was strongly opposed to both Catholic beliefs and Catholic practices. His opposition should not be denigrated as blind opposition arising from ignorance and stubborn adherence to irrational Confucian principles. Instead, his opposition should be evaluated as both well informed and rational, given the premises on which his Confucian rationality was based.

Ahn, as is clear in *A Conversation on Catholicism*, had learned a lot about Catholic teachings, so he cannot be accused of being ill informed. Nor can he be accused of being irrational. His arguments were rational and based on the Confucian assumption that the most important criterion in evaluating a philosophical or religious claim was the impact belief in that claim had on behavior. Since Confucians held as a core principle that the distinction between the moral and the immoral was the difference between the pursuit of the common good and the pursuit of individual self-interest, Catholicism appeared immoral in Ahn's eyes because it focused on individual salvation rather than the overall good of society. He also criticized Catholicism as irrational (the word he used for "irrational" is "contrary to *li* [理]," in other words, contrary to the patterns of appropriate interactions) because he believed that, with its talk of Heaven and Hell, it distracted people from the hard work of cooperating with their fellow human beings to create a harmonious society on this earth. In Ahn's view, a view shared by most of his Confucian contemporaries, Catholicism was irrational because it was selfish and therefore was immoral. We can disagree with Ahn's judgment, but we can hardly accuse him of being irrational when he was faithful to the understanding of reason and rationality of his Confucian tradition.

It is only when we allow ourselves to understand both why some Koreans in the late eighteenth century became Catholics and were willing to die for their beliefs and why some others were so opposed to Catholicism that they were willing to kill their fellow Koreans in order to eradicate what they believed was a threat to the moral foundations of their civilization that we can claim to have an accurate understanding of Korea at the beginning of the nineteenth century. Understanding Korea's past accurately is important because only if we understand the past can we understand the present that emerged from it.

Both the *Silk Letter* and, to a lesser extent, *A Conversation on Catholicism* help us understand how recent Korean nationalism is. A careful reading of *A Conversation on Catholicism* reveals that Ahn did not focus on Catholicism as a threat to Korea but on Catholicism as a threat to Confucian civilization. He drew on examples from both Chinese and Korean history to argue that Catholicism is irrational and dangerous. He was not worried about a possible threat to Korea's independence. He was more concerned about the threat he believed Catholicism posed to Korea's moral fiber, which he defined with terms adopted from China. He knew that historically and politically Korea was a different country from China, but his prime concern was Korea's Confucian civilization. He focused more on protecting Korea's claim to civilized (i.e., moral) status than on securing Korea's political independence against potential foreign threats. That is, Ahn was concerned about culturalism, not nationalism.

Hwang's *Silk Letter*, as already shown, is equally lacking in nationalistic content. Even though Hwang challenged the traditional Sinocentric international order, he still remained more traditional than modern. Both texts translated here show us that Korea as a country was conceived differently in 1801 than it is today. They also help us understand that Korea did not move from protonationalism to modern nationalism along the same path Europeans followed. Though Koreans may have had a strong sense of a distinct and separate identity earlier than Europeans did, the way Koreans two centuries ago conceived of their kingdom was not all that different from the way Europeans had conceived of their kingdoms until around four centuries ago. However, the process through which Koreans redefined Korea was very different from the process Europeans went through to reach the same type of modern nation-state.

Compared to Europe, in Korea religion was not a strong factor in the assertion of a separate and distinct national identity. Korean nationalism, when it finally emerged at the end of the nineteenth century, was secular nationalism. Ahn Chŏngbok had emphasized the Confucianism that China and Korea had in common to highlight Korea's status as a civilized country. Korea's first modern nationalists wanted to establish a separate identity. To do that, they felt they had to reject Confucianism, since that made up much of what China and Korea had had in common. However, they did not replace Confucianism with a religion that they hoped would give them a distinctive identity and accentuate their differences with their neighbors. Their nationalism was nonreligious rather than based on the sort of religious identity we saw employed in early stages of the development of the notion of independent states in Europe.

Rather than an attempt to end religious wars, the desire to create a truly autonomous Korean state was stimulated by the recognition that others (the Japanese as well as Westerners) whom Koreans had long considered separate and distinct from them had constructed modern nation-states, and therefore they could and should do the same. Hwang had hoped his Catholicism would link Korea to the broader world within a global hierarchy defined by that religion. A century later, Korean nationalists had a very different vision. They also wanted to join the outside world, but not on religious terms. They wanted Korea to be recognized as a separate and distinct member of a secular community of nations in which all members were considered equal. The aim of Korea's nationalists was to strengthen Korean autonomy and institutionalize their political differences with other countries, not highlight religious components of their identity. Korea carved its own path to the modern nation-state it is today, one quite different from the path Europe followed.

In tracing Korea's path to modernity we should not confuse the starting point with the finish line. Neither Hwang Sayŏng nor Ahn Chŏngbok were nationalists in the modern sense. But the debate that began in their time between Catholics and Confucians over how to define Korea's place in the world, as a proud member of the Confucian world centered on China or as a member of a Christian world centered on Europe, stimulated the first questioning of the traditional worldview and led eventually to attempts, beginning at the end of the nineteenth century, for Korea to be independent of both of those premodern world orders and to stand on its own. Because Hwang and Ahn give us a glimpse of two different starting points two centuries ago, their texts merit reading today. They help us understand how far Korea has traveled to become the modern nation-state South Korea is today, and how distinctive Korea's journey to modernity has been.

PART II

IN THEIR OWN WORDS

CHAPTER 6

A Conversation on Catholicism
by Sunam Ahn Chŏngbok

Someone asked me, "Did what we nowadays refer to as 'celestial learning' exist in ancient times?" I answered, "Yes, it did. The *Book of History* says 'The August Lord on High [*Hwang Sangje* 皇上帝] has endowed human beings with an innate moral compass. Those who keep this ability to distinguish right from wrong unchanged can rest assured in acting in accordance with it.'[1] The *Book of Odes* says, 'King Wen was very careful and respectful and served the Lord on High [*Sangje*]'[2] and 'Stay in awe of Heaven and it will protect you.'[3] Confucius said, 'Respect what Heaven has ordained for you.'[4] Zisi explained 'What Heaven has ordained is human nature.'[5] Mencius said, 'To preserve the heart-and-mind Heaven has given you and nourish that human nature is the way to serve Heaven.'[6] What we Confucians study, after all, is nothing other than how to serve Heaven. As Master Dong Zhongshu said, 'the ultimate origin of the Dao is none other than Heaven itself.'"[7]

Q: If what we Confucians study is nothing other than how to serve Heaven, then why do you condemn those Western scholars for teaching the same thing?

Ahn: Though both sides talk about "serving Heaven," we use that phrase correctly, but they distort its true meaning. That is why I criticize them.

Q: These Europeans priests live celibate lives, and that is more than virtuous Chinese scholars are capable of. Moreover, the breadth and depth of their knowledge makes them truly exceptional men. They are able to map the heavens, calculate calendars, and make such useful items as a cannon that can pierce the nine layers of heaven and shoot projectiles as far as 80 *li* away. (When our King Injo [r. 1623–1649] was on the throne, the diplomat Chŏng Tuwŏn [1581–?] sent a memorial to the throne that reported that a Westerner named Rodrigues [1561?–1633] had made a cannon that could fire a cannon ball 80 *li* away. Rodrigues was a friend of Matteo Ricci.) These Europeans are also able to circumnavigate the globe. When they enter a strange country, they are able to speak and read that country's language after just a short while. And their astronomical calculations are accurate in every particular. They truly are wise and holy men. Since they are so sage-like, then how can you not trust them?[8]

Ahn: What you say may be true, but let's look at where they come from. Europe lies at the foot of the Kunlun mountains.[9] That is right in the middle of the world. Because of its location, the climate is invigorating, the people are unusually sturdy and tall, and they enjoy an abundance of natural resources. We can compare Europe to the abdomen in the human body. Just as the blood gathers in the abdomen to obtain nourishment before it returns to its job of providing the sustenance necessary to keep its body alive, the essentials for maintaining the human body come together in Europe.

China, on the other hand, is in the southeast corner of the world. The sun's rays are especially strong there. As a result, Sages appear among those whose bodies and minds are formed from the vitalizing matter-and-energy [*ki*] of that place. Yao, Shun, Yu, Tang, King Wen, King Wu, the Duke of Zhou, and Confucius are just some of the Sages China has produced. China is like the heart in the human chest that serves as the organ of perceptive awareness and makes it possible for human beings to conceptualize the myriad transformations. If you keep this in mind, then you can see why the sagely teachings of China are sound, but the "Celestial Learning" of Europe, though there are some who call it the true way and a sagely teaching, does not deserve the label "sagely teaching."

Q: How can you say that the "celestial learning" of the West is all that different from the sagely teachings of China?

Ahn: It's obvious. Each of us is born with a mind-and-heart that is grounded in the human nature Heaven provides us. The way to serve Heaven is to manage to keep that mind-and-heart in the pristine condition it was when Heaven gave it to us, keeping our true human nature healthy and strong by never forgetting what the Lord on High has provided us. There's nothing more to serving Heaven than that. What need is there to do as these Europeans do and pray to God morning and night, begging forgiveness for their sins so that they won't go to Hell when they die? How is their behavior any different from the way shamans constantly beseech their spirits for favors? These Europeans bow in prayer to Heaven five times a day, and every seventh day they refrain from eating meat. What does that have to do with serving Heaven?

Q: We say that there are three basic teachings in this world: Confucianism, Buddhism, and Daoism. These Europeans have added a fourth, attaching the name of Heaven to what they teach. What reason would they have for doing that?

Ahn: There is only one True Way of the Sages. How can there be three teachings? This term, "three teachings," is the fruit of the vulgar thinking of recent generations. Buddhism is something that originally was taught in the Western regions. It undermines the fundamental human ties that are the basis of morality. Daoism is an otherworldly teaching that has nothing to offer in the way of advice for living in the real world. How can you speak of them in the same breath with Confucianism?

The very idea of these Europeans claiming the word "Celestial" for their teachings is presumptuous, indeed. As you know, in the West since ancient times there have been as many strange teachings as there are spines on the back of a hedgehog. We can see from a number of different historical records that there have been many religions besides Buddhism there. The reason these Europeans call their particular product of the West "Celestial Learning" is that they realize that there is nothing we respect more than Heaven. They think that if they call what they teach "Celestial Learning," no one will dare criticize it. Their scheme is just like that of someone who seizes control of the imperial throne and then proceeds to issue orders to the various feudal lords in the name of the Emperor. It is quite a clever scheme.

What we Confucians teach is nothing more than what the Sages, accepting the responsibility Heaven had given them, used to bring order to the human realm in Heaven's stead. Everything that they did or decreed came from Heaven. That is how the will of Heaven came to prevail in this part of the world. How can those

Europeans expect that they can make us think that what they teach is the true way of sagely teachings just because they have attached the word "Celestial" to it?

Q: Haven't there been others, besides these Europeans, who talked about Heaven?

Ahn: Yes, there have. For example, there is a chapter in the *Mozi* titled, "The Will of Heaven.[10] In that chapter, Mozi is quoted as saying,

> Those who abide by the will of Heaven, such that their interactions with their fellow human beings are characterized by mutual love and mutual benefit, will surely be rewarded. But those who act contrary to the will of Heaven, such that their interactions with their fellow human beings are characterized by mutual animosity and a desire to benefit at the expense of others, will surely suffer for it. Yu, Tang, Wen, and Wu, the sage kings of the Three Dynasties of antiquity, complied with the will of Heaven and were rewarded for doing so. Jie, Zhou, You, and Li went against the will of Heaven and suffered because they did so. . . . Above Yu, Tang, Wen, and Wu served August Heaven, in the middle realm they served the spirits, and below they showed love for their fellow human beings. . . . Everything Heaven loved, they loved as well, and everything Heaven benefited, they benefited as well, all without partiality or favoritism.[11]

When Mozi talked about Heaven, he was referring to universal love and universal benefit. When the Europeans talk about putting enmity aside and loving your enemies instead, they sound a lot like Mozi talking about universal love and universal benefit. Moreover, the diligence and self-control they advocate sounds a lot like the frugality Mozi promoted. However, the Heaven Mozi talks about and the "Heaven" these Europeans talk about are not the same. When Mozi talks about Heaven, he is talking about the here and now. However, when the Europeans talk about Heaven, they are talking about the world to come. They are even more absurd than Mozi.

Basically, what those Europeans say about the world to come is just some tangential ideas they lifted from some Buddhist writings. Moreover, what they say about universal love and respecting frugality is just something they picked up from Mozi and his followers. Is any of this something anyone who has studied the Duke of Zhou or Confucius can learn from? These people who call themselves Confucians today have already condemned the Buddhists and Daoists for talking about paradise and hell and have also criticized the Mohists for advocacy of universal love. Why don't they repeat those criticisms when those Europeans spout similar nonsense? All this talk about the teachings of the "Lord of Heaven" is really absurd. Although we hold the Sages of ancient China in the highest esteem, we never think of giving them a lofty title like "Lord of Heaven." That would be ridiculous. These Europeans and those who admire them really need to think about the consequences of saying and writing such irresponsible language.

Q: Jesus is the name of the Messiah, the savior of the world. He was just like the Sages in that he wanted to promote moral behavior. There is no difference.

Ahn: How can you say that? When Jesus worked on "saving the world," he focused on a world after this one. He tantalized people with promises of Heaven if they did good and threatened people with Hell if they did evil. In promoting moral behavior, the Sages, however, focus on this world. They illuminate virtue and revitalize the people in order to help them become better human beings. Jesus encouraged people to focus on what they thought would benefit them the most personally. Our Sages fostered a concern for what was best for everyone. Therein lies the difference.

If what the Westerners say is true and there really is a Heaven and a Hell, then those who do good and avoid evil in this life will go to Heaven anyway, and those who are not virtuous and act improperly will end up in Hell anyway after they die. In the meantime, people should simply continue to do what is right and not turn their backs on the moral nature Heaven has given them. They should not pay the slightest attention to the possibility of some reward in the next life for what they do in this life. Master Cheng[12] said that Buddhists seek escape from what they believe is a never-ending cycle of birth, death, and rebirth only because they think it is in their own personal self-interest to do so. Don't the prayers of Catholics to avoid Hell also represent their pursuit of individual self-interest?

Q: In both ancient and recent times haven't there been other people who have talked about "Celestial Learning"? For example, one such person was Zou Yan, in ancient China. A more recent example is our own Hŏ Kyun (1569–1618). I'd like to hear what you think about them.

Ahn: Zou Yan spoke of a Heaven as deep and as broad as the ocean. He said it was impossible to make exact measurements of Heaven since it had no fixed points we could use to make such measurements. This is not the same as the Heaven European astronomers refer to when they talk about a celestial grid that they say corresponds perfectly to a similar grid on the terrestrial globe below.

As for Hŏ Kyun, he was intelligent and could write really well. However, he did have one fatal flaw. He did not always behave as he should have. While he was supposed to be in mourning, he ate meat and fathered a child. Because of that, his contemporaries scorned him. He was aware he was acting in ways that were inappropriate for a member of the scholarly Confucian elite. However, he put his faith in the Buddha rather than in Confucius. Day and night he bowed before Buddhist statues and chanted the sutras so that he would not go to Hell after he died. He also made the outlandish statement that "It is Heaven that has given human beings emotions and desires. Sages created the rules that place restrictions on the expression of those emotions and desires in order to maintain distinctions of gender and social status. Heaven is more worthy of respect than human beings are, even if those human beings are Sages. Therefore I would rather violate the rules imposed by Sages than go against the human nature Heaven has bestowed on me."[13] Since he had such a way with words, and such flippant remarks were popular at that time, he attracted some disciples. Some of those disciples began espousing what they called "Celestial Learning." However, their "Celestial Learning" and the "Celestial Learning" of the Europeans are not at all the same.

Generally speaking, when scholarship goes astray, it falls into the category of *idan*, ideas and practices that are morally unacceptable. We have to be on the lookout for this. Laozi, the Buddha, Yang Zhu, and Mozi were all highly intelligent men. Yet they ended up mired in nihilism and quietism, and no longer paid proper respect to the distinctions between parents and children, and between rulers and subjects.

Wang Yangming [1472–1529] called himself a scholar of Confucianism. Yet he, too, was guilty of straying from the true Confucian path. As a result, he had disciples such as Yan Shannong [Yan Jun, 1504–1596], who believed that "desires are a manifestation of human nature" was the key point to keep in mind when deciding how to behave, and He Xinyin [1517–1579], who adopted the notion of ranking desires, rather than simply restraining them, as his guiding principle. Both Yan and He claimed that when Wang Yangming talked about "innate knowledge of the good," he was advising us to follow the impulses of our own hearts and minds. They said that whenever we felt we should do something, our innate knowledge of the good was speaking to us. Therefore we should do whatever our hearts told us to do. That way of thinking will eventually lead to such fatal errors as joining up with southern Barbarians,[14] rebelling against a rightful government, and in the end being executed. Heed my words. Before you adopt any new ideas, you should first ascertain where those ideas come from and where they will lead. Beware of the evil consequences of bad ideas.

Q: What those Europeans teach is quite different from the sorts of ideas you're talking about. All they teach is that we should do good and avoid evil. What sort of evil consequences could that possibly lead to?

Ahn: That's not a very good argument for accepting what those Europeans teach. Everybody, no matter whether they are ignorant or well educated, whether they are stupid or wise, knows that "good" means what you are supposed to do and "evil" is what you are supposed to avoid. For example, let's say there is someone who is truly evil to the core. Such a person will nevertheless be pleased if he hears someone say to him, "you're really a good man." And if someone says to him, "you are really evil," he will fly into a rage. That proves that even evil people know the difference between good and evil. How could there be any philosophy anywhere in the world that encouraged doing evil and avoiding good?

When you say that these Europeans say we should do good and avoid evil, are you trying to say they are the only people who say that? Don't be ridiculous! Let me tell you why I am so concerned that what these Europeans teach will have dire consequences.

These Europeans don't talk about the world in which we actually live. Instead, they prattle on about what happens after we die, and the rewards in Heaven or punishments in Hell that await us. Isn't such nonsense a threat to what our revered Sages taught? Our Sages only talked about matters of this world, since this is the arena in which we are supposed to act properly. The world in which we must act is right before our eyes. We can see it clearly. There is nothing obscure or confusing about it. This is why Confucius didn't talk about the strange, the bizarre, the unusual, or the supernatural.[15] The strange and bizarre are things we see rarely, if at all. The supernatural are phenomena we never actually see. If we go on and on about things rare and invisible, then we make our listeners all confused and that can lead to them believing in all sorts of absurdities.

Chinese history provides plenty of examples of what happens when people start believing in things bizarre and supernatural. Near the end of the Han dynasty, for example, there was the Daoist Yellow Turban rebellion led by Zhang Jiao. The Tang suffered from the Pang Xun and Huang Chao rebellions in the last decades of the ninth century. The Song faced rebellions instigated by General Fang La and General Wang Ze. In the Yuan dynasty, there was a millenarian Red Turban rebellion. And various bandit bands plagued the Ming, some proclaiming that the arrival of the Maitreya Buddha was imminent and others calling themselves branches of the White Lotus Society. These are all examples of what happens when people start believing in the strange and supernatural. The history of China is filled with accounts of such disturbances, as many as there are spines on the back of a hedgehog. And history doesn't lie.

Even Korea has seen the damage belief in the strange and supernatural can do. During the reign of the previous king, King Yǒngjo [r. 1724–1776], there was such a disturbance. In 1758, a bewitching shaman named Yǒngmu, who lived in Sin'gye[16] county, proclaimed herself an incarnation of Maitreya. As she traveled from county to county, crowds gathered around her to proclaim her a living Buddha. They clasped their hands together and greeted her with bows. She ordered the people to put a complete stop to the worship of other gods and spirits, saying "Buddha has appeared among you. What need is there to serve other gods?" The people, obeying her words, smashed and burned ritual chests and vessels. Within just a few months, this movement spread from Hwanghae province down into the northern part of Koyang country in Kyǒnggi province as well as over into the districts east of Taegwan Pass in Kangwǒn province. It spread over that whole region like leaves blown off a tree in a heavy wind. I don't think the belief in a "Lord of Heaven" that is being promoted by those Europeans will spread any faster than that.

When the court found out about the disturbance this self-proclaimed Buddha was causing, it immediately dispatched the Royal Commissioner Yi Kyŏngok to put a stop to it by executing that shaman. However, it was another month after that before everything quieted down again. This shows that it is easy to agitate the masses but difficult to calm them down again. It is easy to fool and delude people but difficult to enlighten and educate them. That is just the way things usually are.

Those of you who are engaged in the study of "Celestial Learning" these days defend yourself by insisting that maintaining a consistent attitude of reverence for the Lord on High is no different from what Confucians do when they cultivate a reverential mind. You also say that the way you exercise self-control by limiting what you eat and not doing anything to excess is similar to the Confucian practice of self-discipline. You go on to ask why we don't respect you since, although your terminology and practices may be somewhat different from ours, essentially we share the same goal of doing good and avoiding evil.

My response to that is to warn you that it is difficult for people to tell the true from the false in a world in which cunning and deception prevail. If some bewitching person appears and loudly proclaims that "the Lord of Heaven has appeared in the East," or "the Lord of Heaven has appeared in the West," then people will grow accustomed to such outlandish statements. They will start to believe such nonsense and, just like lemmings, will follow those who make such absurd claims. Would the Europeans then be persuasive if they shouted, "Believe what we say but don't trust the others. What we say is true but what the others are saying is misleading and dangerous"? What arrogance! They are not aware that their words are like whirring arrows signaling the start of a bandit attack. Promoters of "Celestial Learning" don't realize that they are just like maggots eating away at our sacred teachings. It is really a pity that some of you willingly follow after those Europeans.

Q: I'd like to hear what you have to say about this world and the next.

Ahn: "This world" means the world in which we are living now. According to Europeans, the "next world" is where we go after our bodies die. Our immortal souls survive the death of our bodies and, if we have been good, will be rewarded with everlasting happiness in Heaven. However, if we have been bad, our souls will descend into Hell, where they will suffer for eternity.

Q: We recognize the importance of this world. Nothing we do or believe contradicts what the Sages of China taught. You really have no grounds for criticizing "Celestial Learning." For example, it is an undeniable fact that we have immortal souls and that Heaven and Hell are real.

Ahn: I can't come up with any specific concrete examples to refute such hazy concepts that have no shape or form. But if we look at in terms of *li* [理, that by which things are and which determines what they should do], and also see what the Confucian classics and histories have to say about it, then it will be not be particularly difficult to come to understand that they are nonsensical.

What we emphasize in our studies is what Confucius said. So let's look at a conversation between Confucius and his disciple Zilu. Zilu asked Confucius about spirits. Confucius answered, "You do not yet know how to serve human beings. Why do you need to learn how to serve spirits?" Zilu then asked about death. Confucius responded, "You do not yet understand life. Why are you asking about death?"[17] What the Great Sage is telling Zilu here is that talking about things that cannot be clearly defined is like swallowing a large fruit in one gulp. You are biting off more than you can chew. Zilu was a top disciple of Confucius. He is far superior to those who study the words of Confucius these days. If he shouldn't talk about spirits and life after death, why should you?

Your questions suggest that you think that life has been granted to us, and is sustained, through the power of the Lord of Heaven. Therefore, you say, human beings should take serving the Lord of Heaven as their primary task. And you say that after we die, even though our body disappears, our immortal soul lives on and, depending on whether we were good or bad while we were alive, that soul will ascend to Heaven or descend into Hell. You say this is all very clear and you wonder why I am still not satisfied.

If what you say is true, then Confucius simply didn't want to talk about spirits, that's all. You think he wasn't really saying that spirits don't exist. But how can you think that? The teachings of Confucius are totally different from what Europeans teach about the Lord of Heaven and the Messiah. Confucius modeled his life after Heaven, so how could his teachings be contrary to what Heaven intends? That is why I use the teachings of Confucius to criticize these strange ideas from the West.

Q: The fact that Europeans condemn this world is nothing more than an idiosyncrasy of their approach to self-cultivation. Why do you criticize them so harshly for that?

Ahn: Why do you say I've been too harsh? All I am doing is clarifying that their disdain for this world is a serious error. When we are born, we are born into this world. Therefore we ought to do the best we can in this world. What does life after death have to do with our obligations in this life?

Let's take a closer look at what those Europeans say. First of all, they call this world a "vale of tears," a place of hard work and suffering. They also say this is only a temporary home, that we are transients who are only passing through this world. Finally, they say this world is not our true home. Instead, it is the home of wild birds and beasts.

These Europeans say that, a long time ago, there was a wise man in the West named Heraclitus [c. 540–c. 480 BCE] who laughed all the time. That's because he was laughing at the way people pursued material vanities. Another wise man, Democritos [c. 460–370 BCE], cried all the time. He cried because he felt sorry for human beings. But is it only in the West that we can find people with such insight?[18] Yu the Great is reported to have said that we are only visitors to this world, and when we die, we return home.[19] Those who came after him have never failed to remember that they are only in this world for a short while. So how can we develop long-lasting attachments to material possessions? So to this extent we can agree with what those Europeans say. However, it is not acceptable to dismiss this world as a realm suitable only for wild animals. To do so would be a major mistake.

Let's look at the way we talk about our Lord on High and what that tells us about the value of this world. We say he "creates" the three realms. The realm that is lofty and awe-inspiring is Heaven. We look up to it with respect. The realm that looks rather commonplace is the earth, and it resides below. Bright and active *yang ki* [energizing matter and physical energy] descends from the heavens. At the same time, dark and passive *yin ki* rises from the earth. These two forms of *ki* come together, intermingle, and coagulate, giving rise to the myriad things. The Lord on High takes the cleanest and most refined congealed *ki* and has it form into human beings. Thus the Three Forces in nature came to be distinguished.[20]

Pointing at the sky, we say "That's Heaven." Pointing at the ground, we say, "This is the earth." As for what it is in between, if there is any plant or animal on the earth that is worth domesticating, we may do so. If there is any plant or animal worth killing, we may do that as well. If there is any plant or animal that appears in any way useful, we may use it. There is nothing on the earth that does not fall under our dominion. So to say that the earth is the home of wild beasts but not the home of human beings does not make any sense. That is such an unreasonable assertion that there is no need to discuss it any further. How could these Europeans convince even the most ignorant among us of such a thing? If what they say is true, then would not it be better if no more human beings were born and the human race became extinct? Then the space between heaven and earth would truly become a vast wilderness inhabited by wild animals only.

Q: These Europeans warn us about the three enemies of humanity. The first is our own body. The sensations of sound and sight, of taste and smell, along with our tendencies toward lust, laziness, and licentiousness, overwhelm us internally without us even being aware of what is happening. Our second enemy, according to them, is the mundane world. Through the lure of wealth, fame, amusements, and frivolities, it openly attacks us from the outside. The third enemy of man is the Devil. He uses our own pride as well as external allurements to bewitch and confuse us and attacks us both internally and externally.[21] How can you not agree with this? Doesn't this make a lot of sense?

Ahn: You have really been deluded. This notion that our body is our enemy is a terrible perversion of morality. It is true that because we have bodies we are beset with desires of the flesh. That is why we Confucians stress the need for self-control. But where do you think your body comes from? We get our bodies from our parents. So, if our bodies are our enemies, then our parents who gave us those bodies must be our enemies as well!

Moreover, since we are all born into this world, it is only natural that some of us will be rich and others poor, some of us will be well-known and respected and others will not, some of us will be successes and others failures, and some will do well in life and others will do not so well. That is just the way things are. But if you do not know how to gain the strength to resist the temptations of this world by engaging in self-examination and exercising self-control but take the world with all its rewards and disappoint-ments as your enemy instead, then you will render all the moral obligations of that world, such as the moral ties between rulers and subjects, meaningless.

As for their talk about a "devil," that is really ridiculous. Human beings are made of tangible *ki*. It is the nature of such flesh and blood to generate desires. Even Sages cannot avoid having desires. But Sages differ from the rest of us in that they do not let their desires get out of control. Such emotional restraint is what we Confucians mean by "self-discipline." All we have to do is use the mind-and-heart that heaven endowed us with at birth, our un-tainted human nature, to control the desires of the flesh so that they are properly channeled and don't get out of control.

Besides, who can see this "devil"? If, perchance, he does happen to exist, he is out there somewhere in the world around us. It cannot be denied that temptations from the world around us can cause us to lose our original untainted nature. That does happen. But the ab-sence of good in human beings is due to desires caused by tangible *ki*, that's all. How can we blame our faults on some "devil"? Their approach of looking for enemies both internal and external to blame is quite different from our Confucian approach of simply exercis-ing self-control. When these Europeans blame the devil rather than their own flesh and blood for their moral failings, they are missing the point and looking in the wrong direction for an expla-nation of human moral frailty. Their ideas are really not worth discussing.

Q: According to the Europeans, their ancient records state that the Lord of Heaven created the heavens and the earth and also created the first human beings, a man called Adam and a woman called Eve, who are the ancestors of all human beings who have lived on this earth since then. Can this be so?

Ahn: If you think about how things actually happen in this world, you can see that such statements cannot possibly be true. I will ad-mit that the supernatural power of a Lord of Heaven would be un-limited. But as far as the creation of heaven and earth is concerned, that comes about when *yin* ascends and *yang* descends and those two forms of *ki* intermingle to produce the transformations that constitute the multitude of things. Human beings are formed from the best *ki*, the *ki* that is clean, clear, and complete. Murkier, defec-tive *ki* becomes the birds and the beasts, the grasses and the trees.

Let's talk about this in terms of what we can see right before our own eyes today. Ask yourself, where do lice come from? Do they come from human beings or from clothing? Suppose that you take a bath and clean yourself so well that there is not a speck of dirt left on your body. Then you put on some new clothes that have just been sewn and have never been worn before. After you wear them for a few days, you will find quite a few lice in your shirt and pants. Where do these lice come from? They come from the intermingling of the *ki* [氣] emanating from your body with the *ki* given off by your clothes. Isn't this proof that things come into existence naturally, through the fertile intermingling and coalescing of *ki*?

Let's take another example from what we can see around us as we go about our daily life. Let's say you have a basket of the sort farmers use to carry things but, in this case, there's nothing in it but some dirt. There is nothing else in it at all, no seeds, no roots or any other form of vegetation, and not any insects either. You place that basket up in the rafters of your home. Then the wind blows and rain falls on it, making that dirt a little damp. Its humid *ki* is unable to evaporate, so that soil remains damp. After just a few days, you will find ants and other sorts of insects and plants growing in that dirt. Isn't this another case of things coming into existence naturally, through the spontaneous transformation of *ki*?

When *ki* transforms itself in this way and assumes concrete configurations, becoming specific living entities, those entities go on to reproduce and multiply. That's the way it is with all living things. Why should human beings be any different? To say that all the human beings on earth are the descendants of Adam doesn't make any sense. If we are all the children of Adam and Eve, then shouldn't we also be able to say that every plant and animal is also descended from a single similar plant or animal? You don't have to think very deeply about this to realize that such a search for first progenitors is absurd. This tale the Westerners tell is not convincing at all.

Q: Those engaged in "Western Learning" say that not only is there an original progenitor for all humanity, there is also a second progenitor. I'd like to hear what you say about that.

Ahn: By the "original progenitor," you mean Adam, whom we just discussed. "Second progenitor" is another way of referring to Jesus, the Lord of Heaven. Matteo Ricci, in his *Tianzhu shiyi* [True meaning of the Lord of Heaven], writes,

In the beginning when the world was created, there were no diseases for human beings to worry about. The weather was constantly spring-like and mild. Those first human beings were always happy. The birds, beasts, and all living things obeyed the commands of human beings. And all human beings had to do to continue living in such a paradise was obey and serve the Lord on High. But because those first human beings disobeyed the commands of the Lord of Heaven, the myriad other things in this world stopped doing the bidding of human beings. This is the reason human beings encounter so many problems in this world today.[22]

Another book written by a European, *Zhendao zizheng* [The true way is self-evident],[23] says,

The Lord of Heaven created the original progenitor. He became the ancestor of all human beings that have ever lived. The Lord granted him the special grace of being able to make his own decisions. His basic nature was that of a good man and his emotions were all admirable ones. Moreover, he had insight into all the patterns of appropriate interaction in the universe. All plants and animals did his bidding as though he were their sovereign. The devil was jealous of that human's good fortune and plotted to get him expelled from paradise. The Lord of Heaven allowed the devil to tempt that first human in order to test him. He failed that test and succumbed to the devil's temptation. As a result, our first ancestor lost his original innate goodness and also lost the good fortune the Lord of Heaven had bestowed on him. The generosity and goodwill the Lord of Heaven had shown him turned into righteous anger. When that first human died, he fell into the torment of hell. Moreover, his descendants generation after generation have suffered the same punishment.[24]

Can that possibly be true? If the Lord on High created Adam as the original progenitor of all humanity, then we would have to say that the Lord on High was really holy and wise. But why would such a Lord on High agree to the devil's proposition and allow the devil to test whether Adam was truly faithful or not? If he knew that Adam had a rebellious side to him, the Lord on High should have had a talk with him, warned him against giving into such impulses, and encouraged him to stay on the path of righteousness.

Adam would have heeded those words and stayed out of trouble. The Lord on High should have done as any wise father would have done for his own son or any good teacher would have done for any of his students.

Could a true Lord on High really have behaved in this way? To even imply that is blasphemy against Heaven. What is even worse is the claim that Adam's descendants, for ten thousand generations, have all been punished for Adam's sin. Only the culprit himself should have been punished. Under our great sage rulers in times past, punishments were never extended even to the next generation. No just ruler would extend punishment for one person's crime to his descendants for thousands of generations. In the *Tianzhu shiyi*, a Chinese scholar is quoted as saying, "Goodness is rewarded with goodness, and evil with evil. If you do not reap the reward or suffer the consequences yourself, then your sons and grandsons will. There is no need to speak of reward in heaven or punishment in hell."[25] The Western scholar responded to that by saying, "Kings and even tyrants do not extend punishments to a criminal's descendants. Would the Lord of Heaven then exempt the criminal himself from punishment and instead punish his sons and grandsons instead?"[26] They contradict themselves. It's really ludicrous.

Q: Can I hear some more of what you have to say about this talk about a second progenitor?

Ahn: This concept is extremely complicated and is difficult to explain. Let me try to give you a brief explanation. The *Tianzhu shiyi* says that Adam caused myriad problems for his descendants. They all ended up just imitating the evil actions of others. Purity and innocence gradually disappeared and the number of sages and saints diminished. The number of those who simply followed their base desires increased, and those who acted in accord with the patterns of appropriate behavior became fewer. Then the Lord of Heaven, manifesting his great compassion, personally descended to this world in order to save it. This was during the reign of Emperor Aidi of the Han dynasty, in the second year after he adopted the reign title Yuanshou. The Lord of Heaven selected a chaste maiden to be his mother. Even though she had never had sexual relations, she became pregnant and gave birth. Her child was named "Jesus." Jesus means "the messiah, he who will save the world." He spread his transforming teachings for thirty-three years and then returned to Heaven.[27]

If it is really true that the Lord of Heaven personally descended to earth to be born as a human being, then while he was here living among human beings, the throne of the Lord of Heaven above must have been empty!

Moreover, *Zhendao zizheng* claims that the sacred writings of the West tell us that the Lord of Heaven chose one of the descendants of the first progenitor to serve as the second progenitor. This second progenitor is called the son of the Lord of Heaven. He is no different from the true Lord of Heaven himself. This is different from the story that the Lord of Heaven personally descended from Heaven to live among human beings. With such contradictions, how can we believe what they are telling us?

This book also says that Jesus took responsibility for the sins of all humanity and offered himself as a sacrifice to redeem humanity and allowed himself to be nailed to the cross on which he died. But they also say that the Lord on High personally descended to earth, and that the Lord of Heaven who thus walked among human beings was the same person as the Lord of Heaven above. So how can they write that he died on a cross, not even dying a natural death! This is about as ridiculous as anything can be and is a grievous affront to the dignity of the Lord on High. I don't see why anybody would believe them just because they insist their claims are true.

Q: If what you say is true, then we cannot trust anything those Europeans say.

Ahn: Let's look at our own China for examples of how to deal with tales of the supernatural. Way back at the beginning of history, much of what was recorded was about the weird and unexplainable. Then the Sages came along and dismissed such tales as worthless. Can we be sure that the same kind of unreliable reporting didn't happen in early Western history as well?

They claim that their sacred writings contain records handed down unaltered from the beginning of time and therefore they trust them completely. It is reasonable to trust something written by someone holy and wise who only wanted to encourage people to behave appropriately. Clearly, these ancient tales were designed to provide a foundation for their spiritual teachings. Nevertheless, the West does not seem to have sages like our Sages who appeared in China and were able to rectify ancient records. (For example, they dismissed as myth such stories as the story of Nü Wa and how she smelted stones to mend the sky and the story of Houyi and how he

shot nine suns out of the sky, whereupon they turned into crows.)
These stories the Europeans tell about Jesus are quite sensational.
However, they are no different from the tales Buddhists tell about
the supernatural powers of their Buddha. Moreover, when they
make such wild claims as that the Lord on High, the true Lord of
Heaven, personally descended to earth, they show without a doubt
that their teachings are rooted in *idan,* ideas that can only lead to
trouble.

Q: This talk about humanity having "three enemies" really is disturb-
ing and extremely dangerous. For example, if we believe that we
should treat our own bodies as our enemies, we would then view
our parents, who gave us those bodies, as our enemies as well. That
would destroy the moral ties that should prevail between parents
and those they brought into this world. If we believe that the world
in which we live is our enemy, that would render meaningless all
the effort the Sages exerted to put the affairs of this world into
proper order. As a result, the proper relationship between rulers
and the subjects would no longer prevail. These Europeans celebrate celibacy, considering it noble. The *Qike*[28] actually talks about
prohibiting marriage. Some ideas threaten to eradicate the moral
bond between a husband and a wife.

> Human beings are born into the world. Therefore they should re-
> spect the Three Bonds (the bonds between a ruler and a subject,
> a parent and a child, and a husband and a wife). However, these
> Europeans say that this world is just our temporary home and we
> should not be overly concerned about it. They urge us to be more
> concerned about whether we are going to Heaven or to Hell after
> we die. This looks like a variation on what the Buddhists teach.
> But their talk of a devil is even more absurd than the sorts of
> things Buddhists say. That is not the sort of thing real Confu-
> cians would bother discussing. That is why it is perfectly appro-
> priate for us to dismiss what those Europeans say as not worthy
> of our time or attention. However, what about the moral effort in
> their "celestial learning"? What do you think about that?

Ahn: I already made some brief comments about that earlier. They
say that every morning they turn their eyes and their hearts toward
Heaven and give a prayer of thanks to the Lord of Heaven for allowing them to be born in this world, for providing them the things
they need, and for teaching them how to live a proper life. His

benevolence, they say, is without limit. Several times during the day they pray to God to help them keep their "three vows," their vows to think no evil, say no evil, and do no evil. In the evening, they prostrate themselves on the ground and give themselves a strict self-examination to see if they have gone astray in thought, word, or deed. If they find that they have thought, spoke, and acted properly that day, they attribute that good record to God helping them, and they thank him for that assistance. If, on the other hand, they realize they have thought, spoke, or acted improperly, they blame themselves. Repenting, they throw themselves on God's merciful benevolence, praying to him to forgive them. That is essentially what they do every day.

There are some who compare such behavior to the way we Confucians cultivate sincerity and say that it is no different from the Confucian approach to self-cultivation, but can that really be so? Think about it a minute or two. Is the way they look and act really in accord with what our Sages taught, or is it different?

Q: Those Europeans say that Buddha stole teachings from the West and used them to set up their own school.[29] Can that be so?

Ahn: Buddha was born during the reign of King Zhao [995–957 BCE] of the Zhou dynasty. Jesus, the Lord of Heaven, was born a thousand years later, during the reign of Emperor Aidi of the Han dynasty [6 BCE–1 CE]. Given who came first and who came second, their assertion is not even worth discussing.

Q: Those Europeans claim that they have a written record of their history all the way back to the time of creation. Those records, totaling 3,600 volumes, include prophecies of the birth of Jesus. This is quite different from the records of Chinese history. Those Chinese records have large gaps in them. Also there are a lot of errors and misstatements in those Chinese records. What do you think about this?

Ahn: I haven't seen the European histories, so I cannot really say whether or not what the Europeans say about them is true or not. But I am sure there must be some mistakes in them as well. I have seen some statements from those records cited in European publications I have looked at. Those statements must have been selected as representing the key points found in those histories. I can tell you that they are quite different from what we see in the writings of the Sages of China. All you have to do is look at them with your own eyes to tell which is more reliable and which is less so.

Q: These Europeans consider it very important to spread their teachings. They sailed the vast, blue ocean for 80,000 to 90,000 *li* [approximately 25,000 to 30,000 miles] to get here. They did not let fear stop them even though they had to pass through countries inhabited by cannibals and spear-wielding tribes. They did not turn back even when they had to face sharks, crocodiles, tigers, and wolves. If they did not have a serious reason for doing that, and if they were not men of unusual determination, could they have done this?

Ahn: According to Chinese histories, Kumārajīva (344–413) was in the kingdom of Latter Qin [384–417] under the ruler Yao Xing [394–416]. Bodhidharma arrived in China during the reign of the Emperor Wu [r. 502–549] of the Liang dynasty [502–577]. They both had to make their way across a vast desert to reach China. Their reason was the same reason those Europeans sailed all the way from Europe to China. Those Buddhists also wanted to spread their teachings to China. How were they any different from the Europeans! Those two monks brought nothing with them but Buddhist sutras. Although those advocating Western Learning brought Western Learning instead of Buddhism to China, what they are promoting is not that different from what those Buddhist monks taught. How can you advocate replacing the teachings of the Confucians with teachings from the West?

Q: Those Europeans say that it has been seventeen hundred or eighteen hundred years since Jesus preached on this earth. Those countries that have adopted his teachings have been free of rebellions and war. The vast area occupied by Western countries is still peaceful today. But, even though China has produced a number of Sages, dynasties have risen and fallen over and over again there. From these we can see that the teachings in China have only scratched the surface and have not produced a solid foundation. When our fellow Confucians have learned about this, they have been dumbfounded and have concluded that Confucian teachings are not at the same high level as Western Learning. What do you say to that?

Ahn: The weather in the Western regions is temperate and mild. This produces decent human beings with hearts free of guile. They are not at all like those cunning Chinese. So it is possible that there is some truth to what you say. Nevertheless, I suspect there is also some exaggeration. If you study Chinese histories, you will see that from the time of Emperor Aidi of the Han on, China has experienced quite a few attacks from Western barbarians. There have also been quite a few instances of Western barbarians seizing Chinese territory. Are you trying to tell me that those Chinese histories are full of lies? You can not convince me of that. Moreover, take the example of Japan. Since the founding of the Japanese state by Emperor Jimmu during the reign of the King Ping [r. 770–720 BCE] of the Zhou dynasty, the same family has held the throne. They have held their country together by allowing fiefdoms. This is also a case of political stability at the top much greater than China has experienced. Yet can you really put Japan on the same level with China? Do you think the Japanese ruling family has held onto that throne for so long because they practice "Celestial Learning"?

Q: Jesus the Savior was nailed to a cross. Even though he had the power to move Heaven and earth and all of creation, he did not harm in the least bit the people who nailed him to the cross. Does not that show the greatest possible love for mankind?

Ahn: What you are talking about is the "put your anger away and instead love your enemy" precept. Ricci in his *Jiren shipian* says, "The scholars who follow the Celestial Way teach that human beings should respond to hatred with virtue instead of responding to hatred with hatred."[30] However, there are two kinds of hatred. If you are talking about dealing with an enemy who has harmed you personally, then I have no problem with this injunction. There are plenty of cases of gentlemen in ancient times who did not respond in kind to someone who acted with malice toward them. However, in the case of those who have harmed your ruler or your parents, to do as those Europeans suggest would be a grave violation of our moral obligations. We owe it to our rulers and our parents to oppose those who have harmed them. What those Europeans say reminds me of Mozi's advocacy of "loving everyone equally." However, the Europeans go even farther than Mozi did.

Q: Those Europeans criticize the Chinese for not realizing that the Lord of Heaven created the Heaven and earth and all that lies in between. But in his "Explanation of the Diagram of the Supreme Polarity," Zhou Dunyi [1017–1073] asserted that *li* [理] is the origin of all things.[31] And Zhu Xi [1130–1200] said that *li* is nothing other than Heaven.[32] What do you think about that?

Ahn: When we talk about *li* functioning as master of the universe, we sometimes call it "the Lord on High." After all, *li* functions as the overall master of all things. So that is the way we Confucians talk. When people use the term "Heaven," they can use it to mean a couple of different things. "Heaven" can refer to the Heaven which functions as *li*, as the master of the universe. That is the sense in which we are using that term when we talk about Heaven bestowing a moral human nature on all human beings. When we encourage people to "respect the mandate of Heaven," we are talking about Heaven as *li*. The second meaning of "heaven" is the heaven that is visible *ki*. That is heaven as the sky, a material entity.

Zhou's discussion of the Diagram of the Supreme Polarity is based on what Confucius said about the Supreme Polarity producing the Two Forces [yin and yang]. If we want to emphasize that it is functioning as master of the universe, then we may call it "the Lord on High." When we highlight the fact that it gives off no sound and emits no smell, in other words, when we focus on the fact that it is immaterial, then we call it "the Supreme Polarity" or just simply "*li*."

Q: So you say we can call *li* both the "Lord on High" or the "Supreme Polarity"? But Matteo Ricci noted that superior men in ancient times worshipped the Lord on High of Heaven and Earth but he never heard of them showing such respect to the Supreme Polarity.[33] Moreover, he pointed out that *li* cannot exist by itself but is always found adhering to something else. It is only when something exists that its *li* [the principle that defines it] can be said to exist. If something has never existed, then its *li* cannot be said to have ever existed, either. It's like the *li* governing the relationship between a ruler and his subject. How can someone be called a ruler if he has no subjects? If you take vacuous *li* to be the origin of the universe, then you have fallen into the same sort of nihilism that Buddha and Laozi promoted.[34]

Ahn: How can you think that such an argument is valid? Think about it a minute. The Lord on High is the source of *li* and he also created Heaven, earth, and everything in between. But the universe could not have simply come into existence through arbitrary coagulations of *ki*. There must have been pre-existing *li* to define what the universe was and how it should operate. How could the Lord on High create the universe if there was no *li* to tell him what a universe should look and act like? Your argument reminds me of the arguments some Confucians have made recently that *ki* precedes *li*. It's not worth even discussing.

Confucius said "The Supreme Polarity produces the Two Forces." He also said "the alternation of yin and yang is what we call the Dao."[35] The Dao is the Way, which is another word for *li*. If this European argument is correct, then Confucius is wrong. We Confucians must clearly and decisively challenge that argument. We should not stop criticizing it for even one minute.

Q: If you read *Tianzhu shiyi* and the *Jiren shipian*, you'll notice that whenever those Europeans speak, the Chinese who listen to them all straighten up their clothes and follow them, having been convinced by what those Europeans say. What do you say to that?

Ahn: Those books were all written by Europeans. They make up the questions, and then write down the answers themselves. That is why it looks like they always best the Chinese with their arguments. However, if they actually had conversations with scholars who were well-versed in the Confucian Way, then you would not see any of them falling for their arguments and becoming believers.

Q: Does that term "Lord of Heaven" appear in any Chinese books?

Ahn: I've never see it in any of the ancient classics. However, in the "Treatise on the Feng and Shan Sacrifices" in the *Shiji* [Records of the Grand Historian], a "Lord of Heaven" is mentioned as one of the eight gods who is worshipped.[36] In the biography of Huo Qubing in the *Han Shu* [The history of the former Han dynasty], there is a statement that in the first year of the Yuanshou era [122 BCE] a king named Xiu Tu worshipped Heaven in the form of a golden statue of a human being. The passage on his son Jin Erdi says that Jin worshipped that golden statue his father had as the "Lord of Heaven."[37] So you can see that the name "Lord of Heaven" has been around for quite a while. The commentator Ru Chun [189–265 CE] glossed that section as "they worshipped heaven by taking that golden statue as their lord." The commentator Yan Shigu [541–645 CE] noted that they made a statue of a human figure from gold and, taking it as a representation of a celestial spirit, worshipped it. The Buddhist practice of making statues of their gods is something the Buddhists picked up from this sort of activity in the former Han.

The book *Hanwu gushi* [Tales of Emperor Wu of the Han dynasty] says that a branch of the Xiongnu killed King Xiu Tu and then surrendered to the Han, taking that golden statue with them. It was placed it in a seat of honor in the Ganquan-gong. That statue was over ten feet tall. When they worshipped, they did not sacrifice ox or sheep. Instead, they only burned incense and bowed. It was the custom of the people who made that statue to offer sacrifice in that way. Yan Shigu said that, although some people think that statue was like the Buddhist statues common in his day, the fact that it was called the "celestial spirit" shows that it was not a Buddhist statue at all.

It seems to me that what the practitioners of "Western Learning" do these days is just like what those barbarians did during the Han dynasty when they made a statue out of gold and worshipped it as the "Lord of Heaven." The way practitioners of "Western Learning" bow before statues and paintings of the "Lord of Heaven" is slightly different only because of the passage of time. I suspect that, because King Shixian of the Xiongnu has some contact with the Western regions, he adopted the worship rituals popular there.

The *Zhendao zizheng* says that Jesus was born of the Holy Mother, who carried him to a sacred hall. There she presented him before the altar of the Lord of Heaven. This tells us that the name "Lord of Heaven" already existed even before the time of Emperor Aidi of the Han, that is to say, even before Jesus was born. So Jesus cannot be the "Lord of Heaven."

Q: In the *Liezi*, there is a passage that reads, "A high official from Shang asked Confucius 'You are a sage, are you not?' 'A sage!' replied Confucius. 'How could I venture to think so?' The Minister then asked: 'Were the Three Primordial Sovereigns, the Five Thearchs, and the Three Founders of the earliest dynasties sages?' Confucius replied, 'People say they were all sages, but I don't know for sure.' That Shang minister then asked, 'If that is the case, then is there anyone you would call a sage?' Confucius replied, 'Among the people of the West a true sage dwells. He governs not, yet there is no disorder. He speaks not, yet he is naturally trusted. He makes no conscious efforts to transform people, yet right conduct is spontaneous and universal. So great and incomprehensible is he that the people can find no name to call him by.'"[38] Buddhists claim that this passage is a reference to Buddha. But when I look at it, it seems to me to be a reference to the Lord of Heaven.

Ahn: You can't trust anything the *Liezi* says. It is full of all sorts of exaggerations and fantasy stories. According to that book, Confucius said that there is a sage in the Western regions who is "so great and incomprehensible that the people can find no name for him."

Do you really think that Confucius would say that there was a sage living in the Western regions but would refuse to say that the Five Thearchs were Sages?

Q: I've heard that practitioners of Western Learning view their leaders as substitute fathers. (The Lord of Heaven is called the "great parent." Therefore someone who acts in Heaven's stead is called a "substitute father.") They also engage in some strange rituals. They set up a tablet to symbolize the presence of the Lord of Heaven. Then each one takes a three-foot-long piece of clean cloth and hangs it around his neck. They also wash their foreheads with their hands, using what Matteo Ricci called "holy water." This is how they wash uncleanliness from their hearts. They light candles on an altar and prostrate themselves on the floor before it. They confess all the wrong things they have done in the past and say they truly repent those mistakes. After they have intoned the "eight teachings,"[39] they resolve to never commit such mistakes again. They also take a special nickname to show their commitment to Western Learning. What do you think about this?

Ahn: This is similar to what Buddhists do. Buddhists have leaders they call "dharma masters" and "vinaya masters." And they are known to burn their wrists as a sign of repentance for past misdeeds, and to place water on their foreheads. So how are those practitioners of Western Learning any different from the Buddhists? What you describe are, in my opinion, simply the vulgar customs associated with Western Learning. They are not the sort of thing those in our China would engage in, if they have learned well what the Sages taught.

Q: Matteo Ricci talks about three kinds of souls, a vegetative soul, a sentient soul, and a cognitive soul. The vegetative soul, the soul of plants and trees, is the lowest ranking of the three. It has life but no awareness or thought. Next in rank is the sentient soul, the soul of birds and beasts. It has life and the ability to sense things around it but no ability to think and reason. The human soul, however, is not only capable of being alive and being aware of its environment, it is also capable of thinking and reasoning. Both the vegetative soul and the sentient soul are inextricably linked to the material forms in which they are encased. When the material form on which such a soul is dependent dies, its soul dies with it. The highest kind of soul is the human soul, the one we call the cognitive soul. It is not bound

to anything material. Although the human body in which it resides will die, the cognitive soul lives on for eternity.[40] What do
you think about that analysis of the three forms of life?

Ahn: That is nothing new. A similar idea has appeared in our China as
well. Long ago Xunzi said, "Water and fire have *ki* [energized matter]
but are not alive. Plants and trees are alive but are incapable of learning anything. Birds and beasts are capable of recognizing changes
in their environment but are not able to tell what sort of behavior is
appropriate. Human beings, however, not only have *ki,* are alive,
and are aware of their environment, they are also capable of telling
the difference between right and wrong. That is why human beings
are the most noble beings on earth."[41] Zhen Xishan [Zhen Dexiu,
1178–1235] is recorded in the *Xingli daquan* [The Great Compendium on Nature and Principle] as saying something similar. What
those Europeans say is not all that different from what Xunzi said.
The only thing novel about what the Europeans say is their claim
that the human soul is immortal. But that is just like what the Buddhists say. It is not something we Confucians should even bother
to discuss.

Q: Recently there was a student at the National Confucian Academy
who was about to take part in the Sŏkchŏnje [the twice-a-year ritual
honoring Confucius and his disciples]. One of his friends who was
practicing "Western Learning" tried to dissuade him from doing
so, saying, "Normally such rituals are directed toward idols, so the
only spirits who show up to enjoy the ritual offerings are evil spirits.
Do you think the spirit of Confucius actually shows up to enjoy
that food and drink? It is the same with family ancestor rituals.
However, if you have no choice and have to participate in such a
ritual, then keep in mind the whole time that the ritual has no real
meaning. Moreover, you should turn your attention heavenward
and silently pray to the Lord of Heaven to forgive you, while taking
in that ritual with the utmost inner reluctance." Isn't this the worst
thing you have ever heard? It is really a perversion of ritual and an
attack on all we have been taught.

Ahn: Yet that is what those Europeans teach! They even go so far as to
say that such ritual displays of respect for those who have preceded
us on this earth are a waste of time. They assert that if those people
we want to honor led good lives, then they are now in Heaven above
and have no reason to leave there to partake of our meager offerings. If they did not behave properly when they were alive, then

they are now in Hell and, even if they would like to come to the ritual and enjoy what we offer them, they are unable to do so. That is what they believe.

Truly, they make themselves a laughingstock, since they engage in similar behavior. Those who practice Western Learning lift their voices in praise of the Lord of Heaven, worship him, and pray to him. But is not that also a case of offering ritual homage to a meaningless idol, and possibly summoning an evil spirit? Our mentor Sŏngho Yi Ik once asked rhetorically how those Europeans can be so sure that miraculous signs of the Lord of Heaven's presence they talk about are not just simply the tricks of evil spirits. Since our respected teacher has already pointed this out, we now know to watch out, and to remain aware that it is another trick of evil spirits to make men appear to be good men though they actually are beguiling and deceiving people. Those Europeans appears to be victims of the same devilish tricks they warned against, and that is why they worship their "god" the way they do. Is not that enough to make you laugh?

I have heard that they say that there is a false "Lord of Heaven," who is nothing more than an illusion woven by evil spirits. If they admit there can be an illusionary "Lord of Heaven," then how can they be so sure that the Lord of Heaven they worship is the real one?

Q: The Daoists, the Buddhists, and the Europeans all talk about evil spirits. But what kind of spirits are these "evil spirits" that the "Lord of Heaven" is unable to stop from engaging in deceptive tricks and evil deeds?

Ahn: Those Europeans claim that when the Lord of Heaven first created spirits, there was nothing wrong with them. They were perfectly admirable creatures, of impeccable character. The Lord of Heaven arranged them in nine ranks and gave them different responsibilities. They were all called "celestial spirits." Unfortunately, one of the celestial spirits in the top rank grew quite proud of himself and thought that he did not need any one to tell him what to do. He began to draw away from the Lord of Heaven and became the leader of a group of rebellious spirits. The Lord of Heaven then expelled him from Heaven and exiled him to Hell below. He's the one we call Satan, the Evil Spirit. The Lord of Heaven occasionally releases him from Hell temporarily so that he can tempt human beings and thereby allow decent human beings to gain merit by resisting evil while allowing evil human beings to suffer the consequences of their own shortcomings. To say that the Lord of Heaven allows good human beings to gain merit by resisting evil means that he sends Satan to try to tempt good men into doing something wrong in order to test how successful they have been at cultivating a moral character. [Ahn notes here that the rest of this section is omitted.]

Q: Now that I have heard what you have to say about Western Learning, I can see that there is no doubt that it is *idan,* something that should be condemned rather than embraced. Our Confucian efforts to illuminate virtue and transform the people all focus on this world. These Europeans, on the other hand, have their eyes on the next world when they talk about doing good and avoiding evil. Since people are born into this world, they should expend all their energy on things of this world and try to be the best person they can be in this world, without concerning themselves the least bit with reaping a reward after they die. The Catholic approach is really different from our Confucian approach. All they really care about is what will benefit them personally. How can this compare with our Confucian focus on what is the right thing to do, which we define as what is best for the common good? From now on, I will listen to what you have to say.

Hearing this, I smiled. After that guest left, I wrote down this account of our conversation in the hope that it might be of some benefit to our Confucian Way.

Written in the twelfth month of 1785 by someone who is worried about barbarian influence.

CHAPTER 7

The Silk Letter of Hwang Sayŏng

I, the sinner Thomas,[1] am sending this tearful appeal for help to your Excellency, our Bishop, on behalf of all the Catholics in Korea.[2] We heard from a member of the spring tribute mission last year that you were in good health.[3] The year since then has passed by very quickly. We wonder how your Excellency is now. We trust that the Lord has kept your Excellency hale and hearty and that, with God's help, every day you reap more success in your efforts to bring about the moral transformation of China. When we hear how successful your efforts have been so far, we are overjoyed. It is our devout hope and prayer that your work will continue to go well.

We sinners in Korea have made some very serious mistakes and have incurred the wrath of God Above. Because of our own incompetence, our plans have gone awry. As a result, we are now encountering a major persecution. This persecution is so severe that it has even taken our priest from us. We sinners are incapable of saving ourselves in this crisis situation. We therefore are throwing ourselves on your mercy and pray that you, with the grace of God, will be able to help us.

How could I be so bold as to pick up a brush and write this appeal to you when I am ashamed that I failed to repay God's grace by accepting martyrdom as our priest did? I do so out of desperation. Catholicism is in danger of disappearing from Korea. We are all being killed off. Those of us who have managed to stay alive are not only in dire straits, on top of that we are now bereft of our priest. Moreover, those who have managed to escape being arrested have scattered in all directions. We are unable to meet and discuss what we can do about this terrible situation. The only hope we have left is you, Your Excellency. We turn to you like children to a parent for protection and like villagers who place their trust in a righteous magistrate. Certainly you will be able to pity us and save us. In the depths of our suffering, to whom will we be able to appeal besides your Excellency?

In this letter I will give a general report to your Excellency of what has transpired during the persecution. However, because the persecution unfolded over a long period of time and there are quite a number of loose threads to pull together, it is difficult in just one letter to summarize what is happening to us. Nevertheless, I am going to use the rest of this sheet of silk to try to do just that. I will save a more detailed report for later. In the meantime, I humbly hope that you will take pity on us and carefully consider the plight we are in now.

Here is our situation at the moment. The church has been completely laid waste. As far as I know, only very few of us sinners were fortunate enough to escape with our lives. John Ok Ch'ŏnhŭi has also managed to elude the persecution.[4] Perhaps God has not completely abandoned us after all. Ah! Those who have died already offered their lives in order to witness to the truth of our faith. Those who are still alive are risking their lives to protect the Way. However, we lack ability and are very weak. We do not know what to do.

Recently a few of us met secretly to discuss how to cope with the situation we are in now. Let me be perfectly frank with you and report everything in an orderly fashion. It is my humble wish that after you read this letter and understand how serious our situation is, you will have pity on us, who feel abandoned, and hurry to save us from danger. We sinners are like sheep who have lost their shepherd and are scattering here and there. Some have escaped into remote mountain villages; others, homeless, scurry along the various highways and byways of our land. We are in such heart-rending agony that every one of us is crying inside. Day and night, all we do is hope that the Lord's omnipotent power and Your Excellency's magnanimous compassion will save us. With the deepest sincerity, we pray that we will obtain the Lord's help, that He will take pity on us and rescue us from this torment and provide for us a safe haven.

Catholicism has already spread throughout the whole world to the people of the myriad countries. There is nowhere on earth where songs are not sung to praise the glory of God and drums not beaten to inspire people to dance in joy at the propagation of the Gospel. If Your Excellency looks across the Yellow Sea at the people on the other side, you can see that there is not one of us here who is not a child of the Lord. Unfortunately, however, our country is very small, and is isolated from most of the rest of the world. As a result, we were the last to hear the teachings of the church. Moreover, we Koreans do not have a very strong character and it is very difficult for us to endure hardship. Yet, for the last ten years, since the martyrdom of Paul Yun Chich'ung and James Kwŏn Sang'yŏn in 1791, we have suffered terribly. Then this year our situation grew even worse. It has gone beyond anything that we had dreamed of or thought possible. What a pitiful state of affairs we now find ourselves in! How have things reached this extreme situation? When this persecution finally ends, unless God Above especially favors us with His Divine Providence, the Holy Name of Jesus will never again be heard in Korea.

It tears us apart to tell you this. But we hope that, when our fellow believers in China and in the West learn about the danger facing the church in Korea, they will all be filled with pity for us and share our pain. I am so bold now as to write this appeal to the Pope in the hope that he will inform the whole world so believers everywhere will resolve to use all means possible to rescue us.[5] We ask you to imitate the great compassion of our Lord and display the benevolence of our Holy Church by responding to the sincerity with which we tell you what we so desperately desire. We sinners, pounding our chests and weeping copiously, tearfully plead for you to have mercy on us. All we can do now is stand on our tiptoes and crane our necks, looking for good news to arrive from afar. Please, Your Excellency, have pity on us even though, with just this letter, we are unable to tell you everything that we would like you to know.

After Father Zhou barely escaped arrest in 1795, our king at that time, King Chŏngjo [r. 1756–1800], grew more worried every day about having a Chinese subject illegally in his kingdom. The king secretly ordered a manhunt for Father Zhou but, though the search was quite thorough, our priest was able to stay hidden. Finally, the king ordered Cho Hwajin to pretend to be a believer so that he could infiltrate the Catholic community.[6] Though Cho, too, was unable to locate Father Zhou, he learned who was in the Catholic community in Ch'ungch'ŏng province. This led to a persecution in Ch'ŏngju in the winter of 1799. Most of the devout Catholics there were killed in that persecution.

Let me now tell you in detail what has happened to the Catholics in Korea. There was a *chungin* named Thomas Ch'oe P'ilgong who had an upright character and a steadfast will. He was only concerned about righteousness and did not think much about making money. He appeared to stand head and shoulders above the rest of us in his enthusiasm for the faith and in his determination. Unfortunately, however, in the Sinhae [1791] persecution he was induced to renounce Catholicism. King Chŏngjo was very pleased with his renunciation and rewarded him with both a wife and a government post. Thomas had no alternative but to meekly accept those gifts from the king. However, in recent years, Thomas stayed at home, grieving over the mistake he made in 1791. He kept thinking that he should risk execution in order to make up for that sin. In the eighth month of 1799 King Chŏngjo suddenly summoned him to the Board of Punishments and asked him, "Do you still cling to that perverse way of thinking?" This gave Thomas the chance he had been waiting for. Knowing that it would cost him his life, he did not equivocate but spoke out about how Catholicism taught loyalty and filial piety. This lifted the burden of guilt from his heart. He spoke so clearly and powerfully that all who heard him were moved by his words. However, the officials in the Board of Punishments were alarmed and angry at what he said and sent a report to the king saying that Thomas should be executed. King Chŏngjo, rather than ordering further punishment, commanded instead that Thomas be released. This upset officials in the Office of the Inspector General, who sent a memorial to the throne demanding that Thomas be executed. The king gave a somewhat equivocal response to their demand, showing his inclination to be tolerant. That quieted things down for a while.[7]

There was a man named Martin Yi Chungbae, who was a secondary son of a member of the Disciples Faction. He lived in Kyŏnggi province in Yŏju.[8] He was braver than anyone else and had a vigorous spirit. He spent a lot of time with his close friend Kim Kŏnsun [1776–1801]. After Kim became a Catholic, Martin followed him into the church and was baptized. After his baptism, his enthusiasm for the faith was so strong it was as though he was on fire with love for the Lord and His church. He did not try to hide the fact that he was a Catholic. Instead, he strode boldly about, not caring what people knew about him. In 1800 he prepared to celebrate Easter by cooking some dog meat and brewing some alcohol with fellow believers in his village. They then gathered together along a narrow out-of-the-way mountain path and made a lot of noise singing sacred hymns celebrating the resurrection, beating on gourds and wine jars to keep time. When they finally finished singing, they drank that alcohol and ate that meat. When they finished drinking, they sang again. They went on like this all day.

Before long a hostile family reported to the authorities what they were doing, and Martin, along with eleven of his friends, was arrested and taken to a local government office. Some of his friends were weak and found it difficult to keep their faith when law enforcement officials were vigorously trying to force them to renounce it. However, by relying on the strength Martin displayed to encourage them, they were all able to resist and refused to recant. Though they were severely tortured several times, they remained firm in their faith. As a result, they were kept in prison rather than being released.

Martin knew a little about medicine but had not been known to be particularly skillful in treating illness. After he was imprisoned, however, people came to him for medical treatment. When they did that, he would first pray to God for help and then apply acupuncture or provide medicine. Whenever he did that, in every case, the patient recovered. Soon word began to spread far and wide of his healing power, and people began flocking to the prison to ask for his help. Soon the front gate of the jail was as crowded as a market. The officials could not prevent this from happening. In fact, when one of them was ill, he would come and ask Martin to heal him. Because of this, even though Martin and his friends were in prison, they never lacked for the necessities of life.

Kim Kŏnsun once remarked that, if people asked Martin about his healing skill, out of concern that he might become too well-known, he would deny that he could heal everyone and instead would say that he could only successfully treat about eight or nine of every ten people who came to him. However, in actuality, he was able to cure ten out of ten, and even a hundred out of a hundred. There was no one he failed to treat successfully. One prison official, impressed by his success, asked to look at his book of prescriptions. He answered, "I don't have any medical manuals. The secret of my healing power is in love and devotion to God. If you want to study medicine, you ought to believe in the Lord." The jailer said, "All your books have already been burned, so how can I study them?" Martin smiled and said, "The book I have in my heart was not burnt and it is enough to teach you to receive the faith."

One of their fellow prisoners, John Wŏn, had an old maidservant.[9] She dropped by frequently to take care of him. When she did that, she would always tell him how difficult things were for his family. She kept trying to persuade him to renounce his faith. But John was not moved by her entreaties. However, one time she said something that distressed him greatly. Martin gave her such a sharp look that the old maid was afraid and did not dare to finish what she was saying and left. After that, she finally stopped coming and said, "That piercing glare of scholar Yi is terrifying. I can't go back." In prison Martin wrote down sacred texts from memory and recited prayers aloud. He lectured on the Way and encouraged everyone to become Catholic. One prison guard was so moved by Martin's words that he became a zealous believer.

Kwŏn Ch'ŏlsin was a member of the Southerner [Namin] Faction, a branch of the Easterners. He was a son of a proud lineage.[10] He lived in Yanggŭn in Kyŏnggi province. Originally it was through the study of the classics and ritual that he became a famous scholar. When Catholicism came to Korea, his whole family became believers. Because they were a well-known family, their involvement with Catholicism had attracted a lot of attention and they had come under harsh criticism. His brother Ilsin died in the persecution of the Sinhae (1791) year.[11] After this Ch'ŏlsin did not dare to openly follow the commandments and precepts of the faith.

Nevertheless, the hatred his enemies had for him grew only worse. In the summer of 1799 a band of evil people from his neighborhood made false accusations against him at the local government office. The Kwŏn family children were upset by this, and it turned into a major incident. Because the local official there was bright and good-hearted enough to see through those false accusations, he did not pursue those charges. That evil group did not accept that result and, in an even more insidious plot, secretly joined forces with some officials in the capital.

In the fifth month in the year 1800, a report was made to King Chŏngjo directly that, "In Yanggŭn the evil learning is thriving. There is no one who does not study it and no village where it is not present. But the magistrate is unconcerned and does not even look into the matter.

This region's local government should be censured." The king accepted their recommendation, and the magistrate, accepting responsibility for not doing more to rid his district of Catholicism, resigned. After a new magistrate arrived and assumed responsibility for administering that district, the old charges against Kwŏn and his associates were revived. As a result, quite a few people were arrested. Ch'ŏlsin himself was old and afraid so he went up to Seoul and hid there for a while, so the government imprisoned his son instead of him.[12] The son requested many times to be punished in the place of his beloved father but the magistrate would not allow it. He desperately wanted to put Ch'ŏlsin himself in the jail in Yanggŭn but, in the end, was unable to do so.

Even though the king was suspicious of Kwŏn and worried about the spread of Catholicism, he did not want every minor incident to turn into a major issue. Also, he feared that Father Zhou's presence in Korea, and the government's search for him, could cause problems for Korea's relations with China, if China found out how the Korean government was dealing with a Chinese subject within its borders. Therefore, since 1795, though many of his ministers asked him to be very strict in his prohibition of Catholicism, the king had just left the issue for lower-level officials to deal with, not wanting to become too openly involved. Nevertheless, all the persecutions that occurred in the countryside were the result of direct secret orders from the king, though he pretended he did not know what was going on. He wanted to avoid arousing the Catholic community so that he could have Father Zhou secretly arrested and locked up in a hidden location to put an end to the problem. Before he could carry out that plan, King Chŏngjo suddenly died.[13]

Kim Yŏsam was from Ch'ungch'ŏng province.[14] He and his two brothers were all baptized Catholics. In order to escape persecution, they moved to the capital and lived there, but after that Kim Yŏsam's faith grew cold and he renounced his Catholicism. He even joined a gang of thieves. His two brothers were unable to stop him. There was a man named Yi Anjŏng who was also from Ch'ungch'ŏng province and lived in the capital.[15] He was comfortable financially. Yŏsam was poor, but he was related to Yi Anjŏng through marriage and thought he could take advantage of this relationship to improve his lot in life. However, Anjŏng could not help Yŏsam as much as Yŏsam wanted him to help him, which caused Yŏsam to hold a grudge against him. He constantly ground his teeth in frustration. Then Yŏsam found out that Anjŏng regularly received the sacraments. He foolishly thought, if Father Zhou had encouraged Anjŏng to share his property with him, then Anjŏng would not dare to disobey. So the main reason Anjŏng did not give him any of his property must be that the priest did not encourage him to do so. Thinking this way, Yŏsam transferred his resentment to the priest and came up with a plan to cause trouble for Father Zhou. He secretly informed a head of a local police unit of the whereabouts of Father Zhou.

That police officer and his subordinates had been searching for the priest for five or six years but had not yet been able to catch him. Hearing where the priest was made that police officer very happy, as he could finally end his search successfully. He promised that once he caught the priest, he would give Yŏsam a lucrative government position and then asked Yŏsam where the priest was staying. At that time Father Zhou lived at Columba Kang's house.[16] Yŏsam was also able to figure this out and said to the police officer, "On such and such a day come to our house and I will tell you where the priest is." Before the day they had set, Yŏsam went to a friend's house and suddenly became ill and was unable to return to his own home right away. On the agreed upon day the police officer went to Yŏsam's house but, as it was empty, he did not stick around. Luckily there was one believer who learned that a police officer had gone to Yŏsam's house. Curious about this, he checked around and learned the reason for that policeman's visit. He told Father Zhou what he had learned. Father Zhou then quickly moved to another location. Father Zhou also told Yi Anjŏng to prepare several dozen strings of coins and make amends with Kim Yŏsam. When that was done, Yŏsam calmed down and no longer harbored such anger and resentment. Not many days later, King Chŏngjo passed away. The king's death made government officials so busy that they were unable to follow up on Yŏsam's promise of information.

After this incident, Yŏsam was never again able to find out where Father Zhou was staying. He figured out that he would not be able to catch Father Zhou all by himself and instead started plotting with some disreputable fellows. However, they were no more successful than Yŏsam had been on his own. Frustrated by their lack of success, after a while all they wanted to do was harm Father Zhou.

For about two hundred years, high officials and those related to them have been divided into factions struggling with each other for power. The major factions are the Southerners, the Patriarchs, the Disciples, and the Little Northerners. We call them "the four colors." In the later years of King Chŏngjo's reign, the Southerners split into two subfactions. On one side were people like Yi Kahwan [1742–1801], Chŏng Yagyong [1762–1836], Yi Sŭnghun [1756–1801], and Hong Nangmin [1760–1801].[17] These men had all once been part of the Catholic community but had publically renounced involvement with Catholicism in order to stay safe from persecution. Even though outwardly they did quite a bit of damage afterward to the Catholic community, in their hearts they still held onto core Catholic beliefs and sometimes even entertained the hope that they might be able to earn the crown of martyrdom. However, their faction was small, weak, and isolated and therefore was in a dangerous position. The opposing side of the Southerner Faction included Hong Ŭiho [1758–1826], Mok Manjung [1727–1810], and others who were convinced that Catholicism was a danger to Korea. This group attacked the Catholics.[18] Over the last ten years, since 1791, the animosity between those two sides has grown in intensity.

The Patriarch Faction also split into two subfactions. The one called the "Flexible Faction," so-called because it is seen as the faction that changed with the times, respected the king's wishes and generally supported his policies. They were the high officials whom the king trusted and kept close to his heart. The other is called the "Intransigent Faction," so-called because it is seen as the faction that held firm to its own positions and often challenged the king by advocating policies it preferred to his.[19] That faction considered the Flexible Faction to be its primary enemy. The Intransigent Faction was much stronger than the Flexible Faction, and King Chŏngjo was afraid to cross them. This year the Intransigent Faction got the whole country to listen to them.

Yi Kahwan was the best literary talent of his generation, and Chŏng Yagyong is more talented and has a sharper mind than anyone. Before 1795, the king favored and employed them but after that year gradually grew colder toward them. They were deeply hated by the Intransigent Faction, which wanted to harm them.

Even though Yi Kahwan and his associates had withdrawn from the Catholic community and even attacked Catholicism, the Intransigent

Faction continued to single them out for criticism as being involved with "evil practices." However, King Chŏngjo always protected them, and the Intransigent Faction was not able to do much harm to them. But then King Chŏngjo passed away. Because the heir was still a child, the Queen Dowager of the Kim clan became his regent, ruling behind the throne.[20] The Queen Dowager, who is the stepgrandmother of King Chŏngjo, was aligned with the Intransigent Faction. Her natal family had been kept from political power by King Chŏngjo, and therefore, as the years went by, her resentment of him grew, but she was unable to vent her anger.[21] Then suddenly she found herself in control of the government. She locked arms with the Intransigent Faction and began spreading her poison. In November of 1800, as soon as King Chŏngjo's funeral was over, she expelled members of the Flexible Faction from the government and, in the process, emptied half of the court.

The evil gang that had long attacked Catholicism had close links with the Intransigent Faction. Seeing that the times had changed, they rose up with a roar and caused a great disturbance. In April of 1800 the members of the "Association for Illuminating the Way" [Myŏngdohoe] were actively cultivating their own faith and sharing that faith with others.[22] The Catholics who were not members of that association were greatly moved by their enthusiasm and began to also dedicate themselves to transforming others. From fall through winter the numbers of those converted rose day by day. Women and girls made up two out of three of those converts. The uneducated and those on the lower rungs of society made up another one third. Men from elite families feared persecution, and so they accounted for very few believers.

In the 1795 persecution, the woman believer Columba Kang [1760–1801] did the great service of protecting our priest. She was very talented, and so Father Zhou gave her a lot of responsibility. Columba was very enthusiastic in her duties and converted many people.[23] She was from a relatively high-status family background. This allowed her to work among the wives of officials, many of whom became Catholics. Such women were free to join the Catholic community because, except in cases of treason, married women from yangban families are not normally punished for violations of the criminal code.[24] Therefore such people were not worried about the consequences of becoming Catholics. Indeed, Father Zhou wanted to take advantage of this and make it the foundation for promoting Catholicism and so he was especially generous with his time with them.[25] Much of the success in the spread of Catholicism is because of the efforts of these women. However, this is also the reason a lot of rumors spread about the Catholic community.[26]

Catholicism became the major concern of the court in 1801, as soon as the new king ascended the throne. His officials were determined to clear up that problem right away. However, at first they did not know how to go about doing that. Father Zhou warned us to be more careful. All the believers grew worried. Then, on December 27, officers from the Board of Punishments arrested Thomas Ch'oe and locked him up.[27] He had been briefly arrested earlier last year, and then he had been released without any clear determination of how he was going to be dealt with. So his re-arrest was not a surprise. However, at this time the persecution was limited in scope. The court had not yet strictly prohibited Catholicism and therefore, though the believers were on their guard, they were not too worried.

Two days after Thomas Ch'oe was arrested, his paternal cousin, Peter Ch'oe P'ilche, was arrested at sunrise.[28] That was the day of the Feast of the Presentation.[29] Peter Ch'oe was in a small room inside a pharmacy on the side of a road. He and a number of other people were reciting the scriptures. A squad of policemen who were supposed to keep an ear out for sounds of gambling happened to walk by the window to that room (unsavory elements in society are known to gamble for money and so the ministry of justice has always prohibited it).[30]

The policemen heard the sound of people beating their breasts inside that room and took it to be that of coins being thrown down and clanking against each other, and so they thought they were gambling. They forced open the door and burst into that room but did not find any gambling going on there. They searched everyone in that room and found a Holy Card with a prayer written on it. However, they were unable to read that writing and therefore did not know what sort of object that piece of paper was. Taking it with them, they left the pharmacy to show the Holy Card to an official who could read it. That is when they learned that the writing on it was Catholic writing. The police then came back to arrest them. At that time the day was already bright and the other Catholics had already left. Only Peter and Stephen Oh were arrested and taken to police headquarters, where they were put in the same cell as Thomas.[31] Policemen from the Seoul Police Station then went out and grabbed Kim Yŏsam and other unreliable sorts and made them their spies. They dispatched them all over the country to look for signs of Catholic activity. The Catholic community was in a state of panic, but as the year drew to an end, things calmed down.

On the ninth day of the first month of the lunar year, the general secretary of the Myŏngdohoe, John Ch'oe, was arrested.[32] After that, policemen from the Seoul Police Station were busy arresting people everywhere day and night. They arrested so many people that both of the jails in the capital were full. (There is a jail in the eastern part of the capital as well as in the western part.) Most of those arrested were uneducated people, recent converts, and women from various back alleys, so there were not very many who were strong and brave enough to hold on to their faith.

Two days later, on the eleventh day of the first month of the lunar calendar, the Queen Dowager, in her capacity as Regent, issued an order strictly prohibiting Catholicism. It read,

> The late king always said that if proper learning was widely elucidated, then perverse ways of thinking would disappear on their own. Now we have learned that not much has changed. Perverse scholarship has reached from the capital into Kyŏnggi and Ch'ungch'ŏng provinces. Each day it grows even stronger. How can I not be disheartened about this, and concerned? In the capital and in the provinces we will strengthen and clarify the five-family mutual collective responsibility system. If there is one person inside a five-family group who is Catholic, the group head will report him to the government and that Catholic will be punished. If he does not repent, he will be punished according to the law against rebellion. We will cut out Catholicism at its roots so there will be nothing left to sprout up again later.[33]

Catholics began to be harassed everywhere and the situation grew worse every day. Finally it reached the point where Catholics had no place to go.

The chairman of the Association for Illuminating the Way [Myŏngdohoe] was Augustine Chŏng Yakchong [1760–1801], the youngest of three older brothers of Chŏng Yagyŏng.[34] He first lived in Yanggŭn, but during the persecution in the fifth month of 1800, he brought his entire family up to Seoul. Augustine had long been the subject of severe criticism for his leading role in Korea's Catholic community. In the summer of 1800, there was an evil official who, in an audience with the king, specifically singled out Augustine by name as someone who ought to be put to death.[35] Thanks to the king's scolding of his accuser, the attack on him stopped at that time.

However, Augustine saw that the situation had grown much worse than it had ever been before and that the persecution was likely to become even more intense. He grew worried that he would not be able to escape arrest. He took the holy items and books in his possession and put them in a basket along with Father Zhou's letters and gave them to another family for safekeeping. After a short while, they too became worried about having such items in their home. They wanted to return them but were afraid they might be caught by the police, so they had Thomas Im disguise himself as a seller of firewood and smuggle that basket out of their house covered with dried pine leaves.[36] At dusk on the nineteenth, he went out on the road carrying the basket. It was too big, and the covering of leaves was too thin, so it did not look like he was really carrying a bundle of firewood. A city policeman who was on the lookout for someone illegally selling meat (butchers were not permitted to ply their trade within the city of Seoul) saw him and suspected that he was doing just that. He grabbed Thomas and took him to the local government office. When the basket was opened for inspection, the officials there were astonished to see holy books and statues and even the priest's letters. They forwarded both the basket and Thomas to police headquarters. That discovery was like pouring oil on a fire. What had been a minor persecution suddenly exploded into something much bigger.

After the letters and books were seized, all the Catholics were terrified and feared day and night for their safety. However, ten days or so passed quietly without incident. In the beginning of the second month, Yi Yugyŏng, the commander of the Seoul police headquarters, was given another position in the government.[37] The new police commander, Shin Taehyŏn, looked into how this Catholic problem had been dealt with and released from both prisons everyone who had repudiated Catholicism.[38] Only Ch'oe Thomas P'ilgong, his cousin Ch'oe Peter P'ilche, John Ch'oe Ch'anghyŏn, and Thomas Im Taein were kept in jail.[39] Some people say Shin wanted to beat them and kill them. Others say there was talk of banishing them far away.

Then the arrests stopped for a while. The Catholics were happy and hopeful that there would be no more incidents. But the Little Northerner Faction member Pak Changsŏl, the Patriarch Faction member Yi Sŏgu, and the Southerner Ch'oe Hyŏnjung followed each other in succession with memorials that attacked Catholicism in the harshest terms and proposed that Catholics be punished as traitors.[40] They also asked that Shin Taehyŏn be disciplined for not being harsh enough against the Catholics. The queen was infuriated by what she heard from them and ordered Shin reassigned to the Board of Personnel. She also had the four people he had kept in his jail moved to the State Tribunal.[41]

According to the laws of our country, officials and traitors are under the jurisdiction of the State Tribunal. The police are responsible only for thieves and other common criminals. When commoners commit a crime, the Board of Punishments interrogates and punishes them. Most of the Catholics were commoners and were under the jurisdiction of the police. They should have been dealt with according to the laws for thieves and other common criminals. Instead, they were moved to the State Tribunal, which indicated that they were going to be treated as traitors.[42]

On the ninth day of the second month, Yi Kahwan, Chŏng Yagyong, Yi Sŭnghun, and Hong Nangmin [1751–1801] were imprisoned by the State Tribunal and, on the eleventh day, Kwŏn Ch'ŏlsin and Chŏng Yakchong were also arrested. At the same time, the police were told that they should not have released those Catholics earlier and should now track them down and incarcerate them again. Also all the prisoners who were held at Yŏju and Yanggŭn were transferred to the State Tribunal.

Anyone in the capital or in the countryside who was known to be a Catholic was arrested. No one was able to escape. Policemen rushed down the roads across the country to look for Catholics day and night. It was said that the State Tribunal, both of the jails of the police court, and the jail of the Board of Punishments were so full that there was no room for any more prisoners.[43]

On the twenty-fourth day, Columba Kang and her whole family were imprisoned, and, after this, a large number of married *yangban* women were arrested.[44] However, I was not able to learn much about what happened to them.

When Augustine Chŏng was interrogated, he was asked whom that box of documents belonged to. Augustine acknowledged that it, and everything in it, was his. His interrogator then went through the books and letters one by one and questioned him about each book and letter, but Augustine's lips were sealed and he did not answer.[45] The government then sent someone to Augustine's family to tell them, "All that your husband and your father has to do is tell us the name of the priest and where he is staying. If he does that, he won't die. Instead, he keeps his mouth closed and endures our beatings. Since you are members of his immediate family, you must know what he knows. Think about whether you want the head of your family to die and tell us what you know." Each and every member of the family responded that they didn't know anything.[46]

Then the high officials met and decided that those arrested were guilty of "high treason and immorality." On the twenty-sixth day of the second month,[47] six of the arrested Catholics, including Augustine, John Ch'oe, Thomas Ch'oe, Francis-Xavier Hong,[48] Hong Nangmin, and Yi Sŭnghun, were beheaded together. Later on, another nine people were beheaded.[49] There were three women, one of whom was Columba Kang and two whose names I do not know, and six men whose identities I am not sure of. Those men may have been Peter Ch'oe and his colleagues, but I haven't heard in detail who was in that group, so I do not dare to state that as certain fact.[50] As for the people who were arrested in Yŏju and in Yanggŭn, all were sent back to their hometowns and executed by beheading. However, I have not yet been able to investigate those executions so I cannot provide you with any detailed information about them.

The *chungin* John Ch'oe Ch'anghyŏn [1754–1801] was the general secretary of the Myŏngdohoe. He was a distant relative on his father's side of Matthew Ch'oe, who was martyred in 1795.[51] He was from a family that had for generations defined itself by its adherence to the highest moral standards, so when Catholicism first came to Korea he was among the very first to show an interest in it. John was even tempered, prudent, clear minded, dedicated, and hard working. He was that way twenty years ago, and he was still that way this year. He had not changed at all. He had a face that radiated innocence and sincerity. He did not say much, but when he spoke, it was always appropriate. If someone was worried about something or was distraught with anxiety, with just one look at his face they would realize that their problems were not that great and that it would not be too difficult to overcome them. When they heard just a few words fall from his lips, they would feel as if a heavy burden had been taken from their shoulders. When he expounded on our Way, people who heard him found that what he had to say was quite detailed as well as both interesting and illuminating. Even though he did not talk in a particularly polished manner, and did not prepare in advance to impress his listeners, people enjoyed listening to him and no one was bored by what he had to say. What he said penetrated deeply into their hearts, so they derived a lot of spiritual benefit from his words.

Being meek and modest was a manifestation of his natural character. He did not stand out from a crowd. Nor did he engage in any noticeable improper behavior. He had the reputation as the most virtuous member of our small Catholic community. There was no one who did not love him and trust him. Because his family was from the Ipchŏng district in Seoul, the name he used with believers was Kwanch'ŏn.[52] When Cho Hwajin was spying on Catholics in Ch'ungch'ŏng province, he learned that there was someone known as Kwanch'ŏn who was a leader of the Catholic community. However, Cho did not know his real name or where he lived and therefore was not able to arrest John. About this same time, John realized the persecution was about to get a lot worse and left his own home to hide in the home of a fellow Catholic. However, on the fifth day of the first month of 1801, he became ill and had to return to his home to recuperate.

On the ninth day, in the middle of the night, Kim Yŏsam led a police station commander to his house. They arrested John and took him to the jail. After about ten days, they began interrogating him. He was struck thirteen times with the club that was used to beat only those accused of the most serious offenses.[53] While he was being beaten, he kept completely silent and simply lay still as though he were dead. After the flogging, while an official was enumerating his offenses, John suddenly stood up and began lecturing on the Ten Commandments. One of the officials present said to him, "You say you are filial and respect your parents. Why don't you perform ancestor rites?" John responded, "Please give that question some deep thought. When parents are asleep, they show no interest in eating or drinking, no matter how tasty what is offered them might be. So how could they be interested in sacrificial food or drink when they are dead?" That official did not know how to answer that question. Finally he ordered that John be sent to prison. Nothing was heard of him after that, except that he was beheaded on the same day as Augustine Chŏng. At that time, he was forty-three.[54]

Augustine Chŏng Yakchong had an upright character and a strong determination to do what was right.[55] He surpassed everyone else in his meticulousness. When he was young, he wanted to learn about the immortals and their techniques of prolonging life. At that time, he believed in the false theory of the Great Transformation, the end of this universe and birth of another. But, realizing there was a problem with that theory, he sighed and said, "When the cosmos undergoes this great transformation, even the immortals will not be able to escape destruction. In the end there is no way to live in this body forever. It's not worth studying those techniques."[56] Then he heard of Catholicism and gained new hope for eternal life. He became a sincere Catholic and put his whole body and soul into practicing it.[57] In the 1791 persecution, of his brothers, relatives, and friends, there were few who maintained their faith intact.[58] He was the only one who remained steadfast.

He was not very eloquent in talking about things of this world, but was as happy as he could be when he preached the principles of Catholicism. Even when he was sick or in pain or hungry or poor, he did not pay any attention to his own problems. However, if there were some principles of the Way he felt he did not quite understand completely, he forgot about sleeping and eating and instead devoted all his attention and energy toward trying to understand those principles better. Only after he was satisfied that he finally understood them would he stop. Even when he was riding a horse or traveling in a boat, he would keep his mind busy trying to understand Catholic teachings better.

If he came across someone who was not particularly bright and had trouble grasping some key points of Catholicism, he would exhaust himself trying to enlighten them. He would talk to them until his tongue was sore and his throat hurt without the slightest concern over his own growing fatigue. Even when he was talking to the most dim-witted, it was rare that they did not eventually come to understand the teachings of the church. To help those Catholics who were uneducated in classical Chinese, he prepared a two-volume summary of Catholic teachings in the Korean alphabet.[59] To compose that book, he went through the wide range of Catholic writings available to him and extracted important passages, rewriting them in his own words. He exerted the utmost effort to making Catholic teachings extremely clear so that even uneducated women and young children would also be able to open the books, read them, and understand them completely without running across any points that were hard to comprehend. Father Zhou said it would be more important for Korea than *Shengshi churao* was for China and approved its distribution.[60]

He spent so many years engrossed in studying Catholic teachings that it became second nature to him and was his normal day-to-day activity. Each time he saw a fellow Catholic, once they had exchanged the usual pleasantries, he would expound on church teachings. He could spend the whole day doing that without taking a break or talking about anything else. Sometimes in doing so he would come to an understanding of one or two points that he had had difficulties with before. Then his heart would be filled with joy, and he would pour endless praise on the person who had enlightened him.

Sometimes he would meet someone who was indifferent or not a clear thinker and did not want to listen to what he had to say. He couldn't help but feel sad when that happened. If someone asked him about any aspect of Catholic teachings, he didn't hesitate at all but instead was able to come up with an answer immediately. That appeared as easy to him as reaching into his bag and bringing out whatever was in there. In such a situation, he was never at a loss for words. He could go on and on without any verbal stumbles. Even though someone might argue back and forth with him, trying to trip him up, he was always able to come back with a rejoinder. His arguments were always well organized and clear. On top of that, he had a way with language and sprinkled his arguments with well-turned phrases. Moreover, his arguments were so detailed and precise that they were very convincing. Those who listened to him found their faith strengthened. He inspired them to be better Catholics.

Although his reputation for virtue was not as great as that of Ch'oe Ch'anghyŏn, he exceeded Ch'oe in elucidating our holy principles.

He was concerned that the powers of the Lord of Heaven were so wide ranging and the many principles of our Way were so comprehensive, and information about them was scattered among so many different books, that there was no single book someone could read to understand them all. Even someone who read all of them would find it difficult to comprehend everything. He wanted to compile the notes he had taken from various books, put them in order, and compile them into a single volume, which he would call "A Compendium of the Holy Teachings" and give it to his junior colleagues. He started a draft but did not even get halfway done when the persecution began, so he was not able to complete it.

After Augustine was arrested and put in prison, an official rebuked him for violating the king's commands. Augustine responded by unequivocally laying out for him the incontrovertibly true principles of our sacred teachings. He made it clear that he did not think it should be forbidden. That official was greatly angered that Augustine was challenging the king's orders and declared him to be guilty of high treason and immorality.[61]

Later Augustine was taken from his prison cell and put in a cart that headed off toward the execution grounds. Just before they reached their destination, Augustine, in a loud voice, cried out to the crowd watching that procession, "Don't laugh at us. That human beings are born into this world and then die to glorify the Lord of Heaven is the ways things should be. When we all come before God and He passes judgment on how we have lived our lives, we will cry no more. Instead, we will rejoice. And at that time you will no longer be able to laugh. Instead, you will be cast into the deepest misery. So do not laugh at us now." As he descended from the cart and moved toward the execution site, he turned toward those who were watching him approach his execution and said, "Do not be afraid. This is something we have to do. There is nothing for you to be afraid of. After I have died and it is your turn, imitate the way I faced death." The first chop of the sword cut only halfway through his neck. He then sat up suddenly, made a large sign of the cross with his hand, and then calmly lay back down. He was executed with Thomas Ch'oe. He was forty-two years of age.[62]

Thomas Ch'oe was old and very sick. He was in prison for a long time and had become dejected and listless. When he got into the cart he was no longer concerned about the things of this world. When they came close to the execution ground, however, he began to have a joyful expression. He was the first to be executed. He was fifty-six years old.[63]

Francis-Xavier Hong Kyoman was the maternal uncle of Kwŏn Ch'ŏlsin and lived in Kyŏnggi province in P'och'ŏn district.[64] When he was a young man, he passed the *chinsa* exam and later in life liked to study the classics.[65] The Kwŏn family became Catholics and he also became a believer. He gave up the idea of entering the government and, urging his neighbors to convert to Catholicism, he became the head of his village. His daughter married a son of Augustine Chŏng.[66] This led to him being widely criticized. Subsequently he was arrested and martyred.

Paul Hong Nangmin was originally from Ch'ungch'ŏng province in the Yesan district.[67] While still young he passed the *chinsa* exam and moved to the capital. There he became friends with Yi Sŭnghun and Chŏng Yakchong. Sometime between 1784 and 1785 he began to believe in our holy teachings and passionately elucidated its principles in order to better manage the affairs of the Catholic community. He won praise for doing so. However, so that he did not attract the attention of the broader community, he did not give up taking the civil service exam. In 1799 he passed it and rose as high as the Fourth Censor in the Office of the Censor-General.

During the Sinhae persecution, King Chŏngjo forced him to renounce his faith. As a result of that, he appeared outwardly to be a bad person. Those people who renounced their Catholicism at the same time as Paul did not continue to engage in devotional practices, but Paul did not stop reading the scriptures, and he continued to abstain from meat on the days Catholics are supposed to fast.[68] In 1795, when the arrival of Father Zhou finally made it possible for him to receive the sacraments, he received baptism and was preparing to receive absolution for his sins through the sacrament of confession. He had not yet made that confession when a major persecution broke out. Then someone by the name of Han Yŏngik (1767–?) informed on him, saying that he had reverted back to Catholicism. Paul again publically denounced Catholicism under pressure from the king. From then on, when he was at home he observed all the rules and regulations Catholics are supposed to follow, but when he went out he followed the evil ways of the world.

In 1799 his mother passed away and he did not perform the prescribed ancestor rites that required him to bow before an ancestral tablet. In recent years his faith had grown somewhat stronger and he longed wholeheartedly to return to the Lord.[69] Before this righteous desire could be fulfilled, he was arrested and executed. His situation in prison was kept very secret. Therefore I do not know in detail what happened to him, but considering his intentions, it can be guessed that, because the charges against him were not all that serious, if he had repudiated his faith when he was arrested, then he certainly would not have been killed. However, since he was decapitated, we can be sure that he did not betray the sacred teachings.[70]

Peter Yi Sŭnghun (1756–1801) was the nephew of Yi Kahwan (1742–1801) and was also the brother-in-law of Augustine Chŏng.[71] When he was young he passed the *chinsa* exam. He liked to study and probe into philosophical principles. Yi Pyŏk, a scholar without any official office, was very impressed with him.[72] At that time, Yi Pyŏk was secretly reading Catholic books. Yi Sŭnghun did not know anything about that. In 1783, when Sŭnghun was getting ready to follow his father to Beijing on a diplomatic mission, Yi Pyŏk secretly asked him a favor, saying, "There is a Catholic church in Beijing and in that church there are some missionaries from Europe. Go and see them and ask for religious books. Also ask to be baptized. The Western missionaries will certainly be pleased to see you and will treat you well. Then you will be able to get a lot of interesting and enjoyable things from them. You must not come back empty handed." Sŭnghun did as he was asked and went to the church and requested baptism. Because he did not understand the key points of Catholic doctrine, at first the priests all refused to baptize him. He was able to be baptized only because Father Yang overcame the objections of the other priests and did so.[73] Father Yang then gave him quite a few Catholic books.

After Sŭnghun arrived back home, he began studying these books intensely with Yi Pyŏk and some others. They began to understand for the first time the true principles of our faith and this led them to convert their family and friends. At that time, there were many famous scholars who accepted Catholicism. Yi Sŭnghun became their leader. Afterward, however, his father found out and gave him strict orders to withdraw from that Catholic community. He also had some wicked friends who stirred up trouble by criticizing him. However, Sŭnghun endured and kept the faith.

Our late king thought Yi Sŭnghun was talented and, in the fall of 1790, granting him the *ŭm* privilege, appointed him to be a district magistrate in Pyŏngt'aek.[74] In the Sinhae year (1791) he was arrested because of his association with Catholicism. He then renounced Catholicism and wrote many essays and poems criticizing the faith. But none of that was an expression of how he really felt. In 1795 he heard that a priest had come to Korea. His heart was moved and, repenting, he prepared to receive the grace of the sacraments. A few days later, however, a persecution broke out, and Sŭnghun, just as before, shrunk back with fear. Because he was the very first to bring Catholic books to Korea,[75] the evil gang who attacked Catholicism naturally named him in their attacks and called him a criminal. The king protected him throughout these twists and turns. Though outwardly Sŭnghun followed the ways of the world, sometimes he would meet with a close friend from the old days. He would then remember what he used to share with them, and would want to rejoin the community they had once formed.

Then persecution broke out again. Because he had committed the crime of bringing Catholic books to Korea, even though he had repeatedly renounced Catholicism it was difficult for him to escape execution. Therefore, I do not know if he died a martyr or not. I will soon look into this matter and find out.[76]

Yi Kahwan was recognized even when he was still young as exceptionally talented and he grew even more impressive as he matured.[77] His writing was the best in the country. There was no book that he had not read. His memory was much better than that of a mere mortal. In addition, he was well versed in the study of astronomy and geometry. He used to sigh and say, "When this old man dies, that will be the end of geometry in this Eastern Country."[78] Though not strongly so, he originally believed in the *i-ki* metaphysics.[79] However, every time he looked at the Heavens he would sigh and say, "Seeing this great order, how can it be said that the universe is without a Lord that governs it?"

When he was over thirty, he placed first in the preliminary civil service exam, earning the *chinsa* degree, and King Chŏngjo looked upon him as someone with great promise. Sometime between the end of 1784 and the beginning of 1785 he heard that Yi Pyŏk and some others had converted to Catholicism. He rebuked them, saying "I have also read several volumes of Western works (Yi Kahwan had some Western books at his home, including *Zhifang waiji* [Records of countries not listed in the Records Office] and *Xixue fan* [Scholarship in the West]).[80] They provide some novel information about exotic people and places, but they are only useful for recreational reading. It is true that such books can expand our knowledge, but how can they help us develop a moral character and put us on the right path?" Yi Pyŏk countered with a logical defense of the contents of those books. Kahwan found that he was unable to respond, so he asked if he could borrow some of those books and carefully examined them. Yi Pyŏk had several volumes of *Tianxue chuhan* [An introduction to Heavenly Learning], and at that time he also had a volume of *Shengnian guangyi* [The sacred calendar of the lives of the saints].[81] But he feared that Kahwan would not believe the miraculous tales in that latter book, so he was unwilling to loan it to him to read. Kahwan insisted, and in the end he convinced Yi to lend him the books he had on hand at that time.

Kahwan studied them intensively over and over again and was convinced by them, saying "These contain true moral principles. This is the True Way. If what these Western books say is not correct, then everything in them is slander and blasphemy against Heaven. If what they preach were not true, those Westerners would not cross the ocean to share their teachings with us. They would be struck by lightning and die for their blasphemy against Heaven if what they taught were not true." In the end, he encouraged his students to take seriously what those books said and met secretly in the morning and at night with Yi Pyŏk and his group. His faith was quite strong.

At this time Yi Sŭnghun and the others were illicitly performing the sacraments.[82] Kahwan encouraged people to be baptized, but he himself was not baptized. He wanted to go as an envoy to Beijing and receive baptism from a Westerner there. Before long he saw that the atmosphere of the country at that time was not conducive to such involvement with beliefs and practices from the West, so he stopped studying those Western books. However, since many of his family and relatives were among those who were vilified as Catholics, the evil gang always pointed to him as the leader of the Catholics.

At the time of the 1791 persecution he was the magistrate of Kwangju [in Kyŏnggi province, near Seoul] and took that opportunity to severely persecute the believers there in order to clear his name. The use of the laws against bandit gangs to indict Catholics started with Kahwan.[83] After 1791 King Chŏngjo was inclined to appoint more Southerners to high government posts. Kahwan took advantage of this change in the political situation to assume a number of top government offices.[84] He rose to serve as Minister of Public Works. In 1795, after three Catholics had been martyred, the evil gang charged Yi Sŭnghun and his group, including Kahwan, with pretending they did not know that a priest had entered Korea.[85] The evil gang repeatedly sent memorials to the throne attacking them. King Chŏngjo saw that he could not continue to shield them against those accusations. He exiled Yi Sŭnghun to Yesan. Kahwan was demoted to magistrate of Ch'ungju.

There was a Catholic in Ch'ungju who was often criticized for his faith. Kahwan punished him severely and tried to force him to renounce his Catholicism.[86] The use of the leg screw torture (which is the strongest punishment that can be used on criminals) on Catholic believers began with Kahwan.[87] Moreover, Kahwan brought into his household a government courtesan as his concubine.[88] He hoped doing all this would let him escape the charges that he was a Catholic. However, in the end it was of no use and his official career came to an end. He then stayed at home and entertained himself by reading. His wife always had a deep faith. She converted her daughter, daughter-in-law, his concubine, and the women slaves. Sometimes Kahwan found Catholic books in his house, but he did not investigate further or forbid the women from studying and practicing Catholicism. In 1798 and 1799, he heard that persecutions had arisen, one right after another, in the countryside. He said confidentially that he believed that, "This is like striking ashes with a club. The more you strike, the more they rise up. Though the king wants to eliminate Catholicism, in the end, there is nothing that can be done."

When he was first brought into the State Tribunal for interrogation, he still denied that he was a Catholic. The officials running that the prison were all longtime enemies who hated him and wanted him dead. Kahwan knew that, in the end, he could not escape, and so consequently he confessed what was in his heart. He never again renounced his Catholicism, even when he was facing death. He died from being beaten severely and being branded with a hot iron. He was sixty.[89] This was a few days before the six leaders of the church were executed.[90] Kwon Ch'ŏlsin was also flogged to death, but I do not know whether he had a good or bad death.[91] Please wait until I can learn more about what happened to him.

Peter Ch'oe P'ilche's style name was Chasun. He was the younger paternal cousin of Thomas Ch'oe. His family was poor and his parents were old. He sold medicine to make a living. His prices were reasonable and the material he used was pure, so all the people trusted him. He had a sincere and honest manner and a trustworthy appearance, so when people looked at him they knew that he was a worthy man. Although Thomas was as brave and steadfast as anyone, he was always in awe of Peter. Though Peter was his younger cousin, Thomas consulted with him in all matters before he acted. He did not dare to do things on his own. Thomas had a younger relative who would slander Catholicism and criticize Catholics. However, he did not dare to criticize Peter. He would say that Peter was the only Catholic he respected and the rest of them were worthless. Father Zhou praised Peter, saying, "Among those married couples who express a desire to remain chaste, few are able to succeed in the end.[92] But the determination of Chasun and his wife to live a celibate life together has only grown stronger. They have really worked hard to be good Catholics. They are truly virtuous."

After Peter was arrested, his father, who originally was not a Catholic, was so alarmed and worried that he became sick. Realizing that he was near death, Peter's father confessed belief in the Lord, received baptism, and died. Peter was in prison and heard about his death and asked to be allowed to attend his funeral. The official ordered him to return when the funeral was over. However, Peter could read between the lines and see that that official was hinting that he should just stay away. Peter was not willing to do this. After the funeral, he returned to prison even before he was required to do so. In the end he was decapitated. He was thirty-two years old.[93]

In the past, Peter and his friends had each said that they hoped to be decapitated and die for the faith. He achieved his desire, and it happened as he had said. Some have reported that perhaps Peter could not stand the flogging and betrayed our faith. Others say that, since he was not released from prison, Peter must have continued to proclaim his faith and for that reason was killed. I have not yet found out which is true. Therefore I am still unsure.[94]

Joseph Kim Kŏnsun was a member of a Patriarch Faction family.[95] His family was from Yŏju in Kyŏnggi province. His ancestor Sanghŏn greatly contributed to the preservation of the dynasty.[96] Therefore generation after generation of his descendants were given government posts and were members of our nation's elite. When Joseph was a child he was very clever. At the age of nine, he even intended to study the way of the immortals who were said to live in the mountains.[97] When he was young, he received instruction on the *Analects* at the village school. When they reached the sentence "Respect spirits but keep your distance," he asked, "If we ought to respect the spirits, then we ought not to keep our distance. If we ought to keep our distance, then we ought not to respect them. So how can we both respect them and keep our distance?"[98] His teacher was not able to respond.

In his home he had for a while a copy of *Ten Chapters by a Nonconformer* [*Jiren shipian*].[99] Joseph enjoyed reading it. When he was around ten, he had already written a work entitled "Discussion of Heaven and Hell," proving that they must exist. When he grew a little older, he developed a broad range of knowledge on such subjects as literature, the Confucian classics, history, medicine, geography, Buddhism, Daoism, and military strategy. There was no field of knowledge that he was not familiar with. When he was eighteen, his adopted father died. He saw that the mourning clothes of Korea followed the regulations of the Song Confucians and so had fallen from the ways of the ancient past, so he corrected them. Some ignorant Confucian scholars were surprised at this and sent a letter to him rebuking him. He wrote a book responding to their objections. His citation from the classics showed what was correct and he matched every objection they raised. Yi Kahwan looked at it and sighed and said, "I don't dare compare myself with him."

At home he was faithful, loyal, sincere, and respectful. He became well known in his home region as a virtuous man. His family had long possessed great wealth but he poured out his property joyfully, bestowing it on those who needed it. What he ate and wore was simple, like what the poor ate and wore. He was so very well respected that, each time he went to Seoul, people got in their palanquins and on their horses to go out and catch a glimpse of him. Everyone thought they were fortunate if they had a chance to talk with him.

He had formed a close lifelong friendship with Martin Yi [Chungbae] and five or six other people. That group of friends wanted to board a boat and travel to the province of Zhejiang someday, and then go on to Beijing and meet the Western missionaries face to face. They hoped that they then could learn many useful techniques they could use to lift the living standards in Korea after they returned home and taught them in their own country. Because they became Catholics, their plans did not come to fruition. They were all martyred for the Lord.[100]

At this time, Catholics from the literate class were all members of the Southerners Faction. There was not a single Catholic who was a member of the Patriarch Faction. Although Joseph was really impressed with Catholicism, because of his factional affiliation there was no way for him to join the Catholic community. By happenstance he met a believer in the countryside and was able to see a statue of the archangel Michael. He mistakenly thought Catholicism to be some sort of mystical practice and consequently performed magic with Kang Ich'ŏn (1769–1801).

Kang Ich'ŏn was a well-known member of the Little Northerners [*Sobuk*] Faction, but he was not a very stable person. He thought that the current dynasty was on its last legs and that soon there would be a great upheaval that would cause it to fall. He wanted to learn some mystical practices so that he would be prepared to take advantage of that chaotic situation and gain a powerful position in government.[101] Joseph did not know this and mistakenly befriended him.

Father Zhou heard that Joseph was a wise and virtuous man and sent him some books in the hope that they would convince him to become a Catholic.[102] Joseph was surprised and pleased to receive those books and, when he read them, found them quite persuasive.[103] He discarded everything that he had studied up to that time, and from then on his mind focused only on the Lord. At that time he was twenty-two years of age. Among his close friends, there were none that did not become Catholic. Only Kang Ich'ŏn was unwilling to convert. A few months had passed before what Ich'ŏn had been up to was revealed, and it suddenly became a serious criminal matter. Joseph was implicated in

Kang's plot, but King Chŏngjo, recognizing that Joseph was talented, protected him so that he was able to escape punishment.[104]

After his baptism, his faith was as hot as fire. When his father and his older brothers learned that he had become involved with the Catholic community, they tried to stop him by giving him a strict order forbidding any such religious activity. For three or four years there was not a time in his house during which he did not suffer. The slander against him increased. Joseph looked innocent and humble, like a simple person who did not know anything. Because of this, people respected and listened to him all the more. I am not yet able to learn about the details of his imprisonment and how he held up under torture. I only heard that, when he was about to be executed, he spoke to the people at the execution ground, saying, "Holding office or having a good reputation in this world is of no real significance. I earned some degree of respectability and was able to serve in office, but that is not worth very much. I have cast it all away and will not take it with me. Only this Holy Teaching of the Lord of Heaven is completely true and real. Even if because of this I will die I will not abandon the faith. Adhere to this closely." Finally, he was executed by decapitation. At that time he was twenty-six years old.[105] Among the people in the capital, there were none who did not sigh with regret.

Kim Paeksun (1769–1801) was from Seoul and was a paternal cousin of Kŏnsun. His family was very poor, but he did not care much for worldly honors or riches. His ancestor Sangyong (1561–1637) served the country as a prime minister. In the ninth year of the Ming emperor Chongzhen (1636), the army of the Great Qing [The Manchu] captured Kanghwa province.[106] Sangyong was righteous and refused to surrender to them. Instead, he let himself die in a fire he himself set.[107] Because of this, a shrine was erected in his honor and a red gate proclaiming that he was an exceptionally loyal subject was placed in front of his house. After the fall of the Ming to the Manchu, an Altar of Great Gratitude was installed in the royal palace so that rites could be conducted for the emperors Wanli and Chongzhen of the Ming dynasty. Every year the king would lead the descendants of the loyal subjects who died in 1636–1637 into that shrine and perform a kowtow before that altar.[108]

After that ritual was over, the king would prepare the materials for a special civil service examination and would allow those who had participated in the ritual but had not yet passed a higher level exam to take that examination. This is called the "special examination honoring the loyal and the virtuous."[109] Paeksun was the only eligible person who refused to participate in the ritual, saying, "Taking part in such a ritual is not the proper way to show respect for China. Those who take part in the ritual today only do so in order to have a chance to take the exam. They are not sincere at all. I refuse to join them in this ritual."

For a few years, he went along with the people who criticized and slandered Catholicism. Moreover, he concentrated on studying to become an official. But then he noticed how dangerous a life in public office had become and lost his desire for personal advancement up through the ranks of the bureaucracy. He read the books of the Song Confucians and in his studies plumbed the depths of what they wrote about human nature and principle. However, he found some problems with their discussions of what they called the moral path and decided that he could not rely on what they wrote. Then he turned to the writings of Laozi and Zhuangzi.[110] That is when he began thinking that, though a person may die in that his body ceases to exist, he nevertheless still exists in some form. He discussed this new idea with his friends. They laughed at him, saying, "What you are saying is really weird. You must be some sort of Catholic."

When Paeksun saw that his friends were suspicious of him, he thought to himself, "Obviously, I can see things other people cannot see. However, those who listen to me think I am spouting the Catholic line. If that's the case, then there must be something to this Catholicism." That is when he began making some Catholic friends. After a few years of talking things over with them, he finally became a firm believer. He began to strictly obey the commandments and the precepts. His mother also became a devout Catholic. However, his wife was stubborn by nature and continued to press him to become a worldly success and advance to a high post in the government.

One morning, finally realizing that her dreams would not be realized, she could no longer contain her frustration. She exploded and heaped abuse and insults on him. His family, fellow faction members, relatives, and friends joined in criticizing and cursing him. Paeksun was not swayed even in the slightest by this. His mother's brother even came by to try to persuade him to change his way of thinking, but in the end he, too, was unsuccessful. Frustrated, he said, "Since you won't listen to anything I have to say, I don't want to have anything more to do with you and will no longer consider you a member of my family." Paeksun replied, "If that is the choice you give me, it is better for me to end my relationship with my uncle than end my relationship with the Lord." Among his old friends there was not one who did not write him a letter to him severing their friendship. Even his clan decided to throw him out of the family, but he was unshaken. He always said, "Since I have confessed my belief in the Lord, my heart is as unmovable as a mountain." He was decapitated on the same day as Kŏnsun. He was thirty-two years old. He was not a Catholic for long, so he had not yet received baptism and had no baptismal name.[111]

Luke Yi Hŭiyŏng (1756–1801) was a close friend of Joseph. He first lived in Yŏngju but later moved to Seoul. He was an artist and good at painting holy pictures. He was also executed by decapitation.[112]

Philip Hong P'ilchu was the son of the first wife of the man who later married Columba. He was good and virtuous by nature. He followed his stepmother's examples and became a Catholic. At that time, he was not yet thought of as hardworking and conscientious. However, after helping the priest for a year, he was changed into an extraordinary person. The people all wondered at it. In his home he always assisted our priest when he conducted mass. When he was arrested and put in prison, the officials applied torture in order to get him to tell them where Father Zhou was. Despite that torture, Philip did not tell reveal Father Zhou's whereabouts. Finally he was beheaded. He was twenty-eight years old.[113]

Columba Kang was the daughter of a *yangban* father and a non-*yangban* mother. She was articulate and brave, and never wanted anything other than what was right and proper. When she was young, she stayed in the women's quarters and at that time dreamed of becoming a saintly person, but did not know how to do that. Following those around her, she chanted prayers to the Buddhist "savior" Amit'abul.[114] In her teens she came to understand things better and saw that Buddhism was full of absurdities and hard to believe. At that point, she stopped engaging in Buddhist practices. When she grew a little older, she became the second wife of Hong Jiyŏng of Tŏksan after his first wife died.[115] Her husband was not a particularly bright fellow, and, on top of that, he was not an easy man to get along with. Therefore she was always depressed and wanted to escape from the mundane world. Then, when Catholicism reached Ch'ungch'ŏng province, she heard for the first time the three-character phrase "The Teachings of the Lord of Heaven." She pondered this phrase and said, "The Lord of Heaven is the ruler of heaven and earth. That is a good name for teachings. What it teaches must certainly be true."

As soon as she obtained a Catholic book and took a look at it, her heart was drawn to it and she became a believer. Her intelligence, diligence, passionate faith, and self-control allowed her to overcome the troubles she would come to face. She converted her whole family to Catholicism, and she even went to neighboring villages. However, Jiyŏng was wishy-washy. When his wife encouraged him, then he would say "sure, sure" and act like a Catholic. But then an evil group would come along and sharply criticize Catholic teachings, and he would say "yes, yes" and follow what they had to say. His wife would rebuke him, and then he would cry and repent of his sins and then his friends would come again and he would immediately become like he was before. Columba did everything she could to save him, all to no avail. She finally realized that she could not stay with him any longer.

During the persecution of 1791, which created all sorts of turmoil in her home village, she entrusted her farmland to her husband and took her children to Seoul.[116] From Seoul, she was able to help Sabas Chi when he needed to travel to Beijing.[117] In 1795 she was baptized. When Father Zhou saw her for the first time, he could tell she was a good person. Delighted, he appointed her to be head of the Catholic women's association and made her responsible for managing women's affairs in the Catholic community.

During the persecution of the fifth month of 1795, she took the lead in arranging hiding places for Father Zhou. She took it upon herself to hide him in her home and did everything she could to protect him. When police showed up at her front gate looking for Father Zhou, they always had to go away empty-handed. After that persecution died down, Father Zhou decided to stay in her house.

For six years she helped Father Zhou with the important work of the church, and he really appreciated her help and had a lot of respect for her. There was no one who worked as closely with Father Zhou as

Columba did. Columba regularly provided Father Zhou with food, clothing, and lodging and everything was working out just fine. When necessary, she represented him in church matters outside her home, and she did a good job of managing such matters, never making a single mistake. Many unmarried women came to her home to receive instruction from her. When she had finished teaching them, they went back to their respective homes and encouraged people to believe in the Lord. She herself traveled a bit to attract people to the church. She worked hard night and day and rarely had time for a decent night's sleep. She had a clear understanding of Catholic teachings and was very good at explaining them, so she converted more people than anyone else did. In managing church matters, she was firm, decisive, and stern, and the people all stood in awe of her. However, she was eventually arrested and taken to a police station to be interrogated. The officials there asked her where Father Zhou was. Despite having to endure the leg screw torture six times, her voice and complexion never changed. The two wicked guards standing around her said, "This one is a god, not a person." In the end she was executed by decapitation. She was forty-one years old.[118]

Our late king, King Chŏngjo, had an older half-brother by a royal consort.[119] The son of that royal sibling got caught up in a rebellion and ended up dead. The king then exiled his half-brother to Kanghwa Island. Calls came from all over the country for the king to have his stepbrother put to death, but he refused. The wife of that exiled stepbrother and even the wife of the rebel son were allowed to continue living in the palace that had been their home before this whole unfortunate incident happened.

Around 1791 or 1792 a Catholic woman who had come to pity them began encouraging them to convert. But other people around them warned them that would lead to a lot of trouble, so they avoided contact with Catholics. However, Columba then entered the picture. Eventually she was able to convince them to accept baptism and join the Myŏngdohoe. Everyone who heard about this grew concerned. Just as their friends had feared, government officials eventually learned that they had joined the Catholic community, and they were forced to drink poison. Moreover, the former king's ill-fated stepbrother, though he had never been a Catholic, was also ordered to commit suicide by drinking a cup of poison because his wife and daughter-in-law had become believers. Unfortunately, I do not know the family names or the baptismal names of the two wives.[120] Nor do I know the exact dates for the deaths of those who were martyred after Peter Ch'oe.

Peter Cho (?–1801) was from Yanggŭn. His father, a widower who lived in poverty, struggled to make a living as a farmer. Though Peter was close to thirty years old, because of his family's poverty, he had not yet had his capping ceremony,[121] nor had he been able to find a wife. He did not have a very strong constitution and was frequently ill. Moreover, his overall physical appearance did not leave a very good impression. On top of that, he did not seem very bright. He was the laughingstock of his village. No one thought very much of him. But then he began to study under Augustine Chŏng. Unlike the others, Augustine praised Peter, saying that he was impressed by Peter's dedication to the faith.

In April of 1800 Peter and his father moved to Martin Yi's village in Yŏju. When Martin was arrested, Peter and his father were arrested at the same time. When Peter was being interrogated, he refused to cooperate. That made his interrogator very angry. He shouted at Peter, "If you do not follow my orders, I will kill your father." He then grabbed Peter's father and beat him mercilessly right in front of Peter. Peter could not resist any longer. In order to save his father from being beaten to death, he told the official that he would renounce his Catholic beliefs and practices. Peter was then told he could go home. As he was walking out the gate of the prison, Martin and the others called out to him to think about what he was doing and encouraged him to repudiate his renunciation. Their words caused him to think twice and to regret the sin he had just committed. He turned around and told the man who had just released him that he was withdrawing his renunciation. Angered by this, that official threw Peter back in prison, never to release him again. After that, every time the Catholics in that prison were interrogated, though the others were beaten no more than the law allowed, Peter received extra strokes, and those blows had more force behind them. The people working in that prison had thought of Peter as a weakling who would easily give in, but when they discovered to their surprise how stubbornly he clung to his faith, their hatred for him grew and they wanted to kill him.

He stayed in prison for eleven months. It is said that, during that time, Peter impressed his fellow prisoners with his words and deeds. However, right now I cannot remember the exact details of all he did while he was in prison. If I obtain more information later, I will let you know.

While he was in prison, Peter was baptized by one of his fellow inmates, since no priest was available. In the second month of 1801, he was once again harshly interrogated by the prison officials who, one more time, ordered him to abandon Catholicism. Peter responded by saying "There are not two Lords in heaven above, nor can a human being have two different hearts. I have nothing more to say to you, except through my death." He was locked away again and died several days later in prison on the fourteenth day of the second month.[122]

Louis-Gonzaga Yi Chonch'ang was beheaded in Kongju for the crime of proselytizing in Ch'ungch'ŏng province. However, he had a history of renouncing his faith, so I am not sure what he did right before his execution. Some say that he died a martyr's death. I cannot be sure if that is true or not.[123] I've also heard that one person was martyred in Chŏngsan and another in Yesan, but I still don't know who they are.[124]

In Chŏlla province, the ten years following the 1791 persecution were free of attacks on Catholics, so the numbers of believers there grew substantially. But early in the fourth month of 1801, Augustine Yu of Chŏnju and Francis Yun of Kosan were arrested along with more than two hundred others. Only an impoverished scholar by the name of Han from Kimje, and a commoner named Yŏgyŏm, whose family name was Ch'oe, because they were unwavering in their dedication to the faith, were executed, suffering decapitation.[125] All the rest gave into government pressure and left the church.[126]

Those in the capital who renounced Catholicism as well as those in the provinces who did so were exiled to remote locations. There were a great many of them. However, Augustine Yu and his brother, as well as Francis Yun, because they were leaders, were not sent into exile right away, but were instead moved to a prison in Seoul.[127] After Thomas Kim was arrested, because he confessed that he had carried messages between the Catholics in Korea and the priests in Beijing, was also transferred to the prison in Seoul.[128] I have not been able to find out yet if he died or was sent into exile.

According to some non-Catholics, over three hundred were either executed or died in prison.[129] This does not include those outside the capital region. Since the founding of the Chosŏn dynasty, there has never been a year in which so many people were killed by the government. I do not yet know if I can believe this figure or not. I also do not know who among them died despite renouncing their faith or which of them were actual martyrs. The only ones the Chosŏn court wants to completely eliminate are those of high social standing who are able to write classical Chinese. They do not care about the illiterate lower classes. Even if they knew they were Catholics, it sometimes let them go anyway. If they were punished, their punishment was comparatively light. Most of the Catholic commoners in the capital have managed to stay alive.

As for what happened during the first half of the second month, since I was an actual eyewitness, I can provide you a detailed account. But as for what happened afterward, I can only rely on what I heard from others, and therefore all I can report is rather sketchy and I cannot vouch for its reliability. The accounts I have provided of martyrs are based on reliable reports I have personally heard and on things I have known for quite some time. However, all I can provide you is a general account of what happened. I do not dare to give you a report that goes beyond what the evidence allows. However, I am afraid there may still be some errors in what I have written. I will keep investigating and will let you know when I learn more details about what has happened here in Korea to our small Catholic community.

I can tell you that Father Zhou spent most of the time after 1795 inside Columba's house. Sometimes he would travel around to different places, but only Columba, and no one else, knew where he went. When the persecution was just getting started, one Catholic man, seeing that the situation was growing dangerous, became worried that it would be difficult to keep Father Zhou safe.[130] He went out to the countryside to get in touch with some believers who were in hiding. They prepared a couple of good hiding places for our priest. That Catholic then returned to the capital, visited Columba, and implored her to let him have a meeting with the priest. He wanted to tell Father Zhou about this plan so our priest could escape the persecution and stay safe. But Columba told him, "We have already found a safe place for him. There is no need for him to move again." This believer did not give up at first but kept pleading with Columba until he finally realized his pleas were in vain and left. Five or six days later, the full-scale persecution erupted. That Catholic, fearing for his own safety, fled far away with his family.

As for Augustine Chŏng, when he was captured by the government and subjected to intense interrogation, he did not reveal anything about Father Zhou's whereabouts. When the government also seized Columba and her son and subjected them to severe interrogation as well, even when they knew their lives were in danger, they refused to say anything about where our pastor might be hiding. Then the government brought Columba's female slave in for questioning.[131] They used the leg screws on her when they interrogated her. She could not endure such torture and gave them the information they wanted, including Father Zhou's age and a description of what he looked like. One of the government officials then went back to Columba and said, "Your slave has told us the priest was in your home. You can't keep things from us anymore. You must confess where the priest has gone." She responded, "It is true that at one time the priest stayed in my home but he left quite awhile ago. I don't know where he is now."

The government then distributed notices with a sketch of the priest on them, offering a reward to whomever turned him in. They searched for him all over the country. Sometime around the middle of the third month, Father Zhou surrendered himself to the authorities (I do not yet know at whose house he stayed, how he came to give himself up, or the exact date of when he turned himself in).[132] He walked right through the gate of the State Tribunal. The staff there were surprised and asked who he was. He responded, "I, too, am a Catholic. I've heard now that the Chosŏn government has issued strict orders outlawing Catholicism. A lot of innocent people have been killed because of this. My staying alive won't help them at all. Therefore I have come to die with them." They then dragged him inside, where an official recognized that he was the priest they had been looking for and threw him in jail. At that time, they only shackled his feet and did not subject him to harsh interrogation. I've heard that while he was in prison, since his Korean was not very good, he was interrogated in writing many times, but none of the other Catholics who were in prison were actually able to see him.[133] However, some non-Catholics were saying that someone who called himself a Westerner had turned himself in to the authorities.[134]

Six of the Koreans I discussed earlier were all executed on the charge of treason.[135] But, after the priest turned himself in, word spread among people in the capital that a certain "Western scholar" who had been thrown into prison insisted that Catholics are not traitors. It was also reported that he did not want to die quietly but wanted to first explain his beliefs and his conduct. Such reports are probably true.

After the middle of the fourth month, the Chosŏn court ordered the commander of the Royal Guards to execute our priest by cutting off his head, which he was then to display on the front gate of the military headquarters (This was often done after a criminal was beheaded). Saying that he was ill, the commander did not go to his office for three whole days. After those three days, the government dismissed that "ill" commander and replaced him with a new commander, who then carried out the sentence.[136]

Our priest was first dragged out of the prison and subjected to torture. They struck him on his shins thirty times. They then carried him through the streets of Seoul to the execution ground. Seeing a crowd gathered to watch him, he called out that he was thirsty and asked for something to drink. His military escorts gave him a cup of alcohol, and he drank all of it. They then took him ten *li* south of the city walls, to a military training site (it was a sandy spot above the river and was called Noryang).[137] Once there, they stuck arrows through his ears. The soldiers then had him read the text of the sentence that he had received, detailing what his "crimes" were. There was a lot to read, but he remained composed throughout. When he finished, he stuck out his neck and was immediately decapitated. It was in the afternoon of the nineteenth day of the fourth month, which was the feast day of the Holy Trinity.[138]

As soon as his head was cut off, a wind as strong as a typhoon suddenly blew across the execution ground, black clouds filled the sky and blocked the sun, deafening thunder roared, and blinding lightening flashed.[139] Everyone who was there at the time was startled, and frightened.

One believer who was in flight three hundred *li* away and another, also in flight, who was four hundred *li* away, felt that strange wind and heard that thunder as well.[140] They knew something extraordinary had happened. It was so strange that the date it occurred on was engraved in their memory. Later they heard that was precisely the time when Father Zhou had been executed.

The priest's severed head was put on public display for five days, but it was guarded day and night and no one was allowed to come near it. After a while, the commander ordered the guards to bury it. It was kept under strict guard as before. The Catholics were able to ferret out where the head was buried and began planning to rebury it somewhere else in the future. A certain evil official petitioned the court, saying, "This person ought not to be buried. I request that an order be issued that his head be again exposed to public view." The Queen Dowager directed that this be done. The commander who had ordered the head buried pleaded for this new directive to be rescinded, saying, "We have already buried it. Why do we need to do anything more with it? The matter has already been settled." In the meantime, the guards watching over the tomb, who hated this onerous duty, had secretly moved the grave. A few of the Catholics here have been searching everywhere, but have not yet been able to find it.

When Father Zhou was executed, in the official proclamation of his sentence it was written that he was from Cheju Island. That was done so that they would not have to report his execution to China. They didn't want China to know that they had knowingly executed a Chinese subject.[141] After Father Zhou died, the persecution quieted down a bit, but the investigations and arrests have not yet stopped completely. Many of those who were arrested are still in prison. Among them are nine more people who, it is reported, will be executed. However, this is an unconfirmed rumor. I do not yet know if it is true or false.

When Father Zhou first came to Korea, there was an informant who let the king know there was a foreign priest in his kingdom. Consequently, for the last seven years, there was not a time when our priest did not have to be cautious and apprehensive. He could not dare to offer the sacraments widely. Not many people were able to receive the grace of the sacraments, and most of those who did were women. There were quite a few devout Catholics in the countryside as well as some commoners in Seoul who were not able to benefit from the sacraments. This group of people has patiently gone through hard times, but they continued to hold out hope that the situation here would improve. However, things did not become better, and so, even when they were within their own houses, they did not dare to utter the word "priest."

Because of some evil people, the situation unexpectedly became even worse, and then the priest they had waited so long to meet was executed and his severed head displayed for all to see. After that, ten years of sincere effort came to naught in one morning. We Catholics feel like we have suffered a severe blow to both our bodies and our souls. The pillar we had relied on to support us in both life and death has gone. There is none among us who is not heartbroken and fallen into despair. We have no idea of what to do now.

In order to comfort them, some of us sinners told the other Catholics, those who never got a chance to meet with him,

The only reason our priest came to Korea was to offer us salvation. How could he not have wanted to go about the whole country helping us all be saved? But there were too many obstacles in his path and he couldn't do what we wanted to do and share with all of us the love he felt for us in his heart. Now he has had his life on this earth brought to an abrupt end. But the aid he can offer us from heaven, where he is now, will definitely be greater than what he could do for us when he was on earth. So don't turn your backs on what we have been relying on and don't give up on the hope he gave you. In fact, you should be even more hopeful than you were before. Don't waver the slightest in your dreams.

However, their faith is now mixed with doubt. Even though they were somewhat comforted by my words, they are still in mourning nonetheless. I'm afraid there has never been a situation as bad as this before. Even though the persecutions that occurred in the West in the past were worse than this, some priests survived, and the sacraments were still available. That's how our sacred teachings managed to survive and how souls could still be saved.[142] But the situation here in Korea is totally different. Our situation is much more hopeless. When sheep lose their shepherd, they still are able to find some grass to eat to keep alive. When a newborn baby loses the mother that was nursing her, she still has some chance of survival. But we sinners in this sad land cannot think of any way we can move forward, no matter how hard we try.

We wretched sinners were born in a part of the world that has long been in darkness. Providentially we have become people of God. Because we always remember our good fortune, we have dedicated all of our thoughts and efforts to praising the name of the Lord so that we may repay even one ten-thousandth of the debt we owe for the special grace we have received. We did not expect to suddenly run into the roadblock that is now causing us so much trouble. We had once heard that the blood of martyrs is the seed of the church.[143] But unfortunately our humble country has Japan as a neighbor to the east. Those island barbarians are cruel, and they have cut themselves off from all contact with the Lord. Our government is looking at what the Japanese have done and appears to think that such a successful suppression of Catholicism is possible here as well.[144] How can this not cast a chill of fear over our hearts?

We Koreans are not a very strong people. Nor are our laws as vigorously enforced as they are in Japan. However, there are not many Catholics who have the knowledge or courage to lead us. We are only a few thousand ignorant commoner men, women, and children. There is no one here who can lead us out of this morass. There is no way to rouse our people from their feelings of hopelessness. If things continue like this, we will not be able to go on for much longer. Even if the government does not launch another persecution, in ten years the Catholic Church in Korea will disappear on its own. Alas, how it pains me! How can I endure seeing the complete extinction of the Catholic faith in our country while I am still alive?

We sinners have managed to survive the disasters of this year so far and are both fearful and grateful. We are grateful to the Lord for His grace and for preserving our lives. At the same time we are afraid that our sins are so many that we will not be saved. We sincerely desire to spend the rest of our lives exhausting ourselves in devotion to the Lord but we lack not only wisdom but also strength. How can we die and go into the grave harboring resentment at the loss of our priest and the suffering inflicted on the church in our land? In the midst of our sorrow, who will have pity on us and console us? We only want to come before your merciful throne so we can tell you our tale of woe and appeal to you for help. But rivers and mountainous terrain separate us from Your Excellency. We look up hopefully but cannot reach you. We are frustrated and anxious. How can we go on like this?

We sinners were both shocked and saddened when we learned that Father Zhou had surrendered himself to the government. We fear that if his activities and execution are reported to the Chinese court, then the church in China will be implicated and suffer persecution. If that happens, then there will be no hope for the faith in our country. We worry about this late into the night and are even more anxious about what will happen to the church in China than in our own country. Fortunately, because of the Lord of Heaven's powerful protection, the foundation of the Catholic Church in Korea is unshaken, and we sinners are still alive. John is also safe.[145] It is clear that it is the Lord's will that you, Great Father, are entrusted with shepherding the East. How can we sinners not inform you of what is in our hearts, while looking up to you in the hope that you can help us? We have told you everything and implore that you see what can be done to help us.[146]

Among the many countries of the world, our country here in the East is the poorest, and within it, we Catholics are poorer still. Only a handful of us have escaped poverty. In 1794, we were not able to prepare adequately to welcome Father Zhou into our country and so, after he arrived, we hastily tried to do everything at once and so nothing was done right. We were inexperienced and did not manage things properly. Because of our poverty and inexperience, we failed to do what we should have done and so things turned out as they did.

Nevertheless, in recent years the number of Catholics has gradually increased. Our financial situation grew a little better than it was before but we still did not manage things properly. Moreover, some of the people we brought into our community were unsuitable. As a result, we have suffered severely from these disastrous persecutions. This has led to our current financial difficulties. Those who suffered from this year's persecution have lost their homes and families. Anyone who wanted to live fled to safety. We are poorer now than in 1794, when Father Zhou first came. Even if we had a plan to do something to improve our situation, we do not have the resources to do much of anything. We are pretty much destitute right now. However, if we just had a little more in the way of financial resources, we might be able to do something. There is no one in our small group of survivors who is really outstanding, but there are a couple of people who can help us rebuild the church. We can work together.

We have faced many problems since 1795. There are two reasons for this. The first is that the late king grew very concerned when he learned Father Zhou had entered Korea and wanted to track him down. The second is the intense hatred of the Patriarch Faction toward the Southerners, whom they made great efforts to entrap. Now the person our late king was so worried about is dead and those the Patriarch Faction were jealous of are gone. Catholics who were known to be such are all dead. Therefore it is possible that when this year is over the persecution might die out.

There is also hope for us in the countryside. In Seoul there is now in force a five-family mutual responsibility system.[147] However, the law is strictly enforced only in areas where Catholics live. In areas where there are not any Catholics, it is a law in name only and so the people can relax and do not have to worry about having to take flight.

Regarding the situation in the provinces, originally there were many believers in the provinces of Kyŏnggi, Ch'ungch'ŏng, and Cholla. Those who fled the recent persecutions escaped to Kyŏngsang and Kangwŏn provinces. Therefore government spies are searching all those five provinces thoroughly for Catholics. There were never many Catholics in Hwanghae and P'yŏngan provinces, and no one sought refuge in those places, so they are quiet now and the common people are not on the lookout for Catholics there like they would be if the five-family mutual responsibility system were being enforced. Though those two northwestern provinces are not all that far from Bianmen,[148] and therefore there are border guards nearby, after a couple of years, if nothing attracts their suspicion, the border officials will gradually become careless, making it possible for us to make use of that region.

As for how we can manage the affairs of the church here, before the persecution broke out, we Catholics took it as our duty to spread the good news of the Gospel far and wide. Now we can no longer do that. Instead, we take as our primary duty protecting what remains of the Catholic community in Korea. We have fortified our communities and keep a strict watch over it so as to guard against the dangers posed by spies and informers. Those of us who are already baptized encourage each other to keep the faith. Those who are not yet baptized receive instruction in the teachings and precepts of the faith. Together we reverently pray for help from the Lord and quietly wait for an opportunity to strengthen our threatened church's position so that we will no longer fear for our safety.

In 1794, we were so pleased with our good fortune that Father Zhou had been able to enter our country that we became careless. It was then that we made our first error by allowing Father Zhou to conduct pastoral work and offer the sacraments too openly, bringing us to the government's attention. Eventually we found ourselves in a position where we could not do anything. What's done is done, and we cannot undo the mistakes we made. However, we have learned from our missteps and are now more careful and discrete. If we can avoid being careless in the future then there is no reason for further difficulties to arise.

We cannot accept things the way they are now and simply sit and wait to die. We have to do something. Unfortunately, we need some financial resources before we can even begin talking about a plan for going forward. Never in our wildest dreams did we expect that the survival of Catholicism in Korea as well as the salvation of our very souls would depend on filthy mammon.[149] If it is only because of a lack of money that Catholicism is disappearing in Korea and we are losing our chance for salvation, how can our grief at the injustices we are suffering be alleviated? Therefore, we are so bold as to petition you for assistance.

Prostrating ourselves before you, we beseech you to beg all the countries of Europe in the West to support the Catholic Church in the East and provide us what we need to save our souls. If we are given assistance, we will manage it carefully. Once we have made the proper preparations, we will approach you to ask that you send us another priest, someone who can dispense the sacraments necessary for eternal life. All we ask, Your Excellency, is that you feel compassion for us and look upon us with pity.

We do not want to impose a burden on you or be presumptuous, but if we are silent and therefore do not seek help, or seek help but do not obtain it, it will be as if we were already dead. But if we seek assistance from you, even if you are unable to help us, then we can die without regrets that we did not do enough. That is why we are so bold as to write to Your Holiness in this way. We have bared our souls to you and, looking up with humility, beseech Your Holiness to, in imitation of the Gracious Lord's benevolence and remembering our weakness and destitution, bring our hopes to fruition and fulfill our desires. Doing so would be a great blessing for the Catholic faith and for our souls. If we sinners receive this grace of not being forsaken, we will again be able to walk the road of life and will do our best to do whatever you ask us to do.

However, reviving the church in Korea is not something that can be done in days or months. To set up everything and carry out our plan properly will take at least three years. There are two barriers we have to overcome in order to bring a priest across the border into Korea. The first is that Chinese and Koreans have different hairstyles. Chinese shave the front of their heads while we Koreans do not. However, it is easy enough for people to let the hair on their head grow longer. The second problem is the fact that Chinese and Koreans speak different languages. That is a more intractable problem. However, if you can send a priest here who can speak Korean well, then there will not be any great difficulties for him coming to or working in Korea. We wonder if someone from our country could go to one of your churches and teach some young gentlemen our language. After practicing for a while, they should be sufficiently proficient. What do you think of this plan?

If you agree to this plan, then we will establish a secret signal that the people who will meet can use to identify each other when they meet. They could meet after a winter embassy passes through the Willow Palisade on the way to Beijing, or, if that is inconvenient then, they could try to meet when the embassy passes through the Willow Palisade again on its way home in the spring. Such a plan has a high probability of success. It would be even better if a faithful and prudent Chinese Catholic were to move near the Willow Palisade, making sure to be very careful so as not to give rise to any rumors. If he opens a shop and begins waiting on customers, it will not be difficult to meet with him, pass letters on to him, receive letters from you, and in this way make the arrangements for a priest to be sent to us. Don't you agree that this is an ingenious plan? The lives of those of us who live in this small country in the East are in danger but it should not be too difficult to save us.

If you have the same concern for our country that Father Zhou had, then you will be happy to do this for us. We prostrate ourselves before you and ask that you seek far and wide for pious and judicious people who will lend a hand so that somehow a plan to protect the Catholic Church in Korea and provide our community with a priest can be carried out successfully.

Our country is in a dangerous position right now.[150] No matter what China ordered it to do, it would have no choice but to obey. We can take advantage of this situation. The Pope could write a letter to the emperor that says, "I want to disseminate Catholic teachings in Korea. I heard that this country is a vassal of yours and does not communicate with the outside world. Therefore I am approaching you with a request that Your Highness order this country to welcome missionaries from the West, who will teach the people to be loyal and respectful. The people will then repay with the utmost loyalty the kindness Your Highness has shown them."

If the Pope makes his request in this way, then there is a good chance that the emperor of China, knowing of the loyalty and respect that the missionaries have shown him in the past, will agree. If the emperor does so and orders Korea to accept Catholic missionaries, then the church will be able to carry out its work in peace. Since we do not know the situation in China, we do not know whether this plan would work or not. We just ask that you keep it in mind.

The Lord's grace arrived in Korea in an extraordinary way. No missionaries brought Catholic teachings to Korea. Instead, the Lord himself implanted Catholicism here.[151] After that, He bestowed His grace upon us through the sacraments, and so we have enjoyed more special blessings than we could ever count. The punishment we have suffered this year from persecution is because of our lack of gratitude for these blessings. However, because the Lord is good, our community has not been completely destroyed. Though we are in the midst of a great persecution, He has kept a path to safety open for us, showing clearly His desire to save Korea. Since the Lord desires to help, if all those in China and the West who serve the Lord put their minds together and concentrate on coming up with a plan to rescue us, then how will it not be possible to save our tiny country and so turn our suffering into joy? We sinners can console ourselves and others and continue to risk our lives to keep doing what we have been doing, if we know that you will be coming to our aid. We beseech Your Excellency to act in accordance with the will of the Lord and save us quickly.

We have listened for news of what is going on in China. We have heard that bandits are running rampant in the western part of the empire, that the Chinese military has suffered numerous defeats, and that the empire is losing territory.[152] The emperor must be worried about this. If there is someone who is trusted by the emperor and who can propose an attractive plan to him, then we can use this situation to save the Catholic Church in Korea. Have this person speak to the emperor in this way:

> It has long been a teaching of the Way that, even during times of peace and safety, danger and the threat of destruction should not be forgotten. Originally, our dynasty arose in the East and gradually built a great empire that has lasted for two hundred years. But Your Highness faces an unstable situation. If something terrible happens in the future and you are driven from Beijing, you could return to Ninggǔda.[153] However, it is too isolated and small a place and so, though you might be safe there for awhile, you would not be able to do what needs to be done to regain your power. Chosŏn is only separated from Ninggǔda by a single river that is so narrow that smoke rising from fires on one side of the river is visible from the other side, and people can shout to each other across it. Chosŏn is much larger than Ninggǔda, being three thousand *li* long, and so is more suitable as a base of operations, should you need it. The land in the Southwest is fertile and in the Northwest the men and horses are agile and strong. The mountains stretch for a thousand *li* and can provide an inexhaustible supply of timber. Chosŏn is surrounded by the ocean on three sides, and so there are abundant sources of fish and salt. The ginseng in Kyŏngsang province is abundant, and the good horses of T'amna [Cheju] Island are plentiful. Even though this country has been endowed by Heaven with such riches, the Yi dynasty is frail. However, it lingers on like a thin thread that will not snap. The Queen Dowager now controls the government, and powerful officials abuse their power. As a result, the affairs of state are in disorder. The people resent this.
>
> This would be a good time for China to just absorb Chosŏn into the Manchu homeland. That would impose Qing dress on Koreans. Then people would be able to easily go back and forth over what is now a

border. Chosŏn could be put under the authority of Ninggŭda. That would expand the home territory of the imperial family. If an "Office for Pacifying the People"[154] is established between Anju and P'yŏngyang, and an imperial relative is placed in charge of that office so that he can protect the dynasty, it will be a munificent grace bestowed by Your Majesty that will unite the people's hearts. If conditions in the empire should change for the worse, you can use that as a base to maintain control of Liaodong and Shenyang.[155] That will give you tall and rugged mountains to protect you on your eastern flank. If you raise an army, train it, and send it into action when there is a rift in the forces that oppose you, it will provide a firm foundation that will last for ten thousand generations.

In addition, the king of Korea is young and has not yet taken a queen.[156] If we give a daughter of the imperial house the title of princess and marry her into the Korean royal family, she will become queen of Korea. Then the king will be the emperor's son-in-law, and his successors will be descendants of the imperial house and so they will be completely loyal to it.[157] Moreover, we can check the ambitions of the Mongols in this way. If we lose this opportunity, then someday we may suddenly find that someone else has taken control over Korea. If they then raise a strong army, I fear that not only will we have lost the chance to use Korea to our advantage but, by letting someone else control it, we will face a new threat in our own backyard. We will regret it when that time comes but by then it will be too late. We will not be able to undo our past mistakes. I respectfully request that Your Majesty implement this plan.

You can use this general outline and change the specifics to match the circumstances of the imperial family. If the emperor follows this advice, then we Catholics can act as intermediaries, since we have experience in dealing with China. This will allow the Catholic Church to grow to the point where it will not be possible to destroy it. Since there are many Catholics in China, it will be easy for us to act as go-betweens. We will then be able to give counsel to the emperor, and he will in turn protect us. We heard that last year an eminent scholar was made an imperial envoy to Korea and that he is a relative of the empress, is close to Your Eminence, and has Catholic servants. Perhaps we can rely on him to advance our plans. If there is such a person, and he supports this plan, then hopefully the emperor will accept it.[158]

However, China must find some legitimate grounds for seizing control of Korea. If Korea has violated the terms of its relationship with China as a subordinate state, then such transgressions could be used as an excuse for carrying out this plan. In fact, the Korean state has secretly engaged in many activities that violate this relationship and is fearful lest China learn of them. For instance, Korea has promulgated its own calendar and minted its own currency. This is common knowledge in the Chinese court, but no one has raised such issues officially. If it were to be investigated thoroughly, it would be sufficient to prove that Korea was in violation of its tributary status. Integrating Korea into China would not only be profitable for the imperial family but would also not harm Korea. The Korean court right now is going through a very difficult time and may not be able to maintain its grip on power for much longer. If Korea were absorbed into China, then the disdainful looks of the wicked officials toward the king would cease of their own accord and the royal house of Yi would find itself in a much better position.

This would not only bring peace and stability to the church in Korea but would also be a blessing for the country.

Please do not think this plan is impractical, but rather accept it. In your letter last year, you said that in a few years a galleon would be sent to Korea.[159] Now our situation has become so desperate that, even if such a ship shows up soon, it may not be enough to help us. Here is a better plan. Let's force the government here to tolerate Catholicism. Even though doing so would be rather difficult, I ask you to carefully consider it. Our country's military has long been weak and is in fact weaker than any other country. On top of that, we have had two hundred years of peace, and as a result our people have no idea how to fight.[160] The king is young and without good officials to serve him. If the military should suffer any setbacks, it will crumble like a ball of dry mud or shatter like a thin tile.

Therefore, we can use military power to force Korea to leave Catholics alone. This can be done if we obtain several hundred warships loaded with fifty or sixty thousand elite troops, large cannons, and other dangerous weapons, along with three or four clever Chinese scholars who can write well. Put those Chinese scholars ashore in Korea and have them deliver a letter to the king that says,

We have come to spread Catholicism. We are not here to seize your women or your wealth but have come out of obedience to the command of His Holiness the Pope, who desires the salvation of your people's souls. If your honorable country accepts even just one Catholic missionary, we will not make further demands and will not fire one shell nor shoot one arrow nor even disturb one speck of dust or one blade of grass in your kingdom. We will establish ties of eternal peace and friendship with you, play music and dance in celebration of our new relationship, and sail away. However, if you do not accept this one servant of God into your country, then we will visit the Lord's punishment upon you. You will die, and it will be too late for you to undo what you have done. Oh king, you need to make a choice. Will you allow one man into your country so that it may escape punishment or do you wish to refuse and lose your entire kingdom? Because Catholicism seeks to make people loyal, filial, and compassionate, if Your Highness's entire country respects its teachings, then your kingdom will enjoy boundless fortune. We do not do this out of self-interest. We ask Your Highness not to doubt our words. Once Catholicism is tolerated, the benefits of peace and good governance, which are enjoyed by all the countries of the West because they worship the true Lord, will extend to every country in the East. Therefore, welcoming the missionary from the West will not cause any harm. Instead, it will only bring benefits.

If the Chinese scholars, backed by Western military might, repeatedly proclaim this message, then all the countries of the East will be so afraid that they will not dare to disobey. It would be good if the large number of ships and men I have requested could be obtained so that the plan can be carried out as I have described. However, if that is impossible, then this plan could also work with only ten ships and five or six thousand men. Several years ago a Western merchant vessel drifted close to the coastal town of Tongnae, on our country's southeastern coast. A Catholic went aboard and had a close look at it. He returned and reported, "This one ship would be a match for one hundred of ours."[161]

It is not because Koreans are cruel by nature that they persecute Catholicism. Basically, there are two reasons for the attacks on our faith. The first is the prevalence of factionalism, which leads to Catholicism being used as a pretext for attacks on political enemies. The second is that the ruling scholar class has little experience or knowledge of the outside world beyond Korea. Korean scholars only know Song Neo-Confucianism.[162] If another school of thought diverges from it even the slightest bit, they take it to be very strange and make any difference between the two to be as great as the distance between heaven and earth. Our people can be compared to a little child who was born in an isolated village and grew up spending almost all his time inside a room without seeing strangers. If one day he should accidentally meet a stranger, he would be greatly surprised and begin to cry. This is exactly what we are like. We Koreans are fearful and suspicious, and we have no match when it comes to ignorance and weakness.

It is because of this that, though Father Zhou was sentenced to death, he was not killed right away. The court was afraid his execution might spark a rebellion. Only after the officials realized that we could not launch an uprising did they have the courage to murder him.[163] Even though they have killed our priest, they are still suspicious and fearful. However, we can use their fear to end the persecution of Catholics. If the court is given the above letter by messengers backed up with force, then there is no need for us to fear that the persecution will continue. And if we awaken the scholar officials from their ignorance in this way, then, whether or not they want to see a missionary operating openly in Korea, they will not dare refuse our request, since they will clearly see what a refusal will cost them. Fearing destruction and desiring peace, they will give in to our demands. Though this plan is difficult, I am sure that it would succeed. If the situation is such that we can put this plan into effect, and we do all we can to bring it to fruition, then we will be fortunate, indeed.

There is one Catholic who said he was concerned that, aside from whether carrying out such a plan would be easy or not, we should think about what people would think of us if we followed through with this plan.[164] This sinner responded that we should not worry about that. Many Catholics have been killed in Korea over the last ten years, including our priest as well as some top officials in the government. The evil gang slandered them as traitors, and they were executed, although there did not exist the slightest bit of evidence that they had been disloyal. The fact that such good people were unfairly condemned is widely known. If the Catholics of Korea were to rise up in rebellion, it is true that would confirm the worst things that have been said about us.[165]

However, for two thousand years, Europe has served as a base for Catholicism, and it is from there that Catholicism has spread to so many countries. There is no corner of the world that has not felt Catholicism's transforming influence. Korea alone has rejected it. Korea, this tiny little country, has not only refused to accept Catholicism, it has gone so far as to block its civilizing influence, fiercely persecuting the church and murdering our priest. In the two hundred years since Catholicism came to the East, this is the first time something like this has happened.[166] If an armed force were raised in Europe to punish those responsible for these crimes, how could anyone possibly object? Jesus taught that the sin of refusing to allow the good news of the Gospel to be preached was greater than the sins of Sodom and Gomorrah. If God could destroy those two cities, then how could it harm the image of Catholicism were force brought to bear against Korea?[167]

After all, that force would be used only to awe the government into allowing Catholicism to be preached and practiced openly. It would not harm the people or lead to the seizure of their property, and so it would be a benevolent and righteous use of force. It would make clear for all to see what a good religion our religion is. How then can we be worried that such a use of force would hurt our image? My only fear is that we may not have the strength to carry out this plan.

One Catholic said to me, "I fear that should an armed force come to Korea and attempt to force the Chosŏn government to tolerate Catholicism, it would inform the Chinese court. This would lead to troubles for the Church in China." This sinner responded by saying,

> It will be easy to prevent that. The letter that will be presented to the King of Chosŏn will say "The Pope sent a priest to spread Catholicism to your honorable country but not only did you not accept him, you murdered him. If you do not allow Catholicism to be taught in your country, then I will send an emissary to inform the Chinese court that you have committed a crime by murdering Father Zhou and that we intend to punish you for your crime as well as come to the aid of the people of Korea who are suffering because you persecute Catholicism." The government fears that its crime of executing the priest,

who was a Chinese subject and so should not have been killed without China's permission, will be revealed, which would in turn lead to it being punished by China. Therefore since the Korean government will not risk letting China know about what happened to Father Zhou, you don't need to worry. Since the Chinese court will not find out about this plan, it will not cause any harm to the Catholic Church in China.

It is of the utmost importance that a shop be opened soon near the Willow Palisade; the sooner this happens, the better off we will be. As for the other parts of our plan, they should be implemented within three years or so. Then we will finally be out of the perilous situation we are in now. If we don't act now, who knows how different the world will be tomorrow?

For us sinners, right now each day is like an entire year. We do not have the strength to do anything ourselves and so with great hope we beseech you to take pity on us and quickly send us help.

Few Catholics who were known to be such have escaped this year's persecution. Those who remain have gone into hiding. They hope to keep the Catholic community alive by making it seem as if it has already been destroyed. Some Catholics manage to move around the country as traveling merchants while others have left their villages and are moving to isolated locations where they hope they will not be noticed. Quite a few of us are on the road right now. We have to hide the fact that we are Catholic believers. But every time there is a fast day people can easily guess that the travelers among them are in fact Catholics. Therefore I am so bold to ask that Catholics in Korea who are traveling be granted a dispensation from keeping both the great and small fasts.[168] This would allow us to remain in hiding and so survive.

One Catholic took a vow at his last confession to keep two great fasts a week until his next confession. Because of the persecution, he fled from his home and now wanders from village to village in the mountains. Because he stays as a guest in those villages, and often finds that the kind of food he is allowed during his fast is not available, it would be difficult to fast without revealing that he is a Catholic. Because of this, he is not able to keep the fasts and fears he has committed a sin by breaking his vow. Therefore he asks that he also receive a dispensation.[169] He also has asked whether or not he committed a sin by not keeping his vow in the past.

In this the eighteenth hundredth and first year since the descent of Our Lord, one day after the feast of Saint Simon Thaddeus, this sinner Thomas and his companions bow once more and proffer this letter.[170]

APPENDIX

Dramatis Personae: People who appear in the narrative of the growth of Catholicism in Korea in the late eighteenth century, including those who created the intellectual atmosphere within which both Catholicism and anti-Catholicism arose, those who were Catholic at least for a while, and those who were strongly anti-Catholic.

PRECURSORS: THOSE WHO PROVIDED THE PHILOSOPHICAL FOUNDATION FOR THE ATTACKS ON CATHOLICS

Ahn Chŏngbok (Sunam) 安鼎福 (順庵) (1712–1791) A Southerner (Namin) Faction Confucian scholar, his factional affiliation kept him from being appointed to a high government post. Instead, he focused on scholarship, writing a history of Korea (*Tongsa Kangmok* [An Annotated Account of Korean History]), and came to be seen as the intellectual leader of the Southerners. He also wrote a trenchant criticism of Catholicism in 1785, just as believers in that religion began to appear in Korea. That dialogue, reproduced in its entirety in this volume, was designed to stop the spread of what he feared was a dangerous deviation from Confucian orthodoxy. He was especially concerned about his son-in-law Kwŏn Ilsin.

Chinul 知訥 (1158–1210) Though he lived several hundred years before the first Catholics appeared in Korea, his ideas, particularly his insistence on how difficult it is to cultivate a moral character, continued to influence the contours of philosophical and ethical thought in Korea in the eighteenth century. Chinul is widely considered one of the greatest Buddhist thinkers in the long history of Buddhism in Korea. His argument that we still need to cultivate our Buddha nature after becoming enlightened (known as the "sudden enlightenment/gradual cultivation" argument) in order to overcome the self-centered habits we acquired before our enlightenment is reflected in the tendency of later Korean Confucians, though they criticized Buddhism, to pay more attention than Confucians elsewhere to how difficult it was to become a sage. That may be one reason some Korean Confucians in the late eighteenth century were drawn to Catholic teachings about original sin and human moral weakness, and to the Catholic promise of divine assistance to overcome our sinful nature.

Hwang Tŏkkil 黃德吉 (1750–1827) A Southerner Confucian writer, he was a disciple of Ahn Chŏngbok and agreed with Ahn that the Catholic focus on individual salvation was selfish compared to the Confucian concern for the common good.

Shin Hudam 愼後聃 (1702–1761) As a young scholar of the Southerner Faction, he visited Yi Ik and was advised by Yi to look over some books authored by Westerners that had entered Korea from China. In 1724 Shin wrote his *Sŏhakpyŏn,* a detailed critique of Matteo Ricci's *Tianzhu shiyi* [The true meaning of the Lord of Heaven], Giulio Aleni's *Zhifang waiji* [World geography], and *Lingyan lishao* [On the soul] by Francis Sambiasi. Though he lived for another thirty-five years, he appears to have lost interest in European ideas, since he never wrote anything about them again and instead spent the rest of his life studying the *Book of Changes* and *The Doctrine of the Mean.* Even though he passed the literary licentiate civil service examination, earning a "presented scholar" degree, because of his factional affiliation, he was unable to win appointment to a government post. Instead, he spent his life as a gentleman-scholar.

Yi Hwang (T'oegye) 李 滉 (退 溪) (1501–1570) He is considered to be one of the three greatest Confucian philosophers in Korean history (the other two are Yi I and Chŏng Yagyong). Yi Hwang pushed Neo-Confucianism toward moral psychology, analyzing the differences between our moral impulses and our self-centered emotions in an attempt to discover how best to pursue sagehood. He is known for his insistence that we have to control those emotions generated by *ki* (our psychophysical nature) in order to ensure that our thoughts and actions are directed by *li* (the patterns of appropriate actions and interactions). He advocated "abiding in reverence" as a way to cultivate our ability to act in accordance with *li* rather than *ki*. The Southerner Faction tended to look to Yi Hwang for philosophical advice.

Yi I (Yulgok) 李 珥 (栗 谷) (1536–1584) The Korean philosopher most respected by the Patriarchs (Noron) Faction. He respected Yi Hwang but disagreed with him on the need to sharply distinguish between *li* and *ki*. Yi I insisted that all action, including moral action, had to take place within the material world formed from *ki* and therefore, since Confucianism demanded not just moral thoughts but also moral actions, it was important to work with *ki* rather than try to suppress it. His philosophy is usually considered more activist than the philosophy of Yi Hwang, since he stressed the imperative of "abiding in sincerity," which means to always play the role in society you are supposed to play while keeping your mind-and-heart free of any concern for personal benefits.

Yi Ik (Sŏngho) 李瀷 (星湖) (1681–1763) A leading Confucian philosopher in the Yi Hwang tradition, he was seen as an intellectual guide to the Southerners. Even more than Yi Hwang did, he emphasized the difficulty of developing a moral character that would allow individuals to consistently adhere to the rigorous moral demand of Confucianism that people should let the common good rather than their own individual desires determine their thoughts and actions. Since his Southerner affiliation meant he could not serve in public office, he dedicated his life to scholarship and wrote on a wide variety of topics, including a brief discussion of the Catholic writings that had penetrated Korea from China during his time.

Yi Sugwang 李 睟 光 (1563–1628) He was a writer and Confucian scholar with wide-ranging interests. Among the many subjects he discussed in his multitude of short essays were Catholic publications from China. He is usually seen as the first Korean to take Catholic ideas seriously, though he was much more impressed by European cartography than he was by European philosophy or religion.

THE PERSECUTORS: GOVERNMENT OFFICIALS AND OTHERS WHO ACTED AGAINST THE CATHOLICS

Cho Hwajin 趙 和 鎭 (?–?) Under government orders, he infiltrated the Catholic movement under the guise of being a believer. He was the son of a *yangban* father and a non-*yangban* mother and therefore of slightly lower social status than a full *yangban*. However, under King Chŏngjo he was able to serve as the magistrate of a minor rural administrative district.

Ch'ae Chegong 蔡 濟 恭 (1720–1799) He was the leader of the Southerner Faction in the 1790s and rose to be the chief state councilor on the State Council under King Chŏngjo. He was among the more powerful voices calling for the execution of Yun Chich'ung and Kwŏn Sang'yŏn in 1791, probably because he feared the implications of the growth of Catholicism among the younger members of his Southerner Faction, which under King Chŏngjo had been allowed to fill important government posts for the first time in decades. His son by a secondary wife married a stepsister of the Chŏng brothers. She was the daughter of their father's secondary wife.

Ch'oe Hyŏnjung 崔 顯 重 (1745–?) He was a member of the Southerner Faction who served in several important posts under King Chŏngjo.

Chŏngjo, King 正祖 (r. 1776–1800) The son of a crown prince who never became king because he was killed by his own father, King Yŏngjo (r. 1724–1776), Chŏngjo believed that factional struggles were behind the reason his grandfather killed his father. He was therefore determined to control the factions among the *yangban* by appointing people from various factions to high posts. Though he was a staunchly orthodox Confucian, he tried to take a more moderate approach to the challenge Catholicism posed to Confucian orthodoxy, since many of the more talented members of the Southerner Faction he wanted to use to offset the power of the Patriarchs happened to be involved with Catholicism. He did not want a large-scale purge of everyone who had the taint of association with that Western religion, since that would have made him more reliant on the Patriarchs than he wanted to be. When he died suddenly in 1800, his policy of moderation died with him, the Southerners soon lost their posts in the government, and the Patriarchs launched a full-scale assault on the Catholic community, which, conveniently for them, included many of their Southerner rivals.

Chŏng Minsi 鄭 民 始 (1745–1800) He was the governor of Chŏlla province in 1791 and therefore was responsible for dealing with the Yun Chich'ung and Kwŏn Sang'yŏn affair. He took over responsibility for interrogating Yun and Kwŏn from Magistrate Shin Sawŏn but was no more successful than Shin had been in getting those two men to agree that they were wrong when they refused to use a spirit tablet in mourning Yun's mother. He reported to the throne that Yun and Kwŏn had, in fact, burnt their ancestral tablets, setting the stage for the royal order that led to their execution.

In the 1790s he was considered one of the more prominent members of the Flexible Faction, the same faction to which most of the politically prominent Catholics belonged even though he was a member of the Patriarchs (Noron) Faction rather than the Southerner Faction (Namin) to which most of those Catholics belonged. He held a number of high posts under King Chŏngjo.

Chŏngsun 貞 純, Queen Dowager (1745–1805) Wife of King Yŏngjo and therefore the stepgrandmother of King Chŏngjo, she ran the government as regent after the death of King Chŏngjo until 1804, since King Sunjo was only eleven when he ascended the throne. It was under her name that the 1801 anti-Catholic persecution was launched.

Han Yŏngik 韓 永 益 (1767–?) He was a Confucian scholar who passed the Confucian civil service exam and had once been part of the small Catholic community but acted as an anti-Catholic informer during the 1790s. In 1795 Han Yŏngik learned that Father Zhou was in Korea and informed Yi Sŏk, who promptly informed Ch'oe Chegong, who then informed the king, setting off the unsuccessful search for Father Zhou, which led to the martyrdoms of Yun Yuil, Ch'oe In'gil, and Chi Hwang.

Hong Nagan 洪 樂 安 (1752–?) Later in his life he appears in official records as Hong Hŭiun 洪羲 運. Although he was a Southerner and therefore a member of the same faction as the first Catholics, Hong Nagan is considered the instigator of the 1791 persecution. Hong first called for punishment of Korea's Catholics in 1787, when he learned that some young men who were supposed to be studying for their civil service exams at the National Confucian Academy (the Sŏnggyun'gwan) were meeting to hold Catholic-style rituals. In 1791 Hong, by this time a minor official in the Royal Secretariat, wrote a letter to Shin Sawŏn, the magistrate of Chinsan county, to inform him that Yun Chich'ung had omitted a spirit tablet in the mourning ritual for his mother and therefore deserved severe punishment. He sent a similar letter to Ch'ae Chegong, who was the head of the Southerner Faction and, at that time, the Second

State Councilor. This led to a search of Yun's home, which revealed that, indeed, he did not have a spirit tablet for his mother. This result was the execution of Paul Yun Chich'ung and James Kwǒn Sang'yǒn for ritual impropriety. Hong re-appeared as a major critic of Catholics in the 1801 persecution.

Hong Ŭiho 洪義浩 (1758–1826) He was a Southerner who served as a high government official under kings Chǒngjo and Sunjo. At one point early in his career he and Chǒng Yagyong were friends. However, he became an ardent anti-Catholic. He and Mok Manjung were the two leaders of the anti-Catholic Southerner Faction that joined in the persecution of Catholics in 1801. Afterward, he went on to have an illustrious career, serving as an ambassador to China as well as Minister of Rites and Minister of Public Works.

Kwǒn Ŏm 權欕 (1729–1801) He was a member of the Southerner Faction and is believed by most scholars to have been the father-in-law of Yi Pyǒk. Nevertheless, he was among the loudest voices calling for harsh treatment for Catholics in 1801. During the persecution, he was the Third Minister in the Office of the Ministers-without-Portfolio.

Mok Manjung 睦萬中 (1727–1810) He is another Southerner official who took a strong anti-Catholic line. During the 1801 persecution, he was the Censor-General and worked alongside the Chief State Councilor Sim Hwanji, the leader of the Patriarchs (Noron), in persecuting those suspected of involvement with Catholicism.

Pak Changsǒl 朴長卨 (1729–?) He was an official under kings Chǒngjo and Sunjo and, according to some sources, a member of the Patriarchs Faction. The *Silk Letter* says he was a member of the Little Northerner Faction. He served as both a military officer and an official in the Censorate. In 1790, when he was serving as a junior military commander, he accused Chǒng Yakchǒn of being a secret Catholic because in an exam essay Chǒng mentioned the Four Elements, a Western scientific concept introduced to Korea in books written by Jesuit missionaries in China. In 1801 he was the deputy Third Military Commander of the Five Military Commands and still vehemently anti-Catholic.

Sim Hwanji 沈煥之 (1730–1802) A leading member of the Patriarchs Faction in the last years of King Chǒngjo's reign and into the first year of King Sunjo's reign. He became Chief State Councilor after the death of King Chǒngjo and therefore was the top civil servant during the 1801 persecution. Before that he had served as Chief Minister of the Board of Rites, the Board of War, and the Board of Punishments.

Shin Hŏnjo 申獻朝 (1752–1809) He was a member of the Patriarchs Faction and an anti-Catholic official under kings Chŏngjo and Sunjo.

Shin Ki 申耆 (1741–?) He was the Censor-General in 1791 and sent the king a blistering criticism of Catholics, calling them not just immoral but a threat to the moral foundations of the country. He gradually rose in government service, reaching the level of Second Minister of the Board of Rites in 1807.

Shin Sawŏn 申史源 (1732–1799) He was magistrate of Chinsan in 1791. He was dismissed from his post for failing to stop Yun Chich'ung and Kwŏn Sang'yŏn from violating the requirements of the mourning ritual, although he did not know about their plans to ignore the requirement to use a spirit tablet until after the fact. Before his dismissal, he arrested and interrogated both men. The record of that interrogation shows them both insisting that they had done nothing wrong and, in fact, had adhered to the demands of morality by placing the commands of God above the laws of their king.

Sŏ Yongbo 徐龍輔 (1857–1824) He may have been a member of the weak Disciples Faction but he nevertheless rose to high posts in the government. In 1801 he was the Third State Councilor. He was affiliated with the Intransigent Faction and was adamantly anti-Catholic.

Sunjo, King 純祖 (r. 1800–1834) As the only surviving son of King Chŏngjo, he ascended the throne upon Chŏngjo's death. However, he was not even a teenager at that point, so for the first four years of this reign, his government was actually controlled by the oldest living queen of a previous ruler, Queen Dowager Chŏngsun. She came from a Patriarchs family that was allied with the Intransigent Faction, so her government was filled with Patriarchs officials as well as officials from other factions who were affiliated with the Intransigent Faction. It was in her name, acting as regent, that the 1801 persecution of Catholics was launched.

Yi Kigyŏng 李基慶 (1756–1819) A member of the Southerner Faction, he was originally close friends with Chŏng Yagyong. However, he was disturbed by the interest shown in Catholicism by Chŏng Yagyong and a few other fellow Southerner students at the Sŏnggyun'gwan. He relayed his concerns to Hong Nagan in 1787, who then made Catholicism among some Southerners a public issue by informing the government. Yi participated in the persecution of Catholics in 1801 as a minor government official. He later compiled the collection of anti-Catholic documents known as the *Pyŏgwip'yŏn* [闢 衛編 In defense of the right against the wrong].

Yi Igun 李 益 運 (1748–1817) A member of the Southerner Faction, he was the governor of Kyŏnggi province in 1801 and had been a close associate of the late Ch'ae Chegong. He was friendly with Chŏng Yagyong when they were both young officials but became part of the anti-Catholic group of officials in 1801, demanding that Chŏng Yagyong be interrogated to find out the full extent of his involvement with the Catholic community.

Yi Kyŏngmyŏng 李 景 溟 (1733–?) A member of the Southerner Faction, in 1788 he was the fourth censor in the Office of the Censor-General and, in that capacity, petitioned the king to adopt harsh measures against what he saw as the dangerous spread of Catholic ideas. King Chŏngjo replied that harsh measures were not necessary. Instead, the Confucian Way should be further clarified. If that were done, argued the king, such "strange ideas" as Catholics held would fade away on their own.

Yi Pyŏngmo 李 秉 模 (1742–1806) He was thought to be a member of the Disciples (Soron) Faction. There has been disagreement among scholars over Yi's precise factional affiliation, but there is growing agreement that Yi Pyŏngmo was one of the few members of the Disciples Faction to rise to a powerful position in government in the late eighteenth and early nineteenth century. Though he may have been allied with the Expedient Faction at first, by 1801 he was considered a member of the Intransigent Faction. As a member of the State Council in 1801, he participated in the persecution of Catholics.

Yi Sŏgu 李 書 九 (1754–1825) He was a member of the Patriarchs Faction and was allied with the Intransigent Faction. He was exiled briefly in 1795 on the charge that he was involved with the Catholic community. Nevertheless, he was able serve in a number of high-level government posts under both kings Chŏngjo and Sunjo and took part in the persecution of Catholics in 1801. In 1801 he was Second Magistrate for the State Tribunal. He is also known as one of four great poets of his time.

Yi Sŏk 李 晳 (1769–1829) He passed the military government service exam and slowly rose through the ranks under King Sunjo, eventually serving as an army commander, though he was exiled for a while during the 1801 persecution. He was the younger brother of Yi Pyŏk but was never a Catholic. It was Yi Sŏk who informed Ch'ae Chegong that a priest had been smuggled into Korea.

Yi Yugyŏng 李 儒 慶 (1747–?) He was a military official under King Chŏngjo and into the first year of King Sunjo.

Yun Sidong 尹 著 東 (1729–1797) He was a high official under King Chŏngjo and head of the Patriarchs Faction before Sim Hwanji.

The Persecuted: Dates for the executions of the persecuted are given according to the solar calendar, since that is how those dates are recorded today in Catholic lists of beatified and canonized Koreans. The baptismal name, if known, is given after the Chinese characters and in the normal English form rather than as a transliteration of the Korean version of the name of the saint from whom the baptismal name was taken.

Chi Hwang 池 潢 Sabas (1767–1795) He was born into a family of court musicians in Seoul. He traveled to Beijing in 1793 in the hope that he would be able to escort Father Zhou back to Korea. When they arrived at the Yalu River in 1794, they discovered that the ice had melted and therefore they would have to wait until the next winter for Father Zhou to be smuggled into Korea. Zhou waited near the border until December 1794, when Chi Hwang returned to the Yalu River and escorted him across and into Seoul. He died while being interrogated about Father Zhou's whereabouts on June 28, 1795. He was beatified in 2014.

Cho Yongsam 趙 龍 三 Peter (?–1801) He was the elder of two brothers born into an impoverished *yangban* family from Yanggŭn, a village in Kyŏnggi province. Peter moved to Yŏju, where Martin Yi Chungbae was from. Peter, his father, and his younger brother were arrested before the suppression of 1801 officially began. Peter's unwillingness to repudiate Catholicism even under torture was particularly maddening to his interrogators, who beat him more than the legal limit, leading to his death. He died on March 27, 1801. He was beatified in 2014.

Ch'oe Ch'anghyŏn 崔昌顯 John (1754–1801) He was born into a family of *chungin* translators. He was active in the early Catholic Church in Korea, and was even appointed a priest during the period of the pseudo-ecclesiastical hierarchy. He played an important role in bringing Father Zhou to Korea, served as general secretary of the Myŏngdohoe, and translated a missal (a book of Catholic readings and prayers including extracts from the Bible) into Korean. Because of his reputation as a Catholic leader, the government sought his arrest, and he therefore went into hiding. However, he fell ill and returned home to recuperate. A former Catholic, Kim Yŏsam, informed upon him, and he was arrested. Hwang Sayŏng, though unsure of the circumstances of his death, other than the fact he was beheaded with other Catholics on April 8, 1801, described how even after he was beaten, he gave a stout defense of the Catholic prohibition on ancestor rites. However, according to the interrogation records, under torture he renounced his belief in Catholicism, at least at first. Catholic authorities consider the *Silk Letter* more reliable than government interrogation records and beatified him in 2014.

Ch'oe Inch'ŏl 崔 仁 喆 Ignatius (?–1801) He was the younger brother of Ch'oe In'gil, who introduced him to Catholicism. He contributed to the financial backing for a trip to Beijing to appeal for a missionary to be sent to Korea. After Father Zhou arrived in Korea, he worked together with Hong P'ilju and Hwang Sa-yŏng to assist Father Zhou. After his brother In'gil was martyred in 1795, he continued to play an active role in the Catholic community but was captured in 1801 and beheaded on July 2, 1801. He was beatified in 2014.

Ch'oe In'gil 崔 仁吉 Matthew (1764–1795) Born into a family of official interpreters, he was one of the first members of the Catholic community in Korea, having been introduced to Catholicism by Yi Pyŏk. He provided the first home Father Zhou stayed in after arriving Seoul. He died while being interrogated about Father Zhou's whereabouts on June 28, 1795. He was beatified in 2014.

Ch'oe P'ilche 崔 必 悌 Peter (1770–1801) He was born into a family of medical specialists in Seoul and operated a pharmacy. Ch'oe P'ilgong was his cousin. He learned Catholicism from Yi Chonch'ang and received Peter as his baptismal name in 1790. He was arrested along with Ch'oe P'ilgong in 1791 but gained release by renouncing his faith. However, he soon returned to an active Catholic life and often attended the masses celebrated by Father Zhou. He was arrested in 1800 while he was meeting with some fellow Catholics. While he was in prison, his father passed away and he was let out on parole to attend his father's funeral. After the funeral, he voluntarily returned to prison, saying that he wanted to show that he regretted his earlier renunciation of Catholicism. He was beheaded on May 14, 1801. He was beatified in 2014.

Ch'oe P'ilgong 崔必恭 Thomas (1744–1801) He was the son of a physician in Seoul. That means he was of *chungin* rather than the higher *yangban* status. However, he was unable to find employment as a physician to the court and therefore was without a steady income and therefore unable to get married. In 1790 he was introduced to Catholicism by his cousin Peter Ch'oe P'ilche. He was arrested the first time in 1791 but was released shortly afterward. He was re-arrested in 1798 but again was released. The third time he was arrested, in 1801, was the last time. He was beheaded on April 8, 1801. He was beatified in 2014.

Ch'oe Yŏgyŏm 崔汝謙 Matthew (1762–1801) He was born into a family of rural *yangban*. He was introduced to Catholicism by Yun Chich'ung. Later Yi Chonch'ang convinced him to become a Catholic. He was arrested when someone who had been part of the Catholic community revealed his name to authorities in 1801. He was beheaded on August 27, 1801. He was beatified in 2014.

Chŏng Ch'ŏlsang 丁哲祥 Charles (1781?–1801) He was the oldest son of Chŏng Yakchong and St. Cecilia Yu Sosa. He was beheaded on May 14, 1801. He was beatified in 2014.

Chŏng Chŏnghye 丁情惠 Elizabeth (?–1839) She was the daughter of Augustine Chŏng Yakchong and St. Cecilia Yu Sosa, and the sister of St. Chŏng Hasang. She was beheaded in the 1839 persecution and was proclaimed a saint in 1984.

Chŏng Hasang 丁夏祥 Paul (1795–1839) The son of Chŏng Yakchong and St. Cecilia Yu Sosa, he was a lay leader of the underground church in the 1830s. He was beheaded in the 1839 persecution. He was proclaimed a saint in 1984.

Chŏng Kwangsu 鄭光受 Barnabas (?–1802) He was of *yangban* heritage and studied Catholicism under the direction of Kwŏl Ilsin. His wife Lucia Yun Unhye (?–1801) was beheaded on May 14, 1801. He was beheaded on January 29, 1802. They were both beatified in 2014.

Chŏng Im 丁任 (?–?) She was a slave of Kang Wansuk. Under interrogation that involved torture, she confessed all she had learned about

Father Zhou's presence in Seoul and therefore was exiled instead of executed. She is not among those who were beatified.

Chŏng Yakchŏn 丁 若 銓 (1758–1816) An older brother of Chŏng Yakchong and Chŏng Yagyong, he was one of the first members of the Catholic community that emerged in Korea in the mid-1780s. However, like his brother Yagyong, he cut his ties with that community after his cousin Yun Chich'ung was executed in 1791. Nevertheless, like his brother Yagyong, he was exiled in 1801. He died while still in exile on a remote island off Korea's west coast. While there he compiled a study of the fish he found in the waters around that island. For that reason, he is often hailed as Korea's first modern biologist. He was not among those beatified.

Chŏng Yakchong 丁若 鍾 Augustine (1760–1801) Of *yangban* background (his father had served as a district magistrate), he was one of the three Chŏng brothers (along with Chŏng Yagyong and Chŏng Yakchŏn) who were involved with the Korean Catholic Church in its formative years, and the last one of the three to be baptized. However, he was the only one of the three who remained an active member of the Catholic community after 1791, when his cousin Paul Yun Chich'ung was executed. Father Zhou appointed Augustine the leader of the Myŏngdohoe, the primary confraternity in Seoul for Catholic converts. He thus served as one of the most important members of Korea's Catholic community at the end of the eighteenth century. He is the author of the first Korean-authored catechism, the *Chugyo yoji* [Essential elements of the Lord's Teachings]. He was beheaded on April 8, 1801. He was beatified in 2014.

His wife, Cecilia Yu Sosa (1761–1839), was martyred along with his youngest son, Paul Chŏng Hasang (1795–1839), and his daughter, Elizabeth Chŏng Chŏnghye (1797–1839), in 1839. All three were declared saints in 1984. His older son, Charles Chŏng Ch'ŏlsang, was martyred in 1801. Both Augustine and Charles were beatified in 2014.

Chŏng Yagyong 丁若鏞 (1762–1836) One of the greatest philosophers in Korean history, he was one of those who formed Korea's first Catholic community in 1784. However, he withdrew from involvement with the Catholic community after his cousin Yun Chich'ung was executed in 1791. Despite cutting his ties with the Catholic community, he faced continual criticism over the next decade for being tainted by association with Catholicism even as he rose in the civil service. In 1801 he was exiled as punishment for the Catholic activities of his youth. During the eighteen years he spent in exile he wrote commentaries on all the Confucian classics as well as guides to Confucian government administration. Because he insisted in his commentaries that the Confucian classics spoke of a Lord Above, an actual supernatural personality who observed our every thought and action, some scholars today insist that he remained a Catholic in his heart, though he advocated the use of a spirit tablet in mourning rituals. He was the younger brother of Chŏng Yakchong and Chŏng Yakchŏn. He is often referred to by his pen name, Tasan. According to statements made by some of those interrogated in 1801, when he was a member of the Catholic community he used the baptismal name John. He was not among those beatified.

Han Chŏnghŭm 韓 正 欽 Stanislaus (1756–1801) The son of an impoverished *yangban* family, he was brought into the Catholic community by Augustine Yu Hanggŏm, a distant relative, when he was staying with Yu Hanggŏm in order to teach Yu's children. He was beheaded on August 26, 1801. He was beatified in 2014.

Han Sinae 韓信愛 Agatha (?–1801) She was born in Ch'ungch'ŏng province as the daughter of a secondary wife in a *yangban* household. She later moved to Seoul as the wife of Chang Sŏnghan. There she met Kang Wansuk and was converted to Catholicism. In 1800 she was baptized by Father Zhou. She was arrested in 1801 and was beheaded on July 2, 1801. She was beatified in 2014.

Hong Chŏngho 洪正浩 (?–1801) A close relative of Hong P'ilju, he studied Catholicism under Father Zhou. He was beheaded along with Columba Kang and seven others at Little West Gate on July 2, 1801. He was not among the beatified.

Hong Ingman 洪翼萬 Anthony (?–1802) He was the son of a secondary wife in a *yangban* family, giving him a social status slightly below the *yangban* nobility but above the commoners. He was the father-in-law of two Catholics, Hong P'ilchu and Yi Hyŏn. Francis Xavier Hong Kyoman was his cousin. He was introduced to Catholicism by Kim Pŏmu and was baptized by Yi Sŭng-hun. He was beheaded on January 29, 1802. He was one of those beatified in 2014.

Hong In 洪 鎭 Leo (1758–1802) He was the son of Hong Kyoman. He was executed on January 30, 1802. He was one of those beatified in 2014.

Hong Kyoman 洪 教 萬 Francis Xavier (1738–1801) He was of *yang-ban* descent and was introduced to Catholicism by Kwŏn Ch'ŏlsin, his paternal cousin. His son, Hong In (another martyr of 1801), is said to have convinced him to convert to Catholicism. Father Zhou baptized him and gave him the Christian name of Francis Xavier. He was the father-in-law of Chŏng Ch'ŏlsang. Hong Kyoman was beheaded along with Chŏng Yakchong and Hong Nangmin on April 8 in 1801. Both Hong Kyoman and Hong In were beatified in 2014.

Hong Nangmin 洪 樂 敏 Luke (1751–1801) The *Silk Letter* says his baptismal name was Paul. A member of the Southerner Faction, he studied under Kwŏn Ch'ŏlsin and passed the "presented scholar" level of the civil service exam in 1780, later serving in various government posts. He was among the first baptized by Yi Sŭnghun in 1784. Despite two renunciations of Catholicism in the 1790s, when he was arrested and tortured in 1801, after wavering for a while, he eventually confessed that he actually was still a Catholic. He died still professing his faith on April 8, 1801. He was executed along with Yi Sŭnghun, Chŏng Yakchong, and Ch'oe Ch'anghyŏn. He was among those beatified in 2014.

Hong P'ilchu 洪 弼 周 Phillip (1774–1801) The stepson of Kang Wan-suk, he converted to Catholicism under her influence and moved to Seoul when she did. He helped Kang take care of Father Zhou Wenmo and assisted him when he celebrated the mass. He was arrested and beheaded on October 4, 1801. He was one of those beatified in 2014.

Hwang Sayŏng 黃 嗣 永 Alexius (1775–1801) He is the author of the *Silk Letter.* He passed the "presented scholar" examination in 1790, at the age of fifteen, and was congratulated personally by King Chŏngjo. Normally, that suggests he could have had a long and illustrious career as a government official. Soon afterward, he married the oldest daughter of Chŏng Yakhyŏn and Yi Pyŏk's sister. Though Chŏng Yakhyŏn was not a Catholic himself, three of his brothers were. Though two of them, Yakchŏn and Yagyong, had left the Catholic community because of its refusal to allow the use of spirit tablets in ancestral memorial rites, Chŏng Yakchong was still a fervent Catholic and convinced Hwang to became a Catholic as well. Hwang then abandoned any plans for a career in government and instead dedicated the last decade of his life to the endangered Catholic community in Korea. Because of his authorship of the *Silk Letter,* which included a request for foreign intervention to stop the persecution of Catholics, on December 10, 1801, he was executed by dismemberment, considered a much harsher form of capital punishment since Confucians are enjoined to keep intact the bodies their parents gave them. He was not among those beatified in 2014.

Hwang Sim 黃沁 Thomas (1756–1801) He was a commoner from Ch'ungch'ŏng province. He was introduced to Catholicism by Yi Chonch'ang. He was an official horse handler for the government but had to bribe someone in order to join a tribute mission to Beijing. He visited there as a horse handler for tribute missions in October 1797, October 1798, and October 1799. He was supposed to give the *Silk Letter* to Ok Ch'ŏnhŭi, who would then deliver it to Bishop de Gouvea, but Hwang was arrested before he could do so. Hwang Sayŏng wrote that letter as though he were Hwang Sim, because he knew the missionaries in Beijing were familiar with Hwang Sim, since he had visited Beijing before.

Hwang Sim revealed to the authorities that Hwang Sayŏng was hiding in Paeron because he apparently thought Hwang Sayŏng had already moved to a different location. He was wrong, so his information led to Hwang Sayŏng's capture. Hwang Sim was beheaded on November 30, 1801. It is not known whether or not he renounced his faith when he was being tortured, so he was not among those beatified in 2014.

Hyŏn Kyehŭm 玄啓欽 Paul (1763–1801) He was born into a family of official translators. However, he pursued a career as a pharmacist instead. (Both translators and pharmacists had *chungin* status, placing them below the *yangban* nobility but above commoners.) He was the person who sailed out to and went aboard the British warship, the *Providence*, when it approached Tongnae on the southeastern coast of Korea. He reported back that it was as strong as any one hundred ships Korea had. That gave rise to Catholic hopes that Western warships could sail to Korea and create a "decisive moment" in which the government would be forced to stop persecuting Catholics. When the 1801 persecution broke out, he went into hiding, but when he learned that his relatives were being tortured to reveal his whereabouts, he turned himself in. He was beheaded on December 10, 1801. He was the father of Saint Benedicta Hyŏn Kyŏngnyŏn, who was martyred in the 1839 persecution. He himself was beatified in 2014.

Im Taein 任 大 仁 Thomas (1773–?) He was the servant of Chŏng Yakchong. He was not among those beatified in 2014.

Kang Ich'ŏn 姜 彛 天 (1768–1801) He was executed in 1801 not because he was a Catholic but because he had been caught in attempts, inspired by Daoist ideas and a popular book of prophecy called the *Chŏng Kam Nok* (鄭 鑑 錄, the record of Mr. Chŏng Kam), to prepare for the imminent fall of the Yi family from the Chosŏn throne. He had met Father Zhou through the good graces of Kim Kŏnsun because he thought that Zhou might be the Daoist savior from China he was expecting. However, there is no evidence he was ever a serious Catholic. He was not among those beatified in 2014.

Kang Kyŏngbok 姜 景 福 Susanna (1762–1801) Born into a commoner family, she ended up working as a maid in the palace, where she lived a celibate life. She was assigned to the palace occupied by Maria Song, the wife of the exiled Prince Ŭnŏn, and was converted to Catholicism in 1798 by Maria Song. She was executed on July 2, 1801. She was among those beatified in 2014.

Kang Wansuk 姜 完 淑 Columba (1760–1801) She was the descendant of the son of a *yangban* father and a non-*yangban* mother, giving her a social status above the commoners and just below that of the *yangban* nobility. She came to believe in Catholicism soon after she married but was unable to convince her husband to share her enthusiasm for her faith. However, she converted her mother-in-law, her stepson (Hong P'ilchu), and her daughter (Lucy Hong Sunhŭi). Her husband divorced her, but the Catholics in the family went with her to Seoul. There she became an important Catholic leader. She protected Father Zhou, undertook missionary work among women, and gathered together a community of celibate women, making her home something of a convent. After suffering from interrogation under torture, she was beheaded on July 2, 1801. She was one of those beatified in 2014.

Kim Ch'ŏnae 金 千 愛 Andrew (1760–1801) He was a servant of the Catholic activist Yu Hanggŏm. He was beheaded on August 27, 1801. He was one of those beatified in 2014.

Kim Chŏngdŭk 金 丁 得 Peter (?–1801) He was introduced to Catholicism by his relative Kim Kwangok. He was executed on August 25, 1801. He was one of those beatified in 2014.

Kim Hyŏnu 金顯禹 Matthew (1775–1801) He was born a secondary son in a family of hereditary government translators. Kim Pŏmu was his elder stepbrother. Kim Iu, who died in 1801 from blows suffered while being interrogated under suspicion of being a Catholic, was his brother. He survived his own interrogation to be beheaded on July 2, 1801. He was one of those beatified in 2014.

Kim Kŏnsun 金健淳 Joseph (1776–1801) Unlike most of the Catholics from the educated class, he was from a family affiliated with the Patriarchs (Noron) Faction rather than the Southerner (Namin) Faction). Inspired by curiosity by what he had heard about Catholicism, he approached Kwŏn Ch'ŏlsin to learn more and was inducted into the faith by Father Zhou in 1798. He renounced his faith under torture in 1801 but was executed anyway. The official record of his interrogation confirms that he repeatedly denied any connection with Catholicism. He was not among those beatified in 2014.

Kim Kwangok 金廣玉 Andrew (?–1801) He was born into a rural *chungin* family (rather than technical specialists like the *chungin* in Seoul, rural *chungin* tended to be the clerks for local government offices). He was the father of the martyr Francis Kim Hŭisŏng and was related to Kim Chŏngdŭk. He was one of those converted by Yi Chonch'ang. He was executed on August 25, 1801. He was one of those beatified in 2014.

Kim Paeksun 金伯淳 (no baptismal name) (1769–1801) He was a cousin of Kim Kŏnsun. He had already reached the conclusion that human beings had an immortal soul when he was told, much to his surprise, that Catholicism taught the same thing. That convinced him to become a Catholic. He was arrested in March 1801 and at first renounced his Catholic beliefs under torture. He later retracted his renunciation and was beheaded on May 10, 1801. However, he was not among those beatified in 2014.

Kim Pŏmu 金範禹 Thomas (1751–1787) Born into an interpreter family, he became friends with several of the *yangban* who formed the nucleus of Korea's first Catholic community. It is in his home that some of the first Catholic gatherings were held in the mid-1780s. He was beaten severely for allowing those gatherings and sent into exile. He died of his wounds on his way into exile. Myŏngdong Cathedral in Seoul today stands on what was once the site of Kim Pŏmu's home. He was not among those beatified in 2014.

Kim Yŏni 金連伊 Juliana (?–1801) She was the wife of a commoner and was introduced to Catholicism by Han Sinae. She was baptized by Father Zhou at Kang Wansuk's home sometime after 1795. She was executed along with Kang Wansuk on July 2, 1801. She was one of those beatified in 2014.

Kim Yŏsam 金汝三 (??–??) He was born in Ch'ungch'ŏng province, where he became a Catholic, and moved to Seoul with his two brothers to escape persecution. However, he had a difficult time making ends meet and demanded money from better-off Catholics such as Yi Anchŏng, who was related to him through marriage. After failing in several attempts to get money from Yi, he assumed that Father Zhou might have been behind Yi Anchŏng's refusal to help him financially. Dallet mentions that this animosity toward Father Zhou, caused by Kim's false assumption, resulted in Kim's informing on the church leaders to the police. He was not among those beatified in 2014.

Kim Yusan 金有山 Thomas (1761–1801) He was a man from the base class who lived in a village of servants for a post station. For a while he lived as a monk but was converted to Catholicism by Yi Chonch'ang. He delivered the message to Beijing asking that a Western ship be sent to Korea in 1798. He was arrested along with Yu Hanggŏm and beheaded on October 24, 1801. He was not among those beatified in 2014.

Kwŏn Ch'ŏlsin 權哲身 Ambrose (1736–1801) A Southerner *yangban,* he was converted to Catholicism along with his brother Ilsin by Peter Yi Sŭnghun. However, he severed his ties with the Catholic community in 1791 because of the Catholic prohibition of ancestor rites. He was arrested in 1801 and died in prison on April 4, 1801, as a result of the severe beatings he had received. He was not among those beatified in 2014.

Kwŏn Ilsin 權日身 Francis Xavier (1742–1791) A Southerner *yangban,* he was baptized by Peter Yi Sŭnghun in 1784. He was arrested during the 1791 persecution but refused to denounce Catholicism and was sentenced to banishment on Cheju Island. Fearing for the health of his eighty-year-old mother, he submitted a poem in which he vaguely recanted his Catholicism. This led to a reduction in his sentence to banishment to Yesan, which was closer to his mother than Cheju was.

However, he died from the beatings he had suffered before he arrived in his exile site. He was the older brother of Kwŏn Ch'ŏlsin. He was not among those beatified in 2014.

Kwŏn Sangmun 權 相 門 Sebastian (1768–1801) He was the son of Kwŏn Ilsin but had been adopted by Kwŏn Ch'ŏlsin after Kwŏn Ilsin died. He was executed on December 28, 1801, and was among those beatified in 2014.

Kwŏn Sang'yŏn 權 尙 然 James (1751–1791) Born into a rural *yang-ban* family, he was introduced to Catholicism by his younger cousin Yun Chich'ung. He became a Catholic in 1797 and followed Yun's example by destroying the ancestral tablets in his possession. Yun's mother was his aunt, so he participated in the irregular mourning ritual Yun held for his mother. As a result, Kwŏn was arrested along with Yun and beheaded alongside him on December 8, 1801. He was beatified in 2014.

Mun Yŏngin 文 榮 仁 Vivian (1776–1801) She was the daughter of a *chungin* family living in Seoul. In 1783 she was brought into the palace to work as a maid. Converted by Kang Wansuk, she was baptized by Father Zhou in 1797. She was beheaded on July 2, 1801. She was beatified in 2014.

Ok Ch'ŏnhŭi 玉 千 禧 John (1767–1801) He was a low-level worker in a government post station. Acting as a groom for the horses on tribute missions, he was able to carry messages between Bishop de Gouvea and Korea's Catholic community on three trips, in 1799, 1800, and 1801 (just before full-scale persecution broke out). He was caught on the border between China and Korea in 1801 on his way back from Beijing. Hwang Sayŏng had hoped that Ok could pick up the *Silk Letter* from Hwang Sim and carry it to Bishop de Gouvea in Beijing when Ok accompanied the winter mission to Beijing, which was supposed to leave Korea in October, but that plan failed when first Ok and then Hwang Sim were arrested. Ok was beheaded on December 10, 1801. He was not among those beatified in 2014.

Oh Sŏkch'ung 吳 錫 忠 Stephen (1742–1806) He was at first interested in Catholicism but withdrew during the early stages of the persecution. However, he made some enemies in 1795 when he tried to defend Yi Kahwan against what he considered false charges. In 1801 those enemies had him arrested and his house searched. When one Western book was found in his home, that was taken as evidence that he was still involved with the Catholic community and he was exiled to an island off the western coast. His daughter married the martyr Kwŏn Sangmun, the adopted son of Kwŏn Ch'ŏlsin. He was not among those beatified in 2014.

Shin Maria 申 마리아 (?–1801) She was the daughter-in-law of Maria Song and eldest aunt of King Ch'ŏlchong. Being of royal status through marriage, on April 29, 1801, she was allowed to die by being forced to drink poison rather than being beheaded or strangled. She was not one of those beatified in 2014.

Song Maria 宋 마리아 (?–1801) She was the grandmother of King Ch'ŏlchong as the wife of the exiled Prince Ŭnŏn, the stepbrother of King Chŏngjo. Prince Ŭnŏn had been exiled to Kanghwa Island because of attempts, possibly made without his knowledge, to place him on the throne in place of his stepbrother. Maria Song was able to stay behind in an older palace while her husband was in exile. Because she was of royal status through marriage, on April 29, 1801, she was allowed to die by being forced to drink poison rather than being beheaded or strangled. She was not one of those beatified in 2014.

Wŏn Kyŏngdo 元 景 道 John (1774–1801) Born into a *yangban* family, he was a cousin of Yi Chungbae. He was introduced to Catholicism by Kim Kŏnsun in 1797. He married the daughter of the Catholic Marcellinus Ch'oe Ch'angju (1749–1801). He was arrested along with Yi Chungbae after their public celebration of Easter in 1800. He was jailed along with Yi Chungbae for six months and was beheaded along with him on April 25, 1801. He was one of those beatified in 2014.

Yi Anchŏng 李 安 正 (?–?) Yi was from Ch'ungch'ŏng province and was a devoted Catholic. He had lent money to Kim Yŏsam several times, but when Kim asked for even more, he refused. Kim then became angry with Yi. Since Yi An-chŏng often attended Father Zhou's masses, Kim Yŏsam falsely assumed Father Zhou must have been behind Yi's refusal to lend money to him, which caused Kim to report Father Zhou's existence to the government. Yi was not one of those beatified in 2014.

Yi Chonch'ang 李 存 昌 Louis-Gonzaga (1752–1801) He was also known as Yi Tanwŏn 李 端 源. He was a rural *chungin* who was converted to Catholicism by Kwŏn Ilsin. He then actively propagated Catholicism but was arrested and temporarily withdrew from the Catholic community in 1791. He was arrested again in 1795 and held under strict confinement in his hometown for six years, until he was sent to Seoul in 1801 to be interrogated as part of the investigation of Catholics. He was condemned to death in the same sentence that condemned Augustine Chŏng Yakchong, but Yi Chonch'ang was sent down to Kongju to be executed on April 9, 1801. The first Korean priest, Andrew Kim Taegŏn (1822–1846), was the grandson of his niece, and the second Korean priest, Thomas Ch'oe Yangŏp (1821–1861), was the grandson of his nephew. His name is not on the list of those who were beatified in 2014.

Yi Chunshin 李俊新 (1730–1801) He had been an active Catholic but renounced his faith under torture in 1801. He was executed, nonetheless. He was not among those beatified in 2014.

Yi Chungbae 李中培 Martin (1752?–1801) He was the son of a *yangban* father and a non-*yangban* mother, which barred him from the highest-level civil service posts. He converted to Catholicism in 1797 after studying Catholicism from Kim Kŏnsun along with his cousin Wŏn Kyŏngdo. He celebrated Easter too openly in 1800, exposing the fact that he was a Catholic to his non-Catholic neighbors. As a result, he was arrested and spent six months in prison, during which he was tortured several times. In prison he became known for his skill in treating the medical problems of his fellow prisoners. He was finally beheaded on April 25, 1801. He was one of those beatified in 2014.

Yi Hŭiyŏng 李喜英 Luke (1756–1801) A skilled painter of *yangban* background, he was a cousin of Kim Kŏnsun and an uncle of Yi Hyŏn. He was converted to Catholicism by Father Zhou. He is said to have presented Hwang Sayŏng with sacred images that he painted. He was arrested in 1801 but renounced his Catholic beliefs. Nevertheless, he was beheaded on May 10, 1801, along with Kim Paeksun. He was not among those beatified in 2014.

Yi Hyŏn 李鉉 Anthony (?–1801) He was born into a *yangban* family in Yŏju. He began studying Catholicism from Kim Kŏnsŏn in 1797 and was baptized sometime afterward by Father Zhou. He then married the daughter of Hong Ingman. He wavered in his faith at the beginning of his harsh interrogation in 1801 but then returned to vigorous assertions of this Catholic faith. He was beheaded on July 2, 1801. He was beatified in 2014.

Yi Kahwan 李家煥 (1742–1801) The grandson of the brother of the famous Confucian scholar Yi Ik, he was associated with the Southerner

Faction. He passed the "presented scholar" civil service exam in 1771 and began to move up the ranks of government service. Yi Sŭnghun was his sister's son. Many more of his closest intellectual as well as factional colleagues were Catholic converts. Even though he had studied Catholic teachings, he himself was not a Catholic. He was better known for his deep knowledge of European geometry and astronomical mathematics, which he learned from works published by Jesuit missionaries and their followers in China. Even though he was known to have persecuted Catholics under his jurisdiction when he was placed in charge of various local districts around the peninsula, he was accused of being a Catholic in 1801 and, despite his vehement denials, was tortured and died of his wounds. He was among those beatified in 2014.

Yi Kiyang 李 基 讓 (1744–1802) He had discussed Catholicism with Yi Pyŏk but had not become a member of the Catholic community. After passing the "presented scholar" exam in 1774, he had a successful career in the government, serving as Second Minister of the Board of War, the Board of Punishments, and the Board of Rites, as well as Censor-General, Third Royal Secretary, and Second Royal Secretary. He had risen through the ranks with the support of Ch'ae Chegong. However, in 1801 he was accused of being a secret Catholic and was exiled. He was not one of those beatified in 2014.

His eldest son, Yi Ch'ongŏk 李寵億 (a participant in the 1779 meeting at Ch'ŏnjin Hermitage of Chuŏsa Temple), had married a daughter of Kwŏn Ch'ŏlsin. Yi Kiyang claimed that he had not seen much of them after that marriage and did not know if his son or his daughter-in-law were involved with the Catholic community. A second son married Yi Kahwan's daughter. A daughter married the son of Hong Nangmin. And his younger brother was married to Ahn Chŏngbok's granddaughter.

Yi Pyŏk 李檗 John the Baptist (1754–1786) He was an important early leader in the Korean Catholic Church. Some consider him the founder, since it was at his request that Yi Sŭnghun visited a Catholic church in Beijing and asked for information on Catholic teachings, leading to Yi Sŭnghun's baptism and his subsequent baptism of others back in Korea. Yi Pyŏk abandoned his Catholic activities under strong pressure from his family in the wake of the discovery in 1795 that the small Catholic community was holding meetings at the home of Kim

Pŏmu. Yi Pyŏk's father, alarmed by his son's involvement with such non-Confucian activities, threatened suicide if he did not give up his faith. Yi Pyŏk died of ill health in 1786. Yi Pyŏk's sister was the first wife of Chŏng Yakhyŏn, and therefore the mother-in-law of Hwang Sayŏng, though she never met him, since she died in 1780. Yi Pyŏk himself is said to have married a daughter of Kwŏn Ŏm (1729–1801), an official who later became one of the chief persecutors of Korea's Catholics. However, there is some disagreement over who Yi Pyŏk's wife actually was, with others claiming he married Kwŏn Yuhandang, a daughter of Kwŏn Ilsin. Yi Pyŏk was not among those beatified in 2014.

Yi Sŭnghun 李 承 薰 Peter (1756–1801) The first baptized adult Catholic in Korea, he earned his "presented scholar" degree in 1780. He accompanied his father on a tribute mission to Beijing in 1783 and was baptized there the following year before he returned home. After he returned to Korea, he began to baptize some of his relatives and friends. In 1785, after his Catholic activities were exposed during the Kim Pŏmu incident, he denounced Catholic teachings under pressure from his family. In 1787 he rejoined the small Catholic community and served as a leader, but in 1791 he again renounced Catholicism when he was imprisoned briefly. Nevertheless, he was exiled for a while. In 1795, when Father Zhou entered Korea, he again returned to the church. His relationship with Catholicism at his death on April 8, 1801, is not clear, though under interrogation he denied that he was still a Catholic. As a result of his denying in 1801 that he still believed in Catholic teachings, he was not among those beatified in 2014, even though he is still considered by some a founder of the first Catholic community in Korea.

Yi Suni 李 順 伊 Lutgarda (1882–1802) She was a daughter of Yi Yunha and niece on her mother's side of Kwŏn Ilsin and Kwŏn Ch'ŏlsin. She entered into a celibate marriage with John Yu Chungch'ŏl, the son of Yu Hanggŏm, in 1797. She was beheaded on January 31, 1802. She was beatified along with her husband in 2014.

Yi Ujip 李 宇 集 (1762–1801) He was a relative of Yu Hanggŏm through marriage. He was the one who first revealed to the government that Catholics had tried to get Western warships to sail to Korea to force the government to stop persecuting Catholics. He was beheaded on October 24, 1801. He was not one of those beatified in 2014.

Yi Yunha 李潤夏 Matthew (1757–1793) A Southerner *yangban*, he was an eighth-generation descendant of Yi Sugwang, a grandson of Yi Ik (by adoption), brother-in-law of Kwŏn Ilsin and Kwŏn Ch'ŏlsin, and father of Lutgarda Yi Suni, Charles Yi Kyŏngdo, and Paul Yi Kyŏngŏn. (Lutgarda and Charles were beatified in 2014 because of their martyrdom in 1801. Paul was beatified in 2014 because he died in prison in 1827 still professing his faith in God.) Yi Yunha was part of the group that met at the Ch'ŏnjin hermitage of Chuŏsa temple in 1799 to discuss how best to meet the high moral standards of Neo-Confucianism and also was among those questioned about their possession of Catholic materials and participation in Catholic-style rituals in 1785. He died a natural death in 1793 and was not among those beatified in 2014.

Yu Sosa 柳召史 Cecilia (1761–1839) She was the wife of Blessed Chŏng Yakchong and the mother of Saint Chŏng Hasang. She died in prison during the 1839 persecution and was proclaimed a saint in 1984. When she died in prison, she was seventy-nine years old.

Yu Chungch'ŏl 柳重哲 John (1779–1801) He was the oldest son of Yu Hanggŏm. He entered into a celibate marriage with Yi Suni Lutgarda in 1797. He was executed by strangulation on November 14, 1801. He was beatified in 2014.

Yu Chungsŏng 柳重誠 Matthew (?–1802) His father died when he was still a young man, so he moved into the home of his uncle Yu Hanggŏm. He was a cousin of Yu Chungch'ŏl and Yu Munsŏk. He was beheaded on January 31, 1802. He was beatified in 2014.

Yu Hanggŏm 柳恒儉 Augustine (1756–1801) He was the father of John Yu Chungch'ŏl (1779–1801), who was the celibate husband of Yi Suni Lutgarda, and of John Yu Munsŏk (1784–1801). Both of his sons were among those executed in 1801, as was his daughter-in-law Luthgarde Yi Suni (1782–1801) and his nephew Matthew Yu Chungsŏng (?–1802). All were declared beatified in 2014. He was introduced to Catholicism by his relative Kwŏn Ilsin. Among the first to be converted, he was an important leader of the Catholic community in Chŏlla province. As a wealthy *yangban* landowner, he was able to provide the Catholic community important financial support, including financing secret trips to Beijing to meet with the bishop there. Because he was directly involved in the attempts to have a Western warship sail to Korea, he was denied the simpler execution of beheading and instead was executed by dismemberment. He was executed on October 24, 1801. He was beatified in 2014.

Yu Kwan'gŏm 柳 觀 儉 (1768–1801) His baptismal name is unknown. The younger brother of Yu Hanggŏm, he, too, was a fervent Catholic. During the interrogations of 1801, Yi Ujip revealed that Yu Kwan'gŏm had been the first to say he was waiting for the "decisive moment" when Western warships would sail to Korea and force the government to stop persecuting Catholics. For advocating that Western military might be used to threaten the government, Yu was executed and his body dismembered on October 24, 1801, the same day his brother suffered the same fate. However, unlike his brother, he was not among those beatified in 2014 since he is believed to have renounced his faith when he was being tortured. His wife, Yi Yukhŭi (?–1802) was beheaded along with Yi Suni on January 1802. However, she, too, was left off the list of those beatified in 2014.

Yu Munsŏk 柳文碩 John (1784–1801) He was the younger son of Yu Hanggŏm and brother-in-law of Yi Suni. He was only eleven years old when he met Father Zhou for the first time in 1795. At the age of seventeen, he was executed through strangulation on November 14, 1801. He was beatified in 2014.

Yun Chich'ung 尹持忠 Paul (1759–1791) He was a rural *yangban*, which means that he was a member of the local Confucian scholar elite but had little hope of winning appointment to an official post in the national government, though he passed the entry-level qualifying examination and was awarded the title of "presented scholar." He first learned about Catholicism from his cousins Chŏng Yakchŏn and Chŏng Yagyong. In 1787 he was baptized by Yi Sŭnghun. He lived in the same part of the country as Yu Hanggŏm and worked with him to introduce Catholicism to that southwestern corner of Korea.

When he learned in 1790 that Catholics were not allowed to use spirit tablets in ancestor memorial services, he burnt all the tablets he, as the eldest son, had in his home. When his mother passed away soon afterward, he held a memorial service for her without using a spirit tablet. Soon rumors spread of his irregular mourning ritual, and he was brought in for questioning by the local district magistrate. When he defended his decision not to use a spirit tablet when mourning his mother, he was condemned for lacking respect for his mother and the rest of his ancestors. He was beheaded along with his maternal cousin James Kwŏn Sangyŏn on December 8, 1791. He was beatified in 2014, as was his younger brother Yun Chihŏn.

Yun Chihŏn 尹 持 憲 Francis (1764–1801) was a maternal cousin of Augustine Chŏng Yakchong and was introduced to Catholicism by his older brother, Paul Yun Chich'ung, who was executed in 1791. Yun Chihŏn was baptized by Yi Sŭnghun in 1787. Because of his role in sending messengers to the bishop in Beijing, he was executed and then his body dismembered on October 24, 1801. After his execution, his family was split up, with his wife and his children exiled to separate sites. He was beatified in 2014.

Yun Unhye 尹 雲 惠 Lucia (?–1801) The wife of Chŏng Kwangsu, she was beheaded on May 14, 1801. She was beatified along with her husband in 2014.

Yun Yuil 尹 有一 Paul (1760–1795) He studied Catholicism under the guidance of his neighbor Kwŏn Ilsin. In 1789 and again in 1790, he traveled to Beijing to relay messages between Bishop de Gouvea and the small Catholic community back in Korea. It is Yun Yuil who brought the message from Beijing that it was forbidden for Catholics to erect an ancestral tablet for the spirit of an ancestor being mourned at a mourning ritual. He died on June 28, 1795, while being interrogated for information on the whereabouts of Father Zhou, whom he had guided to Seoul. He was beatified in 2014.

Zhou Wenmo 周文謨 James (1752–1801) He was the priest who was smuggled into Korea in early 1795 to provide the sacraments for Korea's emerging Catholic community. Born in Suzhou in China in 1752, he lost both parents when he was still a child and was adopted by his father's sister. When he was nineteen years old, he married but his wife died two years later. Over a decade later, he enrolled in the newly opened Beijing Diocese Seminary and was ordained sometime between 1791 and 1794. He was soon asked by Bishop de Gouvea to serve as the priest for Korea's Catholics.

On January 3, 1795 (December 3, 1794, by the lunar calendar), he was guided by Chi Hwang across the frozen Yalu River into Korea and reached Seoul less than two weeks later. By April of that year, the government was aware Father Zhou had entered Korea and began searching for him. He was able to hide, but those who had helped him enter

Korea (Chi Hwang, Ch'oe In'gil, and Yun Yunil) were all beaten so severely when they were being questioned about his whereabouts that they died. He spent most of the time between 1795 and 1801 in hiding in Seoul, though occasionally he was able to visit Catholics in rural areas.

He surrendered to the authorities on March 11, 1801 (according to the lunar calendar), and was beheaded a little more than one month later, on May 31, 1801 (April 19 by the lunar calendar). He was beatified in 2014.

OTHER PLAYERS: PEOPLE WHO WERE NOT KOREAN CATHOLICS BUT ARE A PART OF THE STORY OF THE FIRST DECADES OF CATHOLICISM IN KOREA

Broughton, William Robert (1762–1821) A British naval commander who sailed the H.M.S. *Providence* off the east coast of Korea in 1797 as part of his survey of the waters of Northeast Asia.

Chǒng Yakhyǒn 丁若鉉 (1751–1821) The oldest brother of Chǒng Yakchǒn, Chǒng Yakchong, and Chǒng Yagyong, though by a different mother. He was the only one of those four not to be involved with the Catholic community. His first wife, who died in 1780, was a sister of Yi Pyǒk. Before she died, they had a daughter. That daughter married Hwang Sayǒng. As the oldest son, and a non-Catholic, Chǒng Yakhyǒn ensured the spirit tablets of the Chǒng family ancestors were enshrined and used in ancestor memorial rituals.

de Grammont, Jean-Joseph (1736–1812) Originally from France, he moved to China as a Jesuit missionary in 1768. After the Society of Jesus was disbanded in 1773 he stayed on in Beijing as a diocesan priest and served under the authority of Bishop de Gouvea, a Francisan. He is the priest who baptized Yi Sǔnghun, after Yi promised to have only one wife.

de Gouvea, Alexandre (1751–1808) Portuguese Franciscan and bishop of Beijing (1785–1808) The Society of Jesus had been in charge of the Catholic mission in Beijing, but the Jesuit order was disbanded by order of the Pope in 1773, so a Franciscan became the bishop there.

Kim Wǒnsǒng 金源星 (?–?) Born into a *yangban* family affiliated with the Southerners, he was a disciple of Kwǒn Ch'ǒlsin and participated in the 1779 meeting at Ch'ŏnjin Hermitage of Chuŏsa temple. However, he never became a Catholic and even signed a memorial in 1785 asking that Catholicism be banned and Catholics punished. There is a report that someone named Kim Wŏnsŏng was among those executed in the 1801 persecution, but it is not clear if that is the same person.

Shin Taehyŏn 申大顯 (1737–1812) A Commander of the Royal Guards and the warden of the Left Police Bureau, he was ordered to behead Zhou Wenmo but, according to Hwang Sayŏng, claimed to be ill and avoided doing that. As a result, Hwang claims, he was dismissed from his post. However, the *sillok* [annals of the Chosŏn dynasty] has Shin dismissed as Commander of the Royal Guards and warden of the Left Police Bureau a few weeks after Father Zhou was executed.

Ŭnŏn, Prince 恩彦 (1775–1801) He was the grandfather of King Ch'ŏlchong (r. 1849–1863) and a stepbrother of King Chŏngjo. He was exiled to Kanghwa Island when a group of officials plotted to dethrone King Chŏngjo and elevate Ŭnŏn in his place. There is no evidence that he was ever a Catholic, but his wife Maria Song and his daughter-in-law Maria Shin became Catholics when they were living in Seoul while he was in exile.

Yinghe 英和 (1771–1839) He was a Manchu official who was sent to Korea as the deputy emissary from the Qing court in late 1799. He was only twenty-nine years old when he was dispatched to Korea. He later rose to high positions in the Qing court and also won fame as a writer.

NOTES

PREFACE

1. Choe Sang-hun, "Papal Visit That Thrills Catholics Is Unsettling to Protestants in South Korea," *New York Times*, August 16, 2014, http://www.nytimes.com/2014/08/17/world/asia/huge-crowds-watch-in-seoul-as-pope-francis-beatifies-korean-catholics.html.
2. Gallup Korea, ed. *Han'gugin ŭi chonggyo: 1984-yŏn, 1989-yŏn, 1997-yŏn, 2004-yŏn, 2014-yŏn, che 5-ch'a pigyo chosa pogosŏ* [The Religion of Koreans: A report comparing survey results from 1984, 1989, 1987, 2004, and 2014]. Seoul: Gallup Korea Research Center, 2015.
3. For a survey of different evaluations of Hwang Sayŏng's *Silk Letter*, see Chŏng Sŏnghan, "Hwang Sayŏng ŭi *Paeksŏ*-e taehan yŏn'gu: poda t'ongjŏnjŏgin yŏksa haesŏgŭl wihan han siron" [A study of the *Silk Letter* of Hwang Sayŏng: An attempt at a broader historical explanation] *Changshin nondan* 33 (2009): 91–116; and Yi Changu, "Hwang Sayŏng kwa Chosŏn hugi ŭi sahoe pyŏnhwa: Kyŏnggi pukpu chiyŏk kyohoe sajŏk ŭi kich'ojŏk kŏmt'o illye" [Hwang Sayŏng and changes in society in the latter half of the Chosŏn dynasty: A preliminary examination of the sites important for church history in northern Kyŏnggi province] *Kyohoesa yŏn'gu* 31 (December 2008): 79–108.

NOTES ON THE TRANSLATED TEXTS AND ROMANIZATION

1. Kang Mangil et al., eds., *Ch'uan kŭp kugan* [Records of special investigations by the State Tribunal] 25 (Seoul: Asea munhwasa, 1978), 735–790. The truncated version of the *Silk Letter*, the one that was sent to Beijing,

can be found in *Hwang Sayŏng paeksŏ*, edited and translated by Yun Chaeyŏng (Seoul: Chŏngŭmsa, 1975), 139–147.

2. Yi Manch'ae, ed. *Pyŏgwip'yŏn* [In defense of the right against the wrong] (Seoul: Yŏlhwadang, 1971), 329–366; Yŏ Chinch'ŏn, "Hwang Sayŏng 'Paeksŏ' ibon-e taehan pigyo yŏn'gu" [A comparative study of alternative versions of the *Silk Letter* of Hwang Sayŏng], *Kyohoesa yŏn'gu* 28 (June 2007): 11.

CHAPTER 1: KOREA AT THE END OF THE EIGHTEENTH CENTURY

1. See Yi Ik's comments on the *Qike* [Seven victories] of Diego de Pantoja (1571–1618) in *Sŏngho saesŏl* [The classified writings of Yi Ik] (Seoul: Minjok munhwa ch'ujinhoe, 1977–78), 11:2.
2. Don Baker, *Korean Spirituality* (Honolulu: University of Hawai'i Press, 2008), 94–113.
3. Don Baker, "The Religious Revolution in Modern Korean History: From Ethics to Theology and from Ritual Hegemony to Religious Freedom," *Review of Korean Studies* 9, no. 3 (September 2006): 257–261.
4. Kim Yong-duk, "Ancestral Rites," *Korean Cultural Heritage*, vol. 4 (Seoul: Korea Foundation, 1997), 42–49; Chang-Won Park, "Between God and Ancestors: Ancestral Practice in Korean Protestantism," *International Journal for the Study of the Christian Church* 10, no. 4 (2010): 257–273.
5. D. E. Mungello, ed. *The Chinese Rites Controversy: Its History and Meaning* (Nettetal: Steyler Verlag, 1994). That papal decision was reversed in 1939, when the Vatican ruled that those rituals were cultural rather than religious.
6. Don Baker, "The Martyrdom of Paul Yun: Western Religion and Eastern Ritual in Eighteenth-Century Korea," *Transactions of the Royal Asiatic Society, Korea Branch*, no. 54 (1979): 33–58.
7. Yi Nŭnghwa, *Chosŏn musokko* [A study of Korean shamanism] (Seoul: Hangukhak Yeonguso, 1977), 37; Han Ugŭn, "Chosŏn wangjo ch'ogi-e issŏsŏ-ŭi yugyo inyŏm-ŭi silchŏn kwa sinang, chongjo: Saje munje rŭl chungsimŭro" [Religion, religious faith, and the realization of Confucian ideals in the early Chosŏn dynasty: Focusing on the issue of rituals], *Hanguk saron* 3 (1976): 189.
8. Boudewijn Walraven, "Popular Religion in a Confucianized Society," in *Culture and the State in Late Chosŏn Korea*, ed. Jahyun Kim Haboush and Martina Deuchler (Cambridge, MA: Harvard University Press, 1999),

160–198; Ch'oe Chongsŏng, *Chosŏnjo musok kukhaeng irye yŏn'gu* [A study of official shamanic rituals during the Chosŏn dynasty] (Seoul: Iljisa, 2002).

9. See, for example, the 1791 request to the king by the Censor-General Shin Ki (1741–?) that Catholicism be outlawed as a threat to morality: *Chŏngjo sillok,* year 15, tenth month, twentieth day (*sinyu*). Also see the edict that declared the start of the 1801 persecution of Catholics: *Sŭnjsŏngwŏn ilgi, Sunjo sillok,* year 1, first month, tenth day (*chŏnghae*).

10. Robert E. Buswell Jr., *The Collected Works of Chinul* (Honolulu: University of Hawai'i Press, 1983), 144.

11. Yi Ik, *Sŏngho saesŏl,* 26:15a–b.

12. "Chungyong chajam" [Admonitions for myself upon reading the *Doctrine of the Mean*], *Yŏyudang chŏnsŏ* [The complete works of Yŏyudang Chŏng Yagyong], 2:3, 2b.

13. "Maengja youi" [Essential meaning of the *Mencius*], *Yŏyudang chŏnsŏ,* 2:6, 19a.

14. Ibid., 2:5, 33a.

15. "Chungyong chajam," 2:3, 4b–5a.

16. Cho Kwang, *Chosŏn hugi sahoe wa Ch'ŏnjugyo* [Catholicism and society in the latter half of the Chosŏn dynasty] (Seoul: Kyŏngin munhwasa, 2010), 89–118, provides a comprehensive narrative of the Confucian origins of Korea's first Catholic community.

17. Yŏ Chinch'ŏn, *Nuga chŏhŭirŭl wirohae chugessŭmnikka?* [Who will comfort us?] (Seoul: Kibbŭn sosik: 2002), 74.

18. *Sunjo sillok,* year 1, twelfth month, twenty-second day (*kapcha*).

19. Andrew Finch, "The Pursuit of Martyrdom in the Catholic Church in Korea before 1866," *Journal of Ecclesiastical History* 60, no. 1 (January 2009): 95–118.

20. See, for example, King Chŏngjo's complaint that all that talk about the "Catholic problem" was becoming a distraction from more important government matters. *Chŏngjo sillok,* year 15, eleventh month, eighth day (*Kimyo*).

21. Chŏng Yagyong is one example of someone whom the king wanted to keep close at hand yet was forced on several occasions to send away. Don Baker, "Tasan between Catholicism and Confucianism: A Decade Under Suspicion, 1791 to 1801," *Tasanhak* 5 (2004): 55–86.

22. See, for example, the account of the relationship between kings and censors in Sohn Pokee, *Social History of the Early Chosŏn Dynasty: the Functional Aspects of Governmental Structure* (Seoul: Jisik-sanup Publishing, 2000), 197–271.

23. A description of another form of the leg screw torture can be found in Gari Ledyard, "Kollumba Kang Wansuk, an Early Catholic Activist and Martyr," in *Christianity in Korea*, ed. Robert E. Buswell Jr. and Timothy S. Lee (Honolulu: University of Hawai'i Press, 2006), 57.

24. Chŏng Yagyong, *Admonitions for Governing the People: Manual for All Administrators* [*Mongmin shimsŏ*], trans. Choi Byonghyon (Berkeley: University of California Press, 2010), 732.

25. Ibid., 745–746.

26. The *Zuo Zhuan* (The commentary of Zuo) on the *Chunqiu* (Spring and Autumn annals) as cited in James Legge, ed., *The Chinese Classics*, vol. 5, *The Ch'un Ts'ew with the Tso Chuen* (Hong Kong: Hong Kong University Press, 1960), 382.

27. For more on the *chungin*, see Kyung Moon Hwang, *Beyond Birth: Social Status in the Emergence of Modern Korea* (Cambridge, MA: Harvard University Asia Center, 2005), 106–126.

28. Pak Kwang'yong, *Yŏngjo wa Chŏngjo-ŭi nara* [The country of Kings Yŏngjo and Chŏngjo] (Seoul: P'urŭn yŏksa, 1998), 271.

29. Richard Rutt and Chong'un Kim, trans. *Virtuous Women: Three Classic Korean Novels: A Nine Cloud Dream, The True History of Queen Inhyŏn, The Song of a Faithful Wife, Ch'un-hyang* (Seoul: Kwangmyong, 1979).

30. For more on this tragic incident, see the account by the widow of that unfortunate crown prince. JaHyun Kim Haboush, trans., *The Memoirs of Lady Hyegyong: The Autobiographical Writings of a Crown Princess of Eighteenth-Century Korea* (Berkeley: University of California Press, 1996).

31. Yi Sŏngmu, *Chosŏn wangjosa* [The history of the Chosŏn dynasty] (Seoul: Tongbang midiŏ, 1998), 2:856.

32. Kim Sŏng'yun, *Chosŏn hugi t'angp'yŏng chŏngch'i yŏn'gu* [A study of the politics of Grand Harmony in the latter half of the Chosŏn dynasty] (Seoul: Chisik sanŏpsa, 1997), 241–245.

33. *Chŏngjo sillok*, twenty-fourth year, fifth month, thirtieth day (*sinhae*).

CHAPTER 2: CONFUCIAN CRITICISMS OF CATHOLICISM

1. *Analects*, II, 16.

2. Shin Hudam, "Sŏhakpyŏn" [On Western Learning] in Yi Manch'ae, ed., *Pyŏgwip'yŏn* [In defense of the right against the wrong] (Seoul: Yŏlhwadang, 1971), 40.

3. Chŏng Yagyong, "Nonŏ gogŭmju" [Notes on the *Analects*], *Yŏyudang chŏnsŏ* [the complete writing of Yŏyudang Chŏng Yagyong], Seoul: Kyŏngin munhwa sa, 1970–2:7, 31a.

4. Arthur Waley, trans. *The Analects of Confucius* (New York: Vintage Books, 1938), 91. Edward Slingerland, in *Confucius: Analects, with Selections from Traditional Commentaries* (Indianapolis, IN: Hackett Publishing, 2003), 13, translates that phrase instead as "working from the wrong starting point will lead to nothing but harm" and writes that it is an anachronism to read *idan* as "heterodox teachings." Nevertheless, that is close to the way this passage was read by mainstream Korean Confucians in the seventeenth and nineteenth centuries, so I will translate *idan* as "strange teachings," or "harmful teachings," when discussing anti-Catholic rhetoric in Chosŏn dynasty Korea.

5. See Sasoon Yun (Yun Sasun), *Critical Issues in Neo-Confucian Thought: The Philosophy of Yi T'oegye*, trans. Michael C. Kalton (Seoul: Korea University Press, 1990), 31 and 46.

6. Yi Ik, "Idan," in *Sŏngho sasŏl yusŏn* [Selections from the classified writings of Sŏngho Yi Ik], ed. Ahn Chŏngbok, 371–372 (Seoul: Myŏngmundang, 1982).

7. Ahn Chŏngbok, *Sunamjip* [The collected writings of Sunam Ahn Chŏngbok] (Seoul: Sŏnggyun'gwan taehakkyo, Taedong munhwa yŏn'guwŏn, 1970), 8:28b.

8. Martina Deuchler, "Despoilers of the Way—Insulters of the Sages: Controversies over the Classics in Seventeenth-Century Korea," in *Culture and the State in Late Chosŏn Korea*, ed. JaHyun Kim Haboush and Martina Deuchler (Cambridge, MA: Harvard University Asia Center, 1999), 90–133.

9. Ahn, *Sunamjip*, 6:27b.

10. Hwang Tŏkkil, *Haryŏ sŏnsaeng munjip* [The collected writings of Haryŏ Hwang Tŏkkil] (Seoul: Kyujanggak Collection, n.d.), 9:35b.

11. Ahn, *Sunamjip*, 6:29b.

12. Shin, "Sŏhakpyŏn," 90.

13. Matteo Ricci, SJ, *The True Meaning of the Lord of Heaven*, trans. Douglas Lancashire and Peter Hu Kuo-chen, SJ (St. Louis, MO: The Institute of Jesuit Sources, 1985), esp. 104–131.

14. Ahn Chŏngbok, "Ch'ŏnhakko" [An examination of Celestial Learning], *Sunamjip*, 17:1–8a.

15. For an example of the use of the state power to enforce specific interpretations of Confucian ritual obligations, see JaHyun Kim Haboush,

"Constructing the Center: The Ritual Controversy and the Search for a New Identity in Seventeenth-Century Korea," in *Culture and State in Late Chosŏn Korea,* ed. JaHyun Kim Haboush and Martina Deuchler (Cambridge, MA: Harvard University Press, 1999), 46–90.

16. *Taemyŏngnyul chikhae* [The Ming law codes explained] (reprint, Seoul: Pŏpjech'o, 1964), 294–295; J. J. M. de Groot, *Sectarianism and Religious Persecution in China* (New York: Paragon Books, 1970), 137 and 147.

17. Kwang-ching Liu, *Orthodoxy in Late Imperial China* (Berkeley: University of California Press, 1990).

18. David L. Holland, "Heresy, Renaissance and Later," in *Dictionary of the History of Ideas,* ed. Philip P. Wiener (New York: Charles Scribner's Sons, 1968–1974), II, 424–431.

19. Julia Ching, *Confucianism and Christianity* (Tokyo: Kodansha, 1977), xxii.

20. For example, see Ahn Chŏngbok's 1784 letter to Kwŏn Ch'ŏlsin, in *Sunamjip,* 6:29a–b.

21. *Mencius* III, 2, IX.

22. For example, see Hong Nagan's letter to Ch'ae Chegong in Yi Kigyŏng, ed., *Pyŏgwip'yŏn* (Seoul: Kyohoesa yŏn'guso, 1979), 26.

23. Zhu Xi and Liu Zuqian, eds., Wing Tsit-chan, trans., *Reflections on Things at Hand* (New York: Columbia University Press, 1967), 279.

24. Cheng Hao, *I-shu,* 4:4b, as translated by Wing-tsit Chan, *A Sourcebook of Chinese Philosophy* (Princeton, NJ: Princeton University Press, 1969), 535.

25. Martina Deuchler, "Neo-Confucianism: The Impulse for Social Action in Early Yi Korea," *Journal of Korean Studies* 2 (1980): 75–79; Kŭm Changt'ae, "Chungjongjo t'aehaksaeng ŭi pyŏkpul undong" [The anti-Buddhist campaign of Confucian students during the reign of King Chungjong], in *Han'guk yugyo ŭi Chaejomyŏng* [New light on Korean Confucianism] (Seoul: Chŏnmangsa, 1982), 199–208.

26. For example, see Yi Ik as cited by Ahn Chŏngbok, *Sunamjip,* 17:26b.

27. Letter by Yi Hŏn'gyŏng to Hong Yangho before Hong's departure on an official mission to the capital of China, in Yi Hŏn'gyŏng, *Kanongjip* [The works of Yi Hŏn'gyŏng] (Seoul: Han'guk kojŏn pŏnyŏgwon [Institute for the Translation of the Korean Classics], 2013), 9:36a–38a; also note Pak Chiwŏn's criticism of the arrogant assumption of moral and cultural superiority some Koreans displayed in China, "Yŏrha ilgi" [Rehe diary], in *Yŏnamjip* [Yŏnam Pak Chiwŏn's collected works] (Seoul: Kyŏngin munhwasa, 1974), 14:1a–4a.

28. Kŭm Changt'ae, "T'oegye ŭi yangmyŏnghak pip'an" [T'oegye's criticism of the Wang Yangming school], in *Han'guk yugyo ŭi chaejomyŏng* [New

light on Korean Confucianism] (Seoul: Chŏnmangsa, 1982), 209–218; Kim Kilhwan, *Chosŏnjo yuhak sasang yŏn'gu* [A study of Confucianism in the Chosŏn dynasty] (Seoul: Iljisa, 1980), 69–76.

29. Hwang Tŏkkil, *Haryŏ sŏnsaeng munjip*, 16:10a.
30. Ibid., 16:11a.
31. For an illuminating discussion of selfishness and selflessness in Chinese Confucian writings, see Donald Munro, "The Concept of Interest in Chinese Thought," *Journal of the History of Ideas* 41, no. 2 (1980): 179–197.
32. Ibid., 180.
33. On Yang Zhu, see "Mencius," in Legge, *Chinese Classics* (Hong Kong: Hong Kong University Press, 1960), 2:92–99. (Here Yang Zhu appears as Yang Chu.)
34. Shin, "Sŏhakpyŏn," 40–41.
35. Ahn, Letter to Yi Ik, 1757, in *Sunamjip*, 2:16a–b.
36. Two useful studies of Yi Ik's influence on later generations of *Southerners* are Kang Segu, *Sŏngho hakt'ong yŏn'gu* [Studies of Sŏngho's intellectual legacy] (Seoul: Hyean Publishing, 1999) and Wŏn Chaerin, *Chosŏn hugi Sŏngho hakp'a ŭi hakp'ung yŏn'gu* [Studies on the academic accomplishments of the Sŏngho school in the latter half of the Chosŏn dynasty] (Seoul: Hyean Publishing, 2003).
37. Mun Sang Seoh, "Yi Ik, an Eighteenth Century Korean Intellectual," *Journal of Korean Studies* 1 (1969): 9–21; Song Chu-yong, "Yi Ik and Practical Learning," in *Korean Philosophy: Its Tradition and Modern Transformation* ed. Korean National Commission for UNESCO (Seoul: Hollym, 2004), 323–335; Han Ugŭn, *Sŏngho Yi Ik yŏn'gu* [A study of Yi Ik] (Seoul: Seoul University Press, 1980).
38. Han, *Sŏngho Yi Ik yŏn'gu*, 49, lists all the works Yi Ik mentions by name in his writings.
39. Yi Ik, *Sŏngho Sŏnsaeng munjip* [The collected works of Yi Ik] (Seoul: Kyŏngin munhwasa, 1974), 55:24a–26b; 27b; 30a.
40. "*Qike*" can be found in Li Zhizao, ed., *Tianxue chuhan* [An introduction to Celestial Learning] (Taipei: Taiwan xuesheng shuju, 1965), 2:689–1131.
41. Yi Ik, *Sŏngho sasŏl*, 11:2b.
42. Ibid., 13:22a–b; 30:39b–40a.
43. Shin, "Sŏhakpyŏn, 38–103
44. Shin Kyusŏng, "Habin sŏnsaeng yŏnbo" [A chronology of the life of Habin Shin Hudam], *Asea yŏn'gu* [Journal of Asiatic Studies] 15, no. 2 (1972): 197; Yi Ik, "Sŏnggyun'gwan chinsa Shin'gong myojimyŏng" [An obituary for Shin Hudam], *Sŏngho sŏnsaeng munjip* 64:33a.

45. "Habin sŏnsaeng yŏnbo," 197–199; Ch'oe Tonghŭi, "Habin Shin Hudam," *Han'guk inmul yuhaksa* [A history of Confucians in Korea] (Seoul: Han'gilsa, 1996), 3:1459–1480.
46. Yi Ik, "Sŏnggyun'gwan chinsa Sin'gong myojimyŏng," 34b.
47. "Habin sŏnsaeng yŏnbo," 200.
48. Yi Ik, *Sŏngho sŏnsaeng munjip*, 22:30a–31a.
49. Shin Hudam, *Habinjip* [The collected works of Habin Shin Hudam], vol. 2, cited in Kim Yangsŏn, *Maesan kukhak san'go* [Kim Yangsŏn's writings on Korean Studies] (Seoul: Sungjŏn University Museum, 1972), 136–138.
50. Shin's essay is contained in its entirety in Yi Manch'ae, ed., *Pyŏgwip'yŏn*, 38–103. It can also be found in the original literary Chinese as well as in an annotated Korean translation in Kim Sŏnhŭi, trans., *Habin Shin Hudam ŭi Tonwa Sŏhakpyŏn* [The *Tonwa Sŏhakpyŏn* of Habin Shin Hudam] (Seoul: Silsi haksa, 2014). For a philosophical analysis of Shin's critical stance, see Kŭm Changt'ae, "Tonwa Shin Hudam ŭi Sŏhak pip'aniron kwa chaengjŏm" [The theoretical basis for Shin Hudam's criticism of Western Learning and the particular points he raised against it], *Chonggyohak yŏn'gu* [Journal of Religious Studies] 20 (December 2001): 1–25. Also see Ch'oe Tonghŭi, "Shin Hudam ŭi Sŏhak pip'an" [Shin Hudam's criticism of Western Learning], in *Sŏhak-e taehan Han'guk sirhak ŭi panŭng* [The reaction of Korean Practical Learning scholars to Western Learning] (Seoul: Koryŏ Taehakkyo Minjok Munhwa Yŏn'guso, 1988), 59–95, and Ch'oe Tonghŭi, "Shin Hudam ŭi Sŏhakpyŏn-e kwanhan yŏn'gu" [A study of Shin Hudam's "On Western Learning," *Asia yŏn'gu* [Journal of Asiatic Studies], 15:2 (1972), 1–27.
51. "Habin sŏnsaeng yŏnbo," 199.
52. Kim Yangsŏn, 138, citing *Habinjip*, vol. 2.
53. Yi Ik, *Sŏngho sŏnsaeng munjip*, 22:33b–34a.
54. "Habin sŏnsaeng yŏnbo," 216–217.
55. Ahn, *Sunamjip*, 17:26a–27a.
56. Ahn provides a record of that first meeting in his "hanjang nok," *Sunamjip*, 16:13b.
57. Yŏnbo" [A chronological account of Ahn Chŏngbok's life], *Sunamjip*, 33b, 47a.
58. Ibid., 3a.
59. A concise introduction to Ahn's intellectual orientation is Ch'oe Pongyŏng, "Sunam Ahn Chŏngbok," *Han'guk inmul yuhaksa* (Seoul: Han'gilsa, 1996), 3:1507–1521. For a more detailed look at Ahn Chŏngbok's intellectual relationship with Sŏngho, see Kang Segu, *Sunam Ahn Chŏngbok ŭi hangmun kwa sasang yŏn'gu* [The scholarship and philosophy of Ahn

Chŏngbok] (Seoul: Hyean, 1996). For a look at Ahn Chŏngbok's overall approach to Confucian learning as well as his reaction to Western Learning, see Sim Ujun, *Sunam Ahn Chŏngbok yŏn'gu* [A study of Sunam An Chŏngbok] (Seoul: Iljisa, 1985).

60. In a 1757 letter to Sŏngho, Sunam gave his reasons for labeling Catholicism *idan*. *Sunamjip*, 2:16a–17a. In 1758 Sunam wrote Sŏngho to discuss the Catholic concept of the soul. *Sunamjip*, 2:26b–30a.

61. Ahn, "Ch'ŏnhakko," *Sunamjip*, 17:1a–8a.

62. Ibid., 1a–b.

63. Ahn, *Sunamjip*, "Ch'ŏnhak mundap," 17:8a–26a. Ch'oe Tonghŭi, "Ahn Chŏngbok ŭi Sŏhak pip'an" [Ahn Chŏngbok's criticism of Western Learning], in *Sŏhak-e Taehan Han'guk sirhak ŭi panŭng*, 96–135; Kŭm Changt'ae, "Ahn Chŏngbok ŭi Sŏhak pip'an" [Ahn Chŏngbok's criticism of Western Learning], in *Han'guk yugyo ŭi chaejomyŏng* [New light on Korean Confucianism] (Seoul: Chŏnmangsa, 1982).

64. Yi Manch'ae, *Pyŏgwip'yŏn*, 105–108.

65. Ahn, *Sunamjip*, 8:21a.

66. Ibid., 8:24b.

67. Ibid., 5:19b–20a.

68. Yi Manch'ae, *Pyŏgwip'yŏn*, 596–598.

69. Ibid., 489; Yi Kuyong, "Sunam Ahn Chŏngbok ŭi saengae wa sasang" [The life and thought of Ahn Chŏngbok], in *Kangwŏn Taehak yŏn'gu nonmunjip* [Research papers from Kangwŏn University] VI (1972): 374.

70. Ahn, *Sunamjip*, 17:26a–28a.

71. Shin, "Sŏhakpyŏn," 91–92.

72. Ahn, letter to Kwŏn Ch'ŏlsin, 1784, *Sunamjip*, 6:33b–34a.

73. Matteo Ricci and Nicolas Trigault, *China in the Sixteenth Century: The Journals of Matthew Ricci, 1583–1610*. Trans. Louis J. Gallagher, SJ (New York: Random House, 1953), 337.

74. Ibid., 98.

75. Ricci, *The True Meaning of the Lord of Heaven (Tianzhu shiyi)*, 324–337. The phrase Ricci cites from the *Odes* can be found in James Legge, *The Chinese Classics*, vol. 4, *The She King or the Book of Poetry* (Hong Kong: Hong Kong University Press, 1960), 433.

76. Trigault, *China in the Sixteenth Century*, 416, 434.

77. George Minamiki, SJ, *The Chinese Rites Controversy from Its Beginning to Modern Times* (Chicago: Loyola University Press, 1985).

78. *Xingli zhenquan* [A complete explanation of principle and human nature], 305, as cited in Zhu Qienzhi, "Yesuhui duiyu Songru lixue zhi fanxiang" [The Jesuits' reaction to Song Neo-Confucianism], in *Mingdai*

zongjiao [Ming dynasty religion], ed. Tao Xisheng et al. (Taipei: The Student Bookstore, 1968), 158.

79. See, for example, Thomas Aquinas, *Summa Theologica*, Part IIA, question 19, article 9, "the goodness of the will depends on its conformity to the divine will," trans. Anton E. Pegis, in *Basic Writings of St. Thomas Aquinas* (New York: Random House, 1948), 2:346.

80. Ricci, *The True Meaning of the Lord of Heaven*, 308–319.

81. Ahn, *Sunamjip*, 17:15b–16a.

82. Shin, "Sŏhakpyŏn," 100–101.

83. Guilio Aleni, *Zhifang waiji* [World geography], Li Zhizao, ed. *Tianxue chuhan* [An introduction to Celestial Learning], vol. 2. Taipei: Taiwan xuesheng shuju, 1965, 1336–1337.

84. Shin, "Sŏhakpyŏn," 102.

CHAPTER 3: THE BIRTH OF THE KOREAN CATHOLIC CHURCH

1. There is some dispute over whether or not Yi Sŭnghun was present at that retreat. Most scholars who have studied reports of that retreat carefully conclude he was not there. Ch'oe Sŏgu, "Han'guk kyohoe ŭi ch'angsŏl kwa ch'och'anggi Yi Sŭnghun ŭi kyohoe hwaldong" [Yi Sŭnghun's activities during the formative period of the Korean church], *Kyohoesa yŏn'gu* 8 (1992): 9; Yun Min-gu, *Han'guk Ch'ŏnjugyo ŭi kiwŏn* [The origins of the Catholic Church in Korea] (Seoul: Kukhak Charyowŏn, 2002), 170.

2. Charles Dallet, *Histoire de L'église de Corée* (Paris: Librairie Victor Palme, 1874; repr., Seoul: Royal Asiatic Society, 1975), 14–15.

3. Yu Hongnyŏl, *Han'guk sahoe sasangsa non'go* [Studies on the history of Korean social thought] (Seoul: Iljogak, 1980), provides some information on the complex marriage and blood ties linking the *Namin* to each other. On Yi Yunha, see 191–195. On Yi Sŭnghun, see 210–212.

4. This *li* is 里, meaning a unit of distance equal roughly to one-third of a mile, and is different from the *li* 理 referring to the normative patterns of Neo-Confucianism.

5. Chŏng Yagyong, *Yŏyudang chŏnsŏ*, I, 15:35a; 39a.

6. Chan Wing-tsit, trans., *A Sourcebook in Chinese Philosophy* (Princeton, NJ: Princeton University Press, 1969), 497–500. Also see Michael Kalton, *To Become a Sage: Ten Diagrams on Sagely Learning* (New York: Columbia University Press, 1988), 51–58.

7. *Analects*, 12:1.

8. "Four Things Not Done" is found in Chu Hsi (Zhu Xi) and Lu Tsu-chien (Lu Zuqian), eds., Chan Wing-tsit, trans., *Reflections on Things at Hand* (New York: Columbia University Press, 1967), 155–157.

9. Kalton, *To Become a Sage*, 191–209.

10. Ibid., 177–718. I have modified Kalton's translation slightly.

11. Chŏng Yagyong, *Yŏyudang chŏnsŏ* I, 13:37b–38a; II, 2:23a.

12. See, for example, the *Zhongyong*, chap. 22, in Legge, *Chinese Classics*, 1:416.

13. Father Byun Ki-Yung (Pyŏn Kiyŏng) is the most vocal scholarly advocate for this position. See, for example, his *Hanŭnim ŭi kyŏre* [The people of God] (Kwangju, Kyŏnggi-do: Han'guk Ch'ŏnjugyohoe ch'angnipsa yŏn'guwŏn, 1999). He dates the beginning of a Catholic Church in Korea to the first time he believes Koreans began taking Catholic writings seriously, which he believes was at Chuŏsa in 1779. That was a few years before anyone in Korea was baptized a Catholic.

14. Kim Wŏnsŏng was one of the signers of the first memorial attacking Korea's inchoate Catholic community in 1785. See Yi Manch'ae, *Pyŏgwip'yŏn*, 105–106.

15. Sŏ Chongt'ae, "Ch'ŏnjin-am Chuŏsa kanghak kwa Yangmyŏnghak" [Wang Yangming's philosophy and the scholarly meeting at Ch'ŏnjin hermitage of Chuŏ temple], *Yi Kibaek sŏnsaeng kohŭi kinyŏm han'guk sahak nonch'ong* [A collection of articles on Korean history in honor of Yi Kibaek's seventieth birthday] (Seoul: Injogak, 1994), 1265–1293.

16. For a firsthand account of Yi Sŭnghun's conversion, see a letter from the bishop of Beijing at that time, Alexandre de Gouvea. Anthony of Taizé, "Origins of the Catholic Church in Korea: A Letter," *Transactions of the Royal Asiatic Society, Korea Branch* 89 (2014): 175–177.

17. Cho Kwang, "Sinyu kyonan kwa Yi Sŭnghun" [Yi Sŭnghun and the 1801 anti-Catholic persecution], *Kyohoesa yŏn'gu* 8 (1992): 61, 74. There is some disagreement over who Yi Pyŏk's wife actually was, with some claiming she was Kwŏn Yuhandang, a daughter of Kwŏn Ilsin. See Kim Ok-hŭi, *Han'guk Sŏhak sasang-sa yŏn'gu* [Studies in the history of Korean thoughts on Western learning] (Seoul: Kukhak Charyowŏn, 1998), 524–525. A recent rigorous scholarly investigation casts doubt on that assumption. See Yun Min'gu, *Chogi han'guk ch'ŏnju kyohoesa ŭi chaengjŏm yŏn'gu* [Study of the points of contention in the early history of the Roman Catholic Church in Korea] (Seoul: Kukhak charyowŏn, 2014), 388–415.

18. Hwang Sayŏng, *Silk Letter*, lines 44–45. Also see Dallet, *Histoire*, 19–22, for an account of Yi Pyŏk's proselytizing activities.

19. Cho Kwang, "Sinyu kyonan kwa Yi Sŭnghun," 61.

20. Chŏng Yagyong, "Sŏnjungssi myojimyŏng" [An epitaph for my older brother], in *Yŏyudang chŏnsŏ*, I, 15:42a.

21. Yi Manch'ae, *Pyŏgwip'yŏn*, 105–106.

22. Ibid., 105–106; *Sahak chingŭi* [a warning against Catholicism] Han'guksa yŏn'guso, ed. (Seoul: Pulham munhwasa, 1977), 82, 378; Yi Wŏnsun, "Kim Pŏmuga non'go" [A look at the family of Kim Pŏmu], in *Han'guk Kat'ollik munhwa hwaldong kwa kyohoesa* [Church history and the cultural activities of the Korean Catholic Church], ed. Ch'oe Sŏgu sinbu kohŭi kinyŏm saŏp wiwŏnhoe (Seoul: Han'guk kyohoesa yŏn'guso, 1991), 459–476.

23. Yi Manch'ae, *Pyŏgwip'yŏn*, 106.

24. Dallet, *Histoire*, 28–29.

25. Ch'a Kijin, "Manch'ŏn Yi Sŭnghun ŭi kyohoe hwaldong kwa chŏngch'ijŏk ipchi" [Manch'ŏn Yi Sŭnghun's political stance and his activities for the church], *Kyohoesa yŏn'gu* 8 (1992): 45; Ch'oe Chaegŏn, *Chosŏn hugi sŏhak ŭi suyong kwa palchŏn* [The reception and development of Western Learning in the second half of the Chosŏn dynasty] (Seoul: Handŭl Publishing, 2005), 88–91.

26. Yi Manchae, ed., *Pyŏgwip'yŏn*, 113–114.

27. Ibid., 117–118.

28. Yi Kigyŏng, *Pyŏgwip'yŏn*, 7–13.

29. *Chŏngjo sillok* yr. 12, 8th month, 2nd day (*sinmyo*).

30. *Chŏngjo sillok* yr. 12 8th month, 6th day (*ŭlmi*); Park Hyunmo, "King Jeongjo's Political Role in the Conflicts between Confucianism and Catholicism in Eighteenth-Century Korea," *Review of Korean Studies* 7, no. 4 (December 2004): 212–215.

31. Cho Kwang, *Chosŏn hugi sahoe wa Ch'ŏnjugyo*, 388.

32. Han'guk Ch'ŏnjugyo chugyohoe ŭi sibok sisŏng chugyo t'ŭkpyŏl wiwŏnhoe, ed., *Hanŭnim ŭi chong: Yun Chich'ung Paoro wa tongnyo sun'gyoja 123 wi* [Servants of God: Paul Yun Chich'ung and 123 fellow martyrs] (Seoul: Han'guk Ch'ŏnjugyo chugyohoe ŭi sibok sisŏng chugyo t'ŭkpyŏl wiwŏnhoe, 2003), 35; Kim Chinso, *Ch'ŏnjugyo Chŏnju kyogusa* [A history of the Catholic Diocese of Chŏnju] (Chŏnju: The Catholic Diocese of Chŏnju, 1998), 108.

33. Anthony of Taizé, "Origins of the Catholic Church," 180–182.

34. Ch'oe Sŏgu, "Han'guk kyohoe," 29; Ch'a [Ch'a, not Cha] Kijin, "Manch'ŏn Yi Sŭnghun," 47; Sŏ Chongt'ae and Han Kŏn, eds., *Chosŏn hugi Ch'ŏnjugyo sinja chaep'an kirok: ch'uan mit kugan* [Records of the trials of Catholic believers in the latter part of the Chosŏn era: Records of the State Tribunal] (Seoul: Kukhak Charyowŏn, 2004), 940–943; Dallet, *Histoire*, 34–35.

35. Kang Mangil et al., eds., *Ch'uan kŭp kugan* [Records of special investigations by the State Tribunal], vol. 25 (Seoul: Asea munhwasa, 1978), 86–88; Sŏ Chongt'ae and Han Kŏn, *Chosŏn hugi Ch'ŏnjugyo*, 937–940; Dallet, *Histoire*, 24.

36. Minamiki, *The Chinese Rites Controversy*; Ch'oe Kibok, "The Abolition of Ancestral Rites and Tablets by Catholicism in the Chosŏn Dynasty and the Basic Meaning of Confucian Ancestral Rites," *Korea Journal* 24, no. 8 (1984): 41–52.

37. For a look at *chesa* in modern Korea, see Roger L. Janelli and Dawnhee Yim Janelli, *Ancestor Worship and Korean Society* (Stanford, CA: Stanford University Press, 1982). Another detailed description of *chesa* can be found in Griffin Dix, "How to Do Things with Ritual: The Logic of Ancestor Worship and Other Offerings in Rural Korea," in *Studies on Korea in Transition*, ed. David McCann, John Middleton, and Edward Shultz (Honolulu: University of Hawai'i Press, 1979), 57–88.

38. Jonathan D. Spence, *Emperor of China: Self-Portrait of K'ang-hsi* (New York: Vintage Books, 1974), 79.

39. *Li Ji*, as translated by Derk Bodde in Feng Yu-lan, *A History of Chinese Philosophy* (Princeton, NJ: Princeton University Press, 1952), 1:350.

40. C. K. Yang, *Religion in Chinese Society* (Berkeley: University of California Press, 1961), 48.

41. Yi Ik, "Chesa ji li," *Sŏngho sasŏl*, 16:28b–30a.

42. Ahn Chŏngbok, *Sunamjip*, 17:24b–25a.

43. Dallet, *Histoire*, 37–38; Kim Chinso, "Chu Munmo sinbu sŏn'gyo hwaldong chŏnhuŭi sun'gyojadŭl" [Those who were martyred around the time Father Zhou Wenmo was proselytizing in Korea], *Kyohoesa yŏn'gu* 10 (1995): 99–100.

44. Yi Kigyŏng, *Pyŏgwip'yŏn*, 27–29.

45. Ibid., 29–30.

46. Ibid., 39–42.

47. Dallet, *Histoire*, 42–53.

48. Ibid., 48.

49. Ibid., 49.

50. Ibid., 47.

51. Ibid., 43.

52. Ibid., 47.

53. Ibid., 47–48. A version of Yun's statement similar to that found in Dallet can be found in *Chŏngjo sillok*, yr 15, 11th month, 7th day (*muin*) (1791).

54. *Analects*, 3:12.

55. See, for example, the memorial by Shin Ki, *Chŏngjo sillok* yr 15, 10ᵗʰ month, 20ᵗʰ day (*sinyu*).
56. *Chŏngjo sillok* yr 12, 8ᵗʰ month, 6ᵗʰ day (*ŭlmi*).
57. Dallet, *Histoire*, 44.
58. Shin Ki, in *Chŏngjo sillok* yr 15, 10ᵗʰ month, 20ᵗʰ day (*sinyu*), is just one of many who uses this phrase. For more examples of the language used in criticizing Yun and Kwŏn and their Catholic religion, see Yi Kigyŏng, *Pyŏgwip'yŏn*, 17–108.
59. *Chŏngjo sillok*, yr 15, 11ᵗʰ month, 8ᵗʰ day (*kimyo*).
60. See, for example, Magistrate Shin Sawŏn's October 2, 1791, letter to Hong Nagan in which he explains that there was nothing wrong with reading Catholic books and that he took action against Yun only after he had clear evidence that Yun had been led by such books to act improperly. Yi Kigyŏng, *Pyŏgwip'yŏn*, 22–25.
61. For the official condemnation of Yun and Kwŏn, see *Chŏngjo sillok*, yr 15, 11ᵗʰ month, 8ᵗʰ day (*kimyo*).
62. Dallet, *Histoire*, 53–54.
63. Yi Manch'ae, *Pyŏwip'yŏn*, 105–106.
64. Yi Manch'ae, 114–118; Dallet, *Histoire*, 57–59.
65. Yi Kigyŏng, *Pyŏgwip'yŏn*, 218–219; Dallet, *Histoire*, 60–61; *Hanŭnim ŭi chong*, 87–89. For a report by a staunch Neo-Confucian impressed by Ch'oe's integrity and moral courage, see Hong Yangho, *Igye Hong Yangho chŏnsŏ* (Seoul: Minjok Munhwasa, 1982), 27:19b–23a.
66. Dallet, *Histoire*, 61.

CHAPTER 4: A DECADE OF HOPES AND FEARS

1. Ledyard, "Kollumba Kang Wansuk, an Early Catholic Activist and Martyr," 41–42.
2. For more on those three men and the relationship with the Catholic community, see Don Baker, "Tasan between Catholicism and Confucianism: A Decade Under Suspicion, 1791 to 1801," *Tasanhak* 5 (2004): 55–86; Ch'oe Sangch'ŏn, "Yi Kahwan kwa Sŏhak" [Yi Kahwan and Western Learning], in *Han'guk kyohoesa nonmunjp: Han'guk Ch'ŏnjugyohoe ch'angsŏl ibaekchunyŏn kinyŏm*, vol. 2 [A collection of articles on the history of the Catholic Church in Korea in commemoration of the two hundredth anniversary of the founding of the Korean Catholic Church, vol. 2], ed. *Han'guk kyohoesa nonmunjip kanhaeng wiwŏnhoe* [The committee to publish studies of the history of the Korean Church] (Seoul:

Han'guk Ch'ŏnju kyohoesa yŏn'guso, 1985), 41–67; Chŏng Yagyong, "Chŏnghŏn Yi Kahwan myojimyŏng" [a tombstone inscription for Chŏnghŏn Yi Kahwan], in *Yŏyudang chŏnsŏ* I: 15, 15a–28b; Ch'oe Sŏgu, "Han'guk kyohoe ŭi ch'angsŏl kwa ch'ocha'nggi Yi Sŭnghun ŭi kyohoe hwaldong," *Kyohoesa yŏn'gu* 8, 7–31; Ch'a Kijin, "Manch'ŏn Yi Sŭnghun ŭi kyohoe hwaldong kwa chŏngch'ijŏk ipchi," *Kyohoesa yŏn'gu* 8, 33–57.

3. Cho Kwang, "Chu Munmo ŭi Chosŏn ipkuk kwa kŭ hwaldong" [Zhou Wenmo's arrival in Korea and his activities on the peninsula], *Kyohoesa yŏn'gu* 10 (1995): 72.

4. Zhao Ma, "The Anti-Christian Campaign and Imperial Control in Eighteenth-Century China," *Asia-Pacific: Perspectives* 5, no. 1 (2004): 18–20.

5. Nicolas Standaert, *Handbook of Christianity in China*, vol. 1, *635–1800* (Leiden: Brill, 2001), 334.

6. Ibid., 521–526.

7. Ha Sŏngnae, *Sun'gyoja Yun Yuil (Paolo), sungyoja Chŏng Ŭn (Paolo) p'yŏngjŏn* [Critical biographies of the martyrs Paul Yun Yuil and Paul Chŏng Ŭn] (Seoul: The St. Luke Hwang Sŏkdu Library, 1988), 115, 127.

8. Ch'oe Sŏgu, "Han'guk kyohoe ŭi ch'angsŏl," 20–21.

9. Cho Kwang, "Chu Munmo," 55–56.

10. Ibid., 57–59.

11. Ha Sŏngnae, *Sun'gyoja*, 71.

12. Cho Kwang, "Chu Munmo," 60; Ch'aKijin, "Chosŏn hugi Ch'ŏnjugyo sinjadŭl-ŭi sŏngjikcha yŏngip kwa yangbak ch'ŏngnae-e taehan yŏn'gu" [A study of the plans by Catholics in the latter half of the Chosŏn dynasty to invite Western ships and clergy to Korea], *Kyohoesa yŏn'gu* 13 (1998): 34–35.

13. Cho Kwang, "Chu Munmo," 62.

14. Ha Sŏngnae, *Sun'gyoja*, 172.

15. Kim Chinso, "Chu Munmo sinbu sŏn'gyo," 93–122; *Han'guk Ch'ŏnjugyo chugyohoe ŭi sibok sisŏng chugyo t'ŭkpyŏl wiwŏnhoe* [the special committee of the Korean Catholic Bishops' Conference for beatification and canonization], ed, *Hanŭnim ŭi chong: Hanŭnim ŭi chong* (Seoul: Han'guk Ch'ŏnjugyo chugyohoe ŭi sibok sisŏng chugyo t'ŭkpyŏl Wiwŏnhoe, 2003), 7–55.

16. Ch'oe Sŏgu, "Han'guk kyohoe," 29–30.

17. Chŏng Yagyong, "Chach'an myojimyŏng" [An epitaph for myself], in *Yŏyudang chŏnsŏ* 1:16, 7a.

18. Cho Kwang, "Sinyu kyonan kwa Yi Sŭnghun," 71; *Silk Letter*, line 50.

19. *Silk Letter,* line 70; Joo Park, "Catholicism and Women in the Royal Court of King Sunjo in the Late Chosun Dynasty," *Yŏsŏng kwa yŏksa* [Women and History] 8 (2008): 1–19.

20. Yi Suni wrote two letters while she was in prison awaiting execution in which she discussed her faith and her decision to have a celibate marriage before her execution. Modern Korean translations of these documents can be found in Kim Chinso, ed., *Yi Suni Rugalta nammae okchung p'yŏnji* [The Prison Letters of Yi Suni Lutgarda and her Brothers], trans. Yang Hŭich'an and Pyŏn Chusŭng (Naewŏlli: Ch'ŏnjugyo honam kyohŏe yŏn'guso, 2002). Yi Suni's letter is reproduced in Dallet, *Histoire,* 1:182–185. Also see Yi Yujin, "Yi Suni Lugalda okchung p'yŏnji hyŏnjŏn p'ilsabon ŭi charyojŏk kach'i wa haedok ŭi munje" [The value of, and problems interpreting, the extant handwritten version of Lutgarda Yi Suni's letter from prison], *Kyohoesa yŏn'gu* 40 (2012): 173.

21. For an English-language translation and analysis of that work, see Hector Diaz, *A Korean Theology: Chu-gyo Yo-ji, Essentials of the Lord's Teaching by Chŏng Yak-jong Augustine (1760–1801)* (Immensee: Neue Zeitschrift für Missionswissenschaft, 1986). Another English translation has recently become available: Deberniere J. Torrey, trans. *Jugyo Yoji* [Essentials of the Lord's teaching] (Seoul: KIATS, 2012). For the background of that work, see Cho Han'gŏn, "Chugyo yoji wa hanyŏk sŏhak wa ui kwan'gye" [The relationship between the *Chugyo yoji* and Catholic books translated into Chinese], *Kyohoesa yŏn'gu* 26 (2006): 5–74.

22. Chŏng Yakchong, *Chugyo yoji* [Essential Elements of the Lord's teachings] (Seoul: Hwang Sŏkdu Luga sŏwŏn, 1984). This edition contains a complete modern Korean translation by Ha Sŏngnae.

23. Diaz, *Korean Theology,* 297–301.

24. Ibid., 327.

25. Kang Mangil et al., *Ch'uan kŭp kugan,* 48–49; Yi Nŭnghwa, *Chosŏn kidokkyo kŭp oegyosa* [A history of Christianity and foreign relations in Korea] (Seoul: Han'gukhak yŏn'guso, 1977), 118.

26. Ch'a Kijin, "Chosŏn hugi Ch'ŏnjugyo," 36.

27. Ha Sŏngnae, *Sun'gyoja,* 185.

28. Yamaguchi Masayuki, "Hwang Sayŏng Paeksŏ yŏn'gu" [A study of the *Silk Letter* of Hwang Sayŏng], trans. Yi Minwŏn, in *Hwang Sayŏng Paeksŏ nonmun sŏnjip* [A collection of studies of the *Silk Letter* of Hwang Sayŏng], ed. Yŏ Chinch'ŏn (Seoul: Kippŭn sosik, 1994), 47.

29. Ch'a Kijin, "Chosŏn hugi," 39.

30. Yamaguchi, "Hwang Sayŏng Paeksŏ yŏn'gu," 48.

31. Ch'a Kijin, "Chosŏn hugi," 54–55.

32. Ha Sŏngnae, *Sun'gyoja*, 168.
33. Ch'a Kijin, "Chosŏn hugi," 24; Kang Mangil et al., *Ch'uan kŭp kugan*, 569.
34. Yu Pyŏnggi and Chu Myŏngjun, "Ch'ungch'ŏngdo ŭi Ch'ŏnjugyo chŏllae: Yi Chonch'ang ŭi hwaldongŭl chungsimŭru" [The spread of Catholicism to Ch'ungch'ŏng province: Focusing on the activities of Yi Chonch'ang], in *Han'guk kyohoesa nonch'ong: Ch'oe Sŏgu Sinbu hwakap kinyŏm* [A collection of scholarly studies of the history of the Korean Catholic Church in honor of the sixtieth birthday of Father Ch'oe Sŏgu] edited by Ch'oe Sŏgu sinbu hwagap kinyŏm nonmunjp kanhaeng wiwŏnhoe (Seoul: Han'guk Kyohoesa Yŏn'guso, 1982), 27–57.
35. Ledyard, "Kollumba Kang Wansuk," 39.
36. "Martyrs of Korea (1791–1888)," *Hagiography Circle*, http://newsaints .faithweb.com/martyrs/Korea2.htm, accessed May 30, 2011.
37. As described in Chapter 1, the Flexible Faction and the Intransigent Faction had both formed in response to the execution of the crown prince in 1762, over a century after the Patriarchs Faction and the Namin Faction had come into existence. Not all members of the older factions were also members of those two new factional groupings. Moreover, membership in those two new factions sometimes cut across traditional factional lines, though most members of the Flexible Faction were *Namin* (Southerners) and the Intransigent Faction tended to be mostly Patriarchs, although there were a few *Namin* Intransigents.
38. Pak Kwang'yong, "Chu Munmo sinbu sŏn'gyo hwaldong ŭi paegyŏng" [The background to the missionary activities of Father Zhou Wenmo], *Kyohoesa yŏn'gu* 10 (1995): 22–25; Park Hyunmo, "King Jeongjo's Political Role," 205–202.
39. *Silk Letter*, line 19.
40. *Silk Letter*, lines 7–11.
41. Cho Kwang, *Chosŏn hugi*, 405.
42. *Sŭngjŏngwŏn ilgi*, 97:287–289; Sunjo, year 1, 1st month, 10th day (*chŏnghae*).
43. Wŏn Chaeyŏn, *Chosŏn wangjo ŭi pŏp kwa Kŭrisŭdogyo: Tong-Sŏyang ŭi sangho insik kwa munhwa ch'ungdol* [Christianity and the laws of the Chosŏn dynasty: Ideological and cultural conflict between East and West] (Seoul: Handŭl Publishing, 2003), 211.
44. Cho Kwang, *Chosŏn hugi*, 406–407.
45. Ibid., 409–414. These dates are all according to the lunar calendar, which is how these executions were recorded at that time.
46. Cho Kwang, "Sinyu kyonan," 74.
47. Sŏ Chongt'ae and Han Kŏn, eds., *Chosŏn hugi Ch'ŏnjugyo sinja chaep'an kirok*, 940–943.

48. Chŏng Yagyong, *Yŏyudang chŏnsŏ*, I, 15:40a–b.
49. Cho Kwang, "Chu Munmo," 72–75.
50. Ledyard, "Kollumba Kang Wansuk," 57. Ledyard uses the solar date of July 2 for her execution.
51. Kang Man'gil et al., *Ch'uan kŭp kugan* [Records of special investigations by the State Tribunal], vol. 25. (Seoul: Asea munhwasa, 1978), 793, 813.
52. For more on this particularly cruel form of capital punishment, see Timothy Brook, Jerome Bourgon, and Gregory Blue, *Death by a Thousand Cuts* (Cambridge, MA: Harvard University Press, 2008).
53. Yŏ Chinch'ŏn, "Hwang Sayŏng 'Paeksŏ'ibon-e taehan pigyo yŏn'gu" [A comparative study of alternative versions of the *Silk Letter of Hwang Sayŏng*], *Kyohoesa yŏn'gu* 28 (June 2007): 6.

CHAPTER 5: NATIONALISM AND EVALUATIONS OF HWANG SAYŎNG

1. "In'gan ŭi choggŏn: sŏngdang (Seoul. Kyŏnggi.)" [The human condition: churches in Seoul and Kyŏnggi province] http://blog.daum.net/gkdrnd pdlfqjswl39/16522834. Accessed June 17, 2014.
2. "Kat'ollik charyosil—Han'guk ŭi sŏngji wa sajŏkchi—Hwang Sayŏng myo" [Documents regarding Catholicism—Sacred sites and historical sites—the grave of Hwang Sayŏng" http://fr.catholic.or.kr/jhs/holyplace /hwangsayeongmyo.htm. Accessed June 17, 2014.
3. See, for example, photos of the museum and the church that have been built at the foot of a hill holding the tombs of some early Korean Catholic leaders. This site south of Seoul is also claimed by some to be where the Korean Catholic Church began: "Chon Jin Am: The Birthplace of the Catholic Church in Korea," http://www.chonjinam.org/eng. Accessed October 2, 2015.
4. "Kat'ollik charyosil—Han'guk ŭi sŏngji wa sajŏkchi—Hwang Sayŏng saengga t'ŏ" [Documents regarding Catholicism—Sacred sites and historical sites—the site where Hwang Sayŏng was born] http://fr.catholic.or.kr /jhs/holyplace/hwangsayeongsaengga.htm. Accessed October 2, 2015.
5. Ha Sŏngnae, "Hwang Sayŏng ŭi Kyohoe hwaldong kwa sun'gyo-e taehan yŏn'gu" [A study of the religious activities of Hwang Sayŏng and his martyrdom], *Kyohoesa yŏn'gu* 13 (1998): 79–80.
6. For an analysis of the rise of this nationalistic understanding of Korean history, see Henry H. Em, *The Great Enterprise: Sovereignty and Histori-*

ography in Modern Korea (Durham, NC: Duke University Press), 2013. One example of a survey history of Korea that is shaped by an implicit assumption that nationalism in Korea was no different from nationalism in the West is Han Young Woo, *A Review of Korean History* (Paju, ROK: Kyongsaewon, 2010).

7. For a study of how the distinction between the religious and the political arose on the Korean peninsula, and how that process was different in Korea than it was in the West, see Don Baker, "Korea's Path of Secularization," Ranjan Ghosh, ed. *Making Sense of the Secular: Critical Perspectives from Europe to Asia* (New York: Routledge, 2012), 182–194. For a more general study of the rise of the secular state in the world, see Peter Beyer, "Questioning the secular/religious divide in a post-Westphalian world," *International Sociology* 28:6 (2013), 663–679.

8. Bryan S. Turner, *The Religious and the Political: A Comparative Sociology of Religion* (Cambridge, UK: Cambridge University Press, 2013), esp. 64–68.

9. Seminal studies of the rise of modern nationalism around the world include Benedict Anderson, *Imagined Communities: Reflections on the Origin and Spread of Nationalism*. Revised Edition ed. (London and New York: Verso, 1991); Ernest Gellner, *Nations and Nationalism* (Ithaca: Cornell University Press, 1983); and Anthony D. Smith, *The Ethnic Origins of Nations* (Oxford: Blackwell Publishers, 1998).

10. John Duncan, "Proto-nationalism in Pre-modern Korea," in *Perspectives on Korea*, ed. Sang-Oak Lee and Duk-soo Park (Sydney: Wild Peony, 1998), 198–221.

11. Because of its centuries of linguistic, cultural, and political identity, premodern Korea was very different from countries such as Indonesia, which provided the basis for Benedict Anderson's study of the emergence of "Imagined Communities."

12. For a survey of the various ways Hwang Sayŏng and his *Silk Letter* have been evaluated, and one that concludes that he was a modernizer who was unfairly treated by Confucians who were unable to look beyond their own narrow philosophy, see Hŏ Tonghyŏn, "Hwang Sayŏng Paeksŏ-e taehan kŭn-hyŏndae hakkye ŭi p'yŏngga" [The evaluations of the *Silk Letter of Hwang Sayŏng* in modern and contemporary Korea] *Han'guk sinhak madang* [Korean theology forum] http://theologia.kr/board_korea/27438. Accessed October 23, 2016. It is common in survey histories of Korea to describe Catholicism in 18th-century Korea as more a political and social reform movement than a religion; for example, see Han Young Woo, *A*

Review of Korean History, vol. 2, 287. Yi Wŏnsun, *Chosŏn Sŏhaksa yŏn'gu* [Studies of the history of Western Learning in the Chosŏn dynasty] (Seoul: Iljisa, 1986) argues that it was the narrow-minded and inflexible ideological orientation of the Confucian ruling elite that prevented Catholicism from initiating the modernization of Korea in the 18th and 19th centuries.

CHAPTER 6: *A CONVERSATION ON CATHOLICISM*

1. *Shujing*, IV, iii, 2 (The announcement of Tang). James Legge, ed., *The Chinese Classics*, vol. 3, *The Shoo King* (Hong Kong: Hong Kong University Press, 1960), 185.

2. *Shijing*, III, I, II, 3 (Daya, Decade of King Wen, Ta Ming). Legge, *The Chinese Classics*, vol. 4, *The She King or the Book of Poetry*, 433,

3. *Shijing*, IV, I (i), 7 (Zhou Song, Decade of Qing Miao, Wo Jiang). Legge, *The Chinese Classics*, vol. 4, *The She King or the Book of Poetry*, 576.

4. *Analects*, XVI, viii, 1 (Ji Shi).

5. *The Doctrine of the Mean* I: I.

6. *Mencius*, VII, I, I, 2 (Jin Xin A).

7. *Han Shu* [The history of the Han Dynasty] 56:18a, entry on Dong Zhongshu. (This is an ancient text which is normally cited this way.)

8. For more on this encounter between the Jesuit missionary João Rodrigues and Chŏng Tuwon, see Michael Cooper, SJ, *Rodrigues, the Interpreter: An Early Jesuit in Japan and China* (Tokyo: Weatherhill, 1974), 347–350.

9. A mountain range that runs along the western border of China.

10. Mozi was a philosopher during China's Warring States period (479–221 BCE). He was condemned by Mencius as a heretic and therefore was regarded as such by Confucians for two millennia afterward.

11. *Mozi*, 26:4–5. See Ian Johnston, trans., *The Mozi: A Complete Translation* (New York: Columbia University Press, 2010), 236–239.

12. Either Cheng Hao (1032–1085) or his brother Cheng Yi (1033–1107), both considered to be, along with Zhu Xi (1130–1200), the founders of Neo-Confucianism.

13. Hŏ Kyun may not have actually said this. It does not appear in any of his collected writings.

14. This is a reference to the Nanman, an aboriginal people in China's southwest who are portrayed as rebels against rightful authority in *Romance of*

the three Kingdoms (Sanguo yanyi), a popular Chinese novel written during China's Ming dynasty.

15. *Analects*, VII: 21 (Shu Erh).
16. A county in southeastern Hwanghae province.
17. *Analects*, XI: 12 (Xian Jin).
18. Ricci, *The True Meaning of the Lord of Heaven*, 140–143.
19. Yu was a legendary emperor of the Xia dynasty. This remark is attributed to him in the early Han dynasty work *Huainanzi*. See John S. Major, Sarah A. Green, Andrew Seth Meyer, and Harold D. Roth, trans., *The Huainanzi: A Guide to the Theory and Practice of Government in Early Han China* (New York: Columbia University Press, 2010), 252.
20. The Three Forces (*samchae*, Ch. *sancai* are Heaven, earth, and human beings).
21. Matteo Ricci, *Jiren shipian* [Ten chapters by an unusual man], in Li Zhizao, ed., *Tianxue chuhan*, 232. *Jiren shipian* was written by Matteo Ricci and first published in 1608 in Beijing. It can be found in *Tianxue chuhan*, 93–290.
22. Ricci, *The True Meaning of the Lord of Heaven*, 444–447.
23. *Zhendao zizheng* was written by the French missionary Emeric Langlois de Chavagnac (1670–1717) and published in Beijing in 1718.
24. This is a summary of what is said in *Zhendao zizheng*, vol. 2, *Sadao, renleishang*, 101–106, in the edition available online, thanks to Google Books, at https://play.google.com/books/reader?id=LQ9aAAAAcAAJ&printsec =frontcover&output=reader&hl=en&pg=GBS.PT8. Accessed February 13, 2016. The same text can be found at http://archives.catholic.org.hk /Rare%20Books/EZT/index.htm/Ezt-037–39.jpg.
25. Ricci, *The True Meaning of the Lord of Heaven*, 318–319.
26. Ibid., 320–321.
27. Ibid., 446–449.
28. This is the "Seven Victories" written by the Jesuit missionary Diego de Pantoja to warn against the seven cardinal sins and teach techniques for overcoming them. *Qike* can be found in Li Zhizao, ed., *Tianxue chuhan*, 689–1126.
29. Ricci, *True Meaning of the Lord of Heaven*, 142–143.
30. Ricci, *Jiren shipian*, 255.
31. See the translation by Joseph Adler in William Theodore de Bary and Irene Bloom, eds., *Sources of Chinese Tradition* (New York: Columbia University Press, 1999), 1:673–676. Zhou never actually uses the word *li*, but later generations of Neo-Confucians assumed that he was describing how *li* functioned as the origin of the universe.

32. See Wing-tsit Chan, trans., *Reflections on Things at Hand: The Neo-Confucian Anthology*, ed. Zhu Xi and Lu Zuqian (New York: Columbia University Press, 1967), 9.

33. Ricci, *True Meaning of the Lord of Heaven*, 106–107.

34. Ibid., 110–113.

35. Richard John Lynn, trans., *The Classic of Changes*, 53, 64 (*Zicizhuan*, 1:5, 11).

36. Sima Qian, "*Shiji* 28: Treatise on the Feng and Shan Sacrifices." See Burton Watson, trans., *Records of the Grand Historian by Sima Qian, Han Dynasty, II* (rev. ed., New York: Columbia University Press, 1993), 13.

37. *Han Shu*, 71. See Burton Watson, trans., *Courtier and Commoner in Ancient China: Selections from the* History of the Former Han *by Pan Ku* (New York: Columbia University Press, 1974), 157.

38. *Liezi* [The Book of Liezi], book 4. A 1912 translation by Lionel Giles is available at http://www.sacred-texts.com/tao/tt/tt07.htm. Accessed October 29, 2016.

39. The "eight teachings" may be a reference to the "eight beatitudes" found in the Gospel of Matthew 5:3–10.

40. Ricci, *The True Meaning of the Lord of Heaven*, 144–147.

41. Eric L. Hutton, trans. *Xunzi: The Complete Text* (Princeton: Princeton University Press, 2014), 76. (Xunzi, "Wangzhi.")

CHAPTER 7: *THE SILK LETTER OF HWANG SAYŎNG*

1. The actual author of this *Silk Letter* is Alexius Hwang Sayŏng. However, he borrowed the name of Hwang Sim (1756–1801), whose baptismal name was Thomas, since Hwang was better known to the priests in Beijing. When Hwang Sim was then arrested, he revealed where Hwang Sayŏng was hiding, thinking that Hwang Sayŏng had moved to a new hiding place by then. Hwang Sayŏng had not moved, however, and was arrested, leading to the discovery of the *Silk Letter*. See Yi Changu, "Sinyu pakhae wa Hwang Sayŏng paeksŏ sakkŏn" [The 1801 persecution, Hwang Sayŏng, and the *Silk Letter* incident] in *Han'guk Ch'ŏnju kyohoesa*, vol. 2 [Korean Catholic history, vol. 2], ed. Han'guk kyohoesa yŏn'guso (Seoul: Han'guk kyohosesa yŏn'guso, 2010), 55–64; Kang Man'gil et al., *Ch'uan kŭp kugan*, 25:813.

2. The letter was intended for Alexander de Gouvea, bishop of the Beijing diocese from 1782 to 1808. For more on Bishop de Gouvea, a Portuguese

Franciscan, see Standaert, *Handbook of Christianity in China*, 335, 351, 720.

3. Officially, the annual embassy was made to offer tribute to the Qing emperor and receive gifts in return. Unofficially, those who went on it used it as an opportunity to engage in trade. Korean Catholics would arrange to accompany the embassy, often through bribery, in order to maintain contact with the Catholics in China, especially the foreign missionaries and the bishop of Beijing. See Yi Changu, "Chosŏn Ch'ŏnjugyohoe ŭi sŏllip" [The establishment of the Chosŏn Catholic Church] in *Han'guk Ch'ŏnju kyohoesa I*, ed. Han'guk kyohoesa yŏn'guso (Seoul: Han'guk kyohosesa yŏn'guso, 2009), 239–244.

4. John Ok Ch'ŏnhŭi (1764–1801) was a Catholic who had managed to travel to Beijing on several tribute missions, acting as a messenger for the Catholic community. See Yi Changu, "Sinyu pakhae," 56, 60–63, 89, 100.

5. The Pope at this time was Pius VII, who reigned from 1800 to 1828.

6. Under Chŏngjo's orders, Cho infiltrated the Catholic community, claiming to be a merchant named P'ilgong. Though he was responsible for reporting many Catholics to the authorities, after King Chŏngjo died there was no one who could vouch for his claim that he had been an undercover agent. He was put in prison in 1801 and, in despair, hung himself. Yi Manch'ae, *Pyŏgwip'yŏn*, 265–266.

7. Thomas Ch'oe P'ilgong (1744–1801) had converted to Catholicism in 1790. A little more than a year after his release in 1799, he was again arrested and was executed on April 8, 1801. According to Catholic sources, he died still professing his faith. Joseph Ch'ang-mun Kim and John Jae-sun Chung, *Catholic Korea: Yesterday and Today* (Seoul: St. Joseph Publishing Co., 1984), 57–58; and Kang Man'gil et al., *Ch'uan kŭp Kugan*, 29–30, confirm this account. He was among those beatified in 2014. We use solar calendar dates in the footnotes to this translation for the dates Catholics were executed because that is how the dates for the martyrdom of the 124 who were beatified in 2014 are now remembered. At the beginning of the nineteenth century, the solar date was generally around six weeks ahead of the lunar date by which the executions were recorded in official Chosŏn dynasty documents. For example, April 8 was the twenty-sixth day of the second month by the lunar calendar, the calendar used in government records at that time. In the body of the text, we use the lunar dates Hwang Sayŏng used.

8. Martin Yi Chungbae (1752?–1801) converted to Catholicism in 1797. As a secondary son (the offspring of a *yangban* father and a non-*yangban* mother), he was a member of a status group that suffered discrimination.

For instance, he could not sit for the exams that would allow him to earn the Confucian degree that would qualify him to serve in a high government post. For more on such discrimination, see Kyung Moon Hwang, *Beyond Birth*, 208–232.

9. John Wŏn Kyŏngdo was born in 1774 and executed on April 25, 1801. See Yi Changu, "Shinyu pakhae," 36, 40. He was among those beatified in 2014.

10. Ambrose Kwŏn Ch'ŏlsin (1736–1801) was converted to Catholicism by Peter Yi Sŭnghun. However, he cut off ties with the Catholic community in 1791 because of the Catholic prohibition of ancestor rites. Despite distancing himself from the Catholic community, he was arrested in 1801 because of his earlier association with Catholicism and died in prison in Seoul on April 4 as a result of the severe beatings he had undergone during his interrogation. See Yi Changu, "Chosŏn Ch'ŏnjugyo ŭ sŏllip" [The establishment of the Korean Catholic Church], Yi Changsu, et. al, ed. *Han'guk Ch'ŏnju kyohoe sa I* (Korean Catholic History, vol. 1) (Seoul: Han'guk kyohoesa yŏn'guso, 2009), 244–245; Cho Hyŏnbŏm, "Kyohoe ŭi hwaldong kwa kyosae ŭi hwaksan" [The activities of the Church and its expansion], in *Han'guk Ch'ŏnju kyohoesa*, vol. 1, ed. Han'guk kyohoesa yŏn'guso (Seoul: Han'guk kyohosesa yŏn'guso, 2009), 304–305; and Yi Changu, "Sinyu pakhae," 38–39. For more on Kwŏn Ch'ŏlsin, see the "tombstone inscription" Chŏng Yagyong wrote for him: "Nogam Kwŏn Ch'ŏlsin myojimyŏng" [A tombstone inscription for Nogam Kwŏn Ch'ŏlsin], *Yŏyudang chŏnsŏ* 1:15, 33a–36b.

11. For more on Francis Kwŏn Ilsin (1751–1792), see Cho Hyŏnbŏm, "Kyohoe," 305–307; and Ch'ang-mun Kim and John Jae-sun Chung, *Catholic Korea*, 40–41.

12. This is Sebastian Kwŏn Sangmun (1768–1801). He was actually the son of Kwŏn Ilsin but had been adopted by Kwŏn Ch'ŏlsin after Kwŏn Ilsin died. He was executed on January 30, 1802, and was among those beatified in 2014. Yŏ Chinch'ŏn, *Nuga Chŏhŭirŭl wirohae chugessŭmnikka*, 47.

13. King Chŏngjo died on August 18, 1800 (the twenty-eighth day of the sixth month according to the lunar calendar).

14. No information is available on when Kim Yŏsam was born or when he died.

15. No information is available on when Yi Anjŏng was born or when he died.

16. Columba Kang (1761–1801) was an important leader in the early Korean Catholic Church. Because she was a woman of relatively high social status, it was difficult for agents of the government to enter and search her house, as Hwang will explain later. Therefore, Father Zhou hid in her home.

17. Yi Kahwan was an intellectual leader of one branch of the Southerner Faction. Chŏng Yagyong was one of the brightest young members of Yi Kahwan's subfaction. Yi Sŭnghun was also a member of that faction, as well as a nephew of Yi Kahwan and a brother-in-law of Chŏng Yagyong. Hong Nangmin was also a member of the Southerner Faction. He was one of the first Catholics in Korea. His son Hong Chaeyŏng (1780–1840) married a daughter of Chŏng Yakhyŏn (1751–1821) with his first wife, who was a sister of Yi Pyŏk (1754–1786). Hong's daughter-in-law was, therefore, a niece of four of the first Catholics (Chŏng Yagyong, Chŏng Yakchŏn, Chŏng Yakchong [1760–1801], and Yi Pyŏk) as well as the sister-in-law of Hwang Sayŏng.

18. The factions were mutually hostile and hereditary in nature. Most Catholics of elite status were connected to the Southerner Faction. However, there were some non-Southerner Catholics and many Southerners were critical of Catholicism. In fact, Southerners were some of the first critics of Catholicism. For examples of such criticism, see Ahn Chŏngbok's "A Conversation on Catholicism" in Chapter 6 of this volume. Also see Don Baker, "The Use and Abuse of the Sirhak Label: A New Look at Shin Hudam and his Sŏhak Pyŏn," *Kyohoesa Yŏn'gu* 3 (1981): 183–254; and Cho Kwang, *Chosŏn hugi Ch'ŏnjukyosa yŏn'gu* [A study of Catholic history in the late Chosŏn dynasty] (Seoul: Kodae minjok munhwa yŏn'guso, 1988), 197–236.

19. The Flexible Faction, which crossed the normal *Southerner/Patriachs* factional lines and included people from both camps, consisted of those who believed that it was wrong for Yŏngjo to have his son, Prince Sado (1735–1762), who was the father of Chŏngjo, killed. They were therefore close to King Chŏngjo. The Intransigent Faction believed that Yŏngjo was in the right and so were more distant from Chŏngjo. For an overview of factional issues and their connection to the persecution of 1801, see Pyŏn Chusŭng, "Sinyu pakhae ŭi chŏngjijŏk paegyŏng-e kwanhan yŏn'gu," [A study of the political background of the 1801 persecution] in *Sinyu pakhae wa Hwang Sayŏng paeksŏ sakkŏn* [The 1801 persecution and the Hwang Sayŏng *Silk Letter* incident], ed. Ch'oe Ch'anghwa (Seoul: Han'guk sun'gyoja hyŏnyang wiwŏnhoe, 2003), 35–54. Also see the discussion of factionalism in chapter 1.

20. This is Queen Chŏngsun (1745–1805).

21. Her brother Kim Kwiju (d. 1786) had been exiled by King Chŏngjo in 1776. Her cousin Kim Kwanju (1743–1806) was banished from court soon after Chŏngjo ascended the throne. See Haboush, *The Memoirs of Lady Hyegyŏng*, 45.

22. The "Association for Illuminating the Way" was an organization that encouraged Catholics to practice their faith more diligently and to spread it to non-Catholics. It was founded by Father Zhou and patterned on similar organizations in China. There were different chapters that met independently of each other. It seems to have been rather small and appears to have acted as a kind of association for lay leaders. For more information on the Myŏngdohoe, see Pang Sanggŭn, "Ch'ogi kyohoe-e issŏsŏ Myŏngdohoe ŭi kusŏng kwa sŏngkyŏk" [The structure and characteristics of the Association for Illuminating the Way during the early church], *Kyohoesa yon'gu* 11 (December 1996): 213–226.

23. Columba Kang Wansuk converted her mother-in-law, her stepson, and her daughter. Her husband divorced her, but the Catholics in the family went with her to Seoul. There she became an important Catholic leader. She protected Father Zhou, undertook missionary work among women, and gathered together a community of celibate women, making her home something of a convent. See Ledyard, "Kollumba Kang Wansuk," 38–71; and Cho Kwang, Chang Chŏngnan, Kim Chŏngsuk, and Song Chongnye, *Sun'gyoja Kang Wansuk yŏksarŭl wihae ilŏsŏda* [The martyr Kang Wansuk: Standing up for history] (Seoul: Catholic Press, 2006).

24. As described in chapter 1, the *yangban* were the elite of the Chosŏn dynasty from whose ranks high government officials were drawn. To qualify as a *yangban*, a person had to have ancestors who were government officials and had to earn a living from either government service or land holdings rather than commerce or technical expertise. They also had to pass at least the lowest level civil service examination. That meant that *yangban* men had to be able to read and write classical Chinese and be well educated in the Confucian classics. If the husband of a family qualified as *yangban*, his primary wife did as well, especially since the primary wife of a *yangban* was supposed to have come from a *yangban* family, with a *yangban* father and a mother who was the primary wife and herself came from a *yangban* family. The treatment of an individual in Korean law and custom depended on one's status. High-status women, considered to be part of the "inner" world of the home, were not treated as severely in criminal matters as were *yangban* men or commoners, both male and female. See *Kugyŏk taejŏn hoet'ong* [Great collection of administrative codes, translated into Korean] (Seoul: Koryŏ University Press, 1960), 537.

25. It would appear that Father Zhou hoped that female converts to Catholicism would spread their faith to their husbands and their children.

26. The mixing of men and women at Catholic services led to accusations of sexual impropriety. For an example of such an accusation, see *T'osa chumun* (Report to the emperor on the eradication of perversity), *Sunjo sillok*, yr. 1, 10ᵗʰ month, 27ᵗʰ day (*kyŏngo*). When Hwang was interrogated by the government, this same charge was launched against him as well. See Kang Man'gil et al., *Ch'uan kŭp Kugan*, 726–728.

27. This is the same Thomas Ch'oe P'ilgong who was mentioned earlier as having renounced Catholicism in 1791 but then a few years later renounced his renunciation.

28. Peter Ch'oe P'ilche (1770–1801) was a *chungin* who converted to Catholicism in 1790. He was arrested in 1791 but was released after he renounced his Catholicism. He returned to the church in 1793 and was executed on May 14, 1801. See Han'guk Ch'ŏnjugyo, *Hanŭnim ŭi chong*, 103–104. He was beatified in 2014.

29. The Feast of the Presentation celebrates the day Mary, the mother of Jesus, followed Jewish custom and presented the infant Jesus at a temple in Jerusalem. See Yŏ, *Nuga*, 61.

30. See *Chŏngjo sillok* year 15, 9:19 (*Sinmyo*).

31. Stephen Oh is Oh Sŏkch'ung (1742–1806). He later renounced his involvement with Catholicism. See Yŏ Chinch'ŏn, *Hwang Sayŏng "Paeksŏ" yŏn'gu: wŏnbon kwa ibon pigyo kŏmt'o* [The Silk Letter of Hwang Sayŏng: A comparative examination of the original and alternate versions] (Seoul: Han'guk kyohoesa yŏn'guso, 2009), 96–97, n224. For more on Oh Sŏkch'ung, see the "tombstone inscription" Chŏng Yagyong wrote for him: "Maejang O Sŏkch'ung myojimyŏng" [A tombstone inscription for Maejang Oh Sŏkch'ung], *Yŏyudang chŏnsŏ* 1:15, 37a–38b. Oh's daughter married Kwŏn Sangmun (1769–1801), the son of Kwŏn Ch'ŏlsin and one of those beatified in 2014. Oh himself was exiled in 1801.

32. John Ch'oe Ch'anghyŏn (1754–1801) was a *chungin* who converted to Catholicism at the urging of John the Baptist Yi Pyŏk, making him one of Korea's first Catholics. He was one of the few early leaders of the Catholic community to remain as a leader after the 1791 persecution. He translated the missal, a collection of daily Bible readings and prayers, from Chinese into Korean. See *Hanŭnim ŭi chong*, 78–79. He was among those beatified in 2014.

33. Hwang Sayŏng made a slight mistake on the date of the anti-Catholic decree. It was issued on the tenth day of the first month according to the lunar calendar. *Sunjo sillok* year 1, 1ˢᵗ month, 10ᵗʰ day (*chŏnghae*).

34. As discussed in Chapter 1, John Chŏng Yagyŏng (1762–1836) was an early *yangban* member of the Catholic community. However, he distanced

himself from that community after learning of the prohibition against ancestor rites. (Some Catholic scholars argue that he was reconciled to the church on his deathbed.) There has been a lot written about Chŏng Yagyŏng, since he is widely considered one of the most brilliant philosophers in all Korean history. For more on Chŏng Yagyŏng, often referred to by his literary name, Tasan, see Baker, "Shamans, Catholics, and Chŏng Yagyong," 139–179; Baker, "Tasan Between Catholicism and Confucianism," 55–86; and Baker, "Tasan and His Brothers," 172–197.

35. *Chŏngjo sillok* twenty-third year, 5, 25 (*imo*). The "evil official" who called for strict punishment for Chŏng Yakchong, along with Kwŏl Ch'ŏlsin, Yi Kahwan, and others suspected of involvement with Catholicism, was the Censor-General Shin Hŏnjo (1752–1809). Hwang mistook the year Shin called for strict action against Catholics. It was actually 1799.

36. Thomas Im Taein (1773–?) was a Catholic servant of Chŏng Yakchong. He renounced Catholicism after his arrest, but was nevertheless exiled. Yŏ, *Nuga*, 64, n78; Kang Man'gil et al., *Ch'uan kŭp Kugan*, 52–54.

37. Yi Yugyŏng (1747–?) was a Little Northerner who passed the military examination in 1774.

38. Shin Taehyŏn (1737–1812) passed the highest-level civil service exam in 1759 and served in various provincial and central offices.

39. Like his cousin, Ch'oe P'ilche (1770–1801) was a *chungin*, working as a pharmacist. John Ch'oe Ch'anghyŏn (1759–1801) was a *chungin* interpreter.

40. Pak Changsŏl was born in 1729 and rose to the rank of Jr. 2, the fourth-highest civil service rank in the government. Yi Sŏgu (1754–1825) was a member of the Intransigent Faction. He would go on to hold the highest positions in the government. Though Ch'oe Hyŏnjung (1745–?) was a member of the Southerner Faction, he was vehemently anti-Catholic.

41. The four people mentioned here are Ch'oe P'ilkong, Ch'oe P'ilche, Ch'oe Ch'anghyŏn, and Im Taein.

42. The emergence of a Catholic community was considered such a threat to the state that Catholics were treated as traitors rather than as common criminals. See Wŏn Chaeyŏn, *Chosŏn wangjo ŭi pŏp kwa Kŭrisŭdogyo*, 200–228.

43. There were so many Catholics being arrested that it strained the ability of the government to house them all. *Sunjo sillok*, year 1, 2nd month, 12th day (*muo*).

44. Since being a Catholic was considered treason and not an ordinary crime, it was legal to arrest *yangban* women.

45. A record of that interrogation of Augustine Chŏng Yakchong can be found in Kang Man'gil et al., *Ch'uan kŭp Kugan*, 48–52.

46. Augustine's second wife (his first had passed away) Cecilia Yu Sosa (1761–1839), their son, Paul Chŏng Hasang (1795–1839), and their daughter, Elizabeth Chŏng Chŏnghye (1797–1839), would all be executed as Catholics in the 1839 persecution. All three were recognized by Catholic authorities as saints in a canonization ceremony in 1984. Augustine's son by his first wife, Charles Chŏng Ch'ŏlsang, was executed in the 1801 persecution and was beatified in 2014. *Hanŭnim ŭi chong*, 81–83, 111–112; Ch'oe Sŏnhye, "Kihae pakhae" [The 1839 Persecution], *Han'guk Ch'ŏnju kyohoesa III* [Korean Catholic History, vol. 3], ed. Han'guk kyohoesa (Seoul: Han'guk kyohoesa yŏn'guso, 2010), 37–43, 46, and 50.

47. April 8, according to the solar calendar.

48. Francis-Xavier was the Christian name of Hong Kyoman (1737–1801). He was related to Kwŏn Ch'ŏlsin on his mother's side. His daughter married a son of Chŏng Yakchong. Kang Man'gil et al., *Ch'uan kŭp Kugan*, 85–86. He was beatified in 2014 along with his son Hong In (1758–1802).

49. These executions took place almost three months later, on July 2.

50. Hwang makes a mistake here. Of the nine people executed, five were women and four were men. The women were Columba Kang Wansuk, Susannah Kang Kyŏngbok (1762–1801), Agatha Han Sinae (?–1801), Juliana Kim Yŏni (?–1801), and Vivian Mun Yŏngin (1776–1801). The four men were Ignatius Ch'oe Inch'ŏl (?–1801), Matthew Kim Hyŏnu (1775–1801), Anthony Yi Hyŏn (?–1801), and Hong Chŏngho (?–1801). See Yŏ, *Nuga*, 70, n92. All of them, except for Hong Chŏngho, were beatified in 2014. For an official report on their execution, see *Sunjo sillok* year 1, 5, 22 (*chŏngyu*).

51. Matthew Ch'oe Ingil (1765–1795) was a *chungin* interpreter who helped Father Zhou enter Korea. When the priest was threatened with arrest, Matthew dressed up in his clothes and allowed himself to be arrested in his place. Because he could speak Chinese, he was initially thought to be Father Zhou. His ruse gave more time for the priest to escape. He refused to inform on Father Zhou and was beaten to death along with Paul Yun Yuil and Sabas Chi Hwang on June 28, 1795. See Pang Sanggŭn, "Chu Munmo sinpu ŭi ipkuk kwa Chosŏn kyohoe" [Father Zhou Wenmo's entry into Korea and the Chosŏn Church], in *Han'guk Ch'ŏnju kyohoesa*, vol. 1, ed. Han'guk kyohoesa yŏn'guso (Seoul: Han'guk kyohosesa yŏn'guso, 2009), 311–316.

52. That nickname was a pun. Both Ip and Kwan refer to hats. Both *chŏng* and *ch'ŏn* refer to water coming out of the ground.

53. For an article on how the use of physical punishment during the Chosŏn dynasty was systematized and applied to varying degrees according to the seriousness of a crime, including the use of clubs, see Sim Chaeu, "Chŏnghodae 'Hŭmhyul chŏnch'ik' ŭi panp'o wa hyŏnggu chŏngbi," [The provision of instruments for interrogation and punishment, and the distribution of the "Regulations for Judicious Inquiry and Trial" during the reign of King Chŏngjo], *Kyujanggak* 22 (December 1999): 135–153.

54. Hwang's account of Ch'oe Ch'anghyŏn's interrogation is quite different from what is reported in the accounts of the State Tribunal. In those records, he is said to have renounced his "twenty-year" involvement with "perverse practices." Kang Man'gil et al., *Ch'uan kŭp kugan*, 27–29, 42–44, 65–67. Church authorities have decided that he renounced that renunciation and died a faithful Catholic. He was beatified in 2014.

55. One reason Hwang Sayŏng praised Augustine Chŏng Yakchong in such high terms is that Hwang married Augustine's niece, the daughter of Chŏng Yakhyŏn (1751–1821) and Yi Pyŏk's sister, and Augustine played an important role in his conversion to Catholicism. See Yŏ, *Hwang Sayŏng Paeksŏ yŏn'gu*, 37–45.

56. Daoism, unlike the other imports from China, Confucianism and Buddhism, never established much of an institutional presence in Korea. There was no Daoist religion per se, outside of a government Daoist temple that closed in the sixteenth century. However, throughout the Chosŏn dynasty, there were a few scholars who practiced what may be called Daoist techniques of breathing and physical exercises in order to reverse the process of physical decay in their bodies. Chŏng Yakchong appears to have been one of those "Daoists" before he became a Catholic. Ch'a Chuhwan, *Han'guk Togyo sasang yŏn'gu* [A study of Daoist thought in Korea] (Seoul: Seoul National University Press, 1993).

57. Augustine converted in 1786 at the behest of his second-oldest brother, Chŏng Yakchŏn (1758–1816). Yakchŏn would later renounce his Catholicism. Kang Man'gil et al., *Ch'uan kŭp kugan*, 51.

58. Although Chŏng Yakchong (1760–1801) was the last of the three Chŏng brothers who joined the young Catholic community in 1780s, he is the only one who remained an active Catholic after 1791. Both his older brother Yakchŏn (1758–1816) and his younger brother, Yagyong (1762–1836), distanced themselves from Catholicism when they learned Catholics were not allowed to honor their ancestors by bowing before ancestral tablets and offering sacrificial food before them. A fourth brother, Yakhyŏn (1751–1821), who was the father-in-law of Hwang Sayŏng, was never involved with Catholicism.

59. Hwang is here referring to the *Essentials of the Lord's Teachings* [Chugyo yoji], the first Catholic catechism in the Korean vernacular. For an English-language translation and analysis of that work, see Diaz, *A Korean Theology*. A more recent English translation, without as much scholarly analysis, is Torrey, *Jugyo Yoji*. For an in-depth Korean-language look at Yakchong's theological thinking, see the special issue of *Han'guk sasang sahak* 18 (2002). See also Cho Han'gŏn, "*Chyugyo yoji* wa Hanyŏk Sŏhaksŏ," 8–11.

60. *Shengshi churao* [Teachings of the church in everyday language] was written by the French Jesuit Joseph-Anne-Marie de Moyriac de Mailla (1669–1748). It is a five-volume introduction to Catholic teachings, focusing on creation, redemption, the soul, and what happens after death. This work is available online at http://archives.catholic.org.hk/Rare%20Books/RB -index.htm. Accessed October 29, 2016.

    For a comparison of *Chugyo yoji* with *Shengshi churao*, see Wŏn Chaeyŏn, "Chŏng Yakchong 'Chugyo yoji' wa Hanmun sŏhaksŏ ŭi pigyo yŏn'gu: 'Shengshi churao' wa ŭi pigyorŭl chungsimŭro" [A comparison of Chŏng Yakchong's *Chugyo yoji* with Catholic books in classical Chinese, focusing on a comparison to *Shengshi churao*], *Han'guk sasang sahak* 18 (2002): 157–195.

61. In the interrogation records of the State Tribunal, Chŏng Yakchong is quoted as saying, "The Lord of Heaven is the great king of heaven and earth and the great parent, so to refuse to acknowledge the Way of serving the Lord of Heaven is a sin against heaven and earth. Death is better than living in such a state." Kang Man'gil et al., *Ch'uan kŭp Kugan*, 50.

62. Augustine Chŏng's statement that "This is something we have to do" is an echo of what he wrote in chapter 39 of the *Essentials of Catholic Teachings*, "Since Jesus died to serve men, men should not refuse to die to serve the Lord." See the translation by Diaz, 417, and the translation by Torrey, 105.

63. For the life of Thomas Ch'oe P'ilgong, see *Hanŭnim ŭi chong*, 87–89.

64. Francis-Xavier Hong Kyoman learned Catholicism from Kwŏn Ilsin and converted at the urging of his son Leo Hong In. He was executed on April 8, 1801. *Hanŭnim ŭi chong*, 84–85. When he was interrogated, Hong mounted a strong defense of his faith. Kang Man'gil et al., *Ch'uan kŭp Kugan*, 85–86.

65. In Korea, *chinsa* was the title, meaning "presented scholar," awarded to those who passed the lower level of the civil service examinations.

66. Hwang is here referring to Augustine Chŏng's first son by his first wife, Charles Chŏng Ch'ŏlsang (1781?–1801). When his father was arrested, he

lived close to the prison so he could take care of him. He himself was arrested the day Augustine Chŏng was executed and was executed May 14, 1801, in Kwangju in Kyŏnggi province. *Hanŭnim ŭi chong*, 111–112.

67. Paul Hong Nangmin (1751–1801) passed the *chinsa*-level civil service exam in 1788 and served in various government posts. Despite two earlier renunciations of Catholicism, he died still professing his faith on April 8, 1801. Other sources say his baptismal name was Luke, not Paul. *Hanŭnim ŭim chong*, 90–91.

68. This suggests that Paul still believed in Catholicism but was afraid to publicly acknowledge his faith.

69. Hwang might mean here that Paul wanted to partake in the sacrament of confession but was unable to meet with Father Zhou.

70. Hwang's reasoning is somewhat off here, as people such as Yi Kahwan denied they were Catholics but were still executed by decapitation. Hong Nangmin at first denounced Catholicism as "more dangerous than a raging flood or ferocious animals," but Catholic sources say he reaffirmed his Catholic faith before he was executed. Kang Man'gil et al., *Ch'uan kŭp Kugan*, 73. He was beatified in 2014.

71. Yi Sŭnghun earned his presented scholar [*chinsa*] degree in 1780, having passed the preliminary civil service exam. He went to Beijing on a tribute mission in 1783 and was baptized there in the following year before he returned home. After he returned to Korea he began to baptize people. In 1785, after his Catholic activities were exposed during the Kim Pŏmu incident, he denounced Catholic teachings under pressure from his family. In 1787 he was reconciled to the church, but in 1791 he again renounced Catholicism but was exiled nonetheless. In 1795, when Father Zhou entered Korea, he again returned to the church. What his inner thoughts were in the last days of his life are not clear. However, records of his interrogation tell us that, in the weeks before he was executed on April 8, 1801, he denounced Catholic teachings. For an article that contains useful biographical information on him and argues that he should not be considered a martyr, see Cho Kwang, "Sinyu kyonan kwa Yi Sŭnghun," 59–85.

72. John the Baptist Yi Pyŏk (1754–1786) was an important early leader in the Catholic Church. He abandoned his Catholic activities in the wake of the Kim Pŏmu incident of 1785, when his father threatened suicide if he did not give up his faith. He died in 1786. Yi Pyŏk's sister was the first wife of Chŏng Yakhyŏn, and therefore the mother-in-law of Hwang Sayŏng, though she never met him, since she died in 1780. See Yi Changu, "Chosŏn Ch'ŏnjugyohoe ŭi sollip," 244–247; and Cho Hyŏnbŏm, "Kyohoe," 264.

73. Father Yang is the Chinese name for the French priest Father Jean De Grammont (1736–1812). He served in Beijing and Guandong. See Yŏ, *Nuga*, 85, n125.

74. The *ŭm* privilege refers to the sons of high officeholders being appointed to lower-level government posts without having to pass the highest level of the civil service examination. Yi's father had been an official. In fact, it was because his father was an official appointed to the 1783 embassy that Yi was able to travel to Beijing in the first place.

75. That is not quite correct. There had been a few Catholic books in Korea before 1784, but Yi Sŭnghun was the first one to form a community to put into practice what they said.

76. Yi Sŭnghun definitely did not die a martyr's death. He denounced Catholicism several times when he was being interrogated. In Kang Man'gil et al., *Ch'uan kŭp Kugan*, 21, he is recorded as saying "Catholics believe that God came down from heaven and lived as a human being among other human beings. Why would I believe anything that absurd?"

77. After passing a series of civil service exams, Yi Kahwan entered government service and was appointed a magistrate. He enjoyed scholarly discussions with the likes of Ahn Chŏngbok, Chŏng Yagyong, and Kwŏn Ch'ŏlsin and was often considered the intellectual mentor of the younger members of the Southerner Faction. Despite his initial interest in Catholicism, as a government official, he persecuted Catholics. Though never formally a Catholic (he was never baptized), he died in prison on April 8, 1801, from the beatings he had suffered while being interrogated. See Yŏ, *Nuga*, 88, n131.

78. Astronomy and geometry were both more advanced in the West than in Korea at this time, so Jesuit missionaries in China had published treatises on both subjects to convince potential converts of the superiority of Western civilization. Yi Kahwan read some of those publications and become one of the few Koreans who understood Western geometry well. For more on Yi Kahwan and Western astronomy, see Ch'oe Sangch'ŏn, "Yi Kahwan kwa Sŏhak," 41–67.

79. "*I-ki* (理氣) metaphysics" is a reference to Neo-Confucianism, the dominant philosophy among the ruling elite of Korea during the Chosŏn dynasty. *Ki* refers to the basic matter and energy that gives the universe substance and animation. *I* [*li*] refers to the organizing principles of appropriate interaction that give that universe coherence. In *i-ki* metaphysics, the universe is self-organizing, rendering the notion of a creator unnecessary.

80. *Zhifang waiji* was written by the Jesuit missionary Giulio Aleni (1582–1649) in Chinese and published in 1623 in China. It included not only maps but also information on the people, climate, and history of the various countries of the world previously unknown to the Chinese. It also devoted some space to Catholic doctrine. It was one of the books analyzed and criticized by Shin Hudam in his *Sŏhakpyŏn*. *Xixue fan* was also written by Aleni and provides a description of the content of education at European universities.

81. *Tianzue chuhan* was a compilation of books by Catholic missionaries on such subjects as religion, ethics, mathematics, and science. First published in 1629, it also included such important works as *Qike* [The seven victories] and Matteo Ricci's *Tianzhu shiyi* [The true meaning of the Lord of Heaven]. *Shengnian guangyi* was a collection of lives of the saints, with entries for each day of the year, which was translated from the French original by Joseph de Mailla in 1738. See Ricci, *True Meaning of the Lord of Heaven*, for an English translation of *Tianzhu shiyi*. For a Korean translation of the *Seven Victories*, see Diego de Pantoja, *Ch'ilgŭk: ilgop kaji sŭngni ŭi kil*, trans. Pak Wansik (Chŏnju: Chŏnju Tehakkyo ch'ulp'anbu, 1996); or *Ch'ilgŭk*, trans. Pak Yuri (Seoul: Ilchogak, 1998).

82. In 1786 Korean Catholic leaders selected their own bishop and priests and began performing the sacraments of confession and the mass. They did not realize that only a bishop, himself ordained by another bishop who was in the line of succession to the apostles, can validly ordain priests. They later had doubts about what they were doing and asked the bishop of Beijing for advice. When they were scolded and told that what they had done was against Catholic doctrine, they obeyed those instructions from Beijing and ceased performing these rituals. They also asked that a validly ordained priest be sent to them as soon as possible. This incident reveals that Korea's first Catholics understood the importance of the sacraments, although they were not yet well informed on the details of church doctrine regarding those sacraments. See Cho Hyŏnbŏm, "Kyohoe," 271–289.

83. This is evidence of state officials taking a harsher line against Catholicism, as well as Yi Kahwan's efforts to distance himself from the religion.

84. The Southerners were a relatively weak faction whom the king hoped could be used to balance the powerful Patriarch Faction without, in turn, being so powerful as to dominate him.

85. The three people referred to here were Chi Hwang (1767–1795), Yun Yuil (1760–1795), and Ch'oe Ingil (1765–1795). They were interrogated about

their role in smuggling Father Zhou and were beaten to death in an un-successful attempt to get them to tell the authorities where he was.

86. It is not clear who this Catholic was.

87. As described in Chapter 1, the leg screw torture involved the tying to-gether of the subject's ankles followed by the insertion of two wooden sticks between the person's legs, which were then pulled in such a way as to bend the shin bones out of shape. This itself was excruciatingly painful, but the agony was compounded after the sticks were removed and the shin bones returned to their old position. It had been banned in 1733, but it appears that it was still used at times. Catholicism was likely considered so dangerous that it was acceptable to use a form of torture previously thought inhumane. See William Shaw, *Legal Norms in a Confucian State* (Berkeley: University of California, Institute of East Asian Studies/Center for Korean Studies, 1981), 97–98.

88. Korea's first Catholics knew that they could have only one spouse at a time and were strictly forbidden from taking concubines. It is likely that his acquiring a concubine was in part to distance himself from Catholicism.

89. According to the official government interrogation records, Yi Kahwan in fact repudiated Catholicism. See Kang Man'gil et al., *Ch'uan kŭp Kugan*, 9–13, 102–104. For more on Yi Kahwan, see the tombstone inscription Chŏng Yagyong wrote for him: "Chŏnghŏn Yi Kahwan myojimyŏng" [A tombstone inscription for Chŏnghŏn Yi Kahwan], *Yŏyudang chŏnsŏ*, 1:15, 15a–28b.

90. These six people were Chŏng Yakchong, Ch'oe P'ilkong, Hong Kyoman, Hong Nangmin, and Yi Sŭnghun. They were executed on April 8, 1801.

91. Kwŏn Ch'ŏlsin on April 4 died from the beatings he suffered under in-terrogation. According to the government interrogation records, he de-nounced Catholicism. See Kang Man'gil et al., *Ch'uan kŭp Kugan*, 32. Chŏng Yagyong agrees. See his epitaph for Kwŏn Ch'ŏlsin: "Nokam myojimyŏng," *Yŏyudang chŏnso*, 1:15, 33a–36b. Church authorities also agree. Kwŏn was not among those beatified in 2014.

92. Hwang Sayŏng seems to be describing a couple who married but decided to remain perpetual virgins. While little is known about this husband and wife, one woman who entered such a marriage, Lutgarda Yi Suni, left two letters in which she discussed her faith and vocation before her execution. Modern Korean translations of these documents can be found in Kim Chinso, ed., *Yi Suni Rugalta nammae okchung p'yŏnji*. English translations of excerpts of her letter to her sisters can be found in Inshil Choe Yoon, trans., "Martyrdom and Social Activism: The Korean Practice

of Catholicism," in *Religions of Korea in Practice*, ed. Robert E. Buswell Jr. (Princeton, NJ: Princeton University Press, 2007), 368–371; and JaHyun Kim Haboush, ed., "Letters of the Catholic Martyrs," in *Epistolary Korea: Letters in the Communicative Space of the Chosŏn, 1392–1910* (New York: Columbia University Press, 2009), 363–369. A complete English translation of her letter to her sisters can also be found in Ch'ang-mun Kim and John Jae-sun Chung, *Catholic Korea*, 63–64, 73–77. A French translation can be found in Dallet, *Historie de l'Église de Corée*, 176–197.

93. The date of his execution was May 14, 1801.

94. Peter Ch'oe Pilche appears to have died still professing his faith. See *Hanŭnim ŭi chong*, 103–104. Church authorities appear to agree. He was among those beatified in 2014.

95. Kim Kŏnsun (1776–1801) converted to Catholicism in 1797. It was quite unusual for someone from a Patriarch Faction family, rather than a Southerner family, to become a Catholic. Father Zhou baptized him in 1799. See Yŏ, *Nuga*, 98, n150.

96. Kim Sanghŏn (1570–1652) was a fiercely anti-Manchu government official. See Yŏ, *Nuga*, 98, n151.

97. Like Augustine Chŏng Yakchong, he seems to have had an interest in philosophies and practices outside of traditional Neo-Confucianism.

98. See *The Analects of Confucius*, book 6, chapter 22.

99. Kim obtained several books from Yi Chunsin (1730–1801) in 1789, including Matteo Ricci's *Ten Chapters by a Non-conformer* [*Jiren shipian*] This book, written in a question-and-answer format and published in Beijing in 1608, criticized Buddhism and asserted that Catholicism was the true religion. See Yŏ, *Nuga*, 99, n153.

100. Those friends, in addition to Joseph Kim Kŏnsun and Martin Yi Chungbae, were John Wŏn Kyŏngdo, Luke Yi Hŭiyŏng, Kang Ich'ŏn, and Kim Ibaek. See Yŏ, *Nuga*, 101, n157. On Kim Ibaek, see Kang Man'gil et al., *Ch'uan kŭp Kugan*, 281. On Kang Ich'ŏn, see Kang Man'gil et al., *Ch'uan kŭp Kugan*, 330. On Kim Kŏnsun, see Kang Man'gil et al., *Ch'uan kŭp Kugan*, 242, 345, 362, 378. For Yi Hŭiyŏng, see Kang Man'gil et al., *Ch'uan kŭp Kugan*, 247–250. Other than Martin Yi and John Won, who were beatified in 2014, all are recorded as renouncing Catholicism.

101. Hwang connects Kang Ich'ŏn (1769–1801) with the growing interest in the *Chŏng Kam Nok* [The prophecies of Chŏng Kam] during the eighteenth century. Kang was known for his plan to raise a private naval force to overthrow the Manchu Qing dynasty in China (Kang Man'gil et al., *Ch'uan kŭp Kugan*, 278) and was likely influenced by his reading of the *Chŏng Kam Nok*. He was arrested in 1798 because of that plot and sent

into exile. He was re-arrested and interrogated in 1801 and died in prison. See Pak Kwang'yong, "Chŏngjodae Ch'ŏnjugyohoe wa Chungam Kang Ich'ŏn ŭi sasang" [The philosophy of Chungam Kang Ich'ŏn and its relationship to Catholicism during the reign of King Chŏngjo], in *Minjoksa wa kyohoesa* [The history of the nation and the history of the Church], ed. (Seoul: Han'guk kyohoesa yŏn'guso, 2000), 107–129. For more information on Kang Ich'ŏn as well as on Kim Kŏnsun, see Paek Sŭngjong, *Chŏngjo wa pullyang sŏnbi Kang Ich'ŏn: 18-seigi Chosŏn ŭi munhwa tujaeng* [Chŏngjo and the rouge scholar Kang Ich'ŏn: Cultural battles in eighteenth-century Chosŏn] (Seoul: P'urŭn yŏksa, 2012).

For the relationship between the *Chŏng Kam Nok* and Catholicism, see Paek Sŭngjong, "Chosŏn hugi Ch'ŏnjugyo wa *Chŏng Kam Nok*: somunhwa chiptan ŭi sangho chagyong" [Catholicism and the *Chŏng Kam Nok* in the latter half of the Chosŏn dynasty: a study of the interaction between two powerful subcultures], *Kyohoesa yŏn'gu* 30 (June 2008): 5–46.

102. Pang Sanggŭn argues that Father Zhou paid special attention to Joseph Kim and sought his conversion in particular because it would help expand the Catholic movement outside of the Southerner Faction. This would have made it less likely for Catholicism to become a factional issue. This did not happen, and the charge of Catholicism was sometimes used in factional struggles against Southerners. See Pang Sanggŭn, "Hwang Sayŏng *Paeksŏ* ŭi punsŏkchŏk ihae" [An analytical understanding of the *Silk Letter* of Hwang Sayŏng], *Kyohoesa yŏn'gu* 13 (July 1998): 161–162.

103. According to Yi Hŭiyŏng (1756–1801), those three books were *Shouren* (a prayer book), *Zhendao zizheng* [The truth is self-evident] by Emeric de Chavagnac, and *Lingyan lishao* [On the nature of the soul] by Francesco Sambiasi. Kang Man'gil et al., *Ch'uan kŭp Kugan*, 279.

104. Specifically, King Chŏngjo protected him by citing his youth and his illustrious ancestors as grounds for leniency. See *Chŏngjo sillok*, year 21, 11th month, 11th day (*pyŏngja*).

105. He in fact appears to have renounced Catholicism. See Kang Man'gil et al., *Ch'uan kŭp Kugan*, 238–243, 345, 362, 378, 506; and Yŏ, *Nuga*, 105n166.

106. Chongzhen (r. 1627–1644) was the last Ming emperor before China was conquered by the Manchu.

107. Kim Sangyong served in several high government posts before he set fire to a fort he had been unable to defend against the invading Manchus rather than surrender it. He died in that fire. See Yŏ, *Nuga*, 106n168.

108. The second, and last, Manchu invasion of Korea took place in 1636 and 1637. Such rituals expressed gratitude to the Wanli Emperor (r. 1572–1620)

for helping Korea resist Hideyoshi's invasions of the 1590s and paid homage to the Chongzhen Emperor (r. 1627–1644) as the last ruler of the Ming dynasty. For more on these rituals, and the political struggles that surrounded them, see JaHyun Kim Haboush, *The Confucian Kingship in Korea: Yŏngjo and the Politics of Sagacity* (New York: Columbia University Press, 2001), 35–43; Seung B. Kye, "The Altar of Great Gratitude: A Korean Memory of Ming China under Manchu Dominance, 1704–1894," *Journal of Korean Religions* 5, no. 2, 71–88.

109. Special civil service examinations were quite common in the Chosŏn dynasty. In fact, they were so numerous that they diminished the importance of the regular exams.

110. Laozi and Zhuangzi are two ancient Chinese writers who are popularly considered the founders of Daoism.

111. Kim Paeksun initially held firm, but after several episodes of interrogation with torture, he renounced his Catholic faith, only to revoke his renunciation, and was therefore executed as a Catholic on May 10, 1801. Kang Man'gil et al., *Ch'uan kŭp Kugan*, 74, 82, 113, 115, 370. Also see Yŏ, *Nuga*, 109n175. He is not among those beatified in 2014.

112. Luke Yi Hŭiyŏng (1756–1801) gained a reputation as a skilled artist of Western-style paintings. He learned about Catholicism from Joseph Kim Kŏnsun in 1797 and was baptized by Father Zhou in 1799. After he converted he painted many holy pictures and gave three paintings of Jesus to Hwang. He was executed on May 10, 1801. See Yŏ, *Nuga*, 110, n176–177. During his interrogation he claimed he had given up the practice of Catholicism before his arrest in the 1801 persecution, Kang Man'gil et al., *Ch'uan kŭp kugan*, 280. He is not among those beatified in 2014.

113. For more on Philip Hong P'ilchu (1774–1801), see *Hanŭnim ŭi chong*, 157–159. He was executed on October 4, 1801. He is among those beatified in 2014.

114. Followers of Pure Land Buddhism rely on the power of Amitabha Buddha to answer their prayers and to take them to the Western Paradise (the Pure Land) when they die. This form of Buddhism was especially popular among laypeople because anyone could engage in its main practice of chanting and so gain the help and protection of Amitabha.

115. Tŏksan was a district in the Naep'o area of Ch'ungch'ŏng province, which is south of the capital district of Seoul. The early convert Yi Chonch'ang was actively promoting Catholicism there in the 1790s.

116. In actuality, her husband divorced her, most likely because of her Catholicism. See Ledyard, "Kollumba Kang," 42–43.

117. Sabas Chi Hwang (1767–1795) met Father Zhou in China and guided him into Korea. He was killed along with Yun Yuil and Ch'oe Ingil in 1795. *Hanŭnim ŭi chong*, 53–55. He was among those beatified in 2014.

118. She was executed outside the Little West Gate of Seoul on July 2. She was beatified in 2014.

119. This is the prince Ŭnŏn (1755–1801). His grandson later ascended the throne as King Ch'ŏlchong (r. 1849–1863).

120. Prince Ŭnŏn's wife's name was Maria Song, and his daughter-in-law's was Maria Shin. They were forced to take poison on April 19, 1801. Neither of them is among those beatified in 2014.

121. A capping ceremony is a Confucian ritual making a young man's entrance into adulthood. In Korea at this time it normally takes place soon after the young man becomes a teenager.

122. Peter Cho, whose personal name was Yongsam, died on March 27, 1801 (according to the solar calendar), as a result of the wounds he suffered under torture while still professing his faith. See *Hanŭnim ŭi chong*, 76–77. He is among those beatified in 2014.

123. Louis-Gonzaga Yi Chonch'ang (1752–1801) was a rural *yangban* who was converted to Catholicism by Kwŏn Ilsin. He actively propagated Catholicism in his area but was arrested and temporarily withdrew from the Catholic community in 1791. He was arrested again in 1795 and held under strict confinement in his hometown for six years, until he was sent to Seoul in 1801 to be interrogated as part of the investigation of Catholics. He was condemned to death in the same sentence that condemned Augustine Chŏng Yakchong, but Yi Chonch'ang was sent down to Kongju to be executed. For more on Yi Chonch'ang, see Yu Pyŏnggi and Chu Myŏngjun, "Ch'ungch'ŏndo ŭi Ch'ŏnjugyo chŏllae," 27–57; Kang Man'gil et al., *Ch'uan kŭp Kugan*, 124–126. The first Korean priest, Andrew Kim Taegŏn (1822–1846), was the grandson of Yi Chonch'ang's niece, and the second Korean priest, Thomas Ch'oe Yangŏp (1821–1861), was the grandson of his nephew. See Yŏ, *Nuga*, 120n196; Kang Man'gil et al., *Ch'uan kŭp Kugan*, 124–126. Church authorities have been unable to determine whether or not Yi Chonch'ang renounced his faith on his way to be executed, so he is not among those beatified in 2014.

124. These two Catholics were, respectively, Peter Kim Chŏngdŭk (?–1801) and Andrew Kim Kwangok (?–1801). See Yŏ, *Nuga*, 121n197; and *Hanŭnim ŭi chong*, 144–148.

125. Stanislaus Han Chŏnghŭm (1756–1801) was converted by Augustine Yu Hanggŏm while he lived at Augustine's house and taught Yu's children. When he was arrested in 1801, he refused to renounce his faith despite

being tortured. He was beheaded on August 26, 1801, at the age of forty-five. Matthew Ch'oe Yŏgyŏm (1762–1801) first heard of Catholicism from Paul Yun Chich'ung and was then converted to Catholicism by Yi Chonch'ang. He was arrested after he was identified as a Catholic by someone who had been a Catholic and had left the church. He was executed on August 27, 1801, in his hometown of Mujang. Hwang identifies him as a commoner but later research has revealed that he probably was from a rural *yangban* family. See Yŏ, *Nuga*, 122n200–201; and *Hanŭnim ŭi chong*, 149–150, 153–154.

126. There was one other person, Andrew Kim Ch'ŏnae, who is reported to have refused to repudiate his faith. He was a servant of Yu Hanggŏm, who introduced him to Catholicism. He was executed on August 17, 1801, in Chŏnju. See Yŏ, *Nuga*, 122n202; and *Hanŭnim ŭi chong*, 151–152.

127. His brother was Yu Kwan'gŏm (1768–1801). Augustine Yu Hanggŏm (1756–1801) was an important early church leader in Chŏlla province. He was a wealthy *yangban* landowner and so was able to provide the Catholic community important financial support. He was involved in the attempts to bring a Western ship to Korea and in maintaining communication with the Catholics in Beijing. He was executed on October 24, 1801, because of his key role in the plan to invite Western warships to Korea. Francis Yun Chihŏn (1764–1801) was a maternal cousin of Augustine Chŏng Yakchong and learned about Catholicism from his older brother, Paul Yun Chich'ung, who had been executed in 1791. He was executed on October 24, 1801. His wife, son, and daughter were all banished to separate sites. Augustine Yu was one of those beatified in 2014. His younger brother Kwan'gŏm was not. See Yŏ, *Nuga*, 121–122n198–199; and *Hanŭnim ŭi chong*, 160–164.

128. Thomas Kim Yusan (1761–1801) was a man of base status [Ch'ŏnmin] who was converted at the urging of Yi Chonch'ang. *Ch'ŏnmin* included butchers, grave diggers, shamans, entertainers, slaves, and others whose hereditary status restricted them to despised occupations. The government relegated them to the bottom of the official social hierarchy, below commoners. He delivered the message to Beijing asking that a Western ship be sent to Korea in 1798. He was arrested along with Yu Hanggŏm and was executed on October 21, 1801. He is not among the beatified. See Yŏ, *Nuga*, 122n203.

129. Another estimate, found in a letter written by Korean Catholics in 1811, has a smaller number. That letter says those who died from the persecution numbered over a hundred. See the 1811 letter from the Korean Catholics

to the Pope, available in the *Scritture Originali riferite nelle Congregazioni* [Collection of primary documents for reference by the General Congregation of the Society of Jesus], 3:837–838, as cited in a Korean translation of this letter in Yun Min-gu, trans., *Han'guk ch'ogi kyohoe-e kwanhan kyohwangch'ŏng charyo moŭmjip* [Collection of Vatican documents related to the early Korean Church] (Seoul: Catholic Press, 2000), 200–213. A partial English translation can be found in Ch'ang-mun Kim and John Jae-sun Chung, *Catholic Korea*, 85–89.

130. This male believer was Barnabas Chŏng Kwangsu. He was caught in the fall of 1801 and executed on January 29, 1802. His wife, Lucia Yun Unhye, was arrested first and was martyred on May 14, 1801. They were both beatified in 2014. Yŏ, *Nuga*, 125n208.

131. This slave was Chŏng Im. Because she provided information about where Father Zhou had been hiding, she was not executed. Instead, she was exiled. See Yŏ, *Nuga*, 126n210.

132. For a description of Father Zhou's voluntary surrender, see Yi Changu, "Sinyu pakhae," 1:41–45.

133. For the record of the interrogation of Zhou, see Kang Man'gil et al., *Ch'uan kŭp Kugan*, 202–225.

134. According to the records of his interrogation, he made no such claim. Instead, he clearly states that he was a Chinese subject and was from Suzhou. Kang Man'gil et al., *Ch'uan kŭp Kugan*, 203.

135. The six Koreans he is referring to are Chŏng Yakchong, Ch'oe Ch'anghyŏn, Ch'oe P'ilgong, Hong Kyoman, Hong Nangmin, and Yi Sŭnghun. They were executed together on April 8, 1801.

136. Hwang appears to be a little confused here. Shin Taehyŏn (1737–1812) was the officer in charge at the time Father Zhou was to be executed. He was not replaced by Shin Taegyŏm (?–1807) until a month later, after Father Zhou had already been executed. If Shin Taehyŏn actually did claim to be ill in an attempt to avoid personally executing Father Zhou, it may have been because he did not want to be involved in the execution of a Chinese subject, which was something Korea was not allowed to do under the terms of its relationship with China. See Yŏ, *Nuga*, 129–130n216–217.

137. *Li* (里) is a unit used for land distances, taking into account both the actual physical distance and the time needed to cover that distance. The ten *li* between the city walls and Noryang would be a little more than three miles. The place where he was executed is now called Saenamt'ŏ, and there is a shrine to Korea's Catholic martyrs on that site.

138. This was May 31, 1801, according to the solar calendar. According to the liturgical year of the Catholic Church, the feast day of the Holy Trinity is celebrated on the Sunday that falls eight weeks after Easter Sunday.

139. Hwang seems to be arranging his description of the death of Father Zhou in accordance with the passion narratives of Jesus. This explains Hwang's curious inclusion of Father Zhou asking for wine (Jesus drank wine before his crucifixion; see John 19:28–30) and the emphasis on the sun being blotted out and the day becoming dark (similar phenomena are described in Mark 27:45–51). Hwang's description of the death of Father Zhou is much more detailed than that of any of the other martyrs and reflects his importance in the early Catholic Church in Korea and underlines that one of the key reasons that Hwang was writing a letter was to acquire another priest so that the Korean Catholics could again have access to the sacraments. See Franklin Rausch, "Wicked Officials and Virtuous Martyrs: An Analysis of the Martyr Biographies in Alexius Hwang Sayŏng's *Silk Letter*," *Kyohoesa yŏn'gu* 32 (July 2009): 20–25.

140. This refers to Hwang Sim and Hwang Sayŏng, respectively. See Yŏ, *Nuga*, 131n221–222.

141. Hwang appears to be mistaken on this point. In the official verdict condemning him to death, it was acknowledged that he came from China. *Sunjo sillok*, year 1, 4th month, 20th day (*pyŏngin*). In the report the Chosŏn court later made to China about the persecution of Catholics and the execution of Father Zhou, it claimed that it did not realize at first that he was Chinese. However, nothing was said about him possibly being from the island of Cheju. *Sunjo Sillok*, year 1, 10th month, 27th day (*kyŏngo*).

142. The sacraments are of great importance in Catholicism as they are believed to be the normal means through which God communicates grace and forgives sins. Without them, it is difficult, according to Catholic doctrine, to lead a normal Christian life and achieve salvation. Hwang argues that the early Christians were able to endure persecution because they had the divine help available through the sacraments. Since Korean Catholics did not have the sacraments as they had no priest to perform them (save for baptism which can be administered by laypeople), Hwang thought they could not endure persecution for much longer.

143. Hwang is referring to what the early Christian writer Tertullian (160–220) wrote in chapter 50 of his *Apologeticus*.

144. Catholicism had been brought to Japan by Portuguese and Spanish missionaries in the sixteenth century and thrived during the chaos of the

"country at war with itself" (J. *sengoku jidai)* period, when there was no central government to carry out a coordinated anti-Catholic policy. However, the rise of Tokugawa Ieyasu (1542–1616), and his establishment of shogunal dominance of the entire country, paved the way for broad attacks on what was viewed as a religion that was a threat to domestic stability because of its foreign connections and its ability to act as a unifying force that could threaten the power of the state. These persecutions killed thousands, and by Hwang's time it was widely believed that Catholicism had been completely wiped out in Japan. In fact, however, some Christians managed to maintain their faith underground and would later reveal themselves after the opening of Japan. See C. R. Boxer, *The Christian Century in Japan* (Berkeley: University of California Press, 1951); George Elison, *Deus Destroyed: The Image of Christianity in Early Modern Japan* (Cambridge, MA: Harvard University Press, 1991); and Ann M. Harrington, *Japan's Hidden Christians* (Chicago: Loyola Press, 1992).

145. Hwang is here referring to John Ok Ch'ŏnhŭi (1767–1801), who had carried messages between Korea and Bishop de Gouvea.

146. At this point in his letter, Hwang Sayŏng begins to share with Bishop de Gouvea various proposals to obtain tolerance for Catholicism and so save the Catholic Church there. For a detailed analysis of these proposals, see Yŏ, *Hwang Sayŏng "Paeksŏ" yŏn'gu*, 128–169.

147. This is a traditional mechanism for maintaining law and order. All families are placed in groups of five families each. If any one member of any of those five families in a group is discovered to have broken the law, and no one else in that group has reported that violation to the authorities, then everyone in all five families is punished.

148. Bianmen (K. Pyŏnmun) refers to a series of gates along the Willow Palisade marking the border with China proper. It was actually not all that close to Korea. Between Korea's northwestern border (the Yalu River) and Bianmen, there was a wide stretch of land reserved for the Manchu, so that neither Koreans nor Chinese were allowed to settle there. However, the Bianmen were the gates Korean diplomats would pass through when they went on diplomatic missions to China.

149. For "mammon," Hwang uses a two-syllable word, pronounced "mamon," which Jesuit missionaries in China had adopted as a rendering for the term used by Jesus with negative connotations to refer to property and money. See Matthew 6:24 and Luke 16:13 as well as Yŏ, *Nuga,* 143n236.

150. Hwang is referring to how China will react if it finds out that Korea executed a Chinese subject.

151. As described above, Peter Yi Sŭnghun, at the urging of John the Baptist Yi Pyŏk, went to Beijing to ask for baptism. He returned to Korea in 1784 and began baptizing Koreans. Thus, when the first foreign missionary arrived in Korea, there were already four thousand Catholics. See Cho Kwang, *Chosŏn hugi Ch'ŏnjugyosa yŏn'gu*, 20–31. It should be pointed out that these were not the first Korean Catholics. Japanese Catholics baptized Korean infants during Hideyoshi's invasions in the 1590s, and some of the Koreans who were kidnapped and taken to Japan later converted. However, if any of those Catholic Koreans returned from Japan, they did not bring their faith with them, and so the Catholic Church started by Yi Sŭnghun in Korea was truly a new beginning. See Yi Changu, "Chosŏn kwa Ch'ŏnjugyo ŭi mannam," 1:107–135.

152. Hwang is here probably referring to the Miao rebellion of 1795–1798 and the White Lotus rebellion of 1796–1801.

153. Ninggŭda is the small settlement from which the ancestors of the rulers of the Qing dynasty emerged. It is located in what is now Liaoning province. It is sometimes confused with a town farther north that has a similar name, Ninguta. Pamela Kyle Crossley, *A Translucent Mirror: History and Identity in Qing Imperial Ideology* (Berkeley: University of California Press, 1999), 20.

154. The official in charge of such an office was sent to help the people in regions affected by natural disasters or social disturbances and to restore social order. The region that Hwang suggests that office assume jurisdiction over was strategically and commercially important for Chosŏn since it lay between Chosŏn's northwestern border with Manchu territory and Chosŏn's capital.

155. Liaodong is a peninsula that juts out of Korea's northwestern border with Manchuria into the waters that it separates into the Gulf of Bohai and the Korea Bay. Shenyang, also known as Mukden, is a major inland city that is north of the Liaodong peninsula and was at one time the Manchu capital.

156. Sunjo was born in 1790, so he was only eleven years old when Hwang made this suggestion. He married the daughter of a powerful *yangban* family the next year, when he was still only twelve.

157. This is essentially the same strategy the Mongol Yüan dynasty used to control Koryŏ dynasty Korea. See David M. Robinson, *Empire's Twilight: Northeast Asia under the Mongols* (Cambridge, MA: Harvard University Press, 2009), 100–105.

158. This appears to be a reference to the Manchu official Yinghe (1771–1839), who visited Korea from late December 1779 through early January 1800

(according to the lunar calendar). Personal communication from Pierre-Emmanuel Roux. See *Chŏngjo sillok* year 23, 12th month, 24th day (*chŏngmi*).

159. Hwang is referring to a letter from Bishop de Gouvea that he had written in 1797 in response to a Catholic request for a large Western warship. For more on this request, see Ch'a Kijin, "Chosŏn hugi Ch'ŏnjugyo sinjadŭl-ŭi," 36–51.

160. After Hideyoshi's invasions of the 1590s and the two Manchu invasions of 1627 and 1636, Korea went for almost two hundred years without any major invasions or rebellions.

161. Hwang is incorrect in describing this as a merchant vessel. This ship, the *Providence*, was commanded by the explorer William Robert Broughton (1762–1821), a commander in the British navy. He had been dispatched to chart the waters of Northeast Asia. The *Providence* was a sloop of sixteen guns and so would have been a significant threat to the Chosŏn navy. The Catholic who went aboard was Paul Hyŏn Kyehŭm (1763–1801). He fled to Tongnae near Pusan when the 1799 persecution broke out. He gave himself up when he saw that his family and relatives were suffering on his account but was released. He was arrested again the next year and martyred on December 10, 1801. He was beatified in 2014. See Yŏ, *Nuga*, 157n262–263; *Hanŭnim ŭi chong*, 170–171; Ch'a Kijin, "Chosŏn hugi Ch'ŏnjugyo sinjadŭl-ŭi," 54; *Chŏngjo sillok*, year 21, 9, 6 (*imsin*). For Broughton's won account, see William Robert Broughton, *A voyage of discovery to the north Pacific Ocean: in which the coast of Asia, from the lat. of 35 ° north to the lat. of 52 ° north, the island of the Insu (commonly known under the name of the land of Jesso,) the north, south, and east coasts of Japan, the Lieuchieux and the adjacent isles, as well as the coast of Corea, have been examined and surveyed. Performed in His Majesty's Sloop* Providence *and her tender, in the years 1795, 1796, 1797, 1798* (London: Printed for T. Cadell and W. Davies, 1804), 328–344.

162. This philosophy emerged during China's Song dynasty (960–1279). It offered a comprehensive explanation of everything from the movements and characteristics of natural objects to the proper political, social, economic, and moral behavior of human beings, and based those explanations on its interpretations of the ancient Confucian classics. The formative forces in the Neo-Confucian universe were *li* (理, dynamic patterns of appropriate interactions) and *ki* (氣, the basic matter and energy out of which the universe is formed). Those who accepted the explanations provided by Song Neo-Confucianism saw no need to

entertain any other philosophies, nor did their philosophy assign any role to God or gods.

163. It appears that Hwang is mistaken about this. The Chosŏn government was hesitant to execute Father Zhou because he was a Chinese subject, not because of fear of a Catholic rebellion. See *Sŭngjŏngwŏn ilgi* year 1, 3ʳᵈ month, 16ᵗʰ day (*imjin*) and year 1, 2ⁿᵈ month, 27ᵗʰ day (*kyemyo*).

164. The unnamed Catholic may have been Thomas Hwang Sim. See Kang Man'gil et al., *Ch'uan kŭp kugan*, 795–796.

165. Hwang appears to be arguing here that, if European Catholics came to Korea and threatened force against the government, it would not look as bad as if Korean Catholics themselves used force against their own government.

166. Hwang is ignoring the persecution of Catholics that began in Japan in the 1600s and continued to his day as well as the intermittent persecution of Catholics in Qing China. For how persecutions in China affected one Catholic community there, see Eugenio Menegon, *Ancestors, Virgins, and Friars: Christianity As a Local Religion in Late Imperial China* (Cambridge, MA: Harvard University Asia Center, 2009).

167. Sodom and Gomorrah were not punished with destruction because they refused to accept missionaries. However, in Matthew 10:11–16, Jesus states that cities who rejected his disciples, who were sent to preach the good news, would be punished on Judgment Day more severely than Sodom and Gomorrah had been. This is probably what Hwang is referring to.

168. Catholics, save for those who were exempted for such reasons as age or health, were expected to fast during Lent, the forty days leading up to Easter. To not fast would be a sin, but fasting might also give away their identities as Catholics, possibly leading to arrest. Therefore Hwang is asking here for a dispensation so that Korean Catholics could miss fast days without committing a sin. According to a Korean catechism first published in 1931, the great fast consisted of abstaining from meat and only eating lunch and, if necessary, a snack at dinnertime. For the small fast, a Catholic was to avoid meat but could eat eggs, fish, milk, and food cooked with animal fat or oil. It is likely the case that alcohol was also excluded in both fasts. Ordinary Fridays were a small fast day, so Catholics would have had to avoid meat at least one day a week, even when it was not Lent. See No Paoro, ed., *Ch'ŏnjugyo yori mundap* [Questions and answers on Catholic doctrine] (1931; repr., Seoul: Kat'ollik ch'ulpansa, 1965), 69–70; Yŏ, *Nuga*, 163n268.

169. This person in question is probably Hwang Sayŏng himself. See Yŏ, *Nuga*, 163n269.
170. Saint Simon Thaddeus was one of the disciples of Jesus. His feast day is on October 28. One day after that would have been October 29, which, according to the lunar calendar, would have been the twenty-second day of the ninth month.

BIBLIOGRAPHY

Ahn Chŏngbok. *Sunamjip* [The collected writings of Sunam Ahn Chŏngbok]. Seoul: Sŏnggyun'gwan taehakkyo, Taedong munhwa yŏn'guwŏn, 1970.

——, ed., *Sŏngho sasŏl yusŏn* [Selections from the classified writings of Sŏngho Yi Ik]. Seoul: Myŏngmundang, 1982.

Ahn Ŭngnyŏl and Ch'oe Sŏgu. *Han'guk Chŏnju kyohoesa* [The history of the Korean Catholic Church]. Seoul: Pundo, 1979. This is an annotated Korean translation, in three volumes, of Charles Dallet, *Histoire de L'Église de Corée.*

Anderson, Benedict. *Imagined Communities: Reflections on the Orign and Spread of Nationalism.* Revised Edition ed. London and New York: Verso, 1991.

Anthony of Taizé. "Origins of the Catholic Church in Korea: A Letter." *Transactions of the Royal Asiatic Society, Korea Branch* 89 (2014): 169–192.

Aquinas, Thomas. *Summa Theologica.* Translated by Anton E. Pegis. In *Basic Writings of St. Thomas Aquinas.* New York: Random House, 1948.

Baker, Don. "A Confucian Confronts Catholicism: Truth Collides with Morality in Eighteenth-century Korea." *Korean Studies Forum,* no. 6 (1979–1980): 1–44.

——. "A Different Thread: Orthodoxy, Heterodoxy, and Catholicism in a Confucian World." In *Culture and State in Late Chosŏn Korea,* edited by JaHyun Kim Haboush, and Martina Deuchler, 199–232. Cambridge, MA: Harvard University Press, 1999.

——. *Korean Spirituality.* Honolulu: University of Hawai'i Press, 2008.

——. "Korea's Path of Secularization," Ranjan Ghosh, ed. *Making Sense of the Secular: Critical Perspectives from Europe to Asia.* New York: Routledge, 2012, pp. 182–194.

——. "The Martyrdom of Paul Yun: Western Religion and Eastern Ritual in Eighteenth-Century Korea." *Transactions of the Royal Asiatic Society, Korea Branch* 54 (1979): 33–58.

———. "The Religious Revolution in Modern Korean History: From Ethics to Theology and from Ritual Hegemony to Religious Freedom." *Review of Korean Studies* 9, no. 3 (September 2006): 259–275.

———. "Shamans, Catholics, and Chŏng Yagyong: Tasan's Defense of the Ritual Hegemony of the Confucian State." *Tasanhak* 15 (December 2009): 139–179.

———. "Tasan between Catholicism and Confucianism: A Decade Under Suspicion, 1791 to 1801." *Tasanhak* 5 (2004): 55–86.

———. "Tasan and His Brothers: How Religion Divided a Korean Confucian Family." In *Perspectives on Korea*, edited by Sang-oak Lee and Duk-so Park, 172–197. Sydney, Australia: Wild Peony Press, 1998.

———. "The Use and Abuse of the Sirhak Label: A New Look at Shin Hu-dam and his Sŏhak Pyŏn," *Kyohoesa Yŏn'gu* [Studies in Catholic Church history] 3 (1981): 183–254.

de Bary, William Theodore, and Irene Bloom, eds. *Sources of Chinese Tradition*. New York: Columbia University Press, 1999.

Peter Beyer, "Questioning the secular/religious divide in a post-Westphalian world," *International Sociology* 28:6 (2013), 663–679.

Biographies of the 124 Koreans who were beatified in 2014: http://www .koreanmartyrs.or.kr/sbss124_en_list.php. Accessed June 25, 2014. In English and Korean. (For more biographies of Korean martyrs, go to http://newsaints.faithweb.com/martyrs/Korea2.htm. Accessed June 26, 2014.)

Boxer, C. R. *The Christian Century in Japan*. Berkeley: University of California Press, 1951.

Brook, Timothy, Jerome Bourgon, and Gregory Blue. *Death by a Thousand Cuts*. Cambridge, MA: Harvard University Press, 2008.

Broughton, William Robert. *A voyage of discovery to the north Pacific Ocean: in which the coast of Asia, from the lat. of 35° north to the lat. of 52° north, the island of the Insu (commonly known under the name of the land of Jesso,) the north, south, and east coasts of Japan, the Lieuchieux and the adjacent isles, as well as the coast of Corea, have been examined and surveyed. Performed in His Majesty's Sloop* Providence *and her tender, in the years 1795, 1796, 1797, 1798*. London: Printed for T. Cadell and W. Davies, 1804.

Buswell, Robert E., Jr. *The Collected Works of Chinul*. Honolulu: University of Hawai'i Press, 1983.

———. *Religions of Korea in Practice*. Princeton, NJ: Princeton University Press, 2007.

Buswell, Robert E., Jr., and Timothy S. Lee, eds. *Christianity in Korea*. Honolulu: University of Hawai'i Press, 2006.

Byun Ki-Yung (Pyŏn Kiyŏng). *Hanŭnim ŭi Kyŏre* [The people of God]. Kwangju, Kyŏngi-do: Han'guk Ch'ŏnjugyohoe ch'angnipsa yŏn'guwŏn, 1999.

Ch'a Chuhwan. *Han'guk Togyo sasang yŏn'gu* [A study of Daoist thought in Korea]. Seoul: Seoul National University Press, 1993.

Ch'a Kijin. "Chosŏn hugi Ch'ŏnjugyo sinjadŭl-ŭi sŏngjikcha yŏngip kwa yangbak ch'ŏngnae-e taehan yŏn'gu" [A study of the plans by Catholics in the latter half of the Chosŏn dynasty to invite Western ships and clergy to Korea]. *Kyohoesa yŏn'gu* 13 (July 1998): 19–71.

———. *Chosŏn hugi ŭi Sŏhak kwa ch'ŏksaron yŏn'gu* [A study of Western Learning and attacks on heterodoxy in the late Chosŏn dynasty]. Seoul: Kyohoesa yŏn'guso, 2002.

———. "Manch'ŏn Yi Sŭnghun ŭi kyohoe hwaldong kwa chŏngch'ijŏk ipchi" [Manch'ŏn Yi Sŭnghun's political stance and his activities for the church]. *Kyohoesa yŏn'gu* 8 (1992): 33–57.

———. "Yi Chonch'ang (Ludovico Gonzaga) ŭi saengae wa sinang" [The life and faith of Yi Chonch'ang Ludovico Gonzaga]. *Kyohoesa yŏn'gu* 19 (2002): 165–182.

———. Chan, Wing-tsit, trans. *Reflections on Things at Hand*, edited by Chu Hsi (Zhu Xi) and Lu Tsu-chien (Lu Zuqian). New York: Columbia University Press, 1967.

Chan, Wing-tsit, trans. and ed. *A Sourcebook of Chinese Philosophy*. Princeton, NJ: Princeton University Press, 1969.

Chang Sŏnghan. "Hwang Sayŏng ŭi 'Paeksŏ-e' taehan yŏn'gu: poda t'ongjŏnjŏgin yŏksa haesŏgŭl wihan han siron" [A study of the *Silk Letter* of Hwang Sayŏng: An attempt at a broader historical explanation]. *Changsin nondan* 33 (2009): 91–116.

Ching, Julia. *Confucianism and Christianity*. Tokyo: Kodansha, 1977.

Cho Han'gŏn. "*Chugyo yoji* wa hanyŏk Sŏhak wa ŭi kwan'gye [The relationship between the *Chugyo yoji* and Catholic books translated into Chinese]. *Kyohoesa yŏn'gu* 26 (June 2006): 5–74.

Cho Hyŏnbŏm, "Kyohoe ŭi hwaldong kwa kyosae ŭi hwaksan" [The activities of the Church and its expansion], *Han'guk Ch'ŏnju kyohoesa I* [Korean Catholic History, vol. 1], Yi Changu, et. al., 255–309. Seoul: Han'guk kyohosesa yŏn'guso, 2009.

Cho Kwang. *Chosŏn hugi Ch'ŏnjugyosa yŏn'gu* [A study of Catholic history in the latter half of the Chosŏn dynasty]. Seoul: Koryŏ Taehakkyo minjok munhwa yŏn'guso, 1988.

———. *Chosŏn hugi Ch'ŏnjugyosa yŏn'gu ŭi kich'o* [A foundation for the study of the history of Catholic Church in the latter half of the Chosŏn dynasty]. Seoul: Kyŏngin Munhwasa, 2010.

———. *Chosŏn hugi sahoe wa Ch'ŏnjugyo* [Catholicism and society in the latter half of the Chosŏn dynasty]. Seoul: Kyŏngin munhwasa, 2010.

———. "Chu Munmo ŭi Chosŏn ipguk kwa kŭ hwaldong" [Zhou Wenmo's arrival in Korea and his activities on the peninsula]. *Kyohoesa yŏn'gu* 10 (1995): 45–92.

———. *Han'guk kŭnhyŏndae Ch'ŏnjugyosa yŏn'gu* [Studies of the history of Catholicism in modern and contemporary Korea]. Seoul: Kyŏngin Munhwasa, 2010.

———. "Sinyu kyonan kwa Yi Sŭnghun" [Yi Sŭnghun and the 1801 Anti-Catholic persecution]. *Kyohoesa yŏn'gu* 8 (1992): 59–85.

———. "Sinyu pakhae ŭi punsŏkchŏk koch'al" [An analysis of the 1801 persecution]. *Kyohoesa yŏn'gu* 1 (1977): 44–74.

Cho Kwang, ed. and trans. *Chosŏn wangjo sillok Ch'ŏnjugyosa charyo moŭm* [Collection of historical materials on Catholicism from the veritable records of the Chosŏn Dynasty]. Seoul: Han'guk sun'gyoja hyŏnyang wiwŏnhoe, 1997.

———. *Sinyu pakhae charyojip* [Collection of materials from the persecution of 1801]. Seoul: Han'guk sun'gyoja hyŏnyang wiwŏnhoe, 1999.

Cho Kwang and Kwŏn Naehyŏn, ed. and trans. *Chŏngjo sidae Ch'ŏnjugyosa charyojip* [Collection of Catholic materials from Chŏngjo's reign]. Seoul: Han'guk sun'gyoja hyŏnyang wiwŏnhoe, 1999.

Cho Kwang, Chang Chŏngnan, Kim Chŏngsuk, and Song Chongnye. *Sun'gyoja Kang Wansuk yŏksarŭl wihae ilŏsŏda* [The martyr Kang Wansuk: Standing up for history]. Seoul: Catholic Press, 2006.

Ch'oe Ch'anghwa, ed. *Sinyu pakhae wa Hwang Sayŏng Paeksŏ sakkŏn* [The 1801 persecution and the Hwang Sayŏng *Silk Letter* incident]. Seoul: Han'guk sun'gyoja hyŏnyang wiwŏnhoe, 2003.

Ch'oe Chaegŏn. *Chosŏn hugi sŏhak ŭi suyong kwa paljŏn* [The reception and development of Western Learning in the second half of the Chosŏn dynasty]. Seoul: Handŭl Publishing, 2005.

Ch'oe Chongsŏng. *Chosŏnjo musok kukhaeng irye yŏn'gu* [A study of official shamanic rituals during the Chosŏn Dynasty]. Seoul: Iljisa, 2002.

Ch'oe Kibok. "The Abolition of Ancestral Rites and Tablets by Catholicism in the Chosŏn Dynasty and the Basic Meaning of Confucian Ancestral Rites." *Korea Journal* 24, no. 8 (1984): 41–52.

Choe Sang-hun. "Papal Visit That Thrills Catholics Is Unsettling to Protestants in South Korea." *New York Times*, August 16, 2014. http://www

.nytimes.com/2014/08/17/world/asia/huge-crowds-watch-in-seoul-as
-pope-francis-beatifies-korean-catholics.html.

Ch'oe Sangch'ŏn. "Yi Kahwan kwa Sŏhak" [Yi Kahwan and Western Learning]. In *Han'guk kyohoesa nonmunjp: Han'guk Ch'ŏnjugyohoe ch'angsŏl ibaekchunyŏn kinyŏm*, vol. 2 [A collection of articles on the history of the Catholic Church in Korea in commemoration of the two hundredth anniversary of the founding of the Korean Catholic Church, vol. 2], edited by Han'guk kyohoesa nonmunjip kanhaeng wiwŏnhoe [The committee for the publication of studies of the history of the Korean Church], 41–68. Seoul: Han'guk kyohoesa yŏn'guso, 1985.

Ch'oe Sŏgu. *Han'guk Ch'ŏnjukyohoe ŭi yŏksa* [Studies in the history of the Catholic Church in Korea]. Seoul: Han'guk kyohoesa yŏn'guso, 1982.

———. *Han'guk Kyohoesa ŭi tam'gu* [Research on the history of the Church in Korea]. Seoul: Han'guk kyohoesa yŏn'guso, 1982.

———. "Han'guk kyohoe ŭi ch'angsŏl kwa ch'ocha'nggi Yi Sŭnghun ŭi kyohoe hwaldong" [Yi Sŭnghun's activities during the formative period of Catholicism in Korea]. *Kyohoesa yŏn'gu* 8 (1992): 7–31.

Ch'oe Sŏgu sinbu kohŭi kinyŏm saŏp wiwŏnhoe [The Committee to commemorate the 70th birthday of Fr. Ch'oe Sŏgu], ed. *Han'guk Kat'ollik munhwa hwaldong kwa kyohoesa* [Church history and the cultural activities of the Korean Catholic Church]. Seoul: Han'guk kyohoesa yŏn'guso, 1991.

Ch'oe Sŏnhye, "Kihae pakhae" [The 1839 Persecution], *Han'guk Ch'ŏnju kyohoesa, III* [Korean Catholic History vol. 3], ed. Han'guk kyohoesa 15–103. Seoul: Han'guk kyohoesa yŏn'guso, 2010.

Ch'oe Tonghŭi. "Habin Shin Hudam." In *Han'guk inmul yuhaksa* [A history of Confucians in Korea], 3:1459–1480. Seoul: Han'gilsa, 1996.

———. *Sŏhak-e taehan Han'guk sirhak ŭi panŭng* [The reaction of Korean Practical Learning scholars to Western Learning]. Seoul: Koryŏ Taehakkyo Minjok Munhwa Yŏn'guso, 1988.

———. "Tasan ŭi sin'gwan" [Tasan's concept of God]. *Han'guk sasang* 15 (1977): 106–134.

Choi, Jai-Keun. *The Origin of the Roman Catholic Church in Korea*. Norwalk, CA: The Hermit Kingdom Press, 2006.

Chŏng Tuhŭi. "Ch'ŏnjugyo sinang kwa yubae ŭi salm, Tasan ŭi hyŏng Chŏng Yakchŏn" [Tasan's brother Yakchŏn, his Catholic faith and his life in exile]. *Yŏksa pip'yŏng* 11 (Fall 1990): 302–317.

Chŏng Yagyong. *Admonitions for Governing the People: Manual for All Administrators* [*Mongmin shimsŏ*]. Translated by Choi Byonghyon. Berkeley: University of California Press, 2010.

————. *Yŏyudang chŏnsŏ* [The complete writings of Yŏyudang Chŏng Ya-gyong]. Seoul: Kyŏngin munhwa sa, 1970.

Chŏng Yakchong. *Chugyo yoji* [Essential Elements of the Lord's Teachings]. Translated by Ha Sŏngnae. Seoul: Hwang Sŏkdu Luga sŏwŏn, 1984.

Chosŏn wangjo sillok [The veritable records of the Chosŏn dynasty]. 48 vols. Seoul: Kuksa P'yŏnch'an Wiwŏnhoe, 1955–58.

Cooper, Michael, SJ. *Rodrigues, the Interpreter: An Early Jesuit in Japan and China*. Tokyo: Weatherhill, 1974.

Crossley, Pamela Kyle. *A Translucent Mirror: History and Identity in Qing Imperial Ideology*. Berkeley: University of California Press, 1999.

Dallet, Charles. *Histoire de L'Église de Corée*. Paris: Victor Palmé, 1874. Reprint, Seoul: Royal Asiatic Society, 1975.

Deuchler, Martina. "Despoilers of the Way—Insulters of the Sages: Controversies over the Classics in Seventeenth-Century Korea." In *Culture and the State in Late Chosŏn Korea*, edited by JaHyun Kim Haboush and Martina Deuchler, 90–133. Cambridge, MA: Harvard University Asia Center, 1999.

————. "Neo-Confucianism: The Impulse for Social Action in Early Yi Korea." *Journal of Korean Studies* 2 (1980): 71–111.

Diaz, Hector. *A Korean Theology: Chu-gyo Yo-ji, Essentials of the Lord's Teaching by Chŏng Yak-jong Augustine (1760–1801)*. Immensee: Neue Seitschrift für Missionswissenschaft, 1986.

Dix, Griffin. "How to Do Things with Ritual: The Logic of Ancestor Worship and Other Offerings in Rural Korea." In *Studies on Korea in Transition*, edited by David McCann, John Middleton, and Edward Shultz, 57–88. Honolulu: University of Hawai'i Press, 1979.

Duncan, John. "Proto-nationalism in Pre-modern Korea." In *Perspectives on Korea*, edited by Sang-Oak Lee and Duk-soo Park, 198–221. Sydney: Wild Peony, 1998.

Elison, George. *Deus Destroyed: The Image of Christianity in Early Modern Japan*. Cambridge, MA: Harvard University Press, 1991.

Feng Yu-lan. *A History of Chinese Philosophy*. Princeton, NJ: Princeton University Press, 1952.

Finch, Andrew. "The Pursuit of Martyrdom in the Catholic Church in Korea before 1866." *Journal of Ecclesiastical History* 60, no. 1 (January 2009): 95–118.

Gallup Korea, ed. *Han'gugin ŭi chonggyo: 1984-yŏn, 1989-yŏn, 1997-yŏn, 2004-yŏn, 2014-yŏn, che 5-ch'a pigyo chosa pogosŏ* [The Religion of Koreans: A report comparing survey results from 1984, 1989, 1987, 2004, and 2014]. Seoul: Gallup Korea Research Center, 2015.

Gellner, Ernest. *Nations and Nationalism*. Ithaca: Cornell University Press, 1983.

Giles, Lionel, trans. *Liezi* [Lie Tzu]. London: J. Murray, 1912. Available at http://www.sacred-texts.com/tao/tt/tt07.htm. Accessed October 29, 2016.

de Groot, J. J. M. *Sectarianism and Religious Persecution in China*. New York: Paragon Books, 1970.

Ha Sŏngnae. "Hwang Sayŏng ŭi kyohoe hwaldong kwa sun'gyo-e taehan yŏn'gu" [A study of the religious activities of Hwang Sayŏng and his martyrdom]. *Kyohoesa yŏn'gu* 13 (1998): 74–144.

———. *Sun'gyoja Yun Yuil (Paolo) sun'gyoja Chŏng Ŭn (Paolo) p'yŏngjŏn* [Critical biographies of the martyrs Paul Yun Yuil and Paul Chŏng Ŭn]. Seoul: The St. Luke Hwang Sŏkdu Library, 1988.

Ha Ubong. "Chŏng Tasan ŭi S'ŏhakgwan'gae ŭi taehan ilgoch'al" [A look at Chŏng Tasan's relationship with Catholicism]. *Kyohoesa yŏn'gu* 1 (1977): 71–112.

Haboush, JaHyun Kim. *The Confucian Kingship in Korea: Yŏngjo and the Politics of Sagacity*. New York: Columbia University Press, 2001.

———. "Constructing the Center: The Ritual Controversy and the Search for a New Identity in Seventeenth-Century Korea." In *Culture and State in Late Chosŏn Korea*, edited by JaHyun Kim Haboush and Martina Deuchler, 46–90. Cambridge, MA: Harvard University Press, 1999.

———, trans. *The Memoirs of Lady Hyegyong: The Autobiographical Writings of a Crown Princess of Eighteenth-Century Korea*. Berkeley: University of California Press, 1996.

———, ed. "Letters of the Catholic Martyrs." In *Epistolary Korea: Letters in the Communicative Space of the Chosŏn, 1392–1910*, Jahyun Kim Haboush, trans., 359–374. New York: Columbia University Press, 2009.

Han Chongman. "Tasan ŭi ch'ŏn'gwan" [Tasan's concept of Heaven]. *Tasan hakbo* 2 (1979): 121–149.

Han Ugŭn. "Chosŏn wangjo ch'ogi-e issŏsŏ-ŭi yugyo inyŏm-ŭi silchŏn kwa sinang, chonggyo: Saje munjerŭl chungsimŭro" [Religion, religious faith, and the realization of Confucian ideals in the early Chosŏn Dynasty: Focusing on the issue of rituals]. *Hanguk saron* 3 (1976): 147–228.

———. *Sŏngho Yi Ik yŏn'gu* [A study of Yi Ik]. Seoul: Seoul University Press, 1980.

Han Young-woo. *A Review of Korean History*. 3 vols. Paju, ROK: Kyongsaewon, 2010.

Han'guk Ch'ŏnjugyo chugyohoe ŭi sibok sisŏng chugyo t'ŭkpyŏl wiwŏnhoe [The special committee of the Korean Catholic Bishops' Conference for beatification and canonization], ed. *Hanŭnim ŭi chong: Yun Chich'ung Paoro wa tongnyo sun'gyoja 123 wi* [Servants of God: Paul Yun Chich'ung and 123 fellow martyrs]. Seoul: Han'guk Ch'ŏnjugyo chugyohoe ŭi sibok sisŏng chugyo t'ŭkpyŏl Wiwŏnhoe, 2003.

Han'guk Kat'ollik Taesajŏn [A Korean dictionary of Catholicism]. Seoul: Han'guk kyohoesa yŏn'guso, 1985.

Han'guk kyohoesa yŏn'guso [Korean Church History Research Institute], ed. *Han'guk Ch'ŏnjugyohoesa,* vol. 1 [The history of Catholicism in Korea, vol. 1]. Seoul: Han'guk kyohosesa yŏn'guso, 2009.

Han'guk sasang sahak 18 (2002). Special issue on "Chŏng Yakchong ŭi sidae wa sasang" [The thought and times of Chŏng Yakchong].

Han'guk sun'gyoja hyŏnyang wiwŏnhoe, ed. *Sinyu Pakhae wa Hwang Sayŏng Paeksŏ Sakkŏn* [The 1801 persecution and the *Silk Letter* of Hwang Sayŏng]. Seoul: Han'guk sun'gyoja hyŏnyang wiwŏnhoe, 2003.

———. *Sinyu Pakhae Yŏn'gu ŭi Pangbŏp kwa saryo* [Methods and materials for research on the 1801 persecution]. Seoul: Han'guk sun'gyoja hyŏnyang wiwŏnhoe, 2003.

Hara, Takemichi. "Korea, China, and Western Barbarians: Diplomacy in Early Nineteenth Century Korea." *Modern Asian Studies* 32, no. 2 (1998): 393–401.

Harrington, Ann M. *Japan's Hidden Christians.* Chicago: Loyola Press, 1992.

Henry H. Em. *The Great Enterprise: Sovereignty and Historiography in Modern Korea.* Durham, NC: Duke University Press, 2013.

Hutton, Eric L., trans. *Xunzi: The Complete Text.* Princeton: Princeton University Press, 2014.

Hŏ Tonghyŏn. "Hwang Sayŏng Paeksŏ-e taehan kŭn-hyŏndae hakkye ŭi p'yŏngga" [The evaluations of the *Silk Letter of Hwang Sayŏng* in modern and contemporary Korea]. *Han'guk sinhak madang* [Korean theology forum] http://theologia.kr/board_korea/27438. Accessed October 23, 2016.

Holland, David L. "Heresy, Renaissance and Later." In *Dictionary of the History of Ideas,* edited by Philip P. Wiener, II, 424–431. New York: Charles Scribner's Sons, 1968–1974.

Hong Yangho. *Igye Hong Yangho chŏnsŏ* [The complete works of Igye Hong Yangho]. Seoul: Minjok Munhwasa, 1982.

Hwang, Alexander Y., and Lydia T. Kim. "The Silk Letter of Alexander Sayông Hwang: Introduction and Abridged Translation." *Missiology: An International Review* 37, no. 2 (April 2009): 165–179.

Hwang, Kyung Moon. *Beyond Birth: Social Status in the Emergence of Modern Korea.* Cambridge, MA: Harvard University Asia Center, 2005.

Hwang Sayŏng. *Hwang Sayŏng paeksŏ* [The *Silk Letter* of Hwang Sayŏng]. Edited and translated by Yun Chaeyŏng. Seoul: Chŏngŭmsa, 1975.

———. *Hwang Sayŏng paeksŏ.* Translated by Kim Yŏngsuk. Seoul: Sŏng Hwang Sŏktu Luga sŏwŏn, 1998.

Hwang Tŏkkil. *Haryŏ sŏnsaeng munjip* [The collected writings of Haryŏ Hwang Tŏkkil]. Seoul: Kyujanggak Collection, n.d.

Janelli, Roger L., and Dawnhee Yim Jamelli. *Ancestor Worship and Korean Society.* Stanford, CA: Stanford University Press, 1982.

Johnston, Ian, trans. *The Mozi: A Complete Translation.* New York: Columbia University Press, 2010.

Kalton, Michael. "Chŏng Tasan's Philosophy of Man: A Radical Critique of the Neo- Confucian World View." *Journal of Korean Studies* 3 (1981): 2–38.

———. *To Become a Sage: Ten Diagrams on Sagely Learning.* New York: Columbia University Press, 1988.

Kang Man'gil et al., eds. *Ch'uan kŭp kugan* [Records of special investigations by the State Tribunal], vol. 25. Seoul: Asea munhwasa, 1978.

Kang Segu. *Sŏngho hakt'ong yŏn'gu* [Studies of Sŏngho's intellectual legacy]. Seoul: Hyean Publishing, 1999.

Kim Chinso. *Ch'ŏnjugyo Chŏnju kyogusa* [A history of the Catholic Diocese of Chŏnju]. Chŏnju: The Catholic Diocese of Chŏnju, 1998.

———. "Chu Munmo sinbu sŏn'gyo hwaldong chŏnhu-ŭi sun'gyojadŭl" [Those who were martyred around the time Father Zhou Wenmo was proselytizing in Korea]. *Kyohoesa yŏn'gu* 10 (1995): 93–122.

———, ed. *Yi Suni Rugalda nammae okchung p'yŏnji* [The Prison Letters of Yi Suni Lutgarda and her Brothers]. Translated by Yang Hŭich'an and Pyŏn Chusŭng. Naewŏlli: Ch'ŏnjugyo Honam kyohŏe yŏn'guso, 2002.

Kim, Joseph Ch'ang-mun, and John Jae-sun Chung. *Catholic Korea: Yesterday and Today.* Seoul: St. Joseph Publishing Co., 1984.

Kim Kilhwan. *Chosŏnjo yuhak sasang yŏn'gu* [A study of Confucianism in the Chosŏn dynasty]. Seoul: Iljisa, 1980.

Kim Ok-hŭi. *Kwangam Yi Pyŏk ŭi Sŏhak sasang* [The Catholic thought of Yi Pyŏk]. Seoul: Catholic Press, 1979.

———. *Han'guk Sŏhak sasangsa yŏn'gu* [Studies in the history of Korean thought on Western learning]. Seoul: Kukhak Charyowŏn, 1998.

———. "Yuhandang Kwŏnssi ŭi 'ŏnhaeng sillok' e kwanhan yŏn'gu" [A study of the records of the life and words of Mrs. Kwŏn Yuhandang]. In *Han'guk Ch'ŏnjugyo yŏsŏngsa* [The history of Korean Catholic women], edited by Kim Ok-hŭi, 34–78. Kyŏngnam Masan-si: Han'guk inmun kwahakwŏn, 1983.

Kim Ok-hy [Kim Ok-hŭi]. "Women in the History of Catholicism in Korea." *Korea Journal* 24, no. 8 (1984): 28–40.

Kim Sanghong. "Tasan ŭi Ch'ŏnjugyo sinbong-e taehan pannon" [Refuting the contention that Tasan Was a Catholic]. In Kim Sanghong, ed *Tasanhak yŏn'gu*, 11–68. Seoul: Kyemyŏng munhwasa, 1990.

Kim Sŏng'yun. *Chosŏn hugi t'angp'yŏng chŏngch'i yŏn'gu* [A study of the politics of Grand Harmony in the latter half of the Chosŏn dynasty]. Seoul: Chisik sanŏpsa, 1997.

Kim Sŏnhŭi, trans. *Habin Shin Hudam ŭi Tonwa Sŏhakpyŏn* [The *Tonwa Sŏhakpyŏn* of Habin Shin Hudam]. Seoul: Silsi haksa, 2014.

Kim T'aeyŏng. "Chŏng Yakchong ŭi Ch'ŏnju kyori ihae" [Chŏng Yakchong's understanding of Catholic doctrine]. *Yŏksa wa Kyŏnggye* 89 (2013): 109–147.

Kim Tuhŏn. "Kim Pŏmu wa kŭ ŭi kagye" [Kim Pŏmu and his family]. *Kyohoesa yŏn'gu* 34 (2010): 5–61.

Kim Yangsŏn. *Maesan kukhak san'go* [Kim Yangsŏn's writings on Korean studies]. Seoul: Sungjŏn University Museum, 1972.

Kim Yŏngil. *Chŏng Yagyong ŭi Sangje Sasang* [The Lord on High in the thought of Chŏng Yagyong]. Seoul: Kyŏngin munhwasa, 2003.

Kim Yong-duk. "Ancestral Rites." In *Korean Cultural Heritage*, 4: 42–49. Seoul: Korea Foundation, 1997.

Kugyŏk taejŏn hoet'ong [Great collection of administrative codes, translated into Korean]. Seoul: Koryŏ University Press, 1960.

Kŭm Chang-t'ae. "Chosŏn hugi Yuhak-Sŏhakgan ŭi kyorironjaeng kwa sasangjŏk sŏng'gyŏk" [The ideological conflict between Confucianism and Catholicism in the later half of the Chosŏn dynasty]. *Kyohoesa yŏn'gu* 2 (1979): 89–139.

———. "Chŏng Yagyong kwa Ch'ŏnjugyo sinang" [Chŏng Yagyong and the Catholic faith]. *Han'guk hak* 24 (1981): 19–29.

———. *Han'guk Yugyo ŭi Chaejomyŏng* [New light on Korean Confucianism]. Seoul: Chŏnmangsa, 1982.

———. "Tonwa Shin Hudam ŭi Sŏhak pip'aniron kwa chaengjŏm" [The theoretical basis for Shin Hudam's criticism of Western Learning and the particular points he raised against it]. *Chonggyohak yŏn'gu* [Journal of religious studies] 20 (December 2001): 1–25.

Kye, Seung B. "The Altar of Great Gratitude: A Korean Memory of Ming China under Manchu Dominance, 1704–1894." *Journal of Korean Religions* 5, no. 2, 71–88.

Ledyard, Gari. "Kollumba Kang Wansuk, an Early Catholic Activist and Martyr." In *Christianity in Korea*, edited by Robert E. Buswell Jr. and Timothy S. Lee, 38–71. Honolulu: University of Hawai'i Press, 2006.

Legge, James, ed. and trans. *The Chinese Classics*. Vols. 1–5. Hong Kong: Hong Kong University Press, 1960.

Li Zhizao, ed. *Tianxue chuhan* [An introduction to Heavenly Learning], vol. 2. Taipei: Taiwan xuesheng shuju, 1965.

Liu, Kwang-ching. *Orthodoxy in Late Imperial China.* Berkeley: University of California Press, 1990.

Lynn, Richard John, trans. *The Classic of Changes.* New York: Columbia University Press, 2004.

Ma, Zhao. "The Anti-Christian Campaign and Imperial Control in Eighteenth-Century China." *Asia-Pacific: Perspectives* 5, no. 1 (2004): 18–20.

Mailla, Joseph-Anne-Marie de Moyriac de. *Shengshi churao* [Teachings of the church in everyday language] http://archives.catholic.org.hk/Rare%20 Books/RB-index.htm. Accessed October 29, 2016.

Major, John S., Sarah A. Green, Andrew Seth Meyer, and Harold D. Roth, trans. *The Huainanzi: A Guide to the Theory and Practice of Government in Early Han China.* New York: Columbia University Press, 2010.

Menegon, Eugenio. *Ancestors, Virgins, and Friars: Christianity As a Local Religion in Late Imperial China.* Cambridge, MA: Harvard University Asia Center, 2009.

Minamiki, George, SJ. *The Chinese Rites Controversy from Its Beginning to Modern Times.* Chicago: Loyola University Press, 1985.

Mungello, D. E., ed. *The Chinese Rites Controversy: Its History and Meaning.* Nettetal: Steyler Verlag, 1994.

Munro, Donald. "The Concept of Interest in Chinese Thought." *Journal of the History of Ideas* 41, no. 2 (1980): 179–197.

No Kilmyŏng. *Kat'ollik kwa Chosŏn hugi sahoe pyŏndong* [The Catholic Church and social change in the latter half of the Chosŏn dynasty]. Seoul: Koryŏ taehakkyo minjok munhwa yŏn'guso, 1988.

No Paoro, ed. *Ch'ŏnjugyo yori mundap.* 1931. Reprint, Seoul: Catholic Press, 1965.

No Yongp'il. *Han'guk Ch'ŏnjugyohoesa ŭi yŏn'gu* [Studies in the history of Korean Catholicism]. Seoul: Han'guk Sahak, 2008.

Pae Ŭnha, ed. *Yŏksa ŭi ttang, paeum ŭi ttang: Paeron* [Paeron: A place of history, a place for learning]. Seoul: St. Paul Publishing, 1992.

Paek Sŭngjong. *Chŏngjo wa pullyang sŏnbi Kang Ich'ŏn: 18-seigi Chosŏn ŭi munhwa tujaeng* [Chŏngjo and the rouge scholar Kang Ich'ŏn: Cultural battles in eighteenth-century Chosŏn]. Seoul: P'urŭn yŏksa, 2012.

———. "Chosŏn hugi Ch'ŏnjugyo wa Chŏng Kam Nok: somunhwa chiptan ŭi sangho chagyong" [Catholicism and the *Chŏng Kam Nok* in the latter half of the Chosŏn dynasty: the interaction between two subcultures]. *Kyohoesa yŏn'gu* 30 (June 2008): 5–46.

Pak Chonch'ŏn. "Chŏng Yagyong ŭi sin'gwan-e taehan chonggyosajŏk haesŏk" [An explanation from the standpoint of religious history of the notion of

God of Chŏng Yagyong]. In *Yugyo wa chonggyohak,* edited by SNU Center for Religious Studies, 3–43. Seoul: Seoul National University Press, 2009.

Pak Chiwŏn. *Yŏnamjip* [Yŏnam Pak Chiwŏn's collected works]. Seoul: Kyŏngin munhwasa, 1974.

Pak, Chonghong. "Sŏgusasang ŭi toip pip'an kwa sŏpch'wi" [The introduction, criticism, and assimilation of Western European thought]. In Asea Munje yŏn'guso, ed., *Sirhak sasang ŭi tamgu,* 172–277. Seoul: Hyŏamsa, 1974.

Pak Kwang'yong. "Chŏngjodae Ch'ŏnjugyohoe wa ŭi Chungam Kang Ich'ŏn ŭi sasang" [The philosophy of Chungam Kang Ich'ŏn and its relationship to Catholicism during the reign of King Chŏngjo]. In *Minjoksa wa kyohoesa* [The history of the nation and the history of the church], edited by Ch'oe Sŏgu Sinbu Sup'um 50-chunyŏn kinyŏm wiwŏnhoe [The committee to celebrate the 50th anniversary of the ordination of Fr. Ch'oe Sŏgu] 107–129. Seoul: Han'guk kyohoesa yŏn'guso, 2000.

———. "Chu Munmo sinbu sŏn'gyo hwaldong ŭi paegyŏng" [The background to the missionary activities of Father Zhou Wenmo]. *Kyohoesa yŏn'gu* 10 (1995): 19–44.

———. *Yŏngjo wa Chŏngjo-ŭi nara* [The country of kings Yŏngjo and Chŏngjo]. Seoul: P'ulŭn yŏksa, 1998.

Pang Sanggŭn. "Ch'ogi kyohoe-e issŏsŏ Myŏngdohoe ŭi kusŏng kwa sŏnggyŏk" [The structure and characteristics of the Association for Illuminating the Way during the early church]. *Kyohoesa yon'gu* 11 (December 1996): 213–226.

———. "Hwang Sayŏng *Paeksŏ* ŭi punsŏkchŏk ihae" [An analytical understanding of the *Silk Letter* of Hwang Sayŏng]. *Kyohoesa yŏn'gu* 13 (July 1998): 145–175.

———. "Chu Munmo sinpu ŭi ipkuk kwa Chosŏn kyohoe" [Father Zhou Wenmo's entry into Korea and the Chosŏn Church], in *Han'guk Ch'ŏnju kyohoesa, I* [Korean Catholic History vol. 1], Yi Changu, et. al. 311–344. Seoul: Han'guk kyohosesa yŏn'guso, 2009.

de Pantoja, Diego. *Chi'ilgŭk: ilgop kaji sŭngni ŭi kil* [Seven victories]. Translated by Pak Wansik. Chŏnju: Chŏnju Taehakkyo ch'ulp'anbu, 1996.

———. *Ch'ilgŭk.* Translated by Pak Yuri. Seoul: Ilchogak, 1998.

Park, Chang-Won. "Between God and Ancestors: Ancestral Practice in Korean Protestantism." *International Journal for the Study of the Christian Church* 10, no. 4 (2010): 257–273.

Park Hyunmo [Pak Hyŏnmo]. "King Jeongjo's Political Role in the Conflicts between Confucianism and Catholicism in Eighteenth-Century Korea." *Review of Korean Studies* 7, no. 4 (December 2004): 205–228.

Park, Joo. "Catholicism and Women in the Royal Court of King Sunjo in the Late Chosun Dynasty." *Yŏsŏng kwa yŏksa* [Women and history] 8 (2008): 1–19.

Pyŏn Chusŭng, "Sinyu pakhae ŭi chŏngjijŏk paegyŏng-e kwanhan yŏn'gu," [A study of the political background of the 1801 persecution] in *Sinyu pakhae wa Hwang Sayŏng paeksŏ sakkŏn* [The 1801 persecution and the Hwang Sayŏng *Silk Letter* incident], ed. Ch'oe Ch'anghwa 35–54. Seoul: Han'guk sun'gyoja hyŏnyang wiwŏnhoe, 2003.

Rausch, Franklin. "Dying for Heaven: Persecution, Martyrdom, and Family in the Early Korean Catholic Church." In *Death, Mourning, and the Afterlife in Korea: From Ancient to Contemporary Times*, edited by Charlotte Horlyck and Michael Pettid, 213–235. Honolulu: University of Hawai'i Press, 2014.

———. "Wicked Officials and Virtuous Martyrs: An Analysis of the Martyr Biographies in Alexius Hwang Sayŏng's *Silk Letter*." *Kyohoesa yŏn'gu* 32 (July 2009): 5–30.

Ricci, Matteo, SJ. *The True Meaning of the Lord of Heaven*. Translated by Douglas Lancashire and Peter Hu Kuo-chen, SJ. St. Louis, MO: Institute of Jesuit Sources, 1985.

Ricci, Matteo and Nicolas Trigault, *China in the Sixteenth Century: The Journals of Matthew Ricci, 1583–1610*. Translated by Louis J. Gallagher, S. J. New York: Random House, 1953.

Robinson, David M. *Empire's Twilight: Northeast Asia Under the Mongols*. Cambridge, MA: Harvard University Press, 2009.

Roux, Pierre-Emmanuel. "The Great Ming Code and the Repression of Catholics in Chosŏn Korea." *Acta Koreana* 15, no. 1 (June 2012): 73–106.

Rutt, Richard, and Chong'un Kim, trans. *Virtuous Women: Three Classic Korean Novels: A Nine Cloud Dream, The True History of Queen Inhyŏn, The Song of a Faithful Wife, Ch'un-hyang*. Seoul: Kwangmyong, 1979.

Sahak chingŭi [A warning against Catholicism]. Han'guk kyohoesa yŏn'guso, ed. Seoul: Pulham munhwasa, 1977.

Scritture originali riferite nelle congregazioni generali (SOCG) [Collection of primary documents for reference by the General Congregation of the Society of Jesus]. 1622–1892. Available in the Vatican Archives, Vatican City.

Seoh, Mun Sang. "Yi Ik, an Eighteenth Century Korean Intellectual." *Journal of Korean Studies* 1 (1969): 9–21.

Shaw, William. *Legal Norms in a Confucian State*. Berkeley: University of California, Institute of East Asian Studies/Center for Korean Studies, 1981.

Sim Chaeu. "Chŏngjodae 'Hŭmhyul chŏnch'ik' ŭi panp'o wa hyŏnggu chŏngbi" [The provision of instruments for interrogation and punishment, and the distribution of the "Regulations for Judicious Inquiry and Trial" during the reign of King Chŏngjo]. *Kyujanggak* 22 (December 1999): 135–153.

Sim Ujun. *Sunam Ahn Chŏngbok yŏn'gu* [A study of Sunam Ahn Chŏngbok]. Seoul: Iljisa, 1985.

Shin Hudam. *Habinjip* [The collected works of Habin Shin Hudam]. Published as *Habin Sŏnsaeng chŏnjip* [The complete works of Habin Shin Hudam] Seoul: Asea munhwasa, 2006.

Smith, Anthony D. *The Ethnic Origins of Nations*. Oxford: Blackwell Publishers, 1998.

Sŏ Chongt'ae. "Ch'ŏnjin-am Chuŏ-sa kanghak kwa Yangmyŏnghak." In *Yi Kibaek sŏnsaeng kohŭi kinyŏm Han'guk sahak nonch'ong* [A collection of articles on Korean history in honor of Professor Yi Kibaek's seventieth birthday], Yi Kibaek sŏnsaeng kohŭi kinyŏm Han'guk sahak nonch'ong kanhaeng wiwŏnhoe, ed. 1265–1293. Seoul: Iljogak, 1994.

———. "Nogam Kwŏn Ch'ŏlsin ŭi Yangmyŏnghak suyong kwa kŭ yŏnghyang" [The influence Kwŏn Ch'ŏlsin's acceptance of Wang Yangming's philosophy had on others]. *Kuksagwan nonch'ong* 34 (1992): 239–260.

———. "Sonam Chŏng Yakchŏn ŭi sirhak sasang" [The practical learning philosophy of Chŏng Yakchŏn]. *Tonga yŭn'gu* 24 (June 1992): 271–311.

———. "Sŏngho hakp'a ŭi Yangmyŏnghak suyong: Pogam Yi Kiyangŭl chungsimŭro." *Han'guk sa yŏn'gu* 66 (September 1989): 75–102.

———. "Sunam Ahn Chŏngbok ŭi 'Ch'ŏnhak sŏlmun' kwa 'Ch'ŏnhakko,' 'Ch'ŏnhak mundap'-e kwanhan yŏn'gu" [A study of the "Questions on Heavenly Learning," "On Heavenly Learning," and "A Conversation on Heavenly Learning" by Sunam Ahn Chŏngbok] *Kyohoesa yŏn'gu* 41 (2013): 5–71.

———. "Yi Ik kwa Shin Hudam ŭi Sŏhak nonjaeng: 'Tonwa Sŏhakpyŏn' ŭi kimunp'yŏnŭl chungsimŭlro" [The argument over Western Learning between Yi Ik and Shin Hudam: Focusing on "Tonwa's On Western Learning" in the "Records of Conversations"]. *Kyohoesa yŏn'gu* 16 (2001): 79–211.

Sŏ Chongt'ae and Han Kŏn, eds. *Chosŏn hugi Ch'ŏnjugyo sinja chaep'an kirok: Ch'uan mit kugan* [Records of the trials of Catholic believers in the latter part of the Chosŏn era: Records of the State Tribunal]. Seoul: Kukhak Charyowŏn, 2004.

Sohn Pokee. *Social History of the Early Chosŏn Dynasty: The Functional Aspects of Governmental Structure*. Seoul: Jisik-sanup Publishing, 2000.

Song Chu-yong. "Yi Ik and Practical Learning." In *Korean Philosophy: Its Tradition and Modern Transformation*, edited by Korean National Commission for UNESCO, 323–335. Seoul: Hollym, 2004.

Spence, Johathan D. *Emperor of China: Self-Portrait of K'ang-hsi.* New York: Vintage Books, 1974.

Standaert, Nicolas. *Handbook of Christianity in China.* Vol. 1, *635–1800.* Leiden: Brill, 2001.

Sŭngjŏngwŏn ilgi [Daily Records of the Royal Secretariat] 126 vols. Seoul: Kuksa P'yŏnch'an Wiwŏnhoe, 1961–1977.

Taemyŏngnyul chikhae [The Ming law codes explained]. Reprint, Seoul: Pŏpjech'o, 1964.

Tao Xisheng et al., eds. *Mingdai zongjiao* [Ming dynasty religion]. Taipei: The Student Bookstore, 1968.

Torrey, Deberniere J., trans. *Jugyo Yoji* [The essentials of the Lord's teaching]. Seoul: KIATS, 2012.

Turner, Bryan S. *The Religious and the Political: A Comparative Sociology of Religion.* Cambridge, UK: Cambridge University Press, 2013.

Walraven, Boudewijn. "Popular Religion in a Confucianized Society." In *Culture and the State in Late Chosŏn Korea,* edited by JaHyun Kim Haboush and Martina Deuchler, 160–198. Cambridge, MA: Harvard University Press, 1999.

Watson, Burton, trans. *Basic Writings of Mo Tzu, Hsün Tzu, and Han Fei tzu.* New York: Columbia University Press, 1967.

——. *Courtier and Commoner in Ancient China: Selections from the History of the Former Han by Pan Ku.* New York: Columbia University Press, 1974.

——. *Records of the Grand Historian by Sima Qian, Han Dynasty, II* (rev. ed., New York: Columbia University Press, 1993).

Wŏn Chaerin. *Chosŏn hugi Sŏngho hakp'a ŭi hakp'ung yŏn'gu* [Studies on the academic accomplishments of the Sŏngho school in the latter half of the Chosŏn dynasty]. Seoul: Hyean Publishing, 2003.

Wŏn Chaeyŏn. *Chosŏn wangjo ŭi pŏp kwa Kŭrisŭdogyo: Tong-Sŏyang ŭi sangho insik kwa munhwa ch'ungdol* [Christianity and the laws of the Chosŏn dynasty: Ideological and cultural conflict between East and West]. Seoul: Handŭl Publishing, 2003.

——. "Chŏng Yakchong 'Chugyo yoji' wa Hanmun sŏhaksŏ ŭi pigyo yŏn'gu: 'Shengshi churao' wa ŭi pigyorŭl chungsimŭro" [A comparison of Chŏng Yakchong's *Chugyo yoji* with Catholic books in classical Chinese, focusing on a comparison to *Shengshi churao*]. *Han'guk sasang sahak* 18 (2002): 157–195.

Yamaguchi Masayuki. *Chōsen seikyōshi* [The history of Korean Catholicism]. Tokyo: Yūzankaku, 1967.

———. *Kō Shiei hakusho no kenkyū. Rōma Hōōcho komonjo-kan shozō* [A study of the *Silk Letter of Hwang Sayŏng*: The copy held in the Vatican archives]. Kyōto: Zenkoku Shobō, 1946. Korean translation by Yi Minwŏn in *Hwang Sayŏng Paeksŏ nonmun sŏnjip* [A collection of studies of the *Silk Letter of Hwang Sayŏng*], ed. Yŏ Chinch'ŏn (Seoul: Kippŭn sosik, 1994), 16–118.

Yang, C. K. *Religion in Chinese Society.* Berkeley: University of California Press, 1961.

Yi Changu. "Chosŏn kwa Ch'ŏnjugyo ŭi mannam" [The meeting of Chosŏn and the Catholic Church]. In *Han'guk Ch'ŏnjugyohoesa* I (Korean Catholic History, vol. 1) 1, Yi Changsu, et. al., 107–135. Seoul: Han'guk kyohosesa yŏn'guso, 2009.

———. "Chosŏn Ch'ŏnjugyo ŭi sŏllip" [The establishment of the Korean Catholic Church]. *Han'guk Ch'ŏnju kyohoesa I* (Korean Catholic History, vol. 1), 227–251. Seoul: Han'guk kyohoesa yŏn'guso, 2009.

———. "Hwang Sayŏng kwa Chosŏn hugi ŭi sahoe pyŏnhwa: Kyŏnggi pukpu chiyŏk kyohoe sajŏk ŭi kich'ojŏk kŏmt'o illye" [Hwang Sayŏng and the changes in later Chosŏn dynasty society: A preliminary examination based on the sites important for church history in northern Kyŏnggi province]. *Kyohoesa yŏn'gu* 31 (2008): 79–108.

———. "Sinyu pakhae wa Hwang Sayŏng paeksŏ sakkŏn" [The 1801 persecution, Hwang Sayŏng, and the *Silk Letter* incident]. In *Han'guk Ch'ŏnjugyohoesa II* [Korean Catholic history, vol. 2], edited by Han'guk kyohoesa yŏn'guso, 20–117. Seoul: Han'guk kyohosesa yŏn'guso, 2010.

Yi Hŏn'gyŏng. *Kanongjip* [The works of Kanong Yi Hŏn'gyŏng]. Seoul: Han'guk kojŏn pŏnyŏgwon [Institute for the Translation of the Korean Classics], 2013. Published as part of the multivolume collection *Han'guk munjip ch'onggan* [The collected works of Korea library].

Yi Ihwa. "Yi Sŭnghun kwan'gye munhŏn ŭi kŏmt'o" [An examination of documents related to Yi Sŭnghun]. *Kyohoesa yŏn'gu* 8 (1992): 105–124.

Yi Ik. *Sŏngho saesŏl* [The miscellaneous writings of Yi Ik]. Seoul: Minjok munhwa ch'ujinhoe, 1977–1978.

Yi Kigyŏng, ed. *Pyŏgwip'yŏn* [In defense of the right against the wrong]. Seoul: Kyohoesa yŏn'guso, 1979. This is the original *Pyŏgwip'yŏn*, compiled shortly after 1801, on which the *Pyŏgwip'yŏn* of Yi Manch'ae is partially based.

Yi Kuyong. "Sunam Ahn Chŏngbok ŭi saengae wa sasang" [The life and thought of Ahn Chŏngbok]. In *Kangwŏn Taehak Yŏn'gu nomunjip* [Research papers from Kangwŏn University] VI (1972).

Yi Manch'ae, ed. *Pyŏgwip'yŏn* [In defense of the right against the wrong]. Seoul: Yŏlhwadang, 1971.

Yi Nŭnghwa. *Chosŏn kidokkyo kŭp oegyosa* [A history of Christianity and foreign relations in Korea]. Seoul: Han'gukhak yŏn'guso, 1977.

———. *Chosŏn musokko* [A study of Korean shamanism]. Seoul: Hangukhak Yŏn'guso, 1977.

Yi Sŏngbae. *Yugyo wa Kŭrisŭdo: Yi Pyŏk ŭi han'gukchŏk sinhak wŏlli* [Confucianism and Christianity: The Korean nature of the theological principles of Yi Pyŏk]. Seoul: Pundo Publishing, 1979.

Yi Sŏngmu. *Chosŏn Wangjosa* [The history of the Chosŏn dynasty]. Vol. 2. Seoul: Tongbang midiŏ, 1998.

Yi Tonghŭi. "Sŏhak suyong ŭi tu kaji panŭng, Shin Hudam kwa Chŏng Yagyong. Mat'eo Lich'i ŭi 'Ch'ŏnju silŭi' suyongŭl chungsimŭro" [Two types of responses to Western Learning, Shin Hudam and Chŏng Yagyong: Focusing on their reception of Matteo Ricci's *The True Meaning of the Lord of Heaven*]. In *Tasan Sasang kwa Sŏhak* [Tasan's philosophy and Western Learning], edited by Kyŏnggi munhwa chaedan sirhak pangmulgwan. 147–181. Seoul: Kyŏngin Munhwasa, 2013.

Yi Tonghwan. "Tasan sasang esŏ-ŭi 'Sangje' toip kyŏngno-e taehan sŏsŏlchŏk koch'al" [A preliminary inquiry into the origins of Tasan's concept of Sangje]. In *Tasan ŭi chŏngch'i kyŏngje sasang* [Tasan's political and economic thought], edited by Kang Man'gil et al., 300–320. Seoul: Ch'angjok kwa pip'yŏngsa, 1990.

Yi Wŏnsun. *Han'guk Ch'ŏnjugyohoesa yŏn'gu* [A study of the history of the Korean Catholic Church]. Seoul: Han'guk kyohoe-sa yŏn'guso, 1986.

———. *Han'guk Ch'ŏnjugyohoesa yŏn'gu, Sok* [A study of the history of the Korean Catholic Church, Supplemented]. Seoul: Han'guk kyohoe-sa yŏn'guso, 2004.

———. "Kim Pŏmuga non'go" [A look at the family of Kim Pŏm]. In *Han'guk Kat'ollik munhwa hwaldong kwa kyohoesa* [Church history and the cultural activities of the Korean Catholic Church], edited by Ch'oe Sŏgu sinbu kohŭi kinyŏm saŏp wiwŏnhoe, 459–476. Seoul: Han'guk kyohoesa yŏn'guso, 1991.

Yi Yujin. "Yi Suni Rugalda okchung p'yŏnji hyŏnjŏn p'ilsabon-ŭi charyojŏk kach'i wa haedok ŭi munje" [The value of, and problems interpreting, the extant handwritten version of Lutgarda Yi Suni's letter from prison]. *Kyohoesa yŏn'gu* 40 (2012): 173–203.

Yŏ Chinch'ŏn. "Han'guk Ch'ŏnjugyo ch'ogi p'yŏngsindo chidojadŭl-ŭi sinang t'ŭksŏng" [The distinctive characteristics of the faith of the lay leaders of the early Korean Catholic Church], *Kyohoesa yŏn'gu* 42 (2013): 5–53.

———. "Hwang Sayŏng 'Paeksŏ' ibon-e taehan pigyo yŏn'gu" [A comparative study of alternative versions of the *Silk Letter* of *Hwang Sayŏng*]. *Kyohoesa yŏn'gu* 28 (June 2007): 5–29.

———. *Hwang Sayŏng "Paeksŏ" yŏn'gu: wŏnbon kwa ibon pigyo kŏmt'o* [The *Silk Letter of Hwang Sayŏng*: A comparative examination of the original and alternate versions]. Seoul: Han'guk kyohoesa yŏn'guso, 2009.

———. *Hwang Sayŏng Paeksŏ wa ibon* [The *Silk Letter of Hwang Sayŏng* and alternate versions]. Seoul: Kukhak Charyowŏn, 2005.

———, ed. *Hwang Sayŏng Paeksŏ nonmun sŏnjip* [A collection of studies of the *Silk Letter of Hwang Sayŏng*]. Seoul: Kippŭn sosik, 1994.

———. *Nuga chŏhŭirŭl wirohae chugessŭmnikka?* [Who will comfort us?]. Seoul: Kibbŭn sosik: 2002. (This is an annotated translation of the *Hwang Sayŏng Paeksŏ*.)

Yoo Kwon Jong. "Dasan's Approach to Ultimate Reality." *Korea Journal* 53, no. 2 (2013): 31–53.

Yoon, Inshil Choe, trans. "Martyrdom and Social Activism: The Korean Practice of Catholicism." In *Religions of Korea in Practice*, ed. Robert E. Buswell Jr., 355–373. Princeton, NJ: Princeton University Press, 2007.

Yu Hongnyŏl. *Han'guk sahoe sasangsa non'go* [Studies on the history of Korean social thought]. Seoul: Iljogak, 1980.

Yu Pyŏnggi and Chu Myŏngjun. "Ch'ungch'ŏngdo ŭi Ch'ŏnjugyo chŏllae: Yi Chonch'ang ŭi hwaldongŭl chungsimŭro" [The spread of Catholicism to Ch'ungch'ŏng province: Focusing on the activities of Yi Chonch'ang]. In *Han'guk kyohoesa nonch'ong: Ch'oe Sŏgu Sinbu hwakap kinyŏm* [A collection of scholarly studies of the history of the Korean Catholic Church in honor of the sixtieth birthday of Fr. Ch'oe Sŏgu], Ch'oe Sŏgu sinbu hwagap kinyŏm nonmunjp kanhaeng wiwŏnhoe, ed. 27–57. Seoul: Han'guk kyohoesa yŏn'guso, 1982.

Yun Min'gu. *Chogi han'guk Ch'ŏnjugyohoesa ŭi chaengjŏm yŏn'gu* [Study of the points of contention in the early history of the Roman Catholic Church in Korea]. Seoul: Kukhak charyowŏn, 2014.

———. *Han'guk ch'ogi kyohoe-e kwanhan kyohwangch'ŏng charyo moŭmjip* [Collection of Vatican documents related to the early Korean Church]. Seoul: Catholic Press, 2000.

———. *Han'guk Ch'ŏnjugyo ŭi kiwŏn* [The origins of the Catholic Church in Korea]. Seoul: Kukhak Charyowŏn, 2002.

Yun, Sasoon [Yun Sasun]. *Critical Issues in Neo-Confucian Thought: The Philosophy of Yi T'oegye*. Translated by Michael C. Kalton. Seoul: Korea University Press, 1990.

Zhu Xi and Liu Zuqian, eds. Chan Wing-tsit, trans. *Reflections on Things at Hand.* New York: Columbia University Press, 1967.

WEBSITES FOR SIGNIFICANT
HISTORICAL SITES

Birthplace of Hwang Sayŏng: "Kat'ollik charyosil—Han'guk ŭi sŏngji wa sajŏkchi—Hwang Sayŏng saengga t'ŏ" [Documents regarding Catholicism—Sacred sites and historical sites—the site where Hwang Sayŏng was born] http://fr.catholic.or.kr/jhs/holyplace/hwangsayeongsaengga.htm. Accessed October 2, 2015. In Korean.

Ch'ŏnjinam, the site of an early meeting associated with some of the early Catholics: "Chon Jin Am: The Birthplace of the Catholic Church in Korea, http://www.chonjinam.org/eng. In English. Accessed October 2, 2015.

Tomb of Hwang Sayŏng: "Kat'ollik charyosil—Han'guk ŭi sŏngji wa sajŏkchi—Hwang Sayŏng myo" [Documents regarding Catholicism—Sacred sites and historical sites—the grave of Hwang Sayŏng] http://fr.catholic.or.kr /jhs/holyplace/hwangsayeongmyo.htm. Accessed June 17, 2014. In Korean.

In'gan ŭi choggŏn: sŏngdang (Seoul. Kyŏnggi.) [The human condition: churches in Seoul and Kyŏnggi province] http://blog.daum.net/gkdrndpdlfqjswl39 /16522834. Accessed June 17, 2014. In Korean.

INDEX

Adam and Eve, 135–138

Ahn Chŏngbok, xii, 39, 117–120; and ancestor memorial rituals, 73–74; criticism of Catholicism, 31–33, 41, 48–52, 55–57, 75; relationship with Yi Ik, 47–48, 51

Aleni, Guilio, 42, 44, 57

Altar of Great Gratitude, 178–179

Analects, 176

ancestor memorial rituals (*chesa*), 6, 8, 70–78, 167, 171

ancestral tablet, 6–8, 54–55, 70–72, 74–77, 80–82

Bodhidharma, 142

Book of Changes [Yijing], 46, 47, 206

Book of History [Shangshu], 123

Book of Odes [Shijing], 123

Buddhism, 3–5, 9, 39, 43, 44, 125, 145, 146; as *idan,* 7, 30, 33–34, 36–37, 41, 145–146; Catholic condemnation of, 54, 180; compared to Catholicism, 45, 48, 53, 126–127, 140, 141–142, 147, 149; Hŏ Kyun, 128; Maitreya, 130–131

Catholicism, and King Chŏngjo, 17; no. of Korean Catholics, ix–x, 85

Celestial Learning [*Ch'ŏnhak*], 33, 36, 41, 43–44, 49, 51–52, 123–132, 143

celibacy, 123, 140

Censorate, 17–18, 70

Ch'ae Chegong, 51, 76, 96; and execution of Yun Chich'ung and Kwŏn Sangyŏn, 93

Chang, Lady, 25–26

Charme, Alexander de la, 55

Chejudo, 82

Chen Bo, 62–63, 127

Cheng Hao, 37, 39, 127

Cheng Yi, 37, 39, 62–63

chesa, 71

China, 27, 49, 51, 64, 99, 107, 118, 124, 130, 139, 143, 148, 179; Buddhism in, 142, Catholic Church, 3, 38, 85, 86–87, 151, 153, 168, 191, 197, 201; Confucianism, 30–39, 62, 127, 132, 141; factionalism, 23–24; Korea's relationship with, xiv, 107, 110–114, 117, 119, 120, 157, 188, 195–198, 201–202; missionaries

ABOUT THE AUTHORS

Don Baker is professor of Korean civilization in the Department of Asian Studies at the University of British Columbia. He received his PhD in Korean history from the University of Washington in 1983. He is the author of *Korean Spirituality* and has written extensively on the life and philosophy of Tasan Chŏng Yagyong and on the history of Christianity, Confucianism, and new religious movements in Korea.

Franklin Rausch is assistant professor in the Department of History and Philosophy at Lander University in Greenwood, South Carolina. He received his PhD from the University of British Columbia in 2011. He has published numerous articles on the history of the Catholic Church in Korea, with a special focus on the life and thought of Ahn Chunggŭn.

HAWAI'I STUDIES ON KOREA